Developer's Digital Media Reference

Developer's Digital Media Reference

New Tools, New Methods

Curtis Poole

Janette Bradley

WITHDRAWN
UTSA Libraries

OXFORD AMSTERDAM BOSTON LONDON NEW YORK PARIS
SAN DIEGO SAN FRANCISCO SINGAPORE SYDNEY TOKYO

Focal Press is an imprint of Elsevier Science.

Copyright © 2003, Elsevier Science (USA). All rights reserved.

Recognizing the importance of preserving what has been written, Elsevier Science
prints its books on acid-free paper whenever possible.

Library of Congress Cataloging-in-Publication Data

Poole, Curtis, 1958–
    developer's digital media reference: new tools, new methods/ Curtis Poole, Janette
Bradley.
        p.   cm.
Includes bibliographical references and index.

ISBN 0-240-80501-1 (alk. paper)
1. Digital video. 2. Multimedia systems. 3. Video recording. 4. Computer
software–Development. I. Bradley, Janette. II. Title.
TK6680.5 .P65 2002
006.7–dc21

2002029751

CIP

British Library Cataloguing-in-Publication Data

A catalogue record for this book is available from the British Library.

The publisher offers special discounts on bulk orders of this book.

For information, please contact:

Manager of Special Sales
Elsevier Science
200 Wheeler Road
Burlington, MA 01803
Tel: 781-313-4700
Fax: 781-313-4882

For information on all Focal Press publications available, contact our World Wide Web
home page at: http://www.focalpress.com.

10 9 8 7 6 5 4 3 2 1

Printed in the United States of America

In memory of my parents, Charles Poole and Claire Linehan Poole.

Curtis Poole

To my husband, who makes all things possible.

Janette Bradley

Acknowledgments

We are very grateful to our editor, Amy Jollymore, for her unwavering enthusiasm and perseverance. Janette also thanks her co-author, Curtis Poole, and Amy, without whose patience this book never would have happened. We would also like to acknowledge Jeffrey Almasol for the generous amount of time he spent on technical review.

Early on in Janette's career, she benefited from a number of people who introduced her to digital media and the power of collaborative tools, including Drs. Gerald Knezek, Mark Mortensen, Paul Schlieve, James Poirot, Cathy Norris, and Jon Young. They gave her the opportunity to participate in groundbreaking work and spurred her long-term interest in this area.

Janette has three additional people to thank — David Krall, Mike Rockwell, and Ethan Jacks of Avid Technology, Inc. all of whom gave her the opportunity in recent years to be involved in some of the most exciting developments in digital media. Most of all, Janette thanks her daughter, Madeline, for her patience when she said she couldn't play right now, and as always, her husband, Peter Scannell, who since 1988 has been the best partner anyone could ever ask for.

Curtis would also like to thank Jeanne Greeley, who edited sections of this book in their former incarnations as column material on the Avid Production Network 'zine. Curtis would also like to thank Tim Vandawalker who founded the Avid Press initiative and helped move this project forward, and co-author Janette, who first got the ball rolling for both the column and the book.

Contents

Chapter 4   Dynamic Web Applications

Section II   Disc-Based Architectures

Chapter 6   Introduction

Chapter 7   DVD-ROM

Chapter 8   DVD Video

Section III   Distribution Architectures

Chapter 10   Introduction

Chapter 11   Metadata for Digital Media Distribution

Chapter 13   Digital Rights Management (DRM)

Section IV   **Merged Architectures**

Chapter 14   **Introduction**

Chapter 15   **All About MPEG**

Chapter 16 **Interactive Television**

Chapter 17   Hybrid DVDs

Appendix   **Additional Resources**

Bibliography and List of Internet Sources

Index

List of Tables

List of Figures

Introduction

Say goodbye to new media — not the technologies or the industries that fall under this category. We're talking about the phrase.

Let's assume that the term "new media" came into use as a desperate attempt to define the breathless march of amazing and sometimes frustrating technologies that flooded our desktops in the late 1990s. Let's say that it stuck because no one could come up with something better before the term started filtering throughout the trades. The problem with the term, and the reason we will be avoiding it in this book, is that it implies from the outset that the technologies that fall under this heading will remain forever "new." Sure, the Web has only been with us since the mid-90s and digital television is just getting its start, but the fact is that CD-ROM technology is now more than 20 years old. If we consider the truism that high-tech time is equivalent to dog years, then we can more accurately state that the CD-ROM industry is already more than 100 years old.

In the wake of the AOL/Time Warner merger in 2000, Jim Nail of Forrester Research was quoted as saying that "There's no such thing as old media or new media anymore. It's all just media." We would take that further. As the age of multipurposed content continues to evolve, in the near future it might be safe to say there's no such thing as print media or Web media or television media anymore. It's all just *multi*media.

Multimedia Redefined

Multimedia is somewhat more descriptive than new media in defining a large group of technologies that have been gradually maturing over the past decade to bring us to this point. But multimedia has also been a difficult term to pin down. Is it the act of combining multiple forms of media technology into one presentation? Then multimedia has been with us since talkies first appeared in theaters. Is it the interactive factor? VCRs are interactive in a rudimentary way — if you can only get your hands on the right remote. Is it digital that makes the difference? Well in fact, the term multimedia got its start describing the ultimate analog presentation: slideshows using old-fashioned slide projectors combined with music and narration.

Let's not go back that far. When we refer to multimedia, we rely on the most common usage, made popular by the CD-ROM industry, as applying to the development and delivery of digital sound, text, and imagery with some interactive aspects. For the purposes of this book, that covers a lot of ground — from streaming media to wireless Web, and from interactive television to hybrid DVD.

We'll also add new meaning to the term "multi":

- *Multiple* platforms: That perennial challenge of the 1990's expands as operating systems proliferate and the World Wide Web presents a new platform.

- *Multiple* bandwidths: Just how broad is broadband? Are we talking cable modem? DSL? Intranet? Internet2? Wireless? And don't forget broadband satellite.

- *Multiple* architectures: How do we deliver to the Web, the box, the PC, and the player in any combination?

- *Multiple* displays: Is it WebTV? HDTV? PC? Choose your windows.

The Future Is Here! Well, Almost . . .

The new millennium brings an even greater impetus to renew our terminology which brings us to the inspiration for this book. Based on the perception that the groundwork that was laid in the last decade is about to yield its greatest fruit in the next, we've set out to write a book about it: a production resource that is meant to be a conduit for the sharing of information and resources.

Despite the worldwide financial and political misfortunes of the year 2001, looking forward this should be a great time for content creators. Multimedia industries are now poised for some big leaps forward in terms of both the means of production and the channels of distribution. It can be said that an era of "in-between" technologies — of limited audience and limited bandwidth — has come to an end, and that the era of digital media will reach its maturity within the next decade. The dust will begin to settle on a number of important technologies. For example:

- Metadata will become a crucial component of all forms of media.

- A powerful new generation of digital TV set-top boxes will become widely available through cable companies and other distributors.

- Recent large mergers between telecommunications, cable, and broadcast giants will begin to yield new fruit in terms of broadband Web and next-generation Internet services.

- DVD should become fully established as a next-generation technology, replacing everything from CD players to CD-ROMs to Video CD and laserdisc players — and eventually VHS.

- Interactive television will offer a new generation of systems providing tighter integration between television and World Wide Web technologies.

- All major television networks will be broadcasting digital television signals and should begin to develop interactive content en masse.

Next-Generation Tools

At the same time, next-generation tools used for production promise to drastically improve the economics and methodology of content creation:

- MPEG-4 and MPEG-7 standards will begin to take hold.

- Internet streaming architectures from Windows, RealMedia, and Apple will continue to advance rapidly, battling it out for market share.

- New tools for the authoring of Web content should make the development process easier and the look and feel of the Web much richer.

- New systems for asset management and distributed media will continue to evolve.

- Standards and applications for next-generation Web languages and tools such as XML, SVG, and SMIL will become widespread.

The authors will strive to consolidate an understanding of the new tools and architectures that are shaping up to be the defining forces of this new era in order to deliver a comprehensive must-have guide for developers who want to stay just ahead of the curve. We will describe current tools as well as best practices and production methods.

We'll also try to answer some crucial questions:

- What exactly is streaming media, and how do I make it work?

- What are the latest tools and techniques for effective cross-media publishing among the various delivery architectures?

- How can I take advantage of broadband delivery without leaving the rest of the narrowband world behind?

- What are the specific challenges of creating content for that strange broadband/low-resolution hybrid called interactive television?

- Is MPEG the video standard of the future, and if so, which flavor?

Subjects will fall under four basic areas defined in terms of underlying technology architectures shown in the chart below: server-based architectures (such as broadband Web and streaming media delivery platforms), disc-based architectures (such as DVD Video and DVD-ROM), distribution architectures (metadata-enhanced broadcast mechanisms), with special emphasis on merging/shared architectures (such as hybrid DVD discs and interactive television) that come out of the first three.

Our emphasis while discussing new trends will be on content creation — not development of the tools themselves but use of the tools to develop the content, with plenty of nuts and bolts.

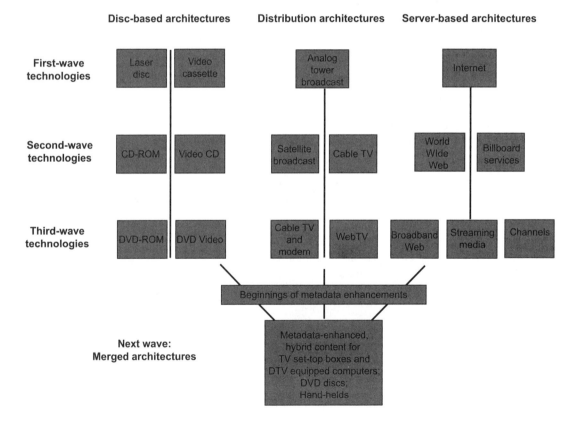

Section I: Server-Based Architectures

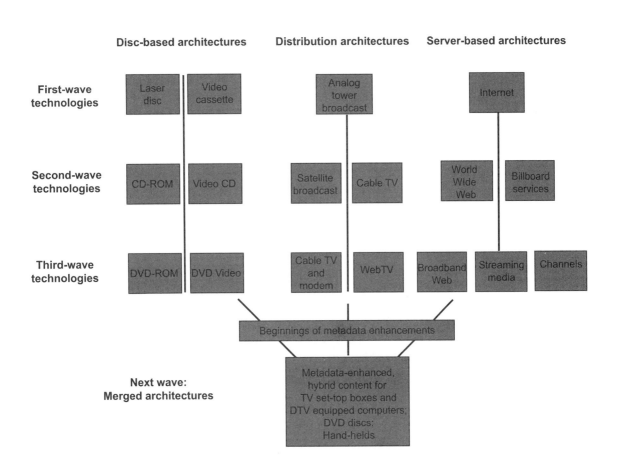

	Disc-based architectures	Distribution architectures	Server-based architectures
First-wave technologies	Laser disc / Video cassette	Analog tower broadcast	Internet
Second-wave technologies	CD-ROM / Video CD	Satellite broadcast / Cable TV	World Wide Web / Billboard services
Third-wave technologies	DVD-ROM / DVD Video	Cable TV and modem / WebTV	Broadband Web / Streaming media / Channels

Beginnings of metadata enhancements

Next wave: Merged architectures

Metadata-enhanced, hybrid content for TV set-top boxes and DTV equipped computers; DVD discs; Hand-helds

Section I: Server-Based Architectures

CHAPTER 1

Introduction

Server-based architectures encompass technologies that most of us associate with the World Wide Web. In this section of the book, we strive to redefine common notions of the Web and Internet to encompass new approaches to delivering content over the public network. Today, the conventional notion of a Website is quickly giving way to something entirely different. The Hypertext Markup Language (HTML), for example, is being overtaken by the next-generation XML and XHTML standards. New forms of hardware all over the infrastructure — from faster server CPUs and data bus technology to broadband optical pipes — also promise to change our networks for the better.

What does this mean for content developers? Fundamentally, two developments are converging at the moment to reshape our concepts, development tools, and approaches: the maturing of dynamic database-driven Web content technologies and the growth of broadband deployment technologies. A third related development is the maturing of digital management and distribution technologies, which is covered in Section III.

From Static to Dynamic Content

The old idea of static Web pages of the late 1990s has given way to a more lively, interactive paradigm in the new millennium. Most of us still use the term "page," even though much of our content has migrated into personalized, active, full-motion windows onto virtual worlds.

Specifically, the types of tools and technologies that are driving this evolution span both the server-side delivery mechanisms as well as the client-side elements. This complicates the development process somewhat from the early days of the Web hacker who could throw up a site in a day. To develop a thoroughly modern Web location today, you might have to work in a larger IT team that includes designers, multimedia authors, and various code and database experts. Content developers are working with a rich range of tools incorporating text, video, animation, HTML, XML, and so forth. Nearly all modern, dynamic Websites are hooked up to some form of database, which requires close cooperation between client and server content. In some cases, the old client-server paradigm is being challenged by new concepts of distributed information and delivery. These topics are covered in the chapters that follow.

Next-Generation Internet: News From the Front Lines

The advent of broadband is another cornerstone of the next wave of multimedia content. What exactly do we mean by broadband? At the moment most of us think of cable or DSL, which represents a major improvement over dial-up modems. But if you have a hard time understanding how postage-stamp Webcasting can ever seriously compete with television and film, you'll be happy to know that our current broadband options do not represent our final destination on the information superhighway. For more than 160 universities as well as several large government institutions involved in the development of Internet2, broadband has a much broader meaning. Existing broadband solutions, for example, are 10 to 50 times faster than standard dial-up modems. Internet2 networks, already in existence, transfer data up to 85,000 times faster. This new system is known as Internet2, or I2.

History Repeats

In 1969 in the United States, helped by funding from the military, four computers were networked together in an effort to create a research network that could survive a military strike. Thirty years later we have the Internet and the World Wide Web.

Today, government and university research institutions are hoping to repeat that performance. You might recall former President Bill Clinton's comments in his 1998 State of the Union address when he urged Congress to "enable all the world's people to explore the far reaches of cyberspace."

That speech launched the Next Generation Internet (NGI) Initiative, which is funded entirely by the U.S. government. The goal is to deliver 100 times the performance of the current Internet, on an end-to-end basis, to at least 100 interconnected federal agencies. No, Al Gore didn't create the original Internet, but through NGI funding as well as activities of the National Science Foundation (NSF), it looks like the Clinton administration can take some credit for the creation of the second one.

Rapid Progress

More than a concept, Internet2 is actually an organization, a not-for-profit consortium led by universities that are developing and deploying advanced network applications and technology. The University Corporation for Advanced Internet Development (UCAID) manages Internet2.

As with the first Internet, government and universities are first in line, but unlike "Internet1," from the start NGI and I2 efforts involve industry leaders from the for-profit sector, such as MCI and Cisco Systems, who will eventually contribute to the development of these services for the general public.

Work is progressing rapidly, and within one to two years we might begin to see deployments of major components of the system in the wider Internet. Some liken this period to the state of the first Internet in the late 1980s and early 1990s. By this timetable we may be rapidly approaching another important watershed moment, like the period of the mid-1990s when the first World Wide Web technologies appeared. Who knows what young Tim Berners-Lee might emerge from this experimental soup to rock our worlds once more.

Building a better Internet is no simple matter. First, of course, you need fatter pipes, but that's not the end of it. Internet2 is looking to address some other aspects of the current system that show weakness, including security and services. But let's start with the hardware.

The Pipes

vBNS

The building of next-generation pipes began in 1995 when construction started on the very-high-performance Backbone Network Service (vBNS), sponsored by the NSF and implemented by MCI WorldCom. The vBNS plays an important role in both NGI and Internet2 initiatives.

Abilene

Cisco Systems, Qwest, Nortel, and IBM, along with Internet2 universities, brought a second high-bandwidth backbone called Abilene (after the railhead in Abilene, Kansas, that opened the West) online in 1999. Abilene operates at 2.4 gigabits a second.

GigaPOPs

An important part of the Internet2 architecture is something called a GigaPOP. The term "GigaPOP" refers to the point of connection between local high-speed networks. Each GigaPOP is connected to other GigaPOPs through the backbone to form Internet2. Just as universities, states, and regions create GigaPOPs, commercial organizations will eventually create and link up using similar technologies and high-speed networking infrastructure.

The Services

IPv6

For Internet2, the IP in TCP/IP has a facelift. Internet Protocol Version 6 (IPv6) is the result of more than six years of work by the Internet Engineering Task Force (IETF). IPv6 is designed to address the major shortcomings of IPv4, the current version at work in the broader Internet. IPv6 uses a different package scheme, the advantage of which is that it incorporates native multicasting, high reliability, and high capacity along with quality controls. IPv6 will allow applications requiring high bandwidth to coexist with each other simultaneously with little or no loss of data.

Because IPv6 includes native multicasting, users are able to send one content packet to many locations — instead of the current method of sending many packets to many locations. Real-time data can now be sent and manipulated in real time, which will allow, for example, television networks to bring their entire digital television offerings onto the Internet, to be delivered at full resolution with full frame accuracy.

QoS

Quality of service (QoS) has become a major issue for the Internet as well as for enterprise data networks due to the increasing importance of Internet service that must be better than best effort, as well as the integration of voice, video, and data. IPv6 includes a number of new QoS technologies designed to ensure more accurate delivery of data.

Routing

New routing schemes, too complex to describe here, are also part of the next-generation networks and will eventually supplement today's IP routing. Large-scale Internet backbones require these enhanced traffic engineering controls under development by MCI, Cisco Systems, and others.

Internet3?

Not surprisingly, there are rumors of an Internet3 in the works. A search for the term on the Web uncovers one Internet3 initiative under way in Sweden that might provide some insight into what additional capabilities engineers are dreaming up.

Documentation for the Internet3 initiative at the Swedish IT Institute (SITI), funded by the Foundation for Knowledge and Competence Development, outlines a few important themes:

- **Everything always connected:** The global community becomes one big virtual computer in which PCs and mobile units will always be connected to the global infrastructure, or at least allow for the rapid creation of spontaneous networks with minimal configuration and protocol implementation for our many Internet devices.

- **Scalable media:** Media distribution involves simultaneous delivery of completely scalable content, ranging from HDTV video (bitrates up to 270 Mbps) to low-bandwidth streams for handheld devices, for example. The scaling of media content becomes invisible to the user, managed by the networks and the devices themselves.

- **Agents for electronic markets:** E-commerce incorporates full-scale agent technologies, which intelligently carry out requests for both businesses and individuals to simplify our navigation through the cornucopia of global markets.

Resources

To learn more about broadband, here are a few links you can follow:

- Next Generation Internet (NGI) Initiative: www.ngi.gov

- Internet2 official site: www.internet2.edu

- IPv6 information: www.ipv6.org

- Internet3: www.cdt.luth.se/I3

Section I:
Server-Based Architectures

CHAPTER 2

Streaming Video

This chapter provides all the information you need to understand the challenges, choose your tools, and then create and distribute video streams on the World Wide Web. For specific information on the various multimedia capabilities of the video platforms, as well as embedding and synchronizing video with graphics and other elements in Web pages, see Chapter 5, Synchronized Media.

Part A: Background

Streaming Content Explosion

Few Web technologies have caused more confusion, and stirred more excitement in recent years, than this thing called streaming video. This frenetic state of affairs is not likely to change soon. Thousands of attendees at streaming media conferences all over the world are living proof that streaming video has arrived at the mainstream for the Web-enabled community, if not the masses. According to the Deutsche Media Metrix Report from BT Alex Brown Research (March 2000), some 234 million hours of streaming content were projected to be delivered on the Web in 2000.

Like all the evolving Web technologies, streaming video involves many variations in terms of competing technologies and standards. But because video holds a certain cache (no pun intended), the stakes are especially high, leaving developers with a rich collection of options and a complex set of decisions to make when choosing technology paths.

Before those decisions can be made, developers must educate themselves on the fundamentals. What follows is a brief primer on the nature of streaming video as it might affect your basic choices of formats and distribution mechanisms. Toward the end of this chapter, you will find a checklist of information that will help you organize your basic technology decisions.

The Storage Challenge

How exactly does streaming video work, and why are the services so darn expensive?

One basic fact about video on the Web that we can all appreciate right away is that it takes a lot more storage space. The first generation of Website developers lived happily with 20 or 30 MB on a server somewhere. Next-wave developers of rich-media content are suddenly dealing in the gigabyte range in many cases. This represents a fundamental shift in storage requirements for Web content.

New high-capacity, high-performance server solutions such as Avid's Trilligent Cluster are geared specifically to this new dynamic at work on the Web. As a developer, expect to pay more for your Web presence as you start to store and deliver streaming content.

It's All in the Protocols

The second and more complex factor is the unique set of software requirements for streaming video. For the first time in the five- or six-year history of the World Wide Web, developers must reach outside of the familiar HTTP and TCP/IP protocols that made the first generation of content possible.

HTTP Streaming: The First Step

A few years ago, after RealAudio captured the imagination of the industry and stirred notions of real-time, full-motion video on the Web, Apple introduced the QuickTime progressive format with QuickTime 3.0 — a precursor to true streaming video that remains popular today for many applications. Also known as HTTP streaming, this type of progressive download allows the user to begin watching a video before the entire file has been transferred. HTTP streaming was meant to be an intermediate step on the road to true streaming, but for a number of reasons, which I will explain a little later, it remains an extremely useful format today in the delivery of short-form video.

As the name suggests, HTTP streaming allows you to deliver video from a traditional HTTP (Hypertext Transfer Protocol) server. When you link to a Web page that includes the embedded video, the contents of the video trickle progressively to the player. From that point on it's a race between the download speed and the rate of playback: after enough of the file is buffered, you can begin to play the file while in the background the remaining content continues to load from the server. If the playback runs beyond the download, playback stops until more of the content gets transferred. You then can resume playback, and so on.

As long as users have a lot of patience and developers use small video files, QuickTime progressive is a quick and simple solution that relies on existing HTTP server technologies. The development of broadband networks makes this solution even more acceptable, allowing for longer high-quality video clips to download quickly and play in something close to real time (a type of HTTP streaming content that has been dubbed DHS, for downloadable high-bandwidth stream). But what happens when you want to stream a one-hour program, without a hitch, in real time?

Real-Time Streaming Protocols

In contrast to HTTP, true streaming servers use real-time streaming protocols that include enhancements for real-time delivery, such as the ability to quickly calculate users' connection speeds and offer up alternate versions of the video with appropriate buffering rates. With true streaming protocols, digital data is transferred, displayed, and then discarded once you've seen it. As mentioned, with HTTP streaming the data is assembled in its entirety on the user's system and can be saved locally. With true streaming, although a 3- to 10-second cache of data is stored on the user's computer to compensate for network delays, at no point is the entire movie stored on the user's computer.

All these unique services and protocols come under the banner of either RTSP (real-time streaming protocol) championed by RealNetworks and others, or Microsoft's protocol for streaming from Windows servers using Windows Media Technologies. RTSP is an open standard backed by the W3C (World Wide Web Consortium). Microsoft's protocol is proprietary.

As I will describe in Chapter 5 dealing with synchronized presentations, HTTP and streaming servers often work hand in hand to combine traditional Web content with streaming content. In most cases, the involvement of a streaming server on a Website is entirely hidden from the user.

Beyond TCP

Real-time streaming protocols vary from traditional Web protocols in some other ways. As you may know, TCP/IP are the dynamic duo, the Starsky and Hutch of first-generation World Wide Web standards, that make the effective transfer of data possible. At the server end, TCP (transmission control protocol) breaks all data into small packets and sends them on their way. At the user's computer — the receiving end — a checksum in the header information tells the receiving computer whether data was lost along the way. If it was, a new request for the missing data is sent to the server, which in turn sends the missing packets again. Once all packets are gathered at the receiving end, TCP reassembles the packets into their original form, as shown in Figure 2-1.

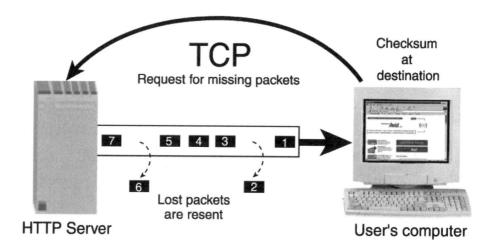

Figure 2-1 Standard Web Content via TCP/IP

As you can imagine, there is a delay here, however miniscule, that does not lend itself well to the steady march of frames that is the hallmark of video. That's where streaming video takes a new turn. Unlike Websites that use TCP, streaming servers use UDP (user datagram protocol). UDP does not check to see if data has been sent, resulting in a more uninterrupted flow, as shown in Figure 2-2.

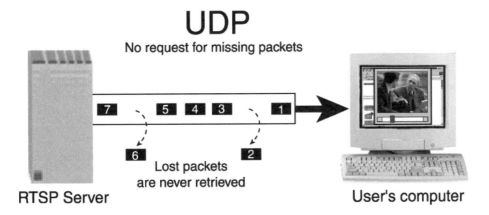

Figure 2-2 Streaming Content via UDP

This is why streaming video is sometimes referred to as a lossy Web technology, in which the user occasionally experiences dropped frames for the sake of uninterrupted flow of the program. When data-oriented applications on the World Wide Web require a high level of accuracy, the video experience is more forgiving, emphasizing overall flow above the loss of granular bits of information that are not always noticeable. With higher-bandwidth delivery, that loss of data occurs less frequently.

Beyond IP

The IP (Internet protocol) part has to do with routing the data from one location to another. The header portion of each packet of data sent on the Web includes information on where to send the data that can be interpreted along the way. You can think of that information as the mailing label, and the protocol at each location that interprets the information and routes it accordingly as the postal system of the information highway. At the moment, the current version of IP that is active across the World Wide Web uses a unicast model with point-to-point communication, which means basically that each computer communicates individually with the source or origin server, and the server in turn addresses data packets to each computer individually.

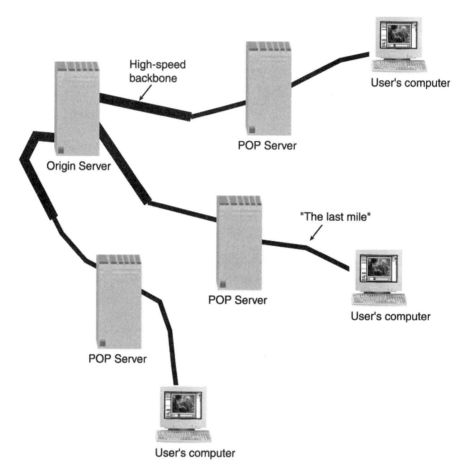

Figure 2-3   Unicast Distribution — Point to Point

Figure 2-3 shows the origin of the data, its transmission over high-speed backbones that make up the core of the Internet, and finally its transmission to the user from servers in a local point of presence (POP) network.

Problems with Unicasting

The unicast model works fine for the first plain-text-oriented generation of Web content. Again, we can easily imagine the problems this creates for video and other forms of streaming content. Coming from a "broadcast" tradition in which content is sent out from a single source, leaving it up to the receiving device to find that content on the airwaves or on the cable, video producers who are turning to the Web have been struggling to find new models that are better suited to the rapid delivery of high-bandwidth streams to large audiences.

To give you a real-world example of the challenge, RealServer 7 is capable of providing 25 simultaneous unicast streams. RealServer Plus provides 60 streams. For most small independent developers with a dedicated T1 line connection to the Internet, 60 or 100 low-bandwidth streams remains the plateau for effective unicast delivery.

Taking It to the Edge

What happens when you need to reach thousands or even millions of simultaneous users? If you remember the Victoria Secret's Webcast fiasco in the year 2000, you know that it's been tried. As useful as that Webcast meltdown was as an education in the technology requirements of Webcasting to the masses, a better example for us to follow might be the NetAid fund-raising broadcast in October 1999. Using RealNetworks' distributed network and Cisco Systems' routers and solutions, the organizers of the NetAid Webcast successfully delivered a fundraising concert worldwide using more than 1,900 servers spread out over several dedicated networks with triple redundancy.

How did they do it? Imagine the unicast packet of data on its journey, traveling from a point of origin through the many wires and routers of the Internet until it reaches its destination. The longer the distance, the more convoluted the journey becomes, with more opportunities for the data to get lost or delayed.

To improve this situation, RealNetworks (www.realnetworks.com, a partner in the NetAid Webcast) and a number of other large players, such as Akamai (www.akamai.com), InfoLibria (www.infolibria.com), Activate (www.activate.com), and Digital Island (www.digitalisland.net,), do something known as network caching, or streaming from the edge. Using various means, these companies push content in advance out to regional servers so that the data is closer to end users; thus data arrives more quickly and more accurately when requested.

The first trick is to move the content around. When the streaming content is not live but is on demand, the content can be sent between other transmissions throughout the day until the full content is cached at the regional data center. Some companies, such as iBeam (www.ibeam.com) and Cidera (www.cidera.com), deliver the content via satellite to local and regional Internet service providers (ISPs). As in television, satellite delivery also allows for the possibility of live Webcasting.

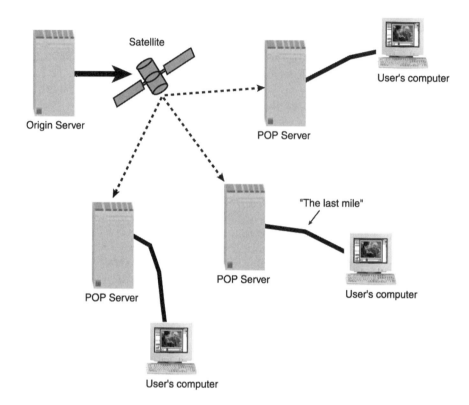

Figure 2-4   Unicast Distribution — Point to Multipoint

In Figure 2-4, satellite transmission is used to bypass a huge portion of the congested Internet to deliver the content directly to multiple servers within local POP networks.

Near-live Webcasting can also be achieved by leveraging some of the broadband infrastructure of Internet2 for at least part of the data journey. In the introduction to this section of the book, we described how Internet2 has developed as a staging ground for the next generation of Internet technologies, due soon at a theater near you.

The second trick is to determine which server will deliver the content to a particular user when that user contacts the Website. This feat is performed by the various proprietary code schemes, combined with mapping of the Internet, that have made these companies very successful and, in most cases, very expensive. With various dedicated servers, satellites, routers, and complex software involved in the task, many of these distributed "edge" delivery network services come with enterprise-level price tags.

Multicasting to the Rescue

If streaming from the edge is so expensive, what hope does a small producer have in reaching a large audience with quality video content? In a word, multicasting.

Another useful experiment conducted during the NetAid Webcast was a 1.5 Mbps stream via multicast on Internet2 to showcase a broadband version of the concert. Multicasting is a built-in feature of IPv6, the next generation of IP already in use on Internet2.

Multicasting, combined with the widespread use of broadband connection speeds among users, the keys for small producers trying to reach large audiences. In one stroke multicasting reduces network congestion, speeds data delivery, and removes the need for costly proprietary hardware solutions.

Multicasting uses a high-capacity Internet backbone, or multicast backbone (Mbone), for transmitting broadcasts using the IP multicast protocol. In multicasting, a single transmission includes the addresses of all those who want to see it. The data then makes copies of itself across the Internet when necessary and delivers copies to the local networks, and eventually to the individual users.

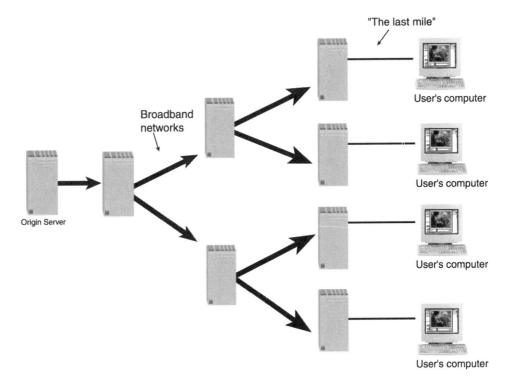

Figure 2-5   Multicast Distribution

As you can see Figure 2-5, the content that you, the developer, place on the origin server requires no further attention or expense. Multicasting allows a single transmission of the data to travel safely to multiple users. As with TCP/IP, the standard is open and free of charge. You can finally reach those thousands or millions of computer users without any trouble. Once those POP networks become GigaPOPs (the term used on Internet2 for local or regional networks with gigabyte-per-second transfer speeds), Webcasting of broadcast-quality video will become affordable and commonplace.

Part B: Tools

Introduction

When it comes to streaming video, look no further than the big three: Real-Networks RealSystems, Microsoft Windows Media Technologies, and Apple QuickTime with the Sorenson codec. These three tool sets are very similar, yet different enough to require a careful review before making your choices.

MPEG-4 is emerging as an important, future-oriented technology that comprises video and several other motion-media technologies. The various MPEG technologies are described in detail in Chapter 15.

General Comparisons

The following tables offer high-level comparisons of various aspects of the big three streaming video tool providers. Table 2-1 shows media player penetration.

Table 2-1: Media Player Penetration*

Player	Number of Home Users
QuickTime	4.7 million (4%)
RealPlayer	32.7 million (28%)
Windows Media Player	22.1 million (22%)

*Source: Jupiter MediaMetrix, June 2001

Basic Features

Table 2-2 compares the availability of basic video technology features in the big three. For a comparison of multimedia features such as Flash support and text track capabilities, see Chapter 5, Synchronized Media.

Table 2-2: Streaming Media Formats — Basic Features

Feature	QuickTime	RealSystems	Windows Media
Automatic bandwidth selection	Requires QuickTime Reference movie creation; works for both HTTP and RTSP streaming	Requires RTSP streaming with Sure-Stream	Requires Windows Media Services streaming with Intelligent Streaming

Table 2-2: Streaming Media Formats — Basic Features (Continued)

Feature	QuickTime	RealSystems	Windows Media
Automatic hinting	Requires addition of hinting track, some manual entry	Automatic	Automatic
De-interlacing	Yes	Yes, with RealVideo 8	Yes, with Windows Media 8
HTTP progressive streaming	Yes, QT 3 and greater	No	No
Inverse telecine	Yes	Yes, with RealVideo 8	Yes, with Windows Media 8
On-the-fly congestion detection and stream adjustment	Yes, with Sorenson 3	Yes	Yes
Platforms — development	Macintosh, Windows	Macintosh, Windows, Linux	Windows
Platforms — playback	Macintosh, Windows	Macintosh, Windows, Linux	Macintosh, Windows
Two-pass encoding	Yes, with Sorenson Developer Edition	Yes, with RealVideo 8	Yes, with Windows Media 8
Variable bit-rate encoding	Yes, with Sorenson Developer Edition	Yes, with RealVideo 8	Yes, with Windows Media 8

Windows Media Technologies

Go to www.microsoft.com/windows/windowsmedia

Quick Review

After much reengineering effort and various name changes — mostly marketing-driven — Windows Media Technologies finally came into its own with Version 7 of the Windows Media Player and Windows Media format 7 with companion authoring and encoding tools. Windows Media 8, which began shipping as a standard feature of Windows XP, consolidates the improvements.

Windows Media Player has been completely transformed, with the addition of skins that allow you to easily customize the look and functionality of the player. The player comprises seven features in a single application: CD player, audio and video player, media jukebox, media guide, Internet radio, portable device music file transfer, and an audio CD burner.

Versions 6.4 through 9 of the Windows Media Player also support Windows Media Video 8 and Audio 8. These most recent versions of the Windows Media formats lower even further the data rates required for delivering high-quality content. The new codecs can deliver near-CD-quality audio at 48 kbps (the same audio quality as typical MP3 encoding in a file nearly one-third the size) and true CD quality at 64 kbps. Windows Media Video 8 delivers near-VHS quality at 250 kbps (the low end of DSL/cable connection speeds) and near-DVD quality video at 500 kbps (full broadband connection speeds). Windows digital rights management features are also built right into Windows Media format 8. The upcoming Windows Media 9 release (codename Corona) promises true broadcast-quality video over broadband connections.

There are a few minor deployment issues to consider with Windows Media: Versions 7 or greater of the player are not supported on the Windows NT operating system, for example, but this can be easily overcome by utilizing Version 6.4 of the player on Windows NT, which supports all the recent formats with downloadable codec updates. The Macintosh version of the player also displays some shortcomings, but if your target audience is primarily the huge installed base of Windows users, Windows Media is an easy choice.

In terms of image quality, Microsoft claims parity, if not superiority, when compared with RealMedia, although RealNetworks presents counter-claims based on research. The new encoders now support de-interlacing to reduce flicker on computer monitors when displaying content that comes from an interlaced source, such as the National Television Standards Committee (NTSC) and phased alternating line (PAL)-based systems. It also supports inverse telecine for the first time, which results in improved playback quality of film-source content at lower bandwidths. Like RealMedia 8, the Windows Media format 8 also supports variable bit-rate (VBR) encoding.

In terms of sound quality, Microsoft strongly claims a superior audio codec, codeveloped with Intel. The Version 8 Windows Media Audio codec provides improved audio quality for narrowband Internet streaming of high-fidelity downloadable music. Improvements in quality over previous codecs have been made at all data rates, from 16 kbps to 192 kbps. Substantial improvements have also been made at 64 kbps and above. Perform your own tests to confirm.

In terms of deployment, Windows Media requires a Windows Media Server for streaming playback, which can be an advantage or a disadvantage depending on your circumstances. For example, if you have a Windows server readily available for deployment (in your workplace or with your ISP), then Windows Media might be a good choice for you. With a minimum of fuss, you can reconfigure the server with Windows Media Services, and you're on your way.

On the other hand, you cannot deploy Windows Media through current versions of RealServer or QuickTime Streaming Server software because

Windows employs its own proprietary streaming technologies, whereas RealServer and QuickTime Streaming Server both conform to the open RTSP standard. Note, however, that the upcoming version of RealNetworks server technology, known as Helix, promises support for all streaming formats, including Real, QuickTime, Windows Media, and MPEG-4, for the first time in a single platform.

Perhaps the biggest draw for Windows Media Technologies is low cost; most of the tools, in fact, are free. However, although the tools are free, RealNetworks rightly points out that there are other expenses involved, depending on the full range of hardware and software requirements, your target audience, and chosen delivery formats — not to mention the fact that you are bound to the Windows platform. You can download the most recent version of the the Windows Media Player, Encoder, and various authoring tools directly from the Microsoft Website.

There isn't a great wealth of third-party tools and information to ease the development process, however. A search at Amazon.com turns up three titles of recent vintage, only two of which provide any useful information for developers (the third is consumer-oriented). In addition, both developer guides are Microsoft publications, so don't expect much mention of or comparison with rival technologies.

Table 2-3 and Table 2-4 cover video codecs and audio codecs, respectively. They also contain descriptions of the codecs.

Table 2-3: Video Codecs for Windows Media Player

Codec	Description
Windows Media Video V8	V8 improves compression efficiency an additional 30 percent over the technically acclaimed Windows Media format 7, according to Microsoft. It provides advanced features such as variable bitrate encoding, de-interlacing, and inverse telecine. Playback using this codec requires modern computers with fast CPU speeds.
Windows Media Video V7	Use the V7 codec when your computer or target computers are not powerful enough to accommodate the performance demands of the Windows Media Video 8 codec. Also use the Windows Media Video 7 codec if your users play content in Windows Media Player 7 and you do not want to force a download of the Windows Media Video 8 codec.
ISO MPEG-4 Video	For most encoding scenarios, you should use Windows Media Video 7 or 8 codecs. The ISO MPEG-4 video codec supports the ISO/IEC standard and enables you to encode and play content that is compatible with ISO MPEG-4.
Microsoft H.263	H.263 is good for providing low to middle bit-rate video. This codec is optimized for videoconferencing, so it is a good choice for presentations and other low-motion video content.

Table 2-4: Audio Codecs Installed with Windows Media Player

Codec	Description
Windows Media Audio V8	The Windows Media Audio 8 codec is appropriate for most uses and encodes audio streams at bit rates of 16 kilobits per second (kbps) to 192 kbps. Use the ACELP codec for voice encoding at low bit rates only.
Windows Media Audio V7	The Windows Media Audio 7 codec can be used for most types of audio streams at bit rates of 16 kbps to 192 kbps. Use the Windows Media Video 7 codec if your users play content in Windows Media Player 7 and you do not want to force a download of the Windows Media Audio 8 codec. Use the ACELP codec for voice encoding at low bit rates only.
Sipro Labs ACELP.net codec	ACELP is a low-bit-rate codec that provides excellent voice compression. ACELP comes with several audio formats, depending on the network bandwidth you choose.

Tools and Tasks

This section provides reference information about Microsoft's free tools for creating Windows Media files, converting other file formats to Windows Media formats, and adding URL flips and other functionality into Windows Media streams.

Windows Media Encoder

Go to www.microsoft.com/windows/windowsmedia/download

The Windows Media Encoder enables both live and on-demand content production with the following features:

- Includes template-based encoding options

- Controls for scaled encoding

- Allows you to insert script commands and URL flips on the fly

- Includes various programmability and administration features

- Supports a variety of capture cards

- Includes special encoding capabilities such as support for de-interlacing, inverse telecine, and screen capture

- Includes an easy process for creating screen capture and training demos using the Windows Media screen capture codec

- Supports multigigabyte files and uncompressed capture directly to Windows Media format and creates archive files that are more than 30 GB in size. This capture feature, combined with support for capturing uncom-

pressed audio and video, provides previously unavailable capture and
archive capabilities

- Enables encoder-based time compression, allowing users to adjust pause
  removal and playback expansion of audio and video files, which further
  reduces playback time

Windows Media Resource Kit

Go to www.microsoft.com/windows/windowsmedia/download

The Windows Media Resource Kit offers a full range of tools for creating
and editing live and on-demand Windows Media–based content. The kit also
includes the popular utilities first introduced in Windows Media 4.1, Digital
Broadcast Manager and Windows Media Tools 4.1. These tools are available
for free.

Table 2-5 lists recommended tools for a variety of common authoring and
editing tasks.

Table 2-5: Windows Media Tools

Task	Recommended Tool	Description
Delete portions of video	ASFChop	This command-line utility crops time periods of a Windows Media file and adds indexes, script commands, markers, and general properties to the file.
Add script commands and events to ASF files	ASF Indexer	This adds properties, markers, script commands, and indexes to an existing Windows Media file.
Distribute encoding among computers	Encoder Controller	It provides frame-accurate playback control for multiple-computer encoding sessions.
Combine multiple video clips	Stitcher	This combines multiple Windows Media files into a single Windows Media file by concatenating the source files in the order defined by the user.
Set up batch encoding	Windows Media Encoder Remote Setup Utility	It is used to automatically configure the DCOM settings for the computer on which it is running, enabling the Windows Media Encoder 7 Automation interfaces to perform properly.
Batch encoding	Windows Media Encoder Batching Utility	It is used to encode multiple files that are not in Windows Media format and save them as Windows Media files with a .wmv extension.

Table 2-5: Windows Media Tools (Continued)

Task	Recommended Tool	Description
Install Windows Media 7 codecs	WMPcdcs	This command-line utility installs the Windows Media Video Version 7 and Windows Media Audio Version 7 codecs on a computer that uses Windows Media Player Version 6.4.
Add script commands and events to WMV or WMA files	Windows Media Advanced Script Indexer	It enables you to edit scripts and markers within any Windows Media file and place those scripts in the header portion of the file.
Play audio files	AudioPlayer	It is used to play Windows Media files through a simple user interface (UI).
Do simple file conversion to WMV	AVIToWMV	This command-line utility is used to convert uncompressed files from either the AVI format or the WAV format to Windows Media format.
Play audio files	WMAPlay	This command-line utility is used to play Windows Media files with a .wma extension.
Modify metadata	WMAttr	This allows you to display and modify the metadata properties for a Windows Media file.
Capture video	WMCap	This is a digital video capture tool.
Display clip properties	WMProp	This command-line utility is used to show some properties of a Windows Media file.
Convert multicast to unicast	WMSProxy	This is a tool to convert a multicast stream to an HTTP unicast stream.
Combine two WMV files	WMVAppend	This command-line utility is used to create an output file from the content of two Windows Media input files.
Simulate streaming of a file	WMVNetWrite	This command-line utility is used to show how a Windows Media file is streamed across the Internet.
Clean up metafiles	Windows Media MetaFile Cleaner	This command-line utility removes unsupported tags and attributes from existing metafiles, which Windows Media Player 7 identifies as not valid and does not support. It then creates valid metafiles.
Create metafiles	Windows Media MetaFile Creator	This tool, through its graphical user interface, is used to automatically create Windows Media files with .asx extensions based on specified information.

Table 2-5: Windows Media Tools (Continued)

Task	Recommended Tool	Description
Verify ASF headers	Windows Media Mobile Utility	This command-line utility is used to verify ASF header section compatibility with mobile terminals from NTT DoCoMo.
Simulate server load	Windows Media Load Simulator	It is used to create a real-world load on a server by simulating Windows Media Player connections.
Monitor streaming connections	Windows Media Monitor	This is a Web page that monitors the connections of up to eight streams simultaneously by using instances of the embedded Windows Media Players.
Get a dynamic IP address over a network	GetDynamicIP	This tool establishes a static port connection between a Windows Media Server hosting a broadcast unicast publishing point and a computer running a Windows Media Encoder that has a dynamically assigned TCP/IP address.
Send an IP address over a network	SendIP	This tool establishes a static port connection between a computer with a dynamically TCP/IP address running Windows Media Encoder and a Windows Media Server hosting a broadcast unicast publishing point.
Encode media	Windows Media Encoder	This tool encodes media content into a Windows Media format stream or file. Content can include stored multimedia files or live input from a microphone or video camera. Windows Media Encoder converts and compresses audio content, video content, and script commands into Windows Media format using state-of-the-art compression technologies.
Broadcast a presentation	Presentation Broadcasting	This feature of Microsoft PowerPoint 2000 integrates with Windows Media Technologies to make it easier to create and publish PowerPoint presentations in Windows Media format. With Presentation Broadcasting, you can broadcast streaming PowerPoint presentations to network users in real time. In addition to broadcasting PowerPoint slides, presenters can broadcast video and audio simultaneously to deliver a live multimedia show online and then store their presentations for on-demand playback.
Generate Windows Media files from within Premiere	Windows Media Plug-in for Adobe Premiere	This tool saves, compresses, and converts your video files into Windows Media format from within Adobe Premiere.
Convert PowerPoint 97 files to WIndows Media	Windows Media Presenter for Power-Point 97	This add-in tool, along with Windows Media Encoder, helps you convert a PowerPoint presentation to a Windows Media format stream.

Table 2-5: Windows Media Tools (Continued)

Task	Recommended Tool	Description
Convert PowerPoint 97 files to ASF	Windows Media Publish to ASF for PowerPoint 97	This add-in tool combines PowerPoint presentations with narration.
Convert video files to ASF	VidToASF	This command-line utility converts .vid or .mov files into Windows Media files. You can use a command-line option to specify script files that add markers, invoke URLs, and execute script commands.
Convert WAV files to ASF	WavToASF	This command-line utility converts .wav or .mp3 files into Windows Media files. You can use a command-line option to specify script files that add markers, invoke URLs, and execute script commands.
Check and repair ASF files	ASFCheck	This command-line utility verifies Windows Media file formats. ASFCheck can identify problems within a Windows Media file and repair some of the identified problems.
Manage Windows Media content	Windows Media Digital Broadcast Manager	This tool enables application service providers (ASPs) and Internet content providers (ICPs) to develop ways to manage, deliver, and sell pay-per-stream and pay-per-download multimedia content over the Internet by using Windows Media Technologies. This component runs on the Windows NT Server and Windows 2000 Server operating systems in conjunction with Windows Media Services, Site Server Commerce Edition, and SQL Server. All of these components must be installed prior to installing Digital Broadcast Manager.

PowerPoint Conversion Tools

The tools described in Table 2-6 are included with the PowerPoint software, available stand-alone or as part of the Microsoft Office suite of products from most software vendors.

Microsoft Producer also allows you to work with PowerPoint in the context of synchronized presentation authoring. For more information, see Chapter 5.

Table 2-6: PowerPoint Conversion Tools

Task	Tool	Features
Create live audio and video synchronized with Microsoft PowerPoint 2000 slides	Presentation Broadcast (part of PowerPoint 2000)	It provides archiving for later on-demand access. Slide changes are synchronized with presenter's audio and video. Only the presenter needs Power-Point 2000. Clients need Windows Media Player and a Web browser.
Create live audio and video synchronized with Power-Point 97 slides	Windows Media Presenter for Microsoft PowerPoint 97	It provides archiving for later on-demand access. Slide changes are synchronized with presenter's audio and video. Only the presenter needs Power-Point 97. Clients need Windows Media Player and a Web browser.

Microsoft Producer

**Go to www.microsoft.com/windows/windowsmedia/
technologies.asp**

Microsoft Producer is a user-friendly environment for building synchronized presentations from a range of Microsoft products and Web technologies such as PowerPoint, Windows Media, HTML, and image files. For more information, see Chapter 5.

Windows Media Services

Windows Media Services is built directly into the Windows 2000 Server, offering easy integration with corporate infrastructures. No additional per-stream or per-seat licensing is required for Windows Media, thus minimizing deployment costs.

In terms of streaming capabilities, ZD Labs has independently documented more than 9,000 concurrent narrowband streams and more than 2,400 broadband streams on a single server running on Windows 2000 Server and Windows Media Services.

The tight integration between Windows Media Services and Windows 2000 creates a highly reliable streaming platform. A streaming server needs to deliver millions of time-sensitive data packets to multiple clients — if a given packet isn't received in time to be played, users experience poor quality. ZD Labs also measured the reliability of Windows Media Services — and reported that Windows Media Services delivered 26 billion packets of data with 99.9999999 percent accuracy over more than 12 days of continuous streaming of more than 2,400 broadband streams.

Windows Media Rights Manager

Go to www.microsoft.com/windows/windowsmedia/download

Microsoft Windows Media Rights Manager is an end-to-end digital rights management (DRM) system that offers content providers and retailers a flexible platform for the secure distribution of digital media files.

Windows Media Rights Manager was first released in August 1999. The latest release includes both server and client software development kits (SDKs) that enable applications to protect and play back digital media files. The SDK is sent to you after Microsoft accepts a signed SDK license agreement from you.

Additional Microsoft Resources

Go to www.microsoft.com/windows/windowsmedia/technologies.asp

You can find the following additional resources at the Microsoft Windows Media Web location noted above:

- Training materials and tutorials
- Downloads
- Developer center
- Additional developer community links

Third-Party Tools

The companies listed in Table 2-7 offer compatible tools for Windows Media authoring, audio and video processing and production, capturing, and compression.

Table 2-7: Windows Media Third-Party Tools

Company	Go To	Product
Adobe Systems, Inc.	www.adobe.com	Adobe Premiere
Avid Technology, Inc.	www.avid.com	Avid Cinema, Avid Xpress DV, ePublisher

Table 2-7: Windows Media Third-Party Tools (Continued)

Company	Go To	Product
Autodesk Inc.	www.discreet.com	Cleaner
Liquid Audio, Inc.	www.liquidaudio.com	Liquifier Pro, Liquid MusicServer, Liquid MusicPlayer
Sonic Foundry, Inc.	www.sonicfoundry.com	Sound Forge 4.5, Stream Anywhere, Vegas Pro
TegoSoft Inc.	www.tegosoft.com	TegoSoft's NetShow-based product
Telos Systems	www.telos-systems.com	Audioactive
Ulead Systems, Inc.	www.ulead.com	MediaStudio Pro 5.0

Before selecting a third-party vendor to provide services or products, you should conduct a thorough independent review of the third-party vendor's ability, skills, experience, and/or products to determine whether the third party can fulfill your particular needs.

RealNetworks RealSystems

Go to www.realnetworks.com/products

Quick Review

In the streaming media arena, RealNetworks has been a company of firsts. The RealAudio format and player, for example, was the first technology to create excitement around the potential of streaming media. Since the success of RealAudio, RealNetworks has continued its role as an innovator, usually coming first to market with each new step up in the quality of streaming media, while also championing the rapid development of various open standards such as RTSP and SMIL.

In terms of image quality, RealNetworks can also stake a claim to delivery of the first VHS-quality broadband streams beginning with RealSystem G7 — although Windows Media and QuickTime, with the Sorenson 3 codec, were not far behind. RealVideo 8 (with the RealSystem iQ platform) and the new Helix family of technologies also stake their claims at the top of the new wave of broadband video content.

RealSystem 8 streaming technologies allow you to target up to eight different bandwidths, while the RealServer software intelligently and dynamically negotiates between them. The full power and control of VBR and two-pass encoding allow you to achieve half-screen VHS quality at only 300 kbps.

The successor to the RealSystem G7 platform is RealSystem iQ, which replaces Version 7 player and server software with Version 8. Version 8 includes modern features such as two-pass VBR encoding and de-interlacing for the first time.

With the RealOne platform, launched in the fall of 2001, RealOne combined a consumer subscription service for viewing and listening to streaming content with a newly integrated media interface that includes the functions of RealPlayer and RealJukebox with a media browser, as well as a content discovery window where related information and links can be displayed. The new Helix platform builds on this model while delivering all the major streaming formats from a single server.

Because RealNetworks is not an OS company, RealSystem software (as you might expect) supports more operating systems than its competitors (including Windows, Linux, Solaris, and Macintosh).

Video and Audio Codecs

RealNetworks keeps things simple when it comes to codecs supported in the RealPlayer: depending on your chosen platform, you have but one set of proprietary codecs, period. So, the only real question is, which audience do you need to reach? Can you target a cutting-edge audience and challenge them to upgrade their players to Version 8 or Helix? Or, do you need to backtrack and capture a larger audience with the RealVideo G7 platform? You might even have that rare case when you must go all the way back to the G2 platform (for example, on a corporate intranet where the IS department has not yet upgraded).

Tools and Tasks

This section provides reference information about RealNetwork's tools for creating, manipulating, and delivering RealMedia files. These tools are also bundled in various special packages that you can learn more about at the RealNetworks.com home page.

RealSystem Producer Plus

Go to www.realnetworks.com/products/producer

Producer Plus (for RealMedia 8) or the newer Producer and Producer Basic for Helix are the standard tools for creating RealSystem audio and video. Producer Plus and the new Producer include the following basic features:

- Encoding for multiple bandwidths: You can simultaneously create one file for up to eight different connection speeds.

- Two-pass, VBR video encoding: Producer can scrutinize the entire video clip before it starts to encode and then assign more bandwidth to complex parts of the presentation — improving quality across all bandwidths.

- RealMedia Editor: It is a timeline-based editing tool that allows you to change start and end times, paste files together, view stream properties, and preview any RealAudio or RealVideo files.

- Bandwidth simulator: This is a feature that allows you to preview and simulate your presentation in a variety of network scenarios.

- Video scaling: It allows you to import video at any size and use Real-Producer Plus to scale the image size down for the Web.

- Multiple platforms: They are available for your choice of a number of Windows, Linux, Sun Solaris, and Apple Macintosh server platforms. Helix adds Free BSD, IBM, Hewlett-Packard, and Compaq platforms.

- Backwards compatibility: RealVideo 8 will stream from any RealServer from Version G2 or later.

- Automation ActiveX/AppleScript/batch encoding: It allows you to integrate RealProducer Plus functionality into your production system using integrated ActiveX or AppleScript components or to utilize the command-line encoder for batch scripting.

RealSlideshow

Go to www.realnetworks.com/products

RealSlideshow allows you to add still images to a stream and synchronize them to RealAudio. RealSlideshow provides the following:

- Layout control, cropping and resizing of images, linking and graphic capabilities: Use these to create dynamic RealAudio slideshows.

- Text captions: Use synchronized text captions to accompany the images and audio.

- Hyperlinks: Add hyperlinks to each image.

- Persistent images: Use a persistent image either to produce a logo for corporate identity or branding or to provide a theme to a particular presentation.

- Images and sounds: Free images and sounds are included.

RealSlideshow can import MP3s or work directly with audio discs in your computer's CD drive. It can work with most common image formats including PNG, JPEG, GIF, and BMP.

RealPresenter

Go to www.realnetworks.com/products

RealPresenter allows you to incorporate Microsoft PowerPoint presentations into your streaming content. RealPresenter includes the following:

- RealVideo 8 support: This allows use of Version 8 RealMedia formats.
- Table of contents: This allows users to jump ahead while viewing their presentation.
- Microsoft PowerPoint 97 and 2000 integration: It allows you to record, broadcast, and publish Internet presentations directly from PowerPoint.
- Free integrated RealSystem Server: You can broadcast live or archived presentations to 25 concurrent users right from your desktop (requires RealPresenter Plus).
- Wizards: These provide simple and intuitive ways to add audio and video to your presentations, edit and rerecord, and then publish them for your audience to see and hear.
- Integrated email capability: It allows you to notify your audience about the presentation and then use email to interact with them in real time during live broadcasts.

RealServer

Go to www.realnetworks.com/products/

RealNetworks provides a variety of server software products to choose from, depending on your needs and budget. Visit the Web location shown above for latest package combinations and pricing.

RealText, RealPix, and RealFlash

These solutions allow you to add various multimedia capabilities to your Real Media streams, and are discussed in detail in Chapter 5, Synchronized Media.

Additional RealNetworks Resources

Go to www.realnetworks.com/devzone

You can find the following additional resources at the RealNetworks DevZone Web location:

- GRiNS Editor Pro (allows you to create and edit RealSystem SMIL presentations)

- RealSystem plug-ins for Dreamweaver and Adobe GoLive
- Additional third-party plug-ins and tools
- Knowledge base, documentation, tutorials, and other useful information

Third-Party Tools

The companies listed in Table 2-8 offer compatible tools for RealMedia authoring, audio and video processing and production, capturing, and compression.

Table 2-8: RealMedia Third-Party Tools

Company	Go To	Product
Adobe Systems, Inc.	www.adobe.com	Adobe Premiere
Avid Technology, Inc.	www.avid.com	Avid Cinema, Avid Xpress DV, Avid ePublisher
Autodesk Inc.	www.discreet.com	Cleaner 5
Liquid Audio, Inc.	www.liquidaudio.com	Liquifier Pro, Liquid MusicServer, Liquid MusicPlayer
Sonic Foundry, Inc.	www.sonicfoundry.com	Sound Forge 4.5, Stream Anywhere, Vegas Pro
TegoSoft Inc.	www.tegosoft.com	TegoSoft's NetShow-based product
Telos Systems	www.telos-systems.com	Audioactive
Ulead Systems, Inc.	www.ulead.com	MediaStudio Pro 5.0

Before selecting a third-party vendor to provide services or products, you should conduct a thorough independent review of the third-party vendor's ability, skills, experience, and/or products to determine whether the third party can fulfill your particular needs.

QuickTime

Go to www.apple.com/quicktime

Quick Review

QuickTime, the granddaddy of multimedia authoring tools, is now more than 12 years old, and after years as the default format for CD-ROM development, QuickTime shows great depth in terms of robustness and richness of features. QuickTime was also the first to go cross-platform, and it took the streaming world by storm when it introduced fast-start HTTP streaming with QuickTime 3 in the early days of streaming video development. Various iterations of QuickTime 4 introduced a slew of solid streaming media features, and the renegade QuickTime Streaming Server went open source in 2000.

But, as the saying goes, what have you done for me lately? A lot. The open-source QuickTime Streaming Server, along with QuickTime 5 and the Sorenson 3 codec plus newcomer On2 Technologies Inc., reestablished QuickTime's parity among the big three, with high-quality, quick, low-bandwidth VBR encoding and playback, as well as a number of enhancements to streaming capabilities including the addition of DSL and cable modem to the list of connection speeds, as well as enhanced skip protection during streaming. QuickTime 6 introduces support for both MPEG-4 and MPEG-2.

QuickTime also retains its lead as a development platform, with a robust hardware-independent container structure and full-featured support for working with the widest range of media types of the big three. See Table 2-9.

Table 2-9: QuickTime Video Codecs

Codec	Description
Animation	For high-quality lossless compression (in which no picture information is lost). Encodes each pixel using a run-length coding scheme. Results in a file that is 70 to 95 percent the size of the uncompressed file. At the maximum quality, this is a lossless compression (in which no picture information is lost).
Apple BMP	A bitmap image format.
Apple Video	Generic desktop video format.
Cinepak	For export at low resolution for use in contexts where high quality is not an issue, such as presentations or educational uses, or for small-screen size playback from CD-ROM or hard drive. Uses compression algorithm optimized for CD-ROM playback.
Component Video	For high-quality lossless compression (in which no picture information is lost). Uses the same algorithm as the Animation method but saves the file in YUV RLE format, which separates the luminance from the chrominance. All QuickTime applications can read this format, but only some can write to this format.
DV NTSC and PAL	Apple's high-quality implementation of the industry-standard DV format for video.
Graphics	For export at low resolution for use in contexts where high quality is not an issue, such as presentations or educational uses, or for small-screen-size playback from CD-ROM or hard drive. Uses a limited color palette version (16 colors) of Animation compression.

Table 2-9: QuickTime Video Codecs (Continued)

Codec	Description
H.261	Video format originally created for videoconferencing purposes, optimized for low data rates with little motion in the picture.
H.263	Video format originally created for videoconferencing purposes, optimized for low data rates with little motion in the picture.
Intel Indeo Video	A video format created by Intel for use primarily on CD-ROM.
Microsoft RLE	A video format created by Microsoft for playback in Windows Media Player.
Microsoft Video 1	Creates files that will play in older versions of the Windows Media Player.
Motion JPEG A	For medium-quality lossy compression (in which some picture information is lost), requiring much storage space and additional hardware support for real-time playback. Motion JPEG (M-JPEG) is a variant of the ISO JPEG specification for use in digital video. Considered the standard for Motion JPEG, format A is supported by chips from Zoran and C-Cubed.
Motion JPEG B	For medium-quality lossy compression (in which some picture information is lost), requiring much storage space and additional hardware support for real-time playback. Motion JPEG (M-JPEG) is a variant of the ISO JPEG specification for use in digital video. Format B cannot use the markers that ISO JPEG and format A do; supported by chips from LSI.
None	For high-quality, lossless compression (in which no picture information is lost). Does not compress the file; results in very large files.
On2 codecs	QuickTime 5 or greater allows you to download and install additional codecs from third parties. The most notable in this category are the codecs from On2 Technologies. These include codecs such as VP3 and VP4, with compression quality that equals or in some cases surpasses Sorenson Video. For more information, visit www.on2.com.
Photo-JPEG	For medium-quality lossy compression (in which some picture information is lost), requiring moderate storage space and data throughput on playback. Uses the Joint Photographic Experts Group (JPEG) algorithm for image compression; results in files that are 20 percent to 30 percent the size of the uncompressed files. Some data is lost during compression, and the export process takes longer to complete (typically six times longer than the Animation compression, for example).

Table 2-9: QuickTime Video Codecs (Continued)

Codec	Description
Planar RGB	For high-quality lossless compression (in which no picture information is lost). Results in large files. Encodes each image plane separately, using a run-length encoding scheme. Used primarily to support Photoshop files, which are usually stored using a planar run-length algorithm.
Sorenson Video	Medium-quality lossy video format optimized for use in low-bandwidth situations on the Web or for broadband use on CD-ROM. The most popular QuickTime multimedia format.

The audio codecs listed in Table 2-10 are installed with QuickTime. MP3 is always a good choice, but it requires greater CPU speed than some others and can prove to be too much of a challenge on older systems. The old standard IMA 4:1 compression remains solidly supported on the widest range of sound cards.

Table 2-10: QuickTime Audio Codecs

Codec	Description
IMA 4:1	An older but highly reliable codec supported on most sound cards.
MP3	MPEG layer 3 audio, the de facto Web audio standard. Always a good choice, but requires greater CPU speeds than some other codecs.
QDesign Music 1 and 2	From QDesign, optimized for use with music tracks.
Qualcomm PureVoice	From QDesign, optimized for use with voice tracks.

Import File Formats

The following formats can be imported directly into the QuickTime Player (requires QuickTime Pro):

- 3DMF
- AIFF
- AU
- Audio CD Data (Macintosh)
- AVI
- BMP
- DV
- FlashPix
- GIF
- JPEG/JFIF
- Karaoke
- MacPaint
- Macromedia Flash
- MIDI
- MPEG-1 (Macintosh)
- MPEG-1, Layer 3 (MP3, M3U)
- Photoshop
- PICS
- PICT
- Pictures
- PNG
- QuickTime Image File
- QuickTime Movie
- SGI
- SMIL
- Sound
- Targa
- Text
- TIFF

- TIFF-fax
- Virtual Reality (VR)
- Wave

QuickTime also supports import of multiple images and layers in TIFF, FlashPix, and Photoshop files.

Export Formats

The following formats can be imported directly into the QuickTime Player (requires QuickTime Pro):

- AIFF
- AU
- AVI
- BMP
- DV Stream
- FLC
- JPEG/JFIF
- MacPaint
- MIDI
- Photoshop
- PICT
- Picture
- PNG
- QuickTime Image
- QuickTime Movie
- SGI
- System 7 Sound
- Targa
- Text
- TIFF
- TIFF-fax
- WAV

Video Effects

The following effects can be used in QuickTime-supported video applications (also in QuickTime Pro):

- Alpha gain
- Blur
- Color balance
- Color style
- Color tint
- Edge detection
- Emboss
- Film noise
- General convolution
- HSL balance
- Lens flare
- RGB balance
- Sharpen
- Zoom

Tools and Tasks

This section provides reference information about Apple's tools for creating, manipulating, and delivering QuickTime files.

QuickTime Pro

Go to www.apple.com/quicktime/products/qt

The QuickTime Pro upgrade for standard QuickTime allows you to work with 35 different file formats, performing basic editing, importing, exporting, and encoding tasks.

iMovie

Go to www.apple.com/imovie

iMovie 2 allows you to capture video from digital camcorders and perform basic editing, importing, exporting, and encoding tasks. You can also add titles, transitions, music, narration, and sound effects to create a finished movie.

Final Cut Pro

Go to www.apple.com/finalcutpro

Final Cut Pro combines professional editing, compositing, and special effects capabilities into one software package that utilizes DV and FireWire standards.

QTVR Authoring Studio

Go to www.apple.com/quicktime/products/qt

The QTVR Authoring Studio allows you to create 360-degree panoramic movies and virtual reality objects and to combine those elements into fully-functional immersive environments.

Additional Apple Resources

Visit the QuickTime Developers area at the Apple Website developer.apple.com/quicktime for knowledge base, documentation, tutorials, and other useful information.

You can find the additional resources shown in the following tables at the Apple QuickTime Web location (www.apple.com).:

Table 2-11: QuickTime Streaming Tools

Tool	Platform	Description
RTSP/RTP Proxy	Mac OS, Win32	Used to give client machines within a protected network access to streaming servers outside that network.
QTPlayer Streaming Info	Mac OS, Win32	This plug-in adds an Info Panel for streaming tracks that shows packet transfer information.
QTStreamSplicer	Mac OS, Win32	This tool allows you to add an image to an audio-only live stream (or in front of a streaming track).
Hint Track Profiler	Mac OS	A diagnostic tool that graphs a streaming movie's hinted packets over time.

Table 2-12: QuickTime Webmaster Tools

Tool	Platform	Description
Plug-In Helper	Mac OS, Win32	Associates URLs as well as stores QuickTime plug-in settings inside a QuickTime movie.

Table 2-12: QuickTime Webmaster Tools (Continued)

Tool	Platform	Description
MakeRefMovie 2.1	Mac OS, Win32	Creates alternate movies for various Internet connection speeds, CPUs, languages, and more.

Table 2-13: QuickTime Effects Tools

Tool	Platform	Description
FlareMaker	Mac OS	This tool allows you to explore different Lens Flare effects for use in other applications.
MakeEffectMovie	Mac OS, Win32	Takes the video tracks from two movies and creates a new movie with an effects track for them.
Effects Teaser	Mac OS, Win32	This utility lets you explore the effects architecture in QuickTime.
MakeEffectSlideShow	Mac OS	Makes a slideshow movie that uses an effect to switch from one video track to the next.

Table 2-14: QuickTime VR Tools

Tool	Platform	Description
QTVR Edit Object	Mac OS	This tool allows you to set many parameters for QTVR Object movies such as column and row settings, pan and tilt controls, auto-play, and animate settings.
QTVR PanoToThumbnail	Mac OS	Allows you to create a small thumbnail-size linear QuickTime movie out of your QTVR panorama.
QTVR Flattener	Mac OS, Win32	Lets you export Web-ready QTVR movies from QuickTime Player.
QTVR Converter	Mac OS, Win32	Converts between 1.0 and 2.0 versions of QTVR files using QuickTime Player's Export command.
QTVR Make Panorama 2	Mac OS	This tool allows you to create QuickTime VR panoramas from panoramic PICT images.

Table 2-15: QuickTime QD3D Tools

Tool	Platform	Description
3D Movie Maker	Mac OS	A tool for quickly creating QuickTime movie files that contain animated 3D models.

Table 2-15: QuickTime QD3D Tools (Continued)

Tool	Platform	Description
QD3D Viewer	Win32	Allows you to open and manipulate Quick-Draw 3D files on Windows 95 and Windows NT systems.
QD3D Scrapbook	Mac OS	Lets you easily view and store text, pictures, movies, and 3DMF models in a scrapbook form.
QD3D to QTVR Converter for Panoramas	Mac OS	Converts QuickDraw 3D files into a sequence of frames that can be turned into QTVR panoramas.
QD3D to QTVR Converter for Objects	Mac OS	Lets you convert QuickDraw 3D files into a QuickTime VR Object using the 'QTVR Edit Objects tool listed in Table 2-14.
TextureEyes	Mac OS, Win32	Let's you apply any picture, movie, or video to the surface of a 3D object, paint on objects in 3D, or select different plug-in renderers.
3Debug	Mac OS	A debugging tool illustrating when and how 3D objects are managed within an application that tracks down possible memory leaks, and more.

Table 2-16: QuickTime Programmer Tools

Tool	Platforms	Description
Dumpster	Mac OS, Win32	Lets you view and edit moov (QuickTime Movie) resources.
HackTV	Mac OS, Win32	A basic movie capture tool that allows you to record audio and/or video.
Reinstaller3	Mac OS	Lets you drag a resource file onto Reinstaller 3 to destroy and re-register any components defined in the file.

Table 2-17: QuickTime Third-Party Tools

Company	Go To	Product
Adobe Systems, Inc.	www.adobe.com	Adobe Premiere, GoLive, After Effects

Table 2-17: QuickTime Third-Party Tools (Continued)

Company	Go To	Product
AutoDesk Inc.	www.discreet.com	EditDV, RotoDV, Cleaner 5, Media Cleaner Pro
Avid Technology, Inc.	www.avid.com	Avid Cinema, Avid Xpress DV, Avid ePublisher
Fidelity Media	www.megaseg.com	MegaSeg
Macromedia	www.macromedia.com	Flash
Media 100	www.media100.com	iFinish
MovieWorks Inc.	www.movieworks.com	MovieWorks
Pinnacle Systems	www.commotionpro.com	CommotionPro
Sorenson Media	www.sorenson.com	Sorenson Broadcaster
Totally Hip	www.totallyhip.com	LiveStage Professional, LiveSlideShow
Tribeworks	www.tribeworks.com	iShell

Before selecting a third-party vendor to provide services or products, you should conduct a thorough independent review of the third-party vendor's ability, skills, experience, and/or products to determine whether the third party can fulfill your particular needs.

Part C: Methods

Choosing Your Technologies

When developing your own approach to streaming video and audio and when contacting service providers, you need to determine the following:

- Which encoding technologies will you use?

- Which media players would be best for your audience?

- Which server platform will you use?

- Will you deliver audio only or audio and video?

- Is your content short form or long form?

- Is your application in business, education, or entertainment?

- Will you provide on-demand, near-live, or live Webcasting?

- Do you require a distributed network solution or just a single unicast origination point?

Your answers to these questions will affect everything from your choice of development tools to your hosting services to your content options, as described below.

Which Encoding Technologies?

- Windows Media Technologies

- QuickTime

- RealNetworks RealMedia

- MPEG

This topic and the next (having to do with players and platforms) go hand in hand, since at the moment the owners of the player technologies all have their own streaming-video encoding schemes. Encoding technologies have advanced significantly in recent years. Those of us who began our multimedia careers with Cinepak can't help but be impressed with the current generation of video encoders from Real, Microsoft, and Apple.

By way of comparison, that 50 MB piece of video that once played off a CD-ROM at 180 kbps with Cinepak is now a 5 MB file that plays over the Internet using the Real Encoder at 18 kbps with similar quality. Amazing.

Experts can argue endlessly about the virtues of Real's encoder over Windows Media Technologies, over the Sorenson codec, but the truth is, they are all pretty close. By comparison with encoding technologies of the recent past, you can't lose. MPEG-4 is a factor that can shake things up a bit, but the standard and its implementation are still a work in progress.

For more information on the specific tools, see Part B: Tools on page 25. The truth is, whatever your choice, encoders are relatively low on the scale of technology factors you must consider when choosing delivery formats.

More important are the underlying technologies used for getting the data from the server to the user's computer, which have a more profound impact on both the data rates at which you can encode and the quality of the end-user experience. Read on.

Which Players and Platforms?

*   Windows
*   QuickTime
*   RealSystem

There are three angles on your choice of players and technologies to this: server-side, client-side (the end user), and development-side.

As a developer, first of all, which culture are you most comfortable with, Windows or Macintosh? Keep in mind that, in this day and age, development and testing of content for most streaming applications will involve both platforms, so the more agnostic you are, the better for your career in streaming media. However, if you have a preference and a set of tools on just one platform, you can simplify your life by focusing on testing and delivery for a single player.

Client-side, you need to consider the audience in your choice of players required to play the video. Are they all Windows users? Windows and Macintosh users? Mostly Mac?

Real, Windows, and QuickTime are all allegedly cross-platform, though common sense and experience suggest that consistent use of each vendor's products will yield fewer snags: RealServer with the RealPlayer (Mac and Windows), QuickTime Streaming Server with QuickTime (where there is a predominance of Mac users), Windows servers with Windows Media Technologies (often in business applications where Windows is ubiquitous).

As an interesting twist in this clash of the titans, Real and Apple recently announced that RealServer 8 will now support the QuickTime streaming format, which opens up opportunities for broader use of QuickTime streaming because there are far more RealServers deployed throughout the world than QuickTime Streaming Servers.

Apple and Windows both have the advantage of including their players with their respective OS software, although users must download and install players on the other platform (QuickTime on Windows or the Windows Media Player on the Macintosh). With RealPlayer, users must download and install the software on either platform if they haven't done so already.

Also, consider that the players themselves support different technologies beyond just video. For example, the QuickTime player supports Flash (SWF format), allowing you to mix video with animated Flash content. Both QuickTime and current versions of RealPlayer support the open SMIL standard for synchronizing video, audio, text, and graphics elements within the player. Most of us are used to thinking of these players as video-only vehicles. You can find links to some fascinating real-world examples of these mixed-format presentations at the Real Website (www.realnetworks.com) and Apple's QuickTime Web location (www.apple.com/quicktime).

Audio Only or Audio and Video?

This choice has a huge impact on deployment of streaming content as a result of the vastly different bandwidth requirements. If your presentation can do with audio only, depending on the length of the material, you can probably get by without a true streaming server and the associated expenses, distributing your content off a standard HTTP server.

Short Form or Long Form?

If video is a must, then you have the next choice to consider: Is the content short form (several minutes) or long form (10 minutes or greater)?

If your video is short form, consider HTTP streaming to deliver your video. Delivery via HTTP in the QuickTime progressive video format, for example, allows you to avoid the added expense of setting up or renting space on a true streaming video server.

HTTP streaming is great for short movies and anything else you intend to play over and over again. The trailer for the *Star Wars* prequel in 2000, for example, was one of the most successful downloads of all time.

In addition, consider that the QuickTime progressive format is not lossy but results in a complete frame-accurate download. The AvidProNet Review & Approval technology, for example, leverages this added accuracy of the progressive download.

Real-time streaming, on the other hand, is a must for full-length movies, lengthy presentations, and live events. In addition to meeting the unique throughput and storage demands of long-form viewing, real-time streaming technologies make it easier for viewers to navigate randomly throughout a long program, another important feature to keep in mind. Navigating randomly in a progressive video download involves long waiting times when moving to a section that has not yet been downloaded.

Which Market: Business, Education, or Entertainment?

The type of content you are delivering also affects your technology requirements. If you are developing business applications, such as corporate training or presentations, then you might not need to spend the money on an expensive distributed network solution, because most businesses already operate close to high-speed Internet backbones, using T1 or T3 lines. If you have the budget, however, and want to use higher-quality video at higher data rates, delivery at the edge is still an option.

If you are delivering distance-learning content to higher-education institutions, the same situation applies. Most colleges are closely linked to a high-speed backbone, and some are part of the Internet2 experiment, making distributed networking solutions unnecessary.

For entertainment, this usually means reaching a mass audience, and depending on the performance requirements and reach of your project, a distributed network solution might be necessary. Apple's close connection with Akamai is a good example of a solid marriage between streaming entertainment content and delivery technology.

On-Demand, Near-Live, or Live Webcasting?

On-demand Webcasting is the most common form of streaming, allowing any combination of users to access the streams whenever they like. On-demand Webcasting is subject to the requirements described in the previous topic.

Live Webcasting is a whole other animal and usually requires significant support from third-party distributed network service and technology providers to handle large audiences. Visit www.netaid.org for more information on the technologies used to deliver the largest live Webcast in history.

Video Preparation Tips

Here are a few tips to keep in mind when shooting video that you will encode for streaming on the Web:

- Shoot on a high-quality format, with the best equipment available. Professional cameras using broadcast-quality tape formats such as BetaSP or Digital Betacam are the best option, followed by prosumer DV formats.

- Make sure the subject is well lit.

- Avoid frequent or rapid movements whenever possible.

- Keep the camera steady as much as possible.

- Closeups generally encode better than wide complex shots.

Here are a few tips to keep in mind when capturing video that you will encode for streaming on the Web:

- If you recorded in a consumer format, consider using an industrial playback deck that has a TimeBase Corrector (TBC).

- Keep your signal transfer path as clean as possible. Use a DV FireWire connection for DV video or an S-Video connection rather than composite RCA jacks whenever possible.

Here are a few tips to keep in mind when preparing captured video clips for encoding:

- Name the clips. For the greatest cross-platform compatibility, be sure to name your movie in a way that does not confuse the Web server's file system, the client computer's file system, or the Web browser. Remove spaces and special characters from filenames; consider making the names lowercase. Make sure to include the proper extension.

- Make movies self-contained (QuickTime only). For prerecorded movies, you'll need to decide whether you want to stream self-contained movies or movies that contain dependencies. Self-contained movies contain all the information for that movie within the movie file. Movies with dependencies contain references to the media tracks in other movies, which would also have to be on the server. Self-contained movies are easier to handle — there's only one file to worry about.

- Hint movies (QuickTime only). Prerecorded and live QuickTime movies must be hinted for streaming. This means creating a hint track for each media track in the movie (except for QuickTime VR and Flash tracks, which cannot be streamed). The hint tracks, which are stored in the movie along with the video, audio, and other tracks, provide Quick-Time Streaming Server software with information about the server, the transmission packet size, and the protocol to be used — in short, how to send the movie data over the network.

Encoding Methods and Target Rates

Topics in this section describe the encoding process, with tips and techniques for producing the best possible results at both low and high data rates.

On-Demand Encoding Workflow

The workflow for encoding on-demand content is roughly the same in all of the big three formats, no matter the output:

- Choose the source.

- Choose the encoding parameters, based on default or customized templates.

- Choose the destination.

- Start encoding.

- Where the three formats differ most is in the postencoding phase prior to deployment, or what is sometimes called late-stage editing. Basic late-stage procedures such as hinting of QuickTime files and preparation of scripts are described in "Late-Stage Editing" on page 64. Additional information on adding URL flips, manipulating tracks, and enabling various multimedia features are described in Chapter 5, Synchronized Media.

- If you use Cleaner to encode your content, you can accomplish a number of basic late-stage editing tasks, such as adding URL flips, during the encoding phase. For more information, consult the Cleaner documentation.

Live Encoding Workflow: Similarities and Differences

The workflow for encoding of live content is similar among the big three formats, with a few differences:

- Carefully set up the live encoding environment from source to output. This includes establishing connection from the source camera or live switcher (when there are several cameras) to the encoding workstation, from the encoding workstation to a streaming server over a high-speed IP network, and from the server to a multicast backbone (MBone), or in some cases from the streaming server to a distributed network of servers when you must reach a national or international audience. Optionally, a third computer is set up to act as a unicast reflector to stream out to areas of the Web not accessible through an Mbone. Some or all of these connections are usually established with the aid of a distributed network service provider.

- Prepare the necessary broadcasting software for live encoding. In the case of Windows Media and RealSystems, live encoding can be accomplished using the same software used to encode on-demand material — specifically, Windows Media Encoder or RealProducer. In the case of QuickTime, live encoding requires Sorenson Broadcaster (available from Sorenson Media; visit www.sorenson.com). The encoding software must be properly configured for live encoding prior to the live event. Use the broadcast software to create a session description protocol (SDP) file on the computer you use to capture and encode the live signal. See the instructions that came with your broadcast software.

- With all systems in place, turn on all devices, open the encoding software, and perform all necessary checks. Copy the SDP file to your streaming server. Be sure to copy the file into the media folder you're using for streaming. If it is not there, streaming will not happen.

- If you want the streamed media to show on a Web page, set up the Web page.

- Make sure streaming services are started.

- Start the capture software by following the instructions that came with the broadcast software.

Effective Encoding Environments

To encode your clips, you need to establish an encoding system using a capable computer along with software tools described in Part B of this chapter. You can encode using the tools provided by the software manufacturer (Microsoft, Apple, or RealNetworks), or you can encode on-demand material using a third-party tool, such as Cleaner from discreet. Various editing products also allow you to encode directly from the application using either plug-ins from the streaming software manufacturer or third-party plug-ins such as Media Cleaner EZ.

Here are some factors to consider when establishing your encoding environment:

- Use the fastest computer available. Encoding is CPU-intensive, but not memory-intensive. The more processing power your system has, the faster your clips will encode.

- Devote the system to the encoding task. Because encoding is CPU-intensive, the less activity that takes place on that system during encoding, the faster it will encode. Encoding live data is the most processor-intensive, so certainly make sure you have a dedicated encoding station during a live Webcast.

- Configuring Microsoft Windows. If you are planning to use Microsoft Windows NT Server instead of Windows NT Workstation, we highly recommend that you change the system setting to reduce the amount of memory that is used for caching files. Otherwise, Windows NT Server attempts to expand the file cache at the expense of Windows Media Encoder. The result is that the encoder gets paged out and falls behind when capturing data from the audio device. The settings for this preference can be found by clicking start > settings > control panel > network > services.

- Standard CPU monitoring tools, such as Microsoft Performance Monitor, cannot precisely measure the CPU load of the encoder because they are not able to show the instantaneous CPU peaks that last just a few milliseconds. When there is high motion in the video, the CPU load can exceed what is available for just one frame time (33 milliseconds at 30 fps), which causes a frame of video to be lost. Such peaks are impossible to observe with a performance monitor that shows average CPU usage over time.

Encoding Target Rates

With streaming media, it's all about bandwidth. No amount of effort can overcome the basic limitations of the pipes. Most encoding software includes templates that take into account the hard realities of the public network and choose the appropriate data rates for you. If you use the manufacturer's templates, in most cases you can't go wrong.

For added control, you can click on the Encode tab in the Cleaner 5 interface or dig more deeply into the manufacturer's encoding software to adjust these data rates directly. In most cases, this is not necessary. In some special cases (for example, when you want to boost the data rate of the audio significantly and reduce the video rate to give priority to sound quality), you can make these changes. Table 2-18 provides a general overview of appropriate data rates to maintain for the various delivery methods.

Table 2-18: Streaming Media Encoding Data Rates

Delivery	Network Data Rate	Aggregate Encode Rate — True Streaming	Aggregate Encode Rate — HTTP Streaming
28.8 modem	28 kbps	20 kbps	17 kbps
56k modem	56 kbps	32 kbps	26 kbps
Single ISDN	64 kbps	48 kbps	45 kbps
Dual ISDN	128 kbps	96 kbps	90 kbps
DSL	64 to 128 kbps	48 to 96 kbps	45 to 90 kbps
Cable modems, low end	100 to 256 kbps	80 to 225 kbps	76 to 210 kbps
Cable modems, high end	256 to 512 kbps	225 to 450 kbps	210 to 420 kbps
Corporate LAN	150 kbps	110 kbps	100 kbps
Gigabit Ethernet network	1500 kbps	1100 kbps	1000 kbps
Local drive	300 to 1,500 kbps	250 to 1,400 kbps	N/A

Tips for Creating Low Bit-Rate Video

Most streaming media professionals consider a 56K modem to be the minimum connection for delivery of any kind of meaningful user experience. If you've ever attempted to view streaming video from home with a 56k modem (or worse, a 28.8 modem), you know that the phrase "good-quality low-bandwidth streaming video" is an oxymoron, not to mention a mouthful.

Creating good-quality video for low-bandwidth situations is not a lost cause. You can make the best impression by paying close attention to these five factors: the quality of the source material, the type of content, the frame rate, the sound and image quality settings, and the image size settings.

To ensure the best-looking content at 56K modem rates or lower, consider making these hard decisions:

- Edit out all motion.

- Edit out all detailed wide shots.

- Drop your frame rate to as low as 10 or 8 fps.

- Encode stereo audio as mono.

If you must deliver streaming content to 28.8 or (gasp!) 14.4 modems, consider delivering audio-only, or when images are necessary, consider showing a single still image of the speaker when the content is simply a talking head or creating a slideshow that combines audio with a series of still images-

Tips for Creating High Bit-Rate Video

At the opposite end of the spectrum is high bit-rate video for delivery in controlled circumstances, such as over a high-speed LAN or a very fast cable-modem system.

Realistic data rates for so-called broadband streaming in various circumstances are listed in Table 2-19.

Table 2-19: Streaming Media Broadband Data Rates

Delivery	Network Data Rate	Aggregate Encode Data Rate
DSL	100 to 256 kbps	80 to 225 kbps
Cable modems, low end	100 to 256 kbps	80 to 225 kbps
Cable modems, high end	256 to 512 kbps	225 to 450 kbps
LAN	150 kbps	110 kbps
Local drive	300 to 1,500 kbps	250 to 1,400 kbps

The rules for producing good-quality high bit-rate video are the same as for low bit-rate content, but because the receiving systems must process more data in the same amount of time, you should be reasonably certain that your audience is using modern computers, with CPU speeds of 300 MHz or greater.

High-end broadband video delivery is relatively new, and therefore most encoding software packages do not include templates covering broadband delivery in the very high range, for local playback or playback over a gigabit Ethernet network, for example.

Windows Media Encoder 7, for example, covers bit rates up to 1,500 kbps, while RealProducer 8 templates go up to 512K cable/DSL/LAN rates. To achieve higher rates, you must create custom templates and make adjustments.

Here are a few tips to keep in mind when creating your broadband encoding templates:

- To reduce the CPU requirements on the client, you can change the audio codec setting to mono.

- Avoid selecting too high a data rate for the audio portion of your stream because it increases both the encoding and decoding processing requirements of the system.

Setup of Multiple Bit-Rate Video

All of the big three formats allow you to set up your video streams so that users receive the one stream that is appropriate for their particular bandwidth. Although your Web location might show a single link to the video, for example, behind the scenes the video technology is able to choose among several video clips encoded at different rates, based on the user's connection speed.

This process of setting up multiple bit-rate video works differently, depending on your choice of streaming video technology:

- RealSystem employs the SureStream technology developed by RealNetworks. SureStream is included as part of RealServer software. Real's templates include SureStream options for encoding multiple streams. No further steps are necessary once the video is encoded and deployed on a RealServer. The RealServer software automatically calculates the user's connection speed and delivers the appropriate media stream.

- Windows Media Technologies employs Intelligent Stream technology developed by Microsoft. Intelligent Stream is included as part of Windows Media Services whenever you set up streaming on a Windows server. Windows Media Technologies templates include Intelligent Stream options for encoding multiple streams. No further steps are necessary once the video is encoded and deployed on a Windows media server. The server software automatically calculates the user's connection speed and delivers the appropriate media stream.

- QuickTime uses a different system for handling multiple bit rates. The QuickTime control panel includes an option for setting the connection speed of the client computer, which users choose when they first install

QuickTime. Content creators must then set up a QuickTime Reference movie that includes references to multiple bandwidth QuickTime streams. The reference movie is able to determine the connection speed settings on the client computer and deliver the appropriate stream.

- Although the QuickTime implementation requires more effort on the part of content creators — and involves the possibility of user error in entering the wrong connection speed into the QuickTime settings — there are also some advantages to this system. For example, this implementation works even when delivering movies from an HTTP server, which makes QuickTime a strong choice for delivery from a standard Web server. You can also use this feature to handle backward-compatibility or to switch among streaming and nonstreaming content based on the user's settings.

Late-Stage Editing

Where the big three streaming formats differ most is in the postencoding phase prior to deployment, or what is sometimes called late-stage editing. Basic late-stage procedures such as preparation of reference movies and scripts and hinting of QuickTime files are described in this section. Additional information on adding URL flips, manipulating tracks, and enabling various multimedia features are described in Chapter 5, Synchronized Media.

Creating QuickTime Reference Movies

When streaming QuickTime video at multiple bit rates, you must use a QuickTime Reference movie to allow the system to intelligently switch among bit rates based on the user's connection speed. The easiest way to create QuickTime Reference movies is with Cleaner or Media Cleaner Pro. The Cleaner documentation describes a procedure for encoding multiple bit-rate video clips and generating a single reference movie along with the encoded clips automatically.

If you do not have Cleaner and must create a QuickTime Reference movie on your own, you'll need the Pro version of QuickTime Player and an application that allows you to make a reference movie, such as Peter Hoddie's XMLtoRefMovie utility or Apple's free MakeRefMovie utility. To make a reference movie using Apple's utility, do as follows.

Make the alternate data rate movies:

- If some of your alternates are streaming movies, make Fast Start movies that point to them, and use the Fast Start movie as the alternate for the stream.

- To create a Fast Start movie that points to a streaming movie, open the streaming movie in QuickTime Player by choosing Open URL from the

File menu and typing in the URL. Then choose Save As from the File menu, name it, and save it as a self-contained movie.

- Also create a default movie that anyone in your audience can see, no matter what connection or computer they are using. It could be a few frames from your movie with a low-bandwidth audio track, a single image with a scrolling text track and no audio, or just a single image. In any case, keep it very small because the browser will download it even if an alternate movie is used.

- Name each movie in a logical way, including the .mov filename suffix. For example, you may want to name your alternate movies altmov01.mov, altmov02.mov, and altmov03.mov. Save as self-contained movies. Store them all in the same folder or directory.

Make the reference movie using Apple's free utility program MakeRef-Movie, available from Apple for Macintosh and Windows. The latest version of MakeRefMovie can also create reference movies that choose among alternate movies based on CPU speed, language, or QuickTime version.

Follow these steps in MakeRefMovie:

1. Open MakeRefMovie.

2. Save your new document in the same folder or directory where the alternates are located. Make sure the reference movie filename contains the .mov extension. This reference movie will call upon the alternates.

3. Drag each of the alternate movies onto the window of MakeRefMovie. An alternate movie will appear for each file you drag and drop. Or you can open each file separately by choosing Add movie file from the Movie menu.

4. Set the minimum connection speed for each alternate movie in the Speedpop-up menu.

5. Set the load order of the movies in the Priority: pop-up. For example, you may want the reference movie to call the highest-quality movie first, then the medium-quality movie, and last the lowest-quality or default movie. If there is more than one movie designed for the same connection speed, set a priority for which movie will load first.

6. Specify the default movie by checking Flatten into output. The default movie should be compressed with a codec supported by older versions of QuickTime for backward compatibility. This checkbox can only be applied to one movie.

Save the reference movie and place it and all the alternate movies in the same directory. Upload the directory or folder to the server.

Hinting QuickTime Movies

Before you can stream an existing QuickTime movie using QuickTime Streaming (from an RTP server), you must Hint it.

Hinting is the QuickTime term for adding instructions to a movie that tell the streaming server how to break the file into tiny packets of data that are sent over the Internet. Hinting also instructs the server when to send a given packet.

The easiest way to hint a movie is by using Cleaner 5 or Media Cleaner Pro. Use the Prepare for Streaming Server option in Cleaner's Advanced Settings dialog.

If you do not have Cleaner, you must hint each movie that you intend to stream on your own using the QuickTime Player:

1. Begin by opening a movie in QuickTime Player by either dragging the movie onto the application icon or launching QuickTime Player and choosing Open Movie... from the File menu option.

2. Choose Export from the File menu.

3. In the Export dialog box, enter a filename with the .mov extension, and from the Format pop-up menu, choose Movie to Hinted Movie.

4. Choose Default Settings from the Use pop-up menu.

5. Click Save to create a hinted movie, or click the Options if you wish to fine tune the hint settings.

Caution: Only those authors with advanced expertise should change the defaults as this may cause poor performance and quality of the stream.

Deployment with HTML

The simplest way to deploy your content is to prepare links on a Web page that cause the player on the client's computer to open and load the video. By simply adding a standard HREF tag into your Web page with a link to the video clip in its location on the server, you are on your way. As mentioned earlier, you must link to a QuickTime Reference movie, in the case of QuickTime.

You can also embed players into Web pages using HTML code that employs Netscape plug-ins or ActiveX Objects to achieve greater control of the user experience. Tools and methods for embedding players and developing interactivity with other elements on the Web are described in Chapter 5, Synchronized Media.

Enhancing Players with Scripting

You can improve the viewer experience, and improve your own workflow as a content creator to some extent, by delving into the various supported script technologies used to add features to the various video players. Each of the big three players supports different script technologies for achieving a variety of results:

- QuickTime: SMIL, JavaScript, AppleScript
- Windows Media Technologies: ASX scripting, JScript
- RealSystem: SMIL, JavaScript

Some of these capabilities are described in more detail in Chapter 5, Synchronized Media.

Deployment Challenges

For simple deployment of streaming video, the basic steps are:

1. Upload the video content to the streaming server.
2. Upload the HTML files containing links to the video to the HTTP server.

Many of the applications described throughout this chapter, such as Cleaner, Windows On-Demand Producer, and RealProducer will do these steps for you automatically after encoding video.

The real challenges of deployment come when seeking to optimize both the hardware and software used to deliver streaming media effectively. The following sections describe a few tips for achieving effective streaming.

The Server

The configuration requirement for the server platform differs depending on whether the content is being streamed live or on demand. Specifically, if the server platform is streaming on-demand content, you must plan on having a high-performance disk subsystem. When streaming live content, the performance of the disk subsystem is not a factor. Also note that a single server can stream out about 50 to 70 Mbps (over a 100-megabit network card). If you have to go beyond this limit, you must use a cluster of servers with some type of load-balancing software.

Once the performance of a single CPU server (about 30 Mbps to 50 Mbps) is exceeded, you should consider using a cluster of computers and load-balancing software.

Microsoft Windows Load Balancing Service (WLBS) allows clustering of TCP/IP-based network services across up to 32 computers, which then appear as a single logical TCP/IP address space. WLBS complements Microsoft Cluster Service (MSCS), which is part of Microsoft Windows NT Server, Enterprise Edition. You can also use a multiprocessor system to increase your throughput, although this creates a single point of failure and is not as reliable as a clustered system.

New servers are appearing in the market to handle the specific needs of streaming media. For example, the Trilligent Cluster systems from Avid Technology, Inc., can achieve extraordinary streaming data throughput and are easy to manage. Monitoring on Trilligent Cluster also allows service providers to track performance of the system. Both RealServer and Microsoft Windows Media Services include a number of performance counters that you or your service provider can use to track performance.

The Client

The requirements for your audience — the client computers — vary depending on the bit rate, video frame size, and frame rate. The most important requirement is a high-performance graphics card followed closely by a high-performance CPU.

The following list shows the minimum client configuration for data rates up to 250 kbps:

- CPU speed of 166 MHz or greater
- 32 MB of memory

If you provide content at bit rates higher than 250 kbps, use the following client configuration — this client computer performs well for data rates of up to 2 Mbps:

- CPU speed of 233 MHz or greater
- 64 MB of memory
- High-performance graphics card

For a client computer that supports the highest data rates, use the following specifications:

- CPU speed of 400 MHz
- 64 MB of memory
- High-performance graphics card

Using Distributed Networks

As described in the section "Taking It to the Edge" on page 21, a number of service providers exist for distributing your streamed content around the world and are closer to users so that the effectiveness of streaming is greatly improved. Networks such as Akamai and RealNetworks provide these services.

Section I: Server-Based Architectures

CHAPTER 3

Motion Graphics

This chapter provides information that will help you to understand the challenges, choose your tools, and then create and distribute dynamic motion graphics content on the World Wide Web.

Part A: Background

Introduction

Let's say, for the sake of this Introduction, that you've authored a fabulous knock-their-socks-off sequence in a state-of-the-art nonlinear video editing or compositing system. After previewing the piece, your client/project manager/executive producer says, "Great. Now how can we get this onto the Web?"

As with most technical challenges today, there is no single solution. The quick option, of course, is to encode your sequence directly to QuickTime, Real Media, or Windows Media — and watch your pristine D1 effects shrink, turn blocky, and sputter during playback. This is where many a motion graphics professional says, "Can't we just wait for broadband?"

There is another way. If you've ever visited the Flash or Shockwave sites showcased at Macromedia's site (www.macromedia.com/showcase), or the Adobe Website (www.adobe.com) and been awed by the beautifully balanced elements of print design, motion graphics, and Web technologies you've seen there, then you've probably wondered, "How do they do it?" This chapter provides a few answers to that question.

The Importance of Parsing

The key, in a word, is parsing. Not the kind of parsing that occurs when a browser interprets HTML code, but "screen parsing," or better yet, "application parsing," if I can coin a term that's more appropriate for the burgeoning field of dynamic media production on the Web.

To be specific, I'm referring to the various tricks and methods used by Website designers and builders to minimize the throughput requirements of a site's display by cutting up, or breaking down, the screen content and targeting specific text, video, or animation technologies to specific regions of the screen to create distinctive effects online. All of this takes place under the hood, invisible to the user, who experiences in some cases the cumulative effect of a rich, interactive CD-ROM, but one with global reach and the potential for more dynamic database-driven content.

This process of "tricking" the browser, if you will, and tricking the user's eye as well, in order to conquer stingy bandwidth situations goes back to the heydays of CD-ROM development during the late 1980s and the early 1990s when multimedia developers first learned similar methods of combining still images with small sprites, for example, to give the effect of a fully animated screen while wrestling with variables of frame rates and color depth. With the shiny silver disc, however, developers wrestle with a bandwidth cap in the 200 to 300 KBps range. Compare that with the 3 to 6 KBps throughput limits in Web applications that must take into account modem users, and you can imagine the dilemma for today's dynamic media professionals.

If the Web is so much poorer in bandwidth, you might ask, why bother with special effects and animation? Some purists believe the Web should stick more closely to its roots as a hypertext medium, with the emphasis on "text." Thankfully, for those of us who welcome the evolution toward richer content, new compression and presentation technologies allow developers to achieve an impressive level of quality even at low bandwidths — provided they know how to maximize the resources. These specific technologies of the World Wide Web have given rise to a new crop of tricksters who combine a broad range of new tools and technologies to achieve stunning effects.

Compiled Versus Uncompiled Applications

In most CD-ROM applications, all the elements in the animation stew are compiled into a single file and then presented to the user through some kind of player. Of course the ultimate compiled application is a piece of video in which all graphics, text, video, and sound are completely interlaced and molded together into a seamless electronic whole.

One of the major differences on the World Wide Web is that the elements remain uncompiled, for the most part — living as a collection of individual files on a single server or several servers — and are presented through the browser, which is the "player," in this case.

There are two common exceptions to this rule: one is the Java applet, which is a compiled application; the second is Flash, but only in those cases where the Flash developers decide to deliver an entire application within the Flash player rather than combining Flash elements with other elements such as DHTML within the browser. There are other instances of compiled content playing through plug-ins in the browser, but these two examples are the most common. Many Websites deliver their content entirely in Flash these days, particularly in the context of interactive television (iTV) as described in Chapter 16.

As with CD-ROM titles — which can employ numerous technologies to achieve effects — from QuickTime to various Director Xtras, for example — Websites also use various supporting players and plug-in technologies. The goal, in all cases, is to combine the best possible tools for the most efficient performance — and the least amount of hassle for the user. Because the elements remain uncompiled in browser-based delivery, you can easily replace low-bandwidth content with higher-bandwidth content and deliver for both the Web and disc using these technologies.

Browser-Native Technologies: GIF Me a Reason

In general, you can think of browser-native technologies as those that are supported and developed by the World Wide Web Consortium (W3C), whose recommendations are eventually supported on most browsers. The great benefit of W3C standards-based technologies is that each standard usually leverages and integrates with other standards. For example, the scalable vector graphics (SVG) standard discussed in this chapter is based in XML and therefore integrates directly with other types of XML content.

In terms of motion graphics, plenty of first-generation Websites took the step toward rich-media delivery with the addition of animated graphics interchange formats (GIFs). Like the still-image GIF format, animated GIFs are browser-native, which means they require no supporting plug-ins. As a result they are not only easy to author but easy for the end user to experience. Spinning logos and banner ads are everywhere now, adding a more dynamic look to the Web. Many Website developers and managers have no reason to change this routine and remain wary of moving beyond this tried-and-true content as everyone waits for new standards and broadband delivery methods to settle.

For many developers, the next step toward fully animated content is some amount of tinkering with Dynamic HTML (DHTML), described in more detail in Chapter 4, along with the Cascading Style Sheets (CSS) standard, which supports text animation and effects. Like animated GIFs, numerous features of DHTML are native to version 4 browsers and later. DHTML is not itself a W3C standard but comprises HTML, JavaScript, and JScript. Three additional effects-oriented technologies from the W3C are scalable vector graphics (SVG) described in this chapter, synchronized multimedia instruction language (SMIL), and XHTML+SMIL, both of which are described in Chapter 5.

The Virtues of Vectors

The first technology to crack the GIF animation barrier as a frequently used dynamic content tool was Flash. Flash introduced vector graphics to the Web, a revolutionary development when you consider that even seasoned CD-ROM developers did not discover the virtues of vectors until Flash came along.

SVG is the open-standard version of vector graphics animation. Yet, while SVG is just starting to emerge, the Flash plug-in (which has been shipping with browsers since Version 4.0 of Navigator and Internet Explorer) is now installed on more than 97 percent of computers, according to Macromedia. Version 5 of the Flash player began shipping with Internet Explorer 6.

Vector-based graphics are to bitmap graphics what Adobe Illustrator is to Adobe Photoshop or Macromedia Freehand is to Procreate Painter, for example. Vector graphics consist of mathematically drawn lines and shapes, which produce smaller source files than bitmap graphics. Because the display of vector graphics is generated dynamically from the mathematical information, the content is scalable to a broad range of display sizes, while bitmap graphics, which consist of collections of individual pixels, become ragged when scaled up from their native size and also lose detail when scaled down. These are great advantages in low-bandwidth situations, and particularly when animating content, since the vector-drawn artwork can bend and reshape and resize without dramatically increasing file sizes.

In contrast to Flash, the SVG specification (released as a Version 1.0 recommendation in September 2001) is an open standard that was developed by the W3C and numerous industry players, including Adobe Systems, IBM, Netscape, Sun, Corel, Hewlett-Packard, and others. The specifics of these technologies are described in Part B: Tools.

Raw Text Versus Vector or Bitmapped Text

While it is tempting to author all of your dynamic content using Flash, many developers still try to use raw text for some of their content within the browser, which is to say text that is drawn using the fonts and text-display technologies that exist on the user's system. Rather than storing the appearance of the text in graphics files or vector formats on the server, developers use basic HTML or CSS to draw text on the user or client system. Cascading Style Sheets (CSS) provide control over the appearance of text displayed in this way, and even the most graphically sophisticated Websites still use basic HTML for some amount of text content. One big difference between SVG and Flash is that SVG, like HTML, remains in script form at all times. Thus, like HTML code, SVG content is completely searchable and can be generated and manipulated dynamically within an SVG browser. Some search agents, but not all, can search within Flash content.

Part B: Tools

General Comparisons

Table 3-1 and Table 3-2 provide a brief summary of the tools and technologies commonly used in today's Web applications to achieve various motion graphics effects.

Table 3-1: Motion Graphics Player Penetration

Player	Number of Web Users
Flash Player	386 million (97.4 %)
Shockwave Player	255 million (64.4%)
SVG Players	Unknown
DHTML and CSS (IE and Netscape 4+ browsers)	Over 394 million (Near 100%)

Source: Macromedia Inc., 2001

Source: Browser News, 2001

Table 3-2: Motion Graphics Authoring — Feature Comparisons

Feature	Flash	Shockwave	SVG	DHTML and CSS
Requires plug-in or ActiveX Control	Yes, but already shipped with most browsers	Yes	Yes, but eventually will become browser-native	No (native support, if inconsistent, in Version 4.0 and greater browsers)
Integration with other Web standards (HTML, CSS, XML, SMIL, scripting, etc.)	Partial	Partial	Complete	Complete
Searchable text	Not in some search agents unless combined with HTML	No, unless combined with HTML	Yes	Yes
WYSIWYG authoring tools	Yes	Yes	No (some primitive tools available; steadily improving)	Yes

Table 3-2: Motion Graphics Authoring — Feature Comparisons (Continued)

Feature	Flash	Shockwave	SVG	DHTML and CSS
Text-based (scripted) authoring	Partial, with ActionScript	No	Yes	Yes
Corporate database integration	Partial (through use of Macromedia Generator)	No	Yes	Yes
Scalable vector graphics and text	Yes	Yes	Yes	Partial
Dynamic manipulation of content within files	Yes	No	Yes	Yes
Support for sound elements	Yes	Yes	Yes, but primitive	Yes, but primitive in CSS1. CSS2 has more advanced controls.
Support for video elements	Yes, in Flash MX or with third-party software	Yes	Yes, but primitive	Yes, but primitive

DHTML and CSS

Quick Review

DHTML and CSS technologies stick nicely to the open standards-based "uncompiled" ethic of the Web but often require a lot of testing and tweaking in order to make animation effects work efficiently cross-platform and cross-browser.

Supported in most Version 4.0 or later browsers, the DIV tag allows for advanced control of placement and layering of elements; CSS style sheets provide an efficient way of controlling text appearance. Animation capabilities are relatively primitive compared to vector-oriented tools such as Flash and SVG.

After you experience a few intractable bugs, you might wish you had just compiled the whole thing in Flash or Shockwave. Use these tools for only the most basic forms of animation in those cases where you wish to keep your content fully native to the browser.

Authoring Tools

- Macromedia Dreamweaver

- Adobe GoLive

- Raw code in any text editor

Resources

- www.macromedia.com/exchange/dreamweaver/
  Extensions for Dreamweaver

- www.macromedia.com/support/dreamweaver/
  Tech notes, downloads, online forums, third-party links, and tutorials
  for Dreamweaver

- www.actionxchange.com/
  Actions, extensions, and modules for Adobe GoLive

- www.adobe.com/support/main.html
  Downloads, online forums, announcements, and tutorials for GoLive

- www.actionext.com/
  Actions and extensions for Adobe GoLive

- www.goliveheaven.com/
  News, links, and tutorials for Adobe GoLive

Macromedia Flash and Shockwave

Go to www.macromedia.com/software/

Quick Review

In the past five years, Flash and the software flash (SWF) file format have
emerged as the Web standard for animation and vector graphics. Unlike the
SVG standard, Flash is now a mature technology and product, with rich
full-featured WYSIWYG authoring environments available from both Macromedia and Adobe Systems, Inc., as well as a very active community of
developers. You can also find loads of publications, tutorials, examples, and
extensions, many of them for little or no cost.

Perhaps the greatest advantage of Flash is the near ubiquity of the player.
Even in those rare cases when a user's browser doesn't have the Flash
plug-in or ActiveX Control, installation from the Macromedia Website takes
a matter of seconds in most cases.

Vector graphics content in Flash files is highly scalable (resizing affects
neither quality nor file size) while bitmap images can also be incorporated
when necessary. Playback is highly efficient, with near-real-time streaming

in those cases where careful attention has been paid to streamlining and pacing the flow of content, among other factors.

Text tools in Flash authoring have steadily improved but remain somewhat limited when compared to SVG or DHTML. In Flash there is no obvious equivalent for Cascading Style Sheets, for example, which provide SVG and HTML authors with direct and dynamic control over the appearance of text from outside the animation files themselves. So, for example, when a style changes in Flash, without a significant programming effort, text attributes or content must be updated manually in every single file. In SVG or DHTML, this process can be semi-automated through use of either CSS or Find/Replace procedures.

This brings us to another limitation of Flash when compared to its standards-based peers: Flash is a compiled, versus an uncompiled or purely script-based, application. It is possible with Flash 5 and greater to script a reasonably complex animation using nothing but ActionScript. In most cases, however, the result of any Flash authoring process is one or a series of published SWF files, each with its fixed content that cannot be changed (except through advanced programming or by returning to the source application and republishing or recompiling). This also means that the internals of a Flash file are not text-searchable by some search agents and cannot easily be localized in multiple languages. The search limitation can be overcome somewhat through incorporation of the Flash content into HTML pages, but localization efforts again require returning to the source application and making the changes manually in each and every file. The fact that Flash files are compiled also means that they are difficult to use as a single source for publishing in multiple contexts such as desktop, PDA, and wireless devices. Formats like SVG are more suited to the task, since developers can program the files to dynamically alter their own contents based on the context.

Versions 4 and 5 of Flash achieve a fair degree of integration with other Web technologies such as XML, HTML, and JavaScript, thanks to the quick evolution of ActionScript, a built-in scripting language that is modeled closely on the ECMA-262 specification, a standard which charts the common ground between JavaScript and JScript. Embedded Flash files can speak to the browser, to other Flash files in the browser, or to other files on the network, and vice versa. Flash files can also interact with server technologies, such as CGI scripts, for handling forms and other data exchanges. Because of its basis in XML, however, the SVG format integrates more easily with industrial-strength database applications.

Flash does a better job of handling sound and video elements, however. Sound files can be directly integrated into the animation and remain accurately synchronized in the final SWF file. SVG and DHTML animations do not always maintain good synchronization and display bugginess when handling sound and video elements.

Until recently, Flash could not incorporate video elements directly within the Flash player, but new third-party tools, such as Flix from Wildform Inc., allow you to integrate a modest amount of video directly into Flash, though this solution is not as robust or effective as streaming video technologies from the big three (Apple QuickTime, RealNetworks Real Media, and Microsoft Windows Media).

By comparison with Flash, the Shockwave player, also from Macromedia, is not as widely distributed. However, you can more easily incorporate a broad variety of elements into Shockwave content, along with highly sophisticated scripting and programming. Shockwave movies can incorporate Flash along with many other elements, including video.

Authoring for Shockwave is done in Macromedia Director, the old standard for multimedia CD-ROM authoring. As a result, CD-ROM content can be easily transferred to the Web but must be carefully fine-tuned for low-bandwidth situations. Also, there is a steep learning curve for authoring in Director with the Lingo scripting language.

An alternative tool for authoring Flash content is LiveMotion from Adobe Systems. As a Version 1.0 product, LiveMotion has a long way to go to reach the sophistication of Macromedia's authoring tools. LiveMotion has just a hint of scripting capability, through a few simple JavaScript implementations. The primary advantages of LiveMotion are its close integration with other Adobe products, such as Photoshop and Illustrator, as well as the many interface features and metaphors that it shares with Adobe After Effects. If you are an Adobe fan and more oriented toward 3D or graphics design than programming, LiveMotion might be a good choice.

Authoring Tools

- Macromedia Flash

- Macromedia Director

- Adobe LiveMotion

Resources

- www.macromedia.com/exchange/flash/
  Extensions for Flash

- www.macromedia.com/support/flash/
  Tech notes, downloads, online forums, third-party links, and tutorials for Flash

- www.macromedia.com/support/director/
  Tech notes, downloads, online forums, third-party links, and tutorials for Director Shockwave Studio

- www.flashkit.com
  Various Flash resources

- www.adobe.com/support/main.html
  Downloads, online forums, announcements, and tutorials for LiveMotion

Scalable Vector Graphics (SVG)

For W3C resources, go to www.w3.org/Graphics/SVG/Overview.htm8

For Adobe Systems Inc. resources, go to www.adobe.com/svg

Quick Review

Developers eagerly anticipated the release of the Version 1.0 recommendation for scalable vector graphics (SVG) in September 2001, endorsed and developed over several years by the W3C and corporate partners such as Adobe, Corel, and RealNetworks. Now that a true, open, thoroughly modern standard is finally in place, developers eagerly anticipate the arrival of a truly full-featured authoring tool, with full implementation in a browser or two. That might take a while.

On paper (or in script form) at least, SVG promises to be the answer to every Web developer's dream. With its foundation in XML and its ambition in the vector graphics space previously conquered by Flash, SVG holds the promise of solving many of the limitations related to integrating a proprietary solution such as Flash with other quickly evolving Web browser standards and back-end, database-driven solutions.

On the design side, the SVG standard incorporates vector graphics, bitmap graphics (GIF, JPEG, and PNG), and text that can be stylized with CSS. Vector mathematics run very close to the technology employed so successfully in Flash. On the application logic side, SVG integrates with all the W3C standards, with direct XML connectivity for database and script-driven charts and graphs, and dynamic manipulation of both content and appearance. Unlike Flash, SVG content always remains in script form, and thus it is completely searchable and scriptable. To that extent, it is an all-purpose format for creating complete Web applications. On paper at least, this also makes SVG an ideal candidate for single-source content that must change dynamically during delivery to multiple platforms and devices, such as desktop systems and wireless devices.

The one great drawback to SVG at the moment is real-world deployment. Authoring tools are primitive at best (although the SVG feature set in Adobe Illustrator is moving along quickly) so developers must be skilled programmers to develop rich content. This could change quickly if SVG catches on. As in the early days of HTML and JavaScript, developers can leverage and adapt code chunks provided by others to speed development. Web developers who are accustomed to coding with XML, JavaScript, and the Document Object Model should feel right at home.

Perhaps of greater concern for developers, the current crop of SVG players are also buggy and do not yet fully implement all the features of the recommendation. The Adobe SVG Viewer relies on JavaScript for most of its dynamic and interactive features, so you might experience problems in Internet Explorer 5 for Macintosh, and it does not support Version 3 browsers. Bugs have been found running the Adobe SVG Viewer with Netscape on both Macintosh and Windows. SVG also has weaknesses when integrating sound and video. Synchronization among elements is not always precise, and manipulations and effects are extremely limited in the current crop of players/browsers.

To a large extent, the weaknesses of SVG are defined by the weaknesses of the available players, not the recommendation itself. As with DHTML, for example, as browsers and players continue to evolve, the bugs and limitations of SVG will gradually lessen. By that time, we should also have some robust tools, including, in all likelihood, SVG export directly from Macromedia Flash.

Authoring Tools

Table 3-3 provides a summary of SVG authoring tools.

Table 3-3: SVG Authoring Tools

Name	Platform	Description
Adobe Illustrator	Macintosh and Windows	Standard SVG authoring tool for working with graphics and adding interactivity
Adobe GoLive	Macintosh and Windows	Placement of SVG in Web applications along with editing of source code
W3C Amaya	Windows 95/98/ME/NT/2000/ XP Linux, Solaris, AIX, HP-UX	Browser and editor for SVG and for mixed namespace XHTML, SVG, and MathML
JASC WebDraw	Win95/98/ME, WinNT/2000	Native SVG editor with import and export of SVG, WYSIWYG visual editing of filter effects, and timeline editing of animations
Beatware e-Picture 2.0	Mac OS 8.5/8.6/9.0, Win98, WinNT/2000	Provides SVG export; can import Adobe Illustrator, Macromedia Freehand, and Adobe Photoshop files

Table 3-3: SVG Authoring Tools (Continued)

Name	Platform	Description
Beez	Win95/98/ME, WinNT/2000/XP	WYSIWYG editor to create a single animated SVG path, consisting of multiple Bezier curves, which can then be used in an SVG file
Bernard Herzog Sketch	Linux, Solaris, FreeBSD, AIX, IRIX	Unix/X drawing program with SVG import and export capability; now bundled with Mandrake Linux 7.0 and written in Python
CadStd Pro 3.51	Win95/98/ME, WinNT/2000	CAD program, reads and writes DXF, exports SVG and written in Delphi
GraPL	Win95/98/ME, WinNT/2000/XP	Graphing and charting program that can take data from spreadsheets and other data sources and generate a wide range of charts including analysis
CorelDraw! 10.0	Win95/98/ME, WinNT/2000	Has SVG import and export capability
Dial Solutions Oak Draw	Win95/98/ME, WinNT/2000/XP	Object-oriented drawing package for Windows 95 and above, designed to be used by children in schools but also to be powerful enough for professional users
ILOG JViews Component Suite	Any Java 2	Java components for application developers and includes optional modules for creating maps, interactive Gantt charts, network diagrams, and graph layout
Sphinx Open Editor	Java Bean, Windows, and Unix environments	Allows creation of animated, dynamic SVG content that uses SMIL Animation features, and many other formats; also provides an API for embedding in custom solutions
Sphinx SVG	Java Bean, Windows, and Unix environments	Based on the full-featured Sphinx Open, allows creation of animated, dynamic SVG content that uses SMIL Animation features and scripting
ITEDO IsoDraw 5	Win95/98/ME, WinNT/2000	Technical illustration package that is especially suited to the production of parallel perspective technical illustrations

Table 3-3: SVG Authoring Tools (Continued)

Name	Platform	Description
Sodipodi	Linux with GNOME	Small vector-based drawing program that loads and saves a subset of SVG
Mayura Draw	Win95/98/ME, WinNT/2000	Drawing program
Gill	Linux 2 with GNOME	Drawing program that has a full DOM; can embed SVG in other GNOME programs (such as Gnumeric, the spreadsheet)
IMS Web Engine	Win95/98/ME, WinNT/2000/ XP	One of a family of products, an interactive animation editor and Web-Top publisher for the creation of content rich, interactive dynamic HTML and SVG
Appligent PDFML Publisher	Solaris, WinNT/2000/XP	Converts from SVG to PDF, and is a server-side SVG converter for on-demand network publishing
Celinea CR2V	Win95/98/ME, WinNT/2000/ XP	Raster-to-vector converter that outputs SVG, with input formats BMP, TIFF, PNG, JPEG and GIF; CR2V combines efficient color segmenting, nonsignificant regions merging, and robust curve fitting
CSIRO SVG Toolkit	Any Java 2	Command-line utility that rasterizes SVG as JPEG, PNG, or other bitmap image formats
CWI SVGGraphics	Any Java 2	SVG generator for Java that extends Java 2D class so any java program can generate SVG
SVGMapMaker	Windows 95, 98, NT, 2000 (MapInfo Professional 5.0 or later is required)	Reads MapInfo mapper and layout windows to export the content to SVG
Gardos Software gsDXF2SVG.dll	Win95/98/ME, WinNT/2000/ XP	ActiveX DLL that converts AutoCAD DXF files to SVG files
KK-Software KVEC	Win9x, WinNT/2000/XP, OS/2, Linux, HP-Unix, Macintosh, BeOS	Command-line raster-to-vector converter that can generate SVG
Oliver Dietzel JPEG to SVG encoder	Web-based	A utility that encodes the JPEG information using the data: URL protocol and returns a small SVG file containing an image element with this URL

Table 3-3: SVG Authoring Tools (Continued)

Name	Platform	Description
SVGmaker	Win95/98/ME, WinNT/2000/XP	Windows printer driver that exports SVG from any application that can print
PS2Web and PS2vector	Win95/98/ME, WinNT/2000 HP-UX Solaris AIX	Converts PostScript and EPS files to SVG; also converts them to WMF, EMF, MIF, and CGM
SteadyState SVGFont	Any Java	Converts TrueType fonts into SVG fonts and generates proof pages; also comes with a servlet that allows a Web server to satisfy font requests on demand
Sun SVG Slide Toolkit	Any Java 2	Transforms an XML file that uses a specific DTD for the structured content of presentations (slides) into an SVG slide presentation
Sun Graphics 2D SVG Generator	Any Java 2	SVG generator for Java that extends Java 2D class; any java program can thus generate SVG; special support for Swing and GLF to improve export; can generate either formatting attributes or CSS
University of Tsukuba fdsSVG	Win95/98/ME, WinNT/2000	Converts indexed raster images (in Windows BMP format) to SVG using an advanced curve-fitting technique

Viewers

Table 3-4 provides a list of SVG viewers. These stand-alone viewers include an XML parser, a CSS parser, a CSS cascading, specificity, and inheritance engine, and an SVG rendering engine to draw the graphics. They may offer print capabilities in addition to display on screen. Interactive SVG viewers typically also include an XML Document Object Model (DOM), a CSS Object Model, and at least one ECMAScript (JavaScript) engine or an implementation of the SYMM/SVG declarative animation.

Any XML browser that implements CSS can be used to get a text view of a SVG graphic (information courtesy of W3C).

Table 3-4: SVG Viewers

Name	Platforms	Description
Adobe SVG Viewer	MacOS 9.x/10.1 Win95/98/ME WinNT/2000/XP	Browser plug-in for Netscape 4.5 to 4.77, MS IE 4 or greater, RealPlayer 8 or greater, and Opera 5.x; also an Active-X control for SVG display in (Windows) MS Office and Visual Basic
Apache Batik SVG browser	Any Java 2	Uses Xerces XML parser, Xalan XSL-T engine, and Koala CSS parser; part of the Apache Batik SVG Toolkit
CSIRO SVG Toolkit	Any Java 2	Uses Xerces XML parser and Steady State CSS parser; can print and convert to raster formats
CSIRO Pocket SVG Viewer	Pocket PC	Low memory footprint (390 K) C++ Active-X control for pocket PC (Windows CE)
Ionic SVG Renderer	Any Java 2	Part of the IONIC Java SVG Component Suite
KDD Labs JaMaPS	PalmOS	Java implementation of SVG for the PalmOS platform
Koala Jackaroo	Any Java 2	Uses the Xerces XML parser and the Flute CSS parser; includes a full DOM 2 implementation; no longer developed, in favor of Batik
SVG in Mozilla project	Windows, MacOS, and Linux binaries	Uses Mozilla XML parser, CSS parser, JavaScript, and DOM
X-Smiles organization, X-Smiles XML browser	Any Java 2	Multi-namespace XML browser that can display SVG, XForms, SMIL 1.0, and XSL-FO and contains an XSL-T engine for styling of other XML document formats (such as well-formed XHTML); also has ECMAScript, support for SIP videoconferencing, and multiskin support (including GTK/KDE skins)

Server-Side Generators

Table 3-5 lists a wide variety of applications that can produce SVG on the fly; these can range in sophistication from a simple Perl CGI script to a full database-backed generation system.

Table 3-5: Server-Side SVG Generators

Name	Platforms	Description
Adobe AlterCast	Interacts with Java, Perl, COM, HTML, and .NET technologies (via XML)	Reduces the time it takes to repurpose images for use in different media, including SVG; scripts can be developed to automate routine tasks, making it quick and easy to apply changes to a large number of files
GraPL.NET	Win95/98/ME, WinNT/2000/XP	.NET application for server-side generation of database-backed SVG graphs; it uses the same charting engine as GraPL
IBM AFP to SVG transcoder	Win95/98, WinNT	On-the-fly transcoding of IBM Advanced Function Print documents into SVG
IBM CGM to SVG transcoder	Win95/98, WinNT	On-the-fly transcoding of Computer Graphics Metafile (CGM) graphics into SVG
SVG.pm	Any Perl 5-compatible system (tested on Solaris, Linux, and Win32 platforms)	100 percent object-oriented Perl 5 library for generating stand-alone or in-line SVG contents; SVG.pm claims to support 100 percent of the SVG 1.0 Recommendation, with embedded SVG, SMIL, and foreignObject support; written by Ronan Oger
DataSlinger	Unix, WinNT/2000/XP	DataSlinger retrieves CAD and mapping drawings (such as AutoCAD DWG and ESRI Shapefiles) and converts them to SVG on the fly; aggregation from multiple data sources is also suported; Java and C++ plug-ins may be used, and there is also XSL-T support
Savage Software SVG Toolkit	Win95/98/ME, WinNT/2000, Linux to come	C++ server-side implementation of the SVG Document Object Model (DOM) including the DOM Level 2 XML DOM and CSS Object model
SVG-PL	Anything with Perl 5	A Perl 5 library to assist writing Perl programs for the creation of error-free SVG documents
Internet Mapper	Unknown	Dynamic database-backed generation of maps, with output in SVG and HTML

Resources

- TextPad.com
  Includes syntax definitions file for SVG

- SVG-PL
  Perl 5 library for creating SVG files

- GNU Plotting Utilities package
  Open-source library for generating and exporting SVG, Adobe Illustrator, or PostScript files

- Nokiko SVG Project
  Tutorials and links to learn, view, and experiment with SVG

- FreeType Project

- SVG101
  SVG articles, forums, samples, tutorials, and utilities

- Levien.com
  Ralph Levien's site documenting his development of SVG support in GNOME, the popular windowing system for Linux

Part C: Methods

Choosing Your Design Architectures

The first task in building motion graphics for the Web is to choose an architecture and the necessary tools, based on the information provided in this chapter.

Audience

Who will be viewing the content, and in what context? The answer to this question can have a great impact on your choice of tools and architectures:

- **Flash for speed, sophistication, and reach:** If you need to reach the largest possible audience in the shortest amount of time but you want your presentation to include sophisticated graphics and effects, then it is a foregone conclusion that Flash is your format, since the Flash player is already widely distributed and the authoring tools more advanced.

- **DHTML for speed, simplicity, and reach:** If you need to reach the largest possible audience in the shortest amount of tim, but your animation requirements are fairly simple, you might be able to parse your interface into elements of bitmap graphics combined with DHTML and even some video to achieve your effects. You will have to deal with cross-browser compatibility issues.

- **SVG for carefully crafted, future-oriented, and focused delivery:** If your audience is fairly sophisticated, and highly concentrated on a specific platform, you can develop in SVG and provide the necessary additional software or instruction to allow the users to prepare for the content. If you have the time to slowly build your architecture over the course of several years, you might want to consider SVG as a more open, scalable, and future-oriented technology.

Compiled or Uncompiled Applications?

Can the motion content be compiled into a single SWF file or a series of files, or would it serve the purpose of the project better if the content remained as an uncompiled script, using SVG, for example? The primary concern is the dynamic generation or manipulation of content: A Flash file can be replaced dynamically using Macromedia Generator software; however, the contents of each SVG and DHTML file can be more thoroughly integrated into back-end systems that use technologies such as XML, Active Server Pages, or Java Server Pages.

If you do choose Flash as your format, consider chunking your content into small elements, units, or topics. This helps both in terms of bandwidth issues (you can program your Flash to load small pieces as needed during the presentation in order to keep file sizes small) and in terms of dynamic control of content (you can use Macromedia Generator, for example, to update or replace content on the fly).

Open-Standards-Based or Proprietary Playback Technologies?

Is it important that your tools interlock and evolve with other standards-based technologies such as HTML and XML, or are you free to mix and match proprietary tools from various vendors? This might be a matter of preference, or company policy.

Scripting Considerations

The most sophisticated scripting technology for motion graphics is SVG. However, you should have solid experience with scripting languages and programming languages, particularly if you need to create your code quickly, while we wait for viable WYSIWYG tools. Director Shockwave Studio software also allows for sophisticated scripting through Lingo, but it is not as modern as SVG in terms of integration with current Web standards such as XML. The current version of Flash includes excellent scripting capabilities through ActionScript. Of these three, Flash is probably the most user-friendly and is thus a good choice for nonprogrammers.

In the case of LiveMotion, an early complaint about this young product has been that there is not much support for scripting when compared with Macromedia Flash. If you take full advantage of LiveMotion's nested Timelines, there's a lot you can do without any scripting at all.

Raw Text, Vector Text, or Bitmapped Text?

Issues to consider are searchability (SVG scripts and DHTML pages are searchable, while Flash content requires special effort in this regard), dynamic generation or manipulation of content (a Flash file can be replaced dynamically using Macromedia Generator software, but the contents of each SVG and DHTML file can be more thoroughly integrated into back-end systems), and whether or not the content of files needs to be updated, for example, for localization purposes or to change the appearance based on changing style guidelines (in many cases, Flash files must be updated manually, while SVG or DHTML files can be linked to external style sheets). When compared with HTML, however, remember that Flash does a better job of scaling text to various sizes within an animation and presents smooth edges when the text elements are vector-based. At the same time, vector text elements do not display as well in very small font sizes, so for readable text at small sizes, consider using HTML text or using the Display fonts option in Flash, which has the same effect.

Deconstructing Your Favorite Site

Do you have a favorite dynamic Website? If not, check out some of the sites featured at the Macromedia showcase or Adobe support locations on the Web (see "Resources" on page 82). How did they do it? Look at the source and break it down. What elements are done in Flash, which are DHTML? What are busy developers discovering about SVG? Can you borrow the code or reverse-engineer it?

Streaming Issues

Try not to load too many bitmap images into your vector-based animations, since these tend to produce larger file sizes. Also avoid animating the position and size of bitmap images, but attempt to keep these elements static within the presentation and animate the vector-based elements instead, since these can scale and reposition through mathematical calculation and, as a result, are more efficient.

Also, there are certain shortcuts you can take in moving bitmapped content to vector-based content, for example, by filtering video or still images with the "posterize" effect and then creating vector images out of these either by using Flash or by running them through the Adobe Streamline application.

Director supports import of Flash content, which you can use to lighten bandwidth requirements in Shockwave. In general, keep a close eye on bandwidth requirements throughout authoring, since Director, which was designed for CD-ROM development, does not automatically produce low-bandwidth titles.

Scaling Up, Not Down

In order to take full advantage of the virtue of vectors in regard to file size and bandwidth performance, you should always start at the smallest possible display size for your animation and then scale up from there. The only exception to this rule arises when your animation also includes bitmap images, which appear blocky when scaled up to sizes larger than the native size. In that case, you could target the middle ground and create your animation at a display size that you expect the majority of users will experience.

Another often-overlooked feature of vector-based animation in Flash or SVG is the fact that display size is dynamic. When embedding these elements into a Web page, for example, you can set the dimensions in the HTML code using percentages rather than actual pixel dimensions. As a result, when the user resizes the window, the animation artwork also resizes along with it, and the vector elements are not distorted or compromised.

Keeping It Simple

Ultimately, creating compelling dynamic media is a matter of good design, whether for the Web, television, or disc. The rule of thumb when bandwidth is limited is to keep it simple. The economy of materials at hand creates its own aesthetic. You have only to look through a high-quality magazine to realize how incredibly evocative simple still images and design can be in the right hands. Even adding a small amount of motion to high-quality design work can be very compelling.

Section I: Server-Based Architectures

CHAPTER 4

Dynamic Web Applications

This chapter describes a new generation of Web applications that combines disciplines and best practices from several industries to arrive at a new category of live content over the public network.

Part A: Background

Introduction

It is no secret that dynamic elements, such as DHTML actions, Flash animation, and streaming video, now play an important role on the World Wide Web. Aside from the piecemeal introduction of individual technologies, however, there is a larger chemistry at work in the evolution of modern Websites. The buzz phrase for a while that hinted at this new chemistry was "application service provider." This phrase referred to companies that created useful full-scale applications out of standard Web technologies that clients and customers could buy or rent out of the box, or in this case straight off the server, with only a minimum of tweaking to serve the specific purpose. Many successful companies continue to offer such services, but the terminology has evolved. We now hear phrases such as "collaboration solutions" and "networked software applications." At the heart of these solutions are robust database infrastructures that can be used to deliver content dynamically through combinations of both client-side and server-side scripting.

In regard to media content creation, we've chosen the term "dynamic Web applications" to describe a new generation of Web content that combines the best practices of business IT departments with new developments in broadband delivery and World Wide Web technologies. The basic formula for this evolution/revolution is as follows:

Broadband + dynamic Web media technologies +
new W3C standards = dynamic Web applications.

The following topics will explain some of this terminology and the ingredients of this new chemistry in greater detail.

Static Versus Dynamic Web Content

The first evidence of the evolution to a new type of Web content came with the arrival of Websites that display information in a stage format, versus the old page metaphor. For examples, view Avid Technology's Website (www.avid.com) and the Discovery Networks family of Websites (www.discovery.com). Rather than experiencing a scrolling page with portrait orientation, on these Websites you find a central stage area (where rich media content and imagery are displayed) with various secondary links and resources surrounding it. The majority of corporate Websites now follow this basic layout. In most cases there is no scrolling; everything is presented in a fixed central space, which provides entry into other similar spaces.

By contrast, the old Website in the narrowband phase included lots of text and images in a portrait orientation, with navigational features concentrated on the top and left side. The best of these sites used a clean, simple layout of graphics elements, often against a white background like paper. Some of these sites veered somewhat from the page metaphor with use of colors, the placement of richer still-image content with links in the middle, along with the occasional animated GIF. Such Websites occupy a virtual world where static imagery predominates, and as a result their design approaches are informed primarily by print industry rules of layout, use of fonts, and so forth.

The new style of Website is a whole different animal. No longer occupying a scrolling space from top to bottom, the site floats in the middle of the screen, with an aspect ratio closer to that of a feature film. In fact, you're not expected to scroll at all, and this is a feature that consistently appears in the new broadband look. Such interactive environments are more akin to the fixed interactive space you find in a CD-ROM or DVD title. The home scene (rather than home page) of these Websites is often dominated by a central display area in which a flash movie presents some new product or service.

DHTML and CSS

The first technologies to promise a more CD-ROM-like experience on the Web were Dynamic HTML (DHTML) and Cascading Style Sheets (CSS). DHTML is really just an amalgam of HTML, CSS, Document Object Model (DOM), and JavaScript/ECMAScript usage.

DHTML is often used for well-known interactive effects such as drop-down menus and rollover buttons. DHTML also makes possible full-scale animation within the browser but is rarely used for this purpose, mostly due to cross-platform compatibility issues. The advantage of DHTML is that it is supported by Internet Explorer and Netscape Version 4 or greater, without the need for plug-ins. The biggest downside is compatibility: The full breadth of DHTML functionality is not supported evenly cross-browser, and those effects that do work reliably usually require testing and tweaking in order to look and act the same in both IE and Netscape.

CSS is an easier choice. CSS is a World Wide Web Consortium standard that provides an elegant way to separate the presentation from the structure of Web page content, by allowing you to determine the styles of fonts and other elements from a single location. That location can be internal (within Web pages) or external (as a separate document on a server). External style sheets are especially helpful in allowing you to avoid embedded <font> tags strewn across multiple pages, with one centralized document that you can use to change or update presentation settings across multiple Web pages.

JavaScript and Beyond

JavaScript, or the Microsoft variant JScript, has been in use since the beginning of the World Wide Web. JavaScript is actually unrelated to the Java language developed by Sun Microsystems, although it was inspired by Java's object-oriented approach. JavaScript was developed by Netscape and was adopted early on as an open standard by the W3C. A new standard, ECMA-Script, was created out of a shared subset of JavaScript and JScript functionalities and therefore represents a true cross-browser standard. The term JavaScript remains popular and is often used to refer to any one of these various flavors.

JavaScript is used everywhere to enable dynamic content as well as to manage various client-side tasks such as forms processing, image rollovers, and cookie processing (cookies are used to store and recall user information).

JavaScript is not the only scripting language at work in Web pages. Internet Explorer, for example, supports Visual Basic Script (VBScript), which can be used for the same purposes as JavaScript. For cross-browser applications, however, JavaScript is the only choice. JavaScript is also more widespread in use, and you can find a wealth of free information and guidance as well as scripts at various locations on the World Wide Web.

Over the years and through browser releases, JavaScript has gained in usefulness, but it still has limitations, primarily in regard to security due to the fact that scripting is performed client-side, within the user's browser. For Web applications that need to access back-end data, server-side processing is usually required.

The Arrival of ASP and JSP

Common Gateway Interface (CGI) scripts have been used as a form of server-side scripting since the earliest days of the World Wide Web. Developed in standard programming languages such as Perl, CGI scripts handle common server-side events, such as the passing of form information between browser and server.

Two additional scripting languages have evolved to handle ever more sophisticated forms of server-side scripting: Active Server Pages (ASP) developed by Microsoft for use on Windows servers, and JavaServer Pages (JSP) developed by Sun Microsystems in an industry-wide collaboration with various leaders in the enterprise software and tools markets. JSP is designed for use on servers running Java 2 Platform, Enterprise Edition (J2EE). Both technologies allow Web developers and designers to create and maintain dynamic Web pages that leverage existing business systems and databases.

Microsoft Active Server Pages allow developers to combine HTML technology, script commands, and COM components to create interactive Web pages or powerful Web-based applications. For development shops that use Microsoft Windows-based Web servers (IIS 4.0 or 5.0), ASP is a very popular choice because it's built in and developers who are familiar with Visual Basic/VBScript can easily pick up ASP. ASP code can also be written in

JScript or other languages, but is predominantly done in VBScript. For more information, visit msdn.Microsoft.com/asp.

JSP, on the other hand, seems to be popular with developers coming from a Java-based background. JSP is part of the Java family (an extension of the Java Servlet technology). JSP uses XML-like tags and scriptlets written in the Java programming language to encapsulate the logic that generates the content for the page. Additionally, the application logic can reside in server-based resources (such as JavaBeans component architecture) that the page accesses with these tags and scriptlets. Any and all formatting (HTML or XML) tags are passed directly back to the response page. For more information, visit www.java.sun.com.

Server-side scripting provides developers with two important features: database access and the ability to script page content on the server. For the purposes of dynamic Web applications, the greatest benefit of these capabilities is that they allow the server to change both the content and the formatting of pages "on the fly," before they are passed to a user's browser. The possibilities seem endless. Web developers can present the user with content that updates at regular intervals, that responds to the user's personal preferences, or that changes dynamically based on any number of variables from the time of day to the user's browser software.

The Database as Lingua Franca

From Website back ends to workgroup solutions, the database has gained great importance in communications environments of all types. Most of us are unaware of the presence of the database behind much of the content we view on the Web. Under the surface, particularly on large enterprise applications using XML to leverage content across applications, the database operates as the true lingua franca — a universal language whose content can be translated into almost any context, with the right technologies (such as XML, server- and client-side scripting) to perform the translations.

As a tool for content developers, the database is crucial. Most developers are accustomed to the technologies used to shape the appearance of content on the Web (Web page authoring tools, graphics design tools, word processing tools, and so forth), but even a basic understanding of database technology is a requirement for most Web development projects these days.

For low-volume needs, you can use entry-level database development tools include Filemaker Pro (www.filemaker.com) and Microsoft Access (www.microsoft.com/office/access), both of which have built-in Web publishing features and capabilities. These solutions have some weaknesses for enterprise applications, such as limitations on the number of simultaneous users and security issues. For higher-volume enterprise-level applications, Microsoft shops that use Windows NT/2000 Server, IIS 4.0/5.0 Web server, often use database solutions that plug easily into Microsoft technologies and skill sets, such as SQL Server (www.microsoft.com/sql). Oracle (www.oracle.com) and IBM (www-3.ibm.com/software/data/db2) provide robust enterprise database technology for use on a broad range of server types.

The Role of XML

Extensible Markup Language (XML) represents the next step beyond HTML in the evolution of World Wide Web standards. But XML is not meant to be a simple tag-based replacement for HTML or XHTML (XML-compliant HTML). XML represents a different approach. XML, in a nutshell, enables the smooth passage of information between disparate Websites and databases that might employ different standards. XML accomplishes this feat by taking the fixed nature of both the tag semantics and the tag set that define page content in HTML and making those tags flexible and customizable, based on a standardized way of defining the customization that any browser or XML-based system can read and understand. Unlike HTML, XML does not specify semantics or a tag set. In fact, XML is really a metalanguage for describing markup languages. In other words, XML provides a facility to define tags and the structural relationships between them. Since there's no predefined tag set, there can't be any preconceived semantics. All of the semantics of an XML document will be defined either by the applications that process them or by style sheets.

By smoothing the way for interoperability between complex Web database systems, the evolving standards of XML conversion will eventually make it possible for content developers to craft complete dynamic Web applications that work easily with and draw content from other resources on the Web. XML will also eventually reduce the problems ensuing from the deployment of different brands and versions of browser software.

Some Websites that currently use news feeds, for example, receive the feeds as XML files that can be parsed and placed into a database, which then handles the dynamic creation of Web pages with up-to-the-minute content. Once XML support can be guaranteed in audience browsers, developers can also serve an XML page that gets processed and styled by the client browser via CSS and eXtensible Stylesheet Language Transformations (XSLT). XSLT is a companion W3C recommendation, a powerful implementation of a tree-oriented transformation language for transmuting instances of XML, using one vocabulary, into either simple text, legacy HTML, or XML instances using any other vocabulary imaginable.

For more information, visit:

- www.w3c.org

- www.xml.com

- www.xml.org

Part B: Tools

General Comparisons

Table 4-1 provides a brief summary of the tools and technologies used commonly in developing today's dynamic Web applications.

Table 4-1: Feature Comparisons — Web Page Authoring Tools

Feature	Dreamweaver	GoLive	FrontPage
Graphics application support	Strong support for round-trip graphics editing with Macromedia Fireworks	Strong support for both round-trip and in-place graphics editing with Adobe Photoshop, Illustrator, and LiveMotion	Includes PowerPoint-like drawing tools
Multimedia application support	Strong Macromedia Generator, Flash, and Shockwave support; RealMedia support	Strong QuickTime plug-in support, including advanced late-stage editing tools for QuickTime; Macromedia Flash and Shockwave; RealMedia; PDF	Like Word and other Office applications, supports integration of Microsoft-centric video and multimedia formats
Standards support	HTML, DHTML, XML,CSS, HTML styles; edit and preserve non-HTML files; view and edit Server-side includes	HTML, DHTML, XML, CSS, SVG; NTT DoCoMo 502i i-mode; CHTML iForm Elements and Emoji Character Authoring; Nokia WAP/WML 1.x Visual Authoring and Phone Terminal Emulation; conversion of HTML to XHTML; convert external style sheets to in-line style code and export in-line styles as an external style sheet	HTML, DHTML, XML,CSS, ASP; Preselect environments (browser, server, FrontPage Server Extensions, ASP, DHTML, CSS, script) to automatically restrict development features
XML features	XML parser; XML-based Tag database; XML-based Design Notes	XML parser	XML parser

Table 4-1: Feature Comparisons — Web Page Authoring Tools (Continued)

Feature	Dreamweaver	GoLive	FrontPage
Database integration	Connect to ODBC and OLE DB databases; works with all ASP-enabled Web servers; preview data-driven pages within GoLive; Supports WebObjects (Java servers); integrates with both ColdFusion for Windows server deployment/database integration and Irun for J2EE	Connect to ODBC, JDBC, and OLE DB databases; JSP and JavaBeans; integrates with Apple WebObjects for J2EE deployment/database integration	Third-party e-commerce applications integrate into FrontPage
WYSIWYG layout and preview	Yes; some line-leading display issues in layout view	Yes; allows selection and drag-and-drop positioning of individual or multiple objects	Yes
Integrated Text Editor	Integrated and bundled with HomeSite; edit and preserve non-HTML files; clean up HTML Command	Built-in HTML source code editor featuring text macro support; edit and preserve non-HTML files; Clean Up HTML Command	Built-in HTML source code editor; edit and preserve non-HTML files; integrated Microsoft Script Editor to debug and test ASP or other script code
Simultaneous access to Visual and Source View	Split View of Design and Code Views	View and/or modify page layout and source code in side-by-side windows	Normal (WYSIWYG) mode, and Reveal Tags command to see code, or author in HTML view
Website management	Asset management and site reporting tools	Diagram information architecture in a visual environment; modify copies of existing pages in site design mode	Site management reports
JavaScript features	Prebuilt JavaScript actions; JavaScript Debugger; JavaScript Code Navigation; JavaScript Reference from O'Reilly	Prebuilt JavaScript actions; validate external links and JavaScript-embedded URLs; export embedded JavaScript to an external document; onboard JavaScript/JScript authoring and debugging; all extensions/actions are cross-platform compatible	Web Components allow automatic insertion of features such as Photo Gallery, Link Bars, Top 10 Lists, List Views from OWS, and Save to Database, and automatic web content such as headlines, stock ticker, and maps

Table 4-1: Feature Comparisons — Web Page Authoring Tools (Continued)

Feature	Dreamweaver	GoLive	FrontPage
Search capabilities	Site-wide search and replace	Site-wide search and replace; Search for files in your site based on file size, modified date, download time, syntax errors, untitled documents, specific links, colors, fonts, address, GoLive components, etc.	Site-wide search and replace
	Reusable library elements; templates with editable and locked regions; template changes automatically propagate site-wide	Reusable library elements; stationary templates	Templates and Wizards available
Source control	File locking with check-in and check-out; WebDAV support; Microsoft Visual Source-Safe support	File locking and checkin and check-out; WebDAV support	Works with Microsoft Visual SourceSafe; built-in "nested subwebs" rights management system; built-in check-in/check-out

Adobe GoLive

Go to www.adobe.com/products/golive

Development platforms: Mac OS Version 9.1, 9.2, 10.1 or Mac OS X; Microsoft Windows 98, Windows 2000, Windows Millennium, or Windows XP

Quick Review

Adobe GoLive and Macromedia Dreamweaver compete hard for the hearts and minds of Web developers. Both products offer a majority of similar features covering the basics of Web content authoring, including prebuilt Java-Script actions, source-code and WYSIWYG layout views, round-trip graphics handling, site management tools, and many other excellent features. Both tools support most of the major Web standards including DHTML, XML, CSS, and so forth. The distinguishing factors tend to run along the lines of user preferences in terms of platforms and integrated design and multimedia tools. For example, users who are accustomed to Adobe design tools will appreciate the tight integration with other Adobe products such as Photoshop, Illustrator, and LiveMotion. Developers who are most comfortable on the Macintosh tend to have a history with Adobe tools and therefore often lean toward GoLive, although both applications run on either platform. In terms of database integration, GoLive includes strong support for integration with Apple WebObjects. If Java server integration is the target, WebObjects support can be a compelling factor in choice of authoring applications.

For a list of features, visit the URL shown above or see "General Comparisons" on page 106.

Resources

*   www.actionxchange.com

*   www.goliveheaven.com

Apple WebObjects

Go to www.apple.com/webobjects

Development platforms: Mac OS X v10.0; Microsoft Windows 2000 Professional Edition

Deployment platforms: Any Java 2 Platform, Standard Edition 1.3 runtime environment, using JDBC 2.0 for universal database connectivity

**The following platforms are fully qualified and supported: Mac OS X Server v10.0, Windows 2000 Pro, Solaris 8
Supported data sources: Oracle 8i**

Quick Review

WebObjects is an object-oriented application server written in Java for use with any Java 2 platform (Java 2 Enterprise Edition). WebObjects is often used with Adobe GoLive, which provides advanced tools supporting it. WebObjects is primarily for large enterprise projects, in the client/server application model. For dynamic Web applications, WebObjects allows you to leverage database content and deliver it dynamically, with the ability to generate HTML from reusable templates. WebObjects handles all the database access and session management. It also greatly reduces the amount of application-specific code you need to write. Because WebObjects 5 uses a pure Java runtime, its application can easily interact with other Java applications.

You can build database applications with WebObjects that have either HTML or Java interfaces, depending on your needs. Included are the code-free Direct to Web and Direct to Java Client technologies that use assistants, preconfigured templates, and dynamically generated user interfaces to generate rich Java client interfaces as easily as HTML clients at the click of a button.

Because of its object-oriented design, WebObjects enables developers to leverage a broad range of reusable system and third-party components as well as create their own corporate component library. Object-Relational Mapping engine lets you write all your business logic using objects. WebObjects will automatically fetch, cache, and update the data for you from any JDBC 2 database, allowing you to avoid writing SQL or JDBC code. WebObjects also provides XML interchange capabilities, allowing the application to interoperate with other XML-based applications. WebObjects also generates dynamic SMIL for use in multimedia applications.

Resources

*   www.apple.com/webobjects/directory.html

Macromedia Dreamweaver

Go to www.macromedia.com/products/dreamweaver

Development platforms: Mac OS Versions 9.1, 9.2, 10.1, or Mac OS X; Microsoft Windows 98, Windows 2000, Windows Millennium, or Windows XP

Quick Review

Adobe GoLive and Macromedia Dreamweaver compete hard for the hearts and minds of Web developers. Both products offer many similar features covering the basics of Web content authoring, including prebuilt JavaScript actions, source-code and WYSIWYG layout views, round-trip graphics handling, site management tools, and many other excellent features. Both tools support most of the major Web standards including DHTML, XML, CSS, and so forth. The distinguishing factors tend to run along the lines of user preferences in terms of platforms and integrated design and multimedia tools. For example, users who are accustomed to Macromedia tools will appreciate the tight integration Dreamweaver shares with Flash, Fireworks, and ColdFusion. Developers who are most comfortable on Windows tend to prefer Dreamweaver over Adobe GoLive, although both applications run on either platform. Dreamweaver's support for Microsoft Visual SourceSafe is one good reason among many. There are also far more extensions for Dreamweaver that function effectively on the Windows side only. Dreamweaver includes strong support for integration with ColdFusion and CFML, another distinguishing factor for those familiar with ColdFusion. Dreamweaver is generally not as strong as GoLive in visual design tools, but it shows a variety of specific strengths in reusable library elements, version control, and Flash and ColdFusion support.

For a list of features, visit the URL shown above or see "General Comparisons" on page 106.

Resources:

*   www.macromedia.com/exchange

*   www.macromediawebworld.com

*   www.templates2go.com

Macromedia ColdFusion

Go to www.macromedia.com/software/cfudstudio

Development platforms: Microsoft Windows 98, Windows 2000, Windows Millennium, or Windows XP

Deployment platforms: ColdFusion server, on Windows NT server platform, Windows 2000 server platform, with IIS and SQL Server

Quick Review

The Macromedia ColdFusion suite of products aimed at Windows-based Web application delivery and includes ColdFusion Studio (a WYSIWYG code-editing environment) ColdFusion server (a Windows server), and the Macromedia ColdFusion UltraDev 4 Studio, which unites JRun Studio with Dreamweaver UltraDev.

Macromedia ColdFusion had its first life as a product of Allaire Corporation, the company that claimed to have created the first Windows NT Web application server. Allaire merged with Macromedia in March 2001. The merger has been a happy one by most accounts. In the Macromedia ColdFusion UltraDev product, Dreamweaver adds powerful visual authoring tools to the development process, while ColdFusion brings robust code-editing and database integration tools for dynamic Web applications.

Throughout its life, ColdFusion has been popular with its audience, particularly during the first wave of e-commerce development because of its unique WYSIWYG, drag-and-drop features designed specifically for database-driven enterprise applications working from Microsoft Windows platforms. ColdFusion provides top-notch support for Windows, IIS, SQL Server, Access, and other Microsoft products. Macromedia's ColdFusion product consists of both a server application and development tools (ColdFusion Studio). You can build sites with ColdFusion that access any database, but tight integration between development tools and the server application can speed development time when building sites specifically for ColdFusion server.

ColdFusion's additional strengths include visual database tools, the ability to create flexible custom tags, and powerful code formatting and multi-language tools for HTML, XHTML, CFML, JSP, WML, SMIL, and XHTML development.

The next planned release of the ColdFusion server will have versions that run on both Windows platforms (including support for Microsoft .NET framework technologies) and Java 2 Enterprise Edition (J2EE) servers.

Resources

- www.macromedia.com/exchange
- devex.macromedia.com/Developer/Gallery/

Macromedia JRun

Go to www.macromedia.com/software/ultradev/resources/ jrudstudio/

Development platforms: Microsoft Windows 98, Windows 2000, Windows Millennium, or Windows XP

Deployment platforms: JRun server, on Java 2 Enterprise Edition server platform

Quick Review

Macromedia's JRun suite of products is aimed at Java-based application delivery and includes JRun Studio (a code-editing environment for developing Web applications for JRun server), JRun Server (a J2EE-based server); and the Macromedia JRun 3 UltraDev 4 Studio, which unites JRun Studio with Dreamweaver UltraDev. JRun's strengths include database integration and debugging tools, including Live Data Preview that shows server-side data while you're working in UltraDev; custom wizards, JSP tags, and free extensions that enable you to customize the work environment and extend functionality.

Certified J2EE-compatible, Macromedia JRun Server 3.1 is a Java application server that empowers you to develop and deploy Java applications quickly using JSP, Java Servlets, EJB, JTA, and JMS. You can rely on JRun for greater productivity, enhanced application performance, and exceptional configuration flexibility.

Resources

*   www.macromedia.com/exchange
*   devex.macromedia.com/Deve loper/Gallery/

Microsoft FrontPage

Go to www.microsoft.com/frontpage

Development platforms: Microsoft Windows 98, Windows 2000, Windows Millennium, or Windows XP

Quick Review

Microsoft FrontPage has long been considered the cheap alternative to the more robust Web authoring applications Macromedia Dreamweaver and Adobe GoLive, but FrontPage continues to gain on its rivals in features and robustness with each new release. FrontPage offers many excellent features covering the basics of Web content authoring and has made great strides in site management as well, including improved reporting features. The addition of Microsoft SharePoint Team Services improves project collaboration in team development environments, while the Microsoft bCentral™ Commerce Manager add-in program adds e-commerce capabilities.

One of the strong suits of FrontPage has always been ease of use. The program looks and acts like other Microsoft Office applications and includes many of the same helpful beginner features such as built-in templates and Wizards, design themes, and image libraries. For more advanced design work, FrontPage includes PowerPoint-like drawing tools that provide simple integrated graphics design and editing, though for more sophisticated design work you will likely turn to a third-party tool.

For quick solutions, FrontPage also includes a host of instant add-ins for your Website, such as automated usage statistics and Top 10 Lists. You can insert Microsoft-centric (naturally) site enhancers such as MSNBC headlines and MSN search directly into pages. There's even a Database Interface Wizard that allows you to quickly create forms and display the contents of a database on a page.

You can accomplish a lot with FrontPage in a very short time to get a site up and running, although serious professional site development teams will usually turn to more advanced tools to cover these areas as a site grows in sophistication. As with many Microsoft products, the greatest advantage of Microsoft FrontPage over its prime competitors Macromedia Dreamweaver and Adobe GoLive is price: To purchase FrontPage stand-alone from Microsoft, the cost is roughly half that of the other two. If you are in the market for a copy of Microsoft Office, the cost is even less if you buy a version of Office that includes FrontPage.

Enterprise-Level Content Development Tools

The explosive growth of the World Wide Web has given rise to a number of successful companies that leverage dynamic Web technologies to service the multimedia communications needs of large corporations. Several of these companies, described and compared in Table 4-2, generally provide both development tools and deployment platforms for delivering full-blown dynamic multimedia content over the Web. In addition to developing dynamic Web applications from the ground up using the other tools described in this chapter, under the right circumstances you can save time and effort by leveraging the services of these companies. There are disadvantages. For example, these service providers usually include their own branding somewhere in the content that you deliver, and affordable pricing for these services usually requires long-term enterprise-level licensing contracts.

Table 4-2: Enterprise-Level Content Development Tools

Vendor	Description	Products and Services	Authoring Tools	Deployment Tools	More Info
BrainShark	On-demand Web-based communications platform for creating, managing, and sharing business documents made more powerful with voice and images	Development software, production and consulting services			www,brain-shark.com
Centra	Real-time and on-demand Web collaboration products, content creation tools, and knowledge delivery systems		Java-based cross-platform development tools		www.centra.com

Table 4-2: Enterprise-Level Content Development Tools (Continued)

Vendor	Description	Products and Services	Authoring Tools	Deployment Tools	More Info
Digital Lava	On-demand rich media software and services for use in e-learning, e-marketing, e-communications and e-commerce applications.	Development software, production and consulting services	Rich media publishing application for linking and synchronizing video, audio, graphics and PowerPoint slides; a PowerPoint add-in for creating synchronized, Web-based presentations with streaming audio	Subscription-based ASP service for storage, management, and deployment for presentations; an out-of-the-box enterprise asset management and deployment system; COM-compliant component that allows you to build a custom host environment behind corporate firewall	www.digitallava.com
OutStart	On-demand enterprise-wide prescriptive and adaptive learning solutions powered by learning platform that encompasses content development and delivery with an e-learning management system	Collaborative development and dynamic delivery environment that also has a tightly integrated learning management system; delivers reusable learning object development and individualized delivery; content development assistance	Evolution Developer (browser-based, distributed content development tools); open to all media formats	Web-based content delivery, individualized delivery, and e-learning management solutions	www.outstart.com

Table 4-2: Enterprise-Level Content Development Tools (Continued)

Vendor	Description	Products and Services	Authoring Tools	Deployment Tools	More Info
PlaceWare	Real-time and on-demand Web conferencing solutions	Choice of two virtual environments: Large auditoriums that can hold up to 2,500 participants or highly interactive online meeting rooms for smaller groups; patented security technology		Web-based solution for Windows, Windows NT, UNIX, and Windows XP; no plug-ins, software, or hardware required	www.placeware.com
Tekadence	Tools for creating networked interactive multimedia content and generating interactive multimedia interfaces	Application and multimedia authoring environment, an enterprise application and multimedia server, an application/communications/computing network, a player/personal server, and platform translators	WYSIWYG editing, drag-and-drop functionality, timelines, object and behavior libraries, and other ease-of-use features common to products such as Macromedia's Director and Flash are core elements of Tekadence's application and multimedia authoring paradigm	Run-time engine that fuses XML, Java, JavaScript, Flash, QuickTime, and other standards-based technologies; incorporates the Java Virtual Machine, a proprietary generic Web server, a proprietary Flash Render, and a proprietary Flash server.	www.tekadence.com

Table 4-2: Enterprise-Level Content Development Tools (Continued)

Vendor	Description	Products and Services	Authoring Tools	Deployment Tools	More Info
WebEx	Real-time and on-demand Web conferencing global interactive network with integrated data, voice and videoconferencing; online meetings, seminars, and events	WebEx Meeting Center for online meetings with customers, prospects, partners, suppliers and colleagues; WebEx OnCall for live, remote, hands-on customer technical support; WebEx OnStage for large online events and seminars			www.webex. com

Part C: Methods

Client-Side Versus Server-Side Processing

One of the key issues in Web development is the question of where processing should be performed: client-side or server-side. Assuming the processing can be done on either the server or at the client application, the developer needs to identify what is being processed, whether there is any business logic that needs to be hidden from the user (for example, preventing the user from doing a View Source on the page to see private formulas), how long it would take to process and present the user with status or additional info, and so on. For example, if a user is given a registration form to fill out, some server-side code (ASP or CGI Perl script that communicates with a database, for example) would integrate the form data into some back-end database, but should data validity checks (Is the phone number in the correct format? Is the date valid? etc.) be done on the client or server? Usually, doing validity checks on the client allows you to pass "clean" and valid values to the back-end system instead of having to do them there. Of course, there might be some checks that cannot be done on the client due to client-side limitations (for example, client-side code could probably check for well-formed email addresses but couldn't tell if there was an invalid one) or business reasons (for example, client-side code shouldn't be checking the validity of product serial numbers because that might give nefarious individuals the ability to crack your software product).

Obviously, sites that rely on user information use back-end databases to store this information, so it's highly important. Some content sites (news, for example) also use back-end databases to store their content but differ on whether they serve the content from the database directly when the user accesses the Web pages or whether the pages are static and just the creation of those pages is done from a database on a staging server. Depending on a site's traffic and the type of information being displayed, database access for each user request might be slow or inefficient. However, if you're on a site that claims to offer real-time stock quotes, you probably don't want your data to be a 30-minute cached version.

Choosing Tools and Technologies

Many organizations with large IT infrastructure choose to create HTML, DHTML, JavaScript, and other code forms by hand. In other words, they avoid some of the WYSIWYG tools described in Part B: Tools on page 105. Others make use of front-end GUI applications such as Dreamweaver or Adobe GoLive for some of their activities, while relying on code experts for others.

Although many WYSIWYG tools advertise the fact that they do not alter preexisting code in documents, minor modifications can take place when the user opens a file within one of these applications and makes a change to an item that involves JavaScript or other coding: The application substitutes code based on its own design. The trick to mixing hand-coded elements with content generated by one of these applications is to isolate the tasks that will not alter the custom code created for the specific purposes of the Web application.

DHTML is often used for well-known interactive effects such as drop-down menus and rollover buttons. DHTML also makes possible full-scale animation within the browser but is rarely used for this purpose, mostly due to cross-platform compatibility issues. The advantage of DHTML is that it is supported by Internet Explorer and Netscape Version 4 or greater, without the need for plug-ins. The biggest downside is compatibility: The full breadth of DHTML functionality is not supported evenly cross-browser, and those effects that do work reliably usually require testing and tweaking in order to look and act the same in both IE and Netscape.

CSS is an easier choice. CSS is a World Wide Web Consortium standard that provides an elegant way to separate the presentation and structure of Web page content by allowing you to determine the styles of fonts and other elements within a single location. That location can be internal (within Web pages) or external (as a separate document on a server). External style sheets are especially helpful in allowing you to avoid embedded <font> tags, strewn across multiple pages, with one centralized document that you can use to change or update presentation settings across multiple Web pages or an entire Website.

Several factors affect your use of technologies such as DHTML or CSS and include target audience, client system requirements, usability concerns, and maintenance. Version 6 or greater of the major browsers are more compliant than in the past, but if a developer cannot restrict the audience to these browsers, some workarounds or design changes might be required to achieve backward compatibility.

Although JavaScript/ECMAScript/JScript exist according to standards, like many other browser technologies, the browser manufacturers implement them inconsistently, so some work is always required to test in the various target browsers.

Template Creation Tips

Templates usually start with design mockups in Photoshop or Illustrator from a graphic/design artist that a code expert or Web page designer can interpret into one or more master pages that represent the various types of structures on the site. The old adage of test early and test often (cross-browser and cross-platform) is important to identify any design issues that might need to be reworked.

A close working relationship between artists and page designers is crucial. Often artists don't have a deep understanding of HTML/Web page limitations, which makes the give-and-take of design versus implementation extremely important from the very beginning of the production. Mock up some working representative pages for signoff before applying templates to an entire site.

Database Integration Tips

Database integration requirements are very specific from organization to organization; therefore, we cannot provide a lot of detail on this subject, except to recommend careful planning from the very early stages of a Web application development that involves back-end integration. Understand the requirements for the site and get the database schema agreed upon by the appropriate stakeholders.

If you have a DBA on your team, sit down with that person to go over the database design completely, and try to plan for extensibility/flexibility, if appropriate. Also, since databases often involve user data and input, reliability, security, backup, and maintenance are important aspects of the planning.

Section I: Server-Based Architectures

CHAPTER 5

Synchronized Media

Synchronized media — interactive combinations of audio, video, illustrations, and text elements in a time-driven sequence — now appears in many forms throughout the corporate, education, and entertainment industries. In interactive presentations, these technologies hold cross-media publishing advantages by utilizing browser-based technologies for simultaneous delivery both on the World Wide Web and on CD-ROM or DVD-ROM. This chapter outlines the fundamentals of the format and the various tools and technologies you can use for authoring.

Part A: Background

Introduction

Most video on the Web looks a lot like video on television, only smaller. The television networks and local stations that use streaming video often launch previews or individual stories from their Websites directly into the player (QuickTime, Windows Media, or RealPlayer). The same is true of many movie trailers on the Web, which makes perfect sense: These more traditional media outlets are simply repurposing their content for the Internet audience.

But there is another way to present your multimedia content: When you embed players and elements within Web pages, these individual components add up to more than the sum of the parts and make possible CD-ROM-like interactive experiences that also take advantage of the unique technologies and opportunities of the World Wide Web.

Why Embed Media?

There are a number of reasons why you might want to break out of the traditional video player mold and combine media elements within a larger browser-based interface.

For example, you might want to:

- **Place your video clips in the context of a Website:** embedding in this case this allows you to maintain consistent design elements and navigational links surrounding the video.

- **Hide the player's identity:** By default, each of the players is heavily identified with its corporate source — with familiar packaging, or "skins," and the company logo displaying boldly during the loading of video. (If you think about this for a minute, it's amazing what we've come to accept in this era of hypermarketing in the high-tech arena; for example, a television network might use a lot of Sony solutions to create and distribute video content, but when was the last time you saw a giant SONY logo popping up between programs?) By embedding video, you can create a custom look for scripted button controls and other packaging elements, while there are also techniques specific to each player for suppressing the logo.

- **Simplify the user experience:** One of the biggest complaints with streaming video at the moment has to do with its complexity in terms of cross-platform, cross-browser, and cross-format decision making, both on the development end and in many cases at the user end. Some developers try and mask this complexity using a combination of embedded video, Dynamic HTML, and JavaScript within the browser to automatically detect browsers, plug-ins, and platforms and instantly deploy the right content for the user behind the scenes, without the user ever knowing about it. At the moment you can only accomplish this feat by embedding.

- **Share resources among formats:** When working with multiple formats, rather than setting up common text and graphics elements to display separately within each of the media players, you can use URL flips (triggers that launch a URL into a specified location in the browser) and other technologies available for QuickTime, Windows Media, or RealVideo — combined with open browser-based standards such as JavaScript or Synchronized Multimedia Integration Language (SMIL) — to synchronize the display of captions or other text or graphics elements elsewhere on the page, thereby sharing those elements among the three.

Moving From Player to Browser

Perhaps the most important reason to remove video from the context of the player and place it in the browser is that this allows you to more freely take advantage of the full range of World Wide Web technologies as we have come to know them.

It's all about context. Think about the look and feel of today's popular media players: With their curvy, textured, ultramodern skin designs, these players have the look, if not yet the feel, of the handheld video devices that have been showing up lately in futuristic technology commercials. Part of the appeal of this image is the compactness: something you can carry in your pocket, fit in your palm, and use anywhere in public.

But in the context of desktop or laptop video, why limit the user to that size? The image of the compact hand held player is an appealing way to downplay the small image sizes required to effectively stream video on today's public network, but given the larger canvas of the browser itself, an embedded video player that interacts with other elements on the page can prove to be a more effective — and more expansive — communications tool for many applications.

Even the word "player" implies certain limitations. As cute as they might be, those wireless handheld video devices of the near future will certainly require some quick thumbwork to manage anything more than the typical playback buttons — and so it is with our current selection of media players on the PC. The word "browser" on the other hand, implies a much wider range of interactive possibilities and controls.

In the larger context of the browser, video can take its place alongside dynamic, user-driven, database-enhanced content including graphics, animation, text, tables, chat boxes, and linked paths to resources anywhere on the Web. One name for this type of program is synchronized presentation — a term we will use in this chapter.

Elements of the Synchronized Presentation

The synchronized presentation can take many forms, but the fundamental feature is the coordination of timing in the display of visual elements to coincide with audio and/or video. The popularity of this key feature is driven primarily by the growing viability of long-form streaming video technologies and delivery platforms, such as Windows Media Technologies, RealSystem G2, and QuickTime Streaming technologies, combined with the growth of broadband delivery mechanisms.

In most cases the synchronization of elements is driven by cue points or events that are interwoven with the video and audio tracks. Various controls can be provided for stopping, starting, and jumping to various points in the presentation. In a sense the synchronized presentation is similar to rich-media content traditionally provided on CD-ROM using authoring tools such as Macromedia Director, but because it is browser-based, the presentation can take advantage of any number of World Wide Web technologies and navigational features, including the specific features of HTML, DHTML, XML, Flash content, and so forth, along with URL links to any location on the Web.

State of the Industry

Now that e-learning — once a novelty — has become standard fare on the Web, it makes sense that Web-based corporate and educational presentations would evolve and benefit from the growth of broadband delivery mechanisms and streaming media technologies.

With the growing appeal of rich-media delivery on the World Wide Web, synchronized presentations have become a major industry force in recent years, as witnessed by the prominence of proprietary solution providers at industry events such as the Streaming Media conferences, as well as the consistent stock performance of companies such as Eloquent, which remains solid even while many other streaming technology players have been suffering the dog days of summer.

Proprietary Solution Providers

Because of the novelty and apparent complexity of the technologies involved, many early adopters have turned to proprietary solution providers in recent years. These companies provide different variations of the format in complete turnkey solutions, allowing their clients to avoid the complexities of development (although a certain amount of time and education is required in order to understand the capabilities and limitations of each solution as well as for preparation of source materials). These companies also provide quick turnaround of content, an especially useful advantage in time-critical applications.

Here's a handful of the most prominent players, with a brief description of the types of content they provide:

- Yahoo! (www.yahoo.com) entered the e-learning space in 2001. Yahoo! is using its familiar three-pane window interface — made popular by Yahoo! FinanceVision — to deliver multimedia presentations to corporate users.

- Eloquent (www.eloquent.com) presentations include video and audio, playback controls, a search capability, volume control, slides, and transcript, as well as the unique ability to speed up the presentation if you are in a hurry. Pitch is automatically adjusted as you speed things up.

- Presenter.com (www.presenter.com) presentations include video and audio, playback controls, slides, thumbnails, and table of contents for navigation. Presenter's iPresentation service also allows you to upload PowerPoint slides to their Website, and then use the telephone to record an audio track for quick turnaround of content.

- HorizonLive (www.horizonlive.com) presentations are geared to real-time meetings with whiteboard, live chat, polls of the participants, and question button for QA, synchronized with PowerPoint slides.

- Digital Lava (www.digitallava.com) provides Hotfoot for PowerPoint, which allows you to add audio narration to your PowerPoint slides, along with a table of contents, search capabilities, and full playback control.

Disadvantages of Proprietary Solutions

The primary disadvantages of proprietary solutions for the synchronized presentation, as with most computer-based technologies, are high costs and lack of flexibility.

In terms of cost, the development resources used to create the proprietary features built into these applications are passed on to clients, as well as the cost for the manufacturing and deployment infrastructure involved. There is also a hidden cost to proprietary solutions when, down the road, as new technologies emerge, the client's content remains embedded within the proprietary platform and cannot be easily extracted or adapted to new situations without the ongoing involvement of the solution provider.

Many of these solutions are also inflexible when the client requires a major restructuring of the interface or addition of features not already included in the package.

Open Standards-Based Solutions

We are now entering a second phase in the evolution of the synchronized presentation in which a new set of affordable open standards-based tools is making it easier for developers and their clients to lower development costs while increasing the flexibility and scalability of their content.

For the past two years or so, QuickTime and RealNetworks have been the leaders in adding synchronizing capabilities to their video technologies. For example, the HREF track in QuickTime allows you to trigger the display of content in target frames elsewhere in the browser when using HTML frames, while Real has championed the development of Synchronized Multimedia Integration Language (SMIL), which I will describe in a later section. Windows Media Technologies has also evolved quickly in Microsoft's bid to reach parity with Real and QuickTime in extending the capabilities of streaming video.

These three big players provide the basic underlying technologies for many synchronized presentations. To ease the authoring process, Real and Microsoft also offer a number of simple authoring tools, while QuickTime Pro and some third-party tools such as Adobe GoLive offer QuickTime authoring tools for building presentations using the QuickTime Player.

On the other hand, Avid ePublisher companion edition, Discreet CineStream, Microsoft Producer, and the SMIL authoring tools from Real-Networks and Oratrix all represent a new breed of tool. Based on the same underlying video technologies just mentioned, these tools offer true drag-and-drop authoring functionality, from the import of assets through to the final publishing stage. ePublisher and CineStream allow you to choose among video technologies (Windows Media, RealSystem, or QuickTime), while Microsoft Publisher and the GRiNs editor for RealPlayer, as you might expect, work with their own media formats.

Affordable packages like these allow you get up to speed quickly and create simple straight-ahead projects such as Web-based re-creations of the corporate presentation with speaker and slideshow, for example. As with many WYSIWYG applications, there are some limitations. As Version 1.0 (or near 1.0) products, these tools lack some of the advanced authoring and layout control capabilities that experienced presentation developers can achieve with manual efforts using raw code or GoLive or Dreamweaver. For example, ePublisher doesn't allow you to publish these synchronized presentations using QuickTime (although you can export the video alone as QuickTime). There is no direct audio-only output in ePublisher, and pixel-accurate graphics design approaches within the generated frame sets of CineStream and ePublisher require a lot of tweaking behind the scenes to remove margins, frame borders, and so forth. (Note that only advanced programmers of HTML and JavaScript should attempt to tweak ePublisher's or CineStreams generated files, as there are chunks of proprietary code that you need to step around.) For straightforward no-nonsense content creation, these tools promise to speed up development cycles significantly.

To overcome the limitations of the WYSIWYG authoring tools — for example, to achieve cross-platform deployment or more advanced functionality beyond the simple table of contents with video and slides — you may want to build all the elements and piece them together using a number of industry-standard tools that are readily available, as described in Part B: Tools on page 135.

Synchronizing Technologies

Here's a brief look at the two main types of technologies (HTML frames and SMIL) you will find under the hood of most open-standards-based presentations.

The HTML Frames-Based Presentation

Many Web-based presentations today use HTML frames as the base technology for layout of content in the browser window. This is the basic technology used by Avid ePublisher, for example. HTML frames technology has been a stable standard since the 3.0 browser versions. While not as flexible and sophisticated in terms of layout as newer technologies such as the SMIL or the DIV tag in Dynamic HTML, frames technology has the advantage of allowing for simple implementation as well as simple drag-and-drop replacement of various HTML components that are referenced in each frame.

With good design, frames can yield a highly professional look, while avoiding the pitfalls of complex SMIL or DHTML implementations that require extensive testing in the various browsers or players. The arrangement of frames and their sizes are completely flexible and can also be adjusted by the user. Figure 5-1 is an example of a frames-based presentation layout.

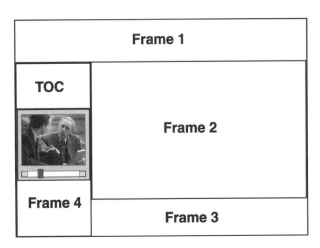

Frame 1: Header
Frame 2: Slides (static or dynamic)
Frame 3: Notes/text
Frame 4: Transcript
Video: Includes play controls
TOC: Table of Contents

Figure 5-1 Synchronized Presentation Example

One of the key benefits of this frames-based model is that each unit of content — whether a transcript page, notes page, slide, etc. — is referenced or pulled into the presentation from an external location. In other words, these presentations are not compiled into a single file but are dynamically assembled as the user watches the presentation in the browser, using relative referencing of resources on the Web.

The benefits of referencing of all elements are as follows:

- Units of content can be replaced with drag-and-drop ease; new content appears instantly within the template.

- Drag-and-drop replacement of content allows for instant scaling of content, from efficient low-bandwidth content for streaming over the Web to high-quality animations and clips for use on CD-ROM.

- Users can print, download, and save the content of each frame, independent of all others.

The greatest disadvantage of the frames-based approach has to do with aesthetics: it takes effort and planning to achieve a rich, layered, pixel-accurate look to your overall layout using frames. There are also more variables to deal with in the process, such as margin widths, user control over background colors, and browser window and frame sizes.

The SMIL-Scripted Presentation

For full CD-ROM-like control over the look and feel of presentation content, many presentation authors are now turning to a new scripting standard that, in its second generation, is bound to make many a developer "smile." Yes, SMIL is pronounced "smile," and it stands for Synchronized Multimedia Integration Language. The SMIL 2.0 standard, a W3C recommendation, is now an accepted scripting language supported in RealPlayer as well as QuickTime and a number of other lesser-known players. In addition, Microsoft supports a cross-over version of the standard in Version 5.5 and later of Internet Explorer known as HTML+Time or in IE 6 or later, XHTML+SMIL. It is possible that, as with JavaScript, all major browsers will natively support the language in the future.

SMIL is specifically designed for just this purpose, combining various types of multimedia elements for delivery on the World Wide Web. In fact, a minimum knowledge of SMIL 1.0 or 2.0 is a necessity for authoring Real-Media content and is also an option for displaying content in the QuickTime Player Version 4.1.2 or greater. According to the W3C Website, SMIL was created in order to "enable simple authoring of TV-like multimedia presentations such as training courses on the Web." A SMIL presentation can be composed of streaming audio, streaming video, images, text, or any other media type.

Because it is an HTML-like scripting language, SMIL presentations can be written using a simple text editor, which makes it much cheaper and easier to deploy than Shockwave content authored in Director, for example. What separates SMIL from a frames-based approach, too, is that developers have pixel-accurate control over placement of elements, complete with layering (z-ordering) of elements on top of each other. And unlike the compiled presentation, SMIL allows you to embed streaming video and audio content, pulled from any streaming server on the Web. You can also enrich existing Web pages by inserting SMIL scripts into standard HTML code. The frames-based approach still holds a couple of advantages, however, such as allowing users to save or print out the content of a single frame rather than the whole page.

You don't have to master the language to author SMIL presentations. A number of authoring tools are now available. But for those experienced with languages like JavaScript, SMIL is simple enough to understand and master fairly quickly. In its 2.0 recommendation, SMIL has evolved into an amazingly powerful tool for rich-media developers, incorporating all the strengths of the full range of open Web standards (including XML, DHTML, and Cascading Style Sheets) into a single motion-media authoring technology. It is, from top to bottom, a true Web technology that will only improve over time with input from some of the best minds in the industry.

Part B: Tools

Media Preparation Tools

Quick Review

If you choose to avoid the limitations of a specific manufacturer's all-in-one solution (as described in "All-in-One Authoring Packages" on page 146), and instead wish to hack out a synchronized presentation from the ground up, the next few sections describe a collection of basic stand-alone tools that you can use.

For initial preparation of the video or audio media, you need the following tools:

- **Video editing tools:** You can accomplish very simple video editing in RealSystem Producer and QuickTime Pro or with Windows Media Tools. More advanced editing requires a nonlinear editing (NLE) system such as Final Cut Pro, Avid Xpress or Media Composer, or Adobe Premiere. For more information on these various tools, see Chapter 2.

- **Video processing and encoding tools:** In this case, processing refers to the conversion of your edited material into Web-friendly formats and data rates as QuickTime, Windows Media, or RealMedia content, while encoding refers to the process of adding events or script commands — such as URL flips or chapter markers — into the video stream. You can process directly to a variety of formats from an Avid editing system, for example, or by passing the sequence to Media Cleaner EZ, Media Cleaner Pro, or Cleaner. Microsoft offers free Windows Media encoders, and you can also purchase RealSystem Producer. For more information on these tools, see Chapter 2.

Late-Stage Editing Tools

Quick Review

This term is used to describe the process of working with video clips that have already been edited and processed in order to achieve various interactive results on the Web or CD-ROM. At this point, you can use tools such as the QuickTime editing features in Adobe GoLive or the specific scripting technologies employed by Windows Media Tools and RealSystem Producer to add functionality such as chapter menus, URL flips, captions, other text elements, and so forth. You can also add or manipulate metadata — such as authorship and copyright data — using these tools. To work successfully at this stage, you must learn (or find a code expert who knows) how to target specific frames in a frame set when encoding URL flips; you must also learn the difference between relative and absolute paths on the World Wide Web and how each of the video formats uses them.

- For more information on QuickTime Pro, Windows Media Tools, and RealNetworks tools, see Chapter 2.

- For more information about Adobe GoLive, visit www.adobe.com/products/golive.

Interface Authoring Tools

Quick Review

This is where you build and design your larger interface in which the encoded video does its magic by calling up images, text, animation, anything you can imagine that is supported by your browser, within areas of the display that you define using HTML frames. For advanced HTML and JavaScript programmers, a simple text editor will do; otherwise you can use authoring tools such as Macromedia Dreamweaver or Adobe GoLive.

GoLive has better QuickTime video integration capabilities and is recommended when building applications with QuickTime, while Dreamweaver, particularly the Windows version, does better with RealMedia and Windows Media, although you can develop using either tool.

- For more information on DHTML authoring, see Chapter 4.

- For more information about Adobe GoLive, visit www.adobe.com/products/golive.

- For more information about Macromedia Dreamweaver, visit www.macromedia.com/software/dreamweaver.

SMIL Tools

Go to www.w3c.org/audiovideo/

Quick Review

Synchronized Multimedia Integration Language (SMIL) 2.0, approved in the fall of 2001 as a W3C recommendation, is a significant extension to the very popular SMIL 1.0 language. Among the key new features of the language are the following:

- Support for media transitions: You can apply visual transitions to all visually rendered media (including images, text, and video), based on a new structured transitions module.

- Support for animations: You can move objects during the presentation and change colors of displayed areas.

- Support for event-based activation: Along with new scheduling primitives, SMIL 2.0 allows object to start relative to user events (such as mouse clicks) or the start/end of other objects in the presentation.

- Support for advanced layout functionality: SMIL 2.0 provides methods for structuring the presentation's layout as a hierarchy of regions. This gives you more design control and makes animating groups of objects easy and efficient.

- New custom test attributes: One of the most powerful features of SMIL 1.0 was the ability to control content based on system test attributes. These attributes are extended in SMIL 2.0 and augmented with user-defined test attributes that allow you unprecedented control over what gets rendered.

SMIL 2.0 also expands existing timing, layout, and synchronization control. The tools described in this section generally allow you to author with some subset of the full range of features described in the SMIL specification.

Authoring Tools

Table 5-1 and Table 5-2 contain information on authoring tools.

Table 5-1: Authoring Tools for Internet Explorer

Microsoft Internet Explorer 6 (XHTML+SMIL)	The XHTML+SMIL profile integrates a subset of the SMIL 2.0 specification with XHTML. It includes SMIL 2.0 modules providing support for animation, content control, media objects, timing and synchronization, and transition effects. The SMIL 2.0 features are integrated directly with XHTML and CSS and can be used to manipulate XHTML and CSS features.	www.microsoft.com/ windows/ie/ www.w3.org/TR/2001/ WD-XHTML-plusSMIL-20010807/
Microsoft Internet Explorer 5.5 (HTML+TIME)	HTML+TIME (Timed Interactive Multimedia Extensions), first released in Microsoft Internet Explorer 5, adds timing and media synchronization support to HTML pages. It supports many of the SMIL 2.0 draft modules including Timing and Synchronization, BasicAnimation, SplineAnimation, BasicMedia, MediaClipping, and BasicContentControl. HTML+TIME 2.0 is based on the HTML+SMIL language profile in the Synchronized Multimedia Integration Language (SMIL) 2.0 working draft. HTML+TIME 2.0 is the successor to HTML+TIME 1.0.	www.microsoft.com/ windows/ie/ msdn.microsoft.com/library/ en-us/dntime/html/html-time.asp

Table 5-2: Cross-Browser Authoring Tools

Tool	Description	Supported Standards	Platforms	More Info
SMILGen	SMIL (and XML) authoring tool designed to ease the process of XML content creation. SMILGen understands XML syntax and handles the nesting and formatting of XML. This allows authors to worry about the content that they are trying to author without having to remember each quote and closing brace. SMILGen also understands the languages it authors; it knows what attributes a specific element uses or what child elements a given element may contain. Both of these features help eliminate a number of common XML syntax errors as well as making it easier to edit without having a reference to the language right by your side.	SMIL 1.0, SMIL 2.0, and RealPix.	Windows	www.realnetworks.com
EZer by SMIL Media	Multimedia integrated SMIL authoring tool that supports the W3C recommended standard SMIL 1.0 with RealPix and RealText. EZer SMIL 1.0 also provides strong editing function for content production. EZer SMIL 1.0 includes a visual/technical timeline and layout display for drag-and-drop ease of use.	SMIL 1.0 and RealSystem-based RM/RA/ RT/RP/JPG/ SWF/MP3/ WAV file support; RealPix/ RealText edit feature	Windows	www.smilmedia.com
Fluition by Confluent Technologies	Easy-to-use interactive multimedia authoring tool oriented toward RealPlayer; it includes Wizards, visual layout display, RealText editor, and user-customizable templates.	SMIL 1.0 and Real System-based RM/RA/ RT/RP/JPG/ SWF/MP3/ WAV file support	Windows and Mac	www.fluition.com

Table 5-2: Cross-Browser Authoring Tools (Continued)

Tool	Description	Supported Standards	Platforms	More Info
Media Access Generator (MAGpie)	Authoring tool for making Web- and CD-ROM-based multimedia accessible to persons with disabilities. Authors can add captions to three multimedia formats: Apple's QuickTime, the World Wide Web Consortium's Synchronized Multimedia Integration Language (SMIL), and Microsoft's Synchronized Accessible Media Interchange (SAMI) format. MAGpie can also integrate audio descriptions into SMIL presentations; it was developed by the CPB/WGBH National Center for Accessible Media (NCAM).	SMIL 1.0	Windows and Mac	www.wgbh.org
Perly SMIL	Used to create dynamic SMIL files using Perl.	SMIL 1.0 Perl module	Windows	

SMIL Players

Table 5-3 and Table 5-4 contain information on SMIL players.

Table 5-3: SMIL 2.0 Players

Player	Description	More Info
RealOne	The RealOne Platform by RealNetworks provides full support for the SMIL 2.0 language profile.	www.realnetworks.com/ solutions/ecosystem/ realone.html
GRiNS for SMIL 2.0	GRiNS for SMIL 2.0 by Oratrix provides a SMIL 2.0 player that supports SMIL 2.0 syntax and semantics.	www.oratrix.com/GRiNS/ SMIL-2.0/

Table 5-3: SMIL 2.0 Players (Continued)

Player	Description	More Info
Microsoft Internet Explorer 6 (XHTML+SMIL)	The XHTML+SMIL profile integrates a subset of the SMIL 2.0 specification with XHTML. It includes SMIL 2.0 modules providing support for animation, content control, media objects, timing and synchronization, and transition effects. The SMIL 2.0 features are integrated directly with XHTML and CSS and can be used to manipulate XHTML and CSS features.	www.microsoft.com/ windows/ie/ www.w3.org/TR/2001/ WD-XHTML- plusSMIL-20010807/
Microsoft Internet Explorer 5.5 (HTML+TIME)	HTML+TIME (Timed Interactive Multimedia Extensions), first released in Microsoft Internet Explorer 5, adds timing and media synchronization support to HTML pages. It supports many of the SMIL 2.0 draft modules including Timing and Synchronization, BasicAnimation, SplineAnimation, BasicMedia, MediaClipping, and Basic- ContentControl. HTML+TIME 2.0 is based on the HTML+SMIL language profile in the Synchro- nized Multimedia Integration Language (SMIL) 2.0 working draft. HTML+TIME 2.0 is the succes- sor to HTML+TIME 1.0.	www.microsoft.com/ windows/ie/ msdn.microsoft.com/library/ en-us/dntime/html/ htmltime.asp

Table 5-4: SMIL 1.0 Players

Player	Description	More Info
QuickTime 4.1 or greater	QuickTime began supporting SMIL 1.0 with Ver- sion 4.1. There are a number of specific exten- sions for using SMIL in QuickTime.	www.apple.com/quicktime/ authoring/qtsmil.html
RealPlayer by Real- Networks	The industry-standard SMIL player. Supports SMIL 1.0 and 2.0.	www.realnetworks.com
Soja	A Java-based SMIL player by Helio. SOJA stands for SMIL Output in Java applets.	www.helio.org
S2M2	A Java applet-based SMIL player by NIST.	smil.nist.gov/player
Schmunzel	A Java player by SunTREC Salzburg.	www.salzburgresearch.at/ suntrec/schmunzel
X-SMILES	A Java-based open browser by TML Laboratory.	www.xsmiles.org

QuickTime SMIL Extensions

To use QuickTime extensions in your SMIL document, include the xmlns: parameter and the URL of the QuickTime extensions as part of the initial <smil> tag like this:

```
<smil xmlns:qt="www.apple.com/quicktime/resources/
smilextensions">
```

QuickTime does not actually access the URL; it is used only to uniquely identify the QuickTime SMIL extensions.

In Table 5-5 that follows, the xmlns: parameter and the URL have been omitted for readability, but they are a required part of the <smil> tag when any QuickTime extensions are used in a SMIL presentation.

Table 5-5: QuickTime SMIL Extensions

SMIL Extension	Description	Example
autoplay	Specifies whether the presentation should play automatically. Legal values are true or false. The default is false.	<smil qt:autoplay="true">
bitrate	Specifies the bandwidth a media object needs in order to play back in real time. This is used to give QuickTime enough information to decide how far in advance to begin loading a media element to provide seamless playback. Possible values are positive integers, in bits per second. Do not confuse qt:bitrate with system-bitrate. Use system-bitrate to select a media element based on the user's connection speed. Use qt:bitrate to help QuickTime determine when to start downloading a media element.	<video src="stream56k.mov" qt:bitrate="56000" />

Table 5-5: QuickTime SMIL Extensions (Continued)

SMIL Extension	Description	Example
chapter	Specifies a chapter name for a media element. Valid values are any character string. Use this to create named points in your presentation that the viewer can jump to interactively. The chapter names appear as a pop-up list in the controller. This allows you to add a QuickTime chapter list to a SMIL presentation. In these examples, the movie controller would have a pop-up menu with three choices: Introduction, Overview, and Under the Hood. The viewer could jump to the corresponding point in the SMIL presentation at any time.	\<seq\> \<video src="Intro.mov" region="r1" qt:chapter="Introduction"/\> \<video src="Chap1.mov" region="r1" qt:chapter="Overview"/\> \<video src="Chap2.mov" region="r1" qt:chapter="Under the Hood" /\> \</seq\>
chapter-mode	Specifies whether the Time slider represents the duration of the whole presentation or the duration of the current chapter. Legal values are all and clip. Specify all for the whole presentation, clip for chapter-at-a-time.	\<smil qt:chapter-mode="clip"/\>
composite-mode	Specifies the graphics mode of a media element. This is used to create partial or complete transparency. The composite-mode attribute goes in any of the media element tags: video, img, or animation. Possible modes are copy, none, direct. These modes all specify no transparency, which is the default for most image formats.	\<img qt:composite-mode="copy"/\>
blend;percent	Specifies a blend between the image and the background, with a required percent integer value specifying the blend weight. 0 percent means complete transparency, 100 percent complete opacity.	\<video qt:composite-mode="blend;50%"/\>
transparent-color;color	Specifies that all pixels of a particular color within the image should be treated as transparent. It accepts a second parameter, color, which specifies the color to be rendered as transparent. The color parameter may be any valid color specification supported by Cascading Style Sheets, level 2.	\<animation qt:composite-mode="transparent-color;black"/\>

Table 5-5: QuickTime SMIL Extensions (Continued)

SMIL Extension	Description	Example
alpha, straight-alpha, premultiplied-white-alpha, premultiplied-black-alpha	Specifies that the image has an internal alpha channel that should be used when compositing. The alpha and straight-alpha modes refer to a separate alpha component; the premultiplied modes refer to an image that has been premultiplied with the alpha against a white or black background, respectively.	\<video qt:composite-mode="straight-alpha;50%"/>
straight-alpha-blend;percent	Specifies that the image has an internal alpha channel as a separate component, and that an additional level of transparency should be applied to the whole image.	\<img qt:composite-mode="straight-alpha-blend;50%"/>
immediate-instantiation	When used in the \<smil> tag, specifies whether all the media elements in the presentation should be downloaded (or streamed) immediately, or whether this should be deferred until each element is about to be played. Legal values are true and false. Default is false. Opening all the media elements at the beginning of the presentation can take considerable time and memory and therefore should be done only for simple presentations with a few small media elements. When used in an element tag, it specifies that this particular element should be downloaded or streamed as soon as the presentation is opened. You might use this to preload an element to be sure it is already in memory when it needs to play.	Example 1: \<smil qt:immediate-instantiation="true"> Example 2: \<img src="bgimg.png" qt:immediate-instantiation="true"/> Example 3: \<video src="bgimg.png" qt: immediate-instantiation="true"/> Example 4: \<text src="bgimg.png" qt: immediate-instantiation="true"/> Example 5: \<audio src="bgimg.png" qt: immediate-instantiation="true"/> Example 6: \<animation src="bgimg.png" qt: immediate-instantiation="true"/>
next	Specifies a presentation to play when this presentation finishes. Legal value is the URL of something QuickTime can play: a media file, a movie, a stream, or a SMIL presentation. This is similar to the QuickTime plug-in's QTNEXT parameter.	\<smil qt:next="nextpresentation.smi">

Table 5-5: QuickTime SMIL Extensions (Continued)

SMIL Extension	Description	Example
system-mime-type-supported	Specifies the MIME type that needs to be supported in order to play a media element. This is normally used in conjunction with the <switch> tag to allow the player software to choose a media element that it can handle. Possible values are character strings matching a valid MIME type.	<switch> <img src="qt.mov" qt:system-mime-type-supported="video/quicktime"/> <img src="someotherformat.suffix" qt:system-mime-type-supported="other/mime-type"/> </switch>
target	Specifies a target for a presentation specified by the href parameter in the anchor tag. Possible targets are an existing browser window, a browser frame, or quicktimeplayer. If the target string is none of these, a new browser window is created. It is used in conjunction with show="new".	<a href="www.server.com/another.smi" show="new" qt:target="quicktime-player"><img src="OpenNewSMIL.gif" region="r2" dur="5:00"/>
time-slider	Specifies whether the movie controller should include a Time slider. During a SMIL presentation, QuickTime dynamically loads media elements as required, so the known duration of the overall presentation can change as a movie is played or navigated. When the known duration changes, the scale of the Time slider changes to reflect that. This can be confusing to the viewer. Because of this, QuickTime movies created from SMIL documents do not normally display a Time slider. Legal values are true and false. Default is false. Note: If you want to import a SMIL presentation into QuickTime and edit it using QuickTime Player's editing features to add a chapter list, for example, you must set time-slider="true". QuickTime Player's editing features rely on the Time slider.	

All-in-One Authoring Packages

Table 5-6 has information on WYSIWYG authoring packages for SMIL.

Table 5-6: Presentation Authoring Packages for SMIL

Product	Description	Output formats	More Info
CineStream	Discreet CineStream combines DV editing and streaming media production software to deliver interactive dynamic media that synchronizes video and HTML. Leveraging streaming technology from Discreet's cleaner software, CineStream uses the EventStream technology to insert interactive commands, such as URL flips, into video directly from the timeline. CineStream software's multiple-composition support offers a singular workflow with editable sub-masters that can be created on the fly, allowing a single project to contain alternate versions of the same movie. Projects can be designed for broadcast and then repurposed for Web delivery.	HTML Frames with Windows Media, RealMedia, or QuickTime	www.discreet.com/products/CineStream
Avid ePublisher Companion Edition	Avid ePublisher Companion Edition is part of the Avid Xpress DV PowerPack. It combines the powerful video editing in Avid Xpress DV with the unique Link & Sync Web authoring of Avid ePublisher. And it's part of a media creation package that includes Avid Xpress DV. It allows you to import audio and video formats, import Web image formats and HTML, import PowerPoint slides, synchronize media elements, lay out Web pages with templates, automatically generate Table of Contents entries, and publish presentations on the Web, CD, or DVD.	HTML Frames with Windows Media or RealMedia (QuickTime output as video only – no synchronization with HTML frames)	www.avid.com/products/avidxpressdv/

Table 5-6: Presentation Authoring Packages for SMIL (Continued)

Product	Description	Output formats	More Info
Microsoft Producer	User-friendly environment for building synchronized presentations from Microsoft products and Web technologies such as PowerPoint, Windows Media, HTML, and image files. It allows you to import several audio and video formats, import Web image formats and HTML, directly edit PowerPoint slides within Microsoft Producer, maintain the compelling animations and effects used in PowerPoint 2002, synchronize media elements, lay out Web pages with templates, automatically generate Table of Contents entries, and publish presentations on the Web or CD.	HTML Frames or scripted Web pages with Windows Media only	www.microsoft.com/ windows/windows-media/ technologies.asp
Oratrix GRiNS Editor Pro	It is based on the newest implementation of the Synchronized Multimedia Integration Language (SMIL 2.0). Along with Real, Oratrix has developed tools to create interactive presentations for the RealPlayer or the Oratrix GRiNS player. It provides a visual, timeline-based Structure Editing with real-time feedback, full drag-and-drop capabilities, bandwidth analysis and feedback, advanced layout editing; transition and animation editor, source view editing, and RealONE export capabilities.	SMIL-based presentations with RealMedia only	www.oratrix.com
Stream Anywhere	Visual timeline-oriented software that allows you to edit and synchronize video with other elements to develop dynamic multimedia presentations that integrate into any Website. It includes Web page layouts and export to Microsoft FrontPage.	HTML-based; Windows Media and RealMedia (no QuickTime)	www.sonic-foundry.com

Part C: Methods

Technology Decisions

Before purchasing a tool set and embarking on your own development efforts, here are a few basic issues to consider regarding the architectures you will use to build and deliver synchronized presentations. Your answers to the following basic questions will affect both your choice of development tools and the look and feel of your final product.

Audio Only, or Audio and Video?

In some cases, you might not need video in your presentation but instead deliver audio only. If your budget is small or if your audience has low bandwidth, in fact, you might want to avoid video.

An audio-only presentation, for example, can be streamed from an HTTP server without the added expense of a streaming server. When you add true streaming video, the requirements change significantly. Streaming video requires a streaming server configuration as well as greater storage capacity on the server. Bandwidth requirements on playback also increase dramatically.

For low-bandwidth audio-only implementations, you can still include navigational features such as playback controls. Using QuickTime as your authoring tool, you can also add chapter menus or text captions.

ePublisher does not support creation of audio-only synchronized presentations, though this feature is planned for a future release. You can, however, cheat the system a bit by creating a small video window that displays low-data-rate white or black content, for example, or a single image such as a logo or title and still achieve the synchronization of events while taking advantage of ePublisher's drag-and-drop authoring features.

User-Driven or Time-Driven?

This question is the same as asking how active or passive do you want your users to be? In other words, do you want the users to move the presentation forward on their own, or will you do it for them by triggering each new chapter and event?

User-Driven Model

In the user-driven model, each unit of content is self-contained, and the user is responsible for moving backward or forward through the presentation — with Next and Previous buttons, for example. Recent versions of Power-Point allow you to quickly generate Web-based presentations with this type of simple navigation, but with very simple visual design based on templates.

Time-Driven Model

Most higher-end synchronized presentations are time-driven, which means that the stream of audio or video advances the content on its own. The user still has the ability to pause or jump to various sections, however, but with the added convenience of watching and absorbing the content passively without intervening to advance the slides and visuals.

Compiled, HTML Frames-Based, or SMIL-Scripted?

This is the most important question you must ask yourself. This section describes the advantages and disadvantages of these options.

A compiled presentation is basically what we know traditionally as the multimedia title, delivered through a player as a single large file. When you create a presentation using Macromedia Shockwave or Flash content, you are delivering a compiled presentation (for more on Shockwave and Flash, see Chapter 4).

One of the advantages of authoring presentations exclusively in Shockwave or Flash is that you know what you are going to get: as long as the user's browser is equipped with the plug-in or ActiveX control, all users will see the same content, with pixel-accurate layout of elements — although the user's bandwidth and monitor settings remain important variables. The major disadvantage is that video is not easily integrated and does not stream using the standard RTSP or Microsoft protocols. Without the benefits of true streaming video, these presentations are somewhat limited when video is a major element. Flash or Shockwave content can, however, be used as elements in the types of presentations described in this chapter.

Interface Considerations

When designing your interface, make sure you address all the usability issues up front. For those of us accustomed to traditional video production, for example, it's easy to overlook how overwhelming the experience can become when synchronizing too many events and information elements on screen all at once. You also need to address how far afield you will allow users to go when following links in your presentation and whether the video should be paused or allowed to play during such explorations.

Embedding Video and Audio

The first step in synchronizing media is embedding the video. As you might guess, there is no one way to embed video clips. The two popular browsers, Netscape and Internet Explorer, both require different code. Netscape uses the embed tag, while Internet Explorer uses Microsoft's object tag with

ActiveX controls. In addition, QuickTime, Windows Media, and RealProducer all use different tags and scripting methods.

You must also decide whether your video content will be uploaded to a standard HTTP server for delivery or whether you will be streaming the video from a streaming server (each format uses its own server technology for streaming — although Quick-Time and RealVideo share the RTSP protocol, and QuickTime files can be streamed from RealVideo 8 servers).

Here's a breakdown of the specific technologies to use when embedding and streaming, with links to resources for specific information on each.

Windows Media Technologies

- For information on embed code and advanced scripting of metadata using ASX files, as well as setting up video streaming using Windows Media Services:

  Microsoft Developer Network workshop
  msdn.microsoft.com/library/default.asp?url=/nhp/
  Default.asp?contentid=28000411

QuickTime

- For information on embed code as well as specific tags and their functionality:

  www.apple.com/quicktime/authoring/embed.html

- For information on SMIL scripting technologies available for QuickTime:

  www.apple.com/quicktime/authoring/qtsmil.html

- For information on setting up QuickTime streaming:

  www.apple.com/quicktime/products/tutorials/
  preparingtostream.html

RealMedia

- For information on embed code, specific tags, and use of SMIL, as well as setup requirements for streaming:

  www.realnetworks.com/resources/media_creation.html

Tips for Video-Based Synchronization

Aside from the well-known issues in dealing with Web video (bandwidth, data rates, and so forth), there are a number of issues to address when creating the type of synchronized presentation described in this column. Here are a few basic tips for starters:

- **Timings are imprecise:** For video and film editors, who are accustomed to frame-accurate production work, the vagaries of Web delivery can be maddening at times. Prepare yourself, and in some cases prepare your client's expectations: Don't expect your carefully encoded URL flips to display your elements at exactly the right time. Net congestion, data routing issues, the size of your files, and the end user's system configuration will all affect the speed with which elements display. Keep your data rates low to speed delivery, but allow for a range of up to 30 seconds in the delivery of synchronized content.

- **URL flips need room:** Don't place events too close together, and don't start events too close to the beginning of a clip; otherwise they might not fire off consistently. In other words, this is not the technology to use to try and re-create those flashy three frame edits in the browser.

- **URL flips must be repeated in Windows Media:** RealMedia and QuickTime allow you to set a time range in which a URL event should trigger, but when working with Windows Media, playback must pass over a specific time location in order to trigger the event. This is not an issue when the video is downloading progressively, but when streaming with the position slider displayed, you can compensate for a user's nonlinear navigation through a clip by repeating appropriate URL flips every 30 seconds, for example, or at the beginning of each new chapter mark.

- **Windows Media and QuickTime chapter menus require streaming:** Keep in mind that those wonderfully useful chapter menus that work so nicely during playback from your local drive will stop work when you upload your video clips to an HTTP server. This is related to the fact that you can only seek randomly into various time locations in a video file when that file is delivered using a streaming protocol.

- **Captions are a challenge:** Caption text, to put it simply, is a bear. RealMedia seems to have the most robust implementation working through SMIL, although we've found that the speed options in SMIL for scrolling text, in increments from 1 to 10, make it difficult to keep the text in sync with some voices. The embedded Windows Media Player, for some reason, only supports one width for the caption window, so that when you turn it on using a PARAM tag for the embedded player, the entire window must conform to that width. The Windows Media Tools provide a template that uses JavaScript to display the captions outside of the embedded player, but you must be a JavaScript expert to go in and customize the template and adjust positions, sizes, and appearances. For QuickTime, we've also discovered recently that scrolling text works fine in a progressive download but does not stream well and can crash the QuickTime Player on Windows.

Section II: Disc-Based Architectures

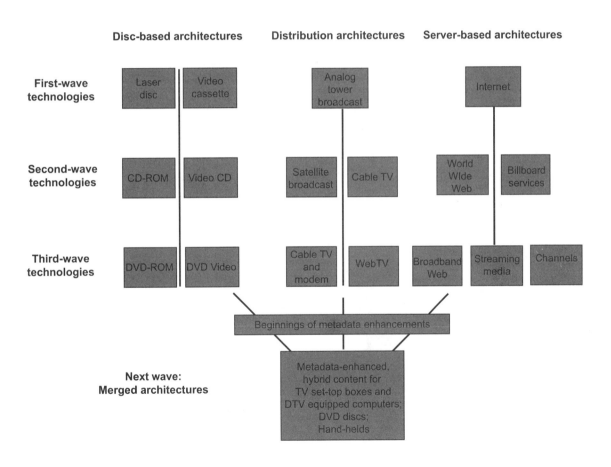

	Disc-based architectures	Distribution architectures	Server-based architectures
First-wave technologies	Laser disc / Video cassette	Analog tower broadcast	Internet
Second-wave technologies	CD-ROM / Video CD	Satellite broadcast / Cable TV	World Wide Web / Billboard services
Third-wave technologies	DVD-ROM / DVD Video	Cable TV and modem / WebTV	Broadband Web / Streaming media / Channels

Beginnings of metadata enhancements

Next wave: Merged architectures

Metadata-enhanced, hybrid content for TV set-top boxes and DTV equipped computers; DVD discs; Hand-helds

Section II: Disc-Based Architectures

CHAPTER 6

Introduction

Since its introduction as a consumer format around 1997, digital versatile disc (DVD) has been a hot topic for most rich-media developers — closely watched in the trades, with a growing number of production houses taking advantage of ever cheaper software tools and equipment for producing DVD.

Because of its ability to combine broadcast-quality video with the kinds of interactivity, we've come to expect in the computer age, DVD has been heralded as the convergent answer to the various limitations of the CD-ROM, the VCR, and the CD player.

Brief History of the DVD Future

The DVD market has grown from nothing in 1996 to more than 28 million units shipped worldwide in 2001. DVD sales will reach new heights over the next several years, according to Cahners In-Stat Group (www.instat.com). In a study conducted in January 2001, Cahners In-Stat found that DVDs will continue as the fastest-growing consumer electronics product in history with 60 million units expected to sell in 2004. New features such as DVD Audio (see Chapter 9), component integration leading to lower prices, and new products incorporating DVD technology, such as hybrid set-top boxes and DVD mini-systems (see Chapter 17), all point to continued growth.

In addition, recording technologies have advanced rapidly, with new products having entered the DVD recorder market in 2001 that included DVD recorders using the DVD-RW and DVD+RW formats.

In-Stat also found that:

- In 2004, DVD player sales in the United States will equal the number of VCRs sold today.

- By 2004, an average DVD player bill of materials (cost for a vendor to supply the drive) will fall below $90.

Though twice as many DVD players sold in the United States than Europe last year, by 2004 the European market will be roughly 80 percent of the U.S. market.

CD and DVD Compared

The basic concept behind DVD data storage is similar to that used in CDs, and to some extent LP recordings on vinyl. Like records and CDs, DVDs store data in microscopic grooves running in a spiral around the disc. Because CDs and DVDs are digital, the stored data is in the form of nonreflective holes (called pits) and reflective bumps (called lands) representing the zeros and ones of digital information. DVD drives use laser beams to scan the grooves.

A DVD can store more than two hours of broadcast-quality video on one layer of the disc. DVD Video storage provides resolution that is far greater than that offered by laser disc media and almost twice the resolution of standard VHS videotape. How do DVDs store so much video at such high quality? DVDs use smaller tracks than CDs (0.74 micron wide compared to 1.6 microns on CDs). DVDs also employ new modulation and error correction methods.

Table 6-1: CD Versus DVD

	CD	DVD
Disc size	12 cm	12 cm
Track size	1.6 microns	0.74 micron
Capacity	650.4 MB	3.75 to 15.9 GB

DVD Playback Formats Compared

This section of the book is divided into three main chapters covering DVD-ROM, DVD Video, and DVD Audio. The main differences among the three formats are summarized in Table 6-2.

Table 6-2: DVD Playback Formats

	DVD-ROM	**DVD Video**	**DVD Audio**
Content	All forms of desktop computer video, audio, and data files	MPEG video, audio, slideshows, menus	MPEG video, audio, slideshows, menus, album lists, lyrics
Key advantages over CDs	More than seven times the storage capacity of CD-ROMs (single-sided)	Twice the image quality, and more than double the play length of Video CDs (VCDs)	More than double the audio fidelity of CDs; much greater play-length
Playback devices	DVD-ROM drives (does not require DVD Video software)	Consumer DVD Video players; DVD-ROM drives with appropriate playback software	Consumer DVD Audio players; DVD-ROM drives with appropriate playback software
Folder structures	Like CD-ROM, does not require a particular structure or multiplexing of the content	Requires VIDEO_TS folder and accompanying standards-compliant structure	Requires AUDIO_TS folder and accompanying standards-compliant structure; can also include VIDEO_TS structure for use in DVD Video players

The Role of MPEG

DVD specifications are tied closely with the evolving Motion Pictures Experts Group (MPEG) standards for video. Where White Book Video CD incorporated the MPEG-1 video standard, DVD incorporates both MPEG-1 and MPEG-2. For more information on all the MPEG video standards, see Chapter 15.

DVD Recording Formats Compared

One of the last aspects of the DVD standard to come together has been recording formats. This remains a highly competitive market, with various industry players seeking to influence the adoption of standards. To date, no one format can call the market its own. The formats and key differences are summarized in Table 6-3.

Table 6-3: DVD Recording Formats

	DVD-R	DVD-RAM	DVD-RW
Content	Originally designed for professional DVD Video and DVD-ROM authoring, a consumer version is now available.	Primarily intended for backup and storage, with random read-write access.	Primarily intended for backup and storage. Features a sequential read-write access more like a phonograph than a hard disc.
Key advantages	The standard for mass-produced consumer titles. As with CD-R, users can write only once to this disc.	Can be re-written more than 100,000 times. Not cost-effective for mass production of titles.	It can be re-written up to about 1,000 times. Not cost-effective for mass production of titles, but could replace VHS as a consumer recording medium.

Enter DVD Multi

As a compromise in the battle over disc formats, the DVD Forum (www.dvdforum.org) championed the development of the DVD Multi set of specifications. These specifications (not a format or a single specification) help define which drives will read and write which discs for the various DVD consumer and computer applications. DVD Multi is meant to help consumers by embracing all existing format versions and thus encouraging broader compatibility across DVD drives and players. The DVD Forum has set up DVD Multi specifications Version 1.0, and has approved the first two test specifications as well as the new Logo for DVD Multi products.

• Version 1.0 is available at the Website of the DVD Format/Logo Licensing Corporation (DVD FLLC): www.dvdfllc.co.jp/

• For more information about all the DVD disc formats, go to www.dvdforum.org/tech-dvdbook.htm

About the DVD Forum

Originally founded in 1995 under the name DVD Consortium, the DVD Forum (www.dvdforum.org) is an international association of hardware manufacturers, software firms, and other users of DVDs. The Forum was created for the purpose of exchanging and disseminating ideas and information about the DVD format and its technical capabilities, improvements, and innovations. Membership is open to any corporation or organization that is engaged in activities related to DVD research, development, and/or manufacturing or any software firms or other users of DVD products that are interested in developing and improving the DVD format. Forum members are not required to support the DVD format to the exclusion of other formats. Ten companies (including Sony, Pioneer, Time Warner, and Toshiba) founded the organization. The Forum provides a wealth of information for developers at its Website.

Additional DVD Resources

For information about hybrid DVDs and DVD devices as well as new upcoming DVD technologies, see Chapter 17.

These links are provided on the DVD Forum Website:

- DVD technical notes by Chad Fogg (www.mpeg.org/MPEG/DVD/)
  Best collection of technical information about DVD

- DVD — at the brink of a successful European launch by Philips (www.news.philips.com/whatsup/19971204-00.html)
  Jan Oosterveld, senior director of Philips Corporate Strategy, addressing the DV Summit in Versailles, France, on December 1, 1997

- Selection of audio coding technologies for Digital Delivery Systems by Dolby
  Comparison of MPEG-2 audio and Dolby AC-3 (www.dolby.com/dvd/sel-code.html)

- International CD-i Association (www.icdia.org/)
  Includes some discussion of DVD

- The OpenDVD Consortium (www.opendvd.org)

- DVD articles by Jeff Gilbert (www.efd.lth.se/~e95jla/soundpic/dvd/Jeffletters.html)

- DVD sidebar: It's the Pits at Columbia University (www.columbia.edu/cu/moment/040396/dvdside.html)

Section II: Disc-Based Architectures

CHAPTER 7

DVD-ROM

This chapter provides information that will help you to understand the challenges, choose your tools, and then create and distribute DVD-ROM discs.

Part A: Background

Introduction

While DVD Video has taken the spotlight in recent years as the format of choice for distribution of Hollywood entertainment titles, DVD-ROM might well prove to be the true star of interactive media (particularly in the corporate world) once the distribution of DVD-ROM drives reaches critical mass.

What exactly is DVD-ROM? Technically speaking, DVD-ROM is no more than a physical disc specification combined with a new file format called the universal disc format (UDF). You can think of DVD-ROM as the foundation, with the various DVD applications (desktop applications, DVD Video, DVD Audio) built as layers on top of it.

For the purposes of this chapter, you can consider DVD-ROM separately from DVD Video as it applies to desktop applications similar to those supplied on CD-ROM in the past. Currently, a small industry is growing up around the process of converting the vast libraries of interactive CD-ROM content to DVD-ROM. The advantages include fitting multidisc CD-ROM games and reference titles onto single DVD-ROM discs, and in some cases reprocessing of video to take advantage of higher-quality MPEG formats. In addition many new titles are targeted specifically for DVD-ROM.

In the corporate space, DVD-ROM allows developers to continue using all the same tools with the same degree of control over advanced interactivity (including use variables, programming logic, and database and Web integration) while resolving the long-standing issues of video quality and reliability.

Universal Disc Format: A New File Standard

In August 1995, the computer industry group working on the DVD Video standard recommended adoption of the universal disc format (UDF) that had been developed by the Optical Storage Technology Association (OSTA). In September of the same year, OSTA announced the final standard, which represented a big improvement over ISO 9660 and included the following:

- Single format for computer and TV-based applications
- Backward-read compatibility with existing CD-ROMs
- Forward compatibility with future R/W discs
- Single file system for all content and disc media types
- Low-cost drives and discs
- No mandatory container
- Reliable data storage and retrieval
- High performance for both sequential and nonsequential data types

    There are several versions of UDF:

- UDF 1.02 is the original specification that handles all the requirements of DVD-ROM and DVD-R.

- UDF 1.5 was developed for adding recording capability based on UDF 1.02 to support DVD-RAM, magneto-optical devices, and other rewritable or erasable media.

- UDF 2.0 is supported on Macintosh System 8.5, Sun Solaris 2.6, and Windows 2000.

- UDF does not have ISO 9660 limitations on filename length (12 characters for ISO Level 1, 31 for ISO Level 2) and the limitation to 8 directory levels. UDF supports unlimited length filenames and unlimited directory levels. Realistically, however, the interpretation of these filenames will probably be limited to 256 characters.

CD-ROM Versus DVD-ROM

DVD-ROM represents a quantum leap over the capacity of CD-ROM. Table 7-1 shows a quick comparison of the two formats.

Table 7-1: CD-ROM Versus DVD-ROM

	CD-ROM	**DVD-ROM**
Disc size	12 cm	12 cm
Track size	1.6 microns	0.74 micron
Capacity	650.4 MB	4.4 GB (single-layer) 8 GB (dual-layer) 8.8 GB (double-sided, single-layer) 15.9 GB (double-sided, dual-layer)
File systems	ISO 9660	UDF
Data transfer rate	Minimum 1.23 million bits per second	Minimum 11.08 million bits per second

DVD-ROM Myths and Facts

DVD-ROM is one of the most misunderstood acronyms in the new media era. Here are a few common misconceptions and related facts:

- **DVD-ROM is just a CD-ROM with more capacity:** Although DVD-ROM is meant to serve many of the same applications as CD-ROM, it is really an entirely different format in both technical and physical details. Although it looks like a CD-ROM drive to the naked eye, DVD-ROM uses an entirely different file format, track size, and manufacturing materials, among other specifics.

- **DVD-ROM drives cannot play CDs:** Most DVD-ROM drives are backward-compatible with most CD formats. There are some CD-ROM formats (such as multisession CDs) that might not play on some DVD-ROM drives. CD-ROM drives, however, cannot play DVD-ROM discs.

- **DVD drives all use the new UDF format:** The UDF format is used for most DVD applications and is required for DVD-R discs. Rerecordable discs, however, such as DVD-RAM and DVD-RW discs can be formatted as Windows-standard FAT32 or Mac HFS.

- **You need new authoring software to produce content for DVD-ROM:** For DVD-ROM authoring, you can use all the same software you've always used when authoring content for CD-ROMs. The only real difference in terms of data is in the file format.

- **DVD-ROMs only use MPEG-2 video:** While most DVD-ROM drives ship with MPEG-2 decoders, in either software or hardware, the fact is that any video format that will play on the desktop can be stored and played from a disc in a DVD-ROM drive.

- **DVD-ROMs require special players:** Only DVD-ROM discs that incorporate MPEG-2 content require DVD Video or MPEG-2 decoding software or hardware. In most cases, a system with a DVD-ROM drive already has such software or hardware installed.

- **DVD Video is better than DVD-ROM:** While DVD Video has quickly become the standard for high-quality feature film and entertainment content, for those applications that require sophisticated interactivity and compatibility with desktop computer environments (such as corporate media and education), DVD-ROM applications can prove to be more useful and effective.

DVD-ROM Specifications

As of April 14, 2000, the DVD Format/Logo Licensing Corporation (DVD FLLC, www.dvdfllc.co.jp) assumed all responsibilities for licensing the various DVD formats and logos. The official specification for DVD is documented in a series of five books covering read-only discs; recordable discs; rewritable discs; rerecordable discs; and DVD-RAM, DVD-RW, and DVD-R for general-purpose discs. Beginning November 11, 2001, a new DVD Multi license became available for development of DVD Multi drives that can handle all of the formats mentioned.

The DVD-ROM, DVD Video, and DVD Audio specifications fall under the read-only disc book.

- For more information about the DVD Video spec, see Chapter 8.

- For more information about the DVD Audio spec, see Chapter 9.

As of June 2001, the DVD-ROM spec Version 1.1 includes:

- Physical Specifications Version 1.0
- File System Specifications Version 1.0

For more complete book information and instructions on how to order a DVD book specification, visit www.dvdfllc.co.jp.

Part B: Tools

DVD-ROM Authoring Tools

There is a wide range of tools you can use to present content on DVD-ROM. Tools include all the software historically used to author CD-ROM content, such as Macromedia Director and Authorware, as well as Web browser content authoring tools for creating everything from simple HTML pages to complex Web applications. You can also simply supply files on disc. Quite simply, you can use any file type that is supported by the target operating system. All the same rules apply in terms of system and software requirements, depending on your content; however, DVD-ROMs generally perform better and with greater reliability than CD-ROM drives.

Tools for Integrating MPEG-2 and DVD Video

If you wish to add MPEG-2 content, you must supply an MPEG playback engine, either as a software player, as a plug-in to another application, or through authoring of DVD Video-compliant content that makes use of the DVD Video player installed with the DVD-ROM drive.

Several tools allow you to display MPEG-2 and DVD Video content within conventional authoring tools. These include Xtra DVD for Macromedia Director, OnStage DVD for Director or ActiveX control environments, and Active DVD for PowerPoint. These tools are discussed in detail in Chapter 17.

DVD Recorders

Table 7-2 provides information on a selection of popular DVD Recorders.

Table 7-2: DVD Recorders

Device	Type	System Interface	Basic Specs	More Info
Pioneer DVR-S201	DVD-R, authoring discs	SCSI external	Compatible with Version 1.0 of the DVD-R standard 3.95 GB or 4.7 GB capacity	www.pioneerusa.com
Pioneer DVR-A03	DVD-R, general-purpose discs	IDE internal and external	Specs	www.pioneerusa.com

Table 7-2: DVD Recorders (Continued)

Device	Type	System Interface	Basic Specs	More Info
Toshiba SD-W1111	DVD-RAM	External	Rewritable 2.6 GB single-sided & 5.2 GB dual-sided Reads DVD-ROM, DVD-R, and all CD-ROM media 1,350 KB/sec DVD-RAM transfer rate 180 ms average random access DVD-RAM read 260 ms average random access DVD-ROM read Large 2 MB data buffer	www.toshiba.com
Toshiba SD-W1101	DVD-RAM drive	External	Rewritable 2.6 GB single-sided & 5.2 GB dual-sided Reads DVD-ROM, DVD-R, and all CD-ROM media 1,350 KB/sec DVD-RAM write and read 270 ms average random access DVD-RAM write 180 ms average random access DVD-RAM read	www.toshiba.com
Toshiba SD-W2002	DVD-RAM	External	Uses rewritable single- or dual-sided media; single-sided 2.6 GB; dual-sided 5.2 GB; single-sided 4.7GB; dual-sided 9.4 GB; Reads DVD-ROM, DVD-R, and all CD-ROM media 1,352 - 2,704 KB/sec DVD-RAM transfer rate 190 ms average random access DVD-RAM read; 120 ms average random access DVD-ROM read Large 8 MB data buffer	www.Toshiba.com

Table 7-2: DVD Recorders (Continued)

Device	Type	System Interface	Basic Specs	More Info
Panasonic LF-D201U	DVD-RAM	SCSI-2	Maximum DVD-ROM read speed 6x Dimensions (HWD, in inches) 5.75 x 1.1 x 7.75 Buffer size 1 MB Maximum CD-ROM read speed 24x PC only Claimed average seek time 65 ms	www.panasonic.com
Hi-Val	DVD-RAM	Internal SCSI	2X/1X	www.hival.com
HP DVD-Writer DVD100i	DVD+RW	Internal EIDE (ATAPI)	Sustained transfer rate: 1x CD = 150 KB/sec (data mode 1), 1x DVD = 1,353 KB/sec Write: CD-R: 4x, 8x, 12x CD-RW: 4x,10x DVD+RW: 2.4x (CLV) Read: CD-R: 4x, 8x, 10x, 20x, 32x (CAV) CD-RW: 2x, 4x, 8x, 20x (CAV) DVD+RW: 8x (CAV) Burst transfer rate: 33 MB/sec Seek time: 125 ms average random access (CD-ROM, DVD-ROM) 250 ms average full-stroke access (CD-ROM, DVD-ROM) Disc finalization time: DVD+RW: up to 3 minutes at 2.4x (1x DVD = 1,353 KB/sec)) CD: 2 minutes typical at 2x (1x CD = 150 KB/sec (data mode 1)) PC only	www.hp.com

Table 7-2: DVD Recorders (Continued)

Device	Type	System Interface	Basic Specs	More Info
Hitachi GF-2000	DVD-RAM drive	SCSI-2	Write capacity: DVD-RAM 4.7 GB per side and 2.6 GB per side, single- or double-sided media Data transfer rate (maximum): DVD-RAM 2.7 MB/sec, DVD-ROM 8.3 MB/sec, CD-ROM 3.6 MB/sec access time (typical): DVD-RAM 210 ms DVD-ROM 165 ms DVD-R 190 ms CD-ROM 140 ms Burst transfer rate: 33.3 MB/sec max Buffer memory: 2 MB DVD-RAM: 4.7 GB per side and 2.6 GB per side, single- or double-sided media DVD-ROM: DVD-ROM, single- or dual-layer, single- or double-sided DVD-R: 4.7 GB/side and 3.95 GB/side CD-ROM: CD-ROM, CD-R, CD-RW, CD-ROM-XA, CD-I, CD Audio (CD-DA), Photo-CD Multi-session, CD-Extra, CD-Text 650 MB (mode 1)/742 MB (mode 2)	www.hitachi.com

Table 7-2: DVD Recorders (Continued)

Device	Type	System Interface	Basic Specs	More Info
Hitachi GF-2050	DVD-RAM Drive	External SCSI-2	Write capacity: DVD-RAM 4.7 GB/side and 2.6 GB/side, single- or double-sided media	www.hitachi.com
			Data transfer rate (maximum): DVD-RAM 2.7 MB/sec, DVD-ROM 8.3 MB/sec, CD-ROM 3.6 MB/sec	
			Access time (typical): DVD-RAM 210 ms, DVD-ROM 165 ms, DVD-R 190 ms, CD-ROM 140 ms	
			Interface: SCSI-2	
			Burst transfer rate: 33.3 MB/sec max	
			Buffer memory: 2 MB	
			Compatible formats (read only): DVD-RAM: 4.7 GB/side and 2.6 GB/side, single- or double-sided media	
			DVD-ROM: DVD-ROM, single- or dual-layer, single- or double-sided	
			DVD-R: 4.7 GB/side and 3.95 GB/side	
			CD-ROM: CD-ROM, CD-R, CD-RW, CD-ROM-XA, CD-I, CD Audio (CD-DA), Photo-CD Multi-session, CD-Extra, CD-Text	
			650 MB (mode 1)/742 MB (mode 2)	

DVD Premastering Software

Table 7-3 provides information on a selection of popular DVD Recorders

Table 7-3: DVD Premastering Software

Product	Operating Systems	Description	More Info
MakeDisc+	UNIX or Windows NT	MakeDisc+ is an updated version of MakeDisc that allows users to generate both CD and DVD disc images. The software premasters your data. During the premastering process, data can be converted to a form compliant with the ISO 9660 standard. Premastering your data to comply with the standard results in a CD-ROM that can be read on the greatest number of computer systems. MakeDisc provides transparent recovery of original UNIX filenames, directories, and symbolic links.	Young Minds Inc. www.ymi.com
Write! DVD Pro	Windows 95, 98, NT, 2000, ME	A UDF file system-based DVD utility, Write! DVD for Windows allows you to set up, run, test, and repair DVD-RAM drives and media on a PC.	Software Architects Inc. www.softarch.com
GEAR Pro DVD	Windows 95, 98, NT	Based on the well-established GEARSoftware product line, GEAR Pro DVD supports DVD/UDF, hybrid ISO 9660/UDF, and CD-Rewritables and is suitable for one-offs, premastering for replication, or archiving.	GEAR Software Inc. www.gearsoftware.com
Instant CD/ DVD	Windows 95, 98, NT, 2000, ME	InstantCD/DVD was created as a very professional product for the high-end market. InstantCD/DVD contains the InstantCD/DVD mastering program and MultiCOPY for professional CD duplication with simultaneous writing to several CD recorders.	VOB www.vob.de/us/

Table 7-3: DVD Premastering Software (Continued)

Product	Operating Systems	Description	More Info
DVD-Rep	Windows 95, 98, NT	DVD Rep is intended for use to master files that are already prepared on your system. DVD Rep prepares the disc using the ISO/UDF bridge: a double file system with ISO-9660 level 2 compatibility with Windows 3.1/95/NT, and UDF 1.02 for compatibility with DVD set-top boxes and Windows 98.	Prassi Software USA, Inc. www.prassi.com
Toast Titanium	Macintosh	Comprehensive all-in-one CD and DVD mastering solution that enables you to record in various formats on CD or DVD on the Macintosh.	Roxio www.roxio.com
VideoPack 5	Windows 95, 98, NT, 2000, ME	Full-featured DVD authoring tool for creative professionals interested in building and burning DVD Videos, Video CDs, and Super-VCDs on PC. VideoPack automatically converts video and still frame files, including AVI, JPEG, BMP, and more, into DVD- or VCD-compatible MPEG-1 and MPEG-2 video files. VideoPack 5 is the powerful authoring software for the sophisticated video professional and anyone who wants to be one.	Roxio www.roxio.com

Part C: Methods

Choosing Your Technologies

Your choice of technologies for authoring DVD-ROM content is virtually limitless, provided you stick to common desktop authoring tools and file formats. Your primary limitation involves use of DVD Video or DVD Audio elements. DVD-ROMs that incorporate MPEG-2, DVD Video, or Dolby Digital audio, for example, require appropriate playback software or hardware; make sure that your target systems have this support or provide the software with your disc. Otherwise, consider delivering the content on CD-ROM using more common media formats.

Also, observe the limitations of the various DVD media formats. The most universal media format is a DVD-ROM disc that's been replicated at a facility. The most widely supported one-off format is a 3.95 GB DVD-R authoring media disc. New formats, such as DVD-R general-purpose discs, require relatively new DVD-ROM drives that support the 2.0 specification.

Taking Advantage of Capacity

DVD-ROM represents a great improvement for multimedia developers who are accustomed to wrestling with the 650 MB capacity of CD-ROM. With roughly seven times the storage capacity, DVD-ROM offers, the following opportunities:

- **Avoid multidisc titles:** You can now produce long-form multimedia content for distribution on a single disc.

- **Distribute multiple titles per disc:** Particularly useful in corporate applications, you can distribute literally hundreds of documents and files or several complete multimedia titles on a single disc.

- **Increase your data rates:** Even while most modern computers can now manage broadband data rates for video and audio media, developers of CD-ROM content often continue to work with mid- or low-range data rates in order to fit the content onto the disc. DVD-ROM allows you to increase data rates for video and audio to match current desktop standards.

- **Conduct more efficient archiving:** Many institutions, large and small, are turning to DVD-ROM for archiving purposes in order to reduce the number of discs required for archiving, thus decreasing both the cost of the media and storage space.

Handling Hybrid Content

The term "hybrid DVD" can refer to a number of combinations of technologies layered onto the DVD-ROM specification. The most common hybrid formats are as follows:

- **DVD discs that play in CD-ROM drives:** These discs use the UDF/ISO bridge format, described in the next section.

- **DVD-ROM titles that incorporate DVD Video:** These discs allow users to play DVD Video-compliant elements combined with DVD-ROM elements on PCs. For more information, see Chapter 17.

- **DVD Video titles that incorporate DVD-ROM elements:** These discs allow users to access DVD-ROM content while viewing the disc on a consumer DVD player or set-top box. For more information, see Chapter 17.

- **DVD titles that interact with the World Wide Web:** Also known as WebDVD discs, these hybrid titles work like standard DVD Video titles but provide additional Web links and Web-enabled features. For more information, see Chapter 17.

Using the UDF/ISO Bridge Format

UDF/ISO bridge is a DVD-R file system that allows for both the newer UDF system and the older ISO 9660 system used by the CD-ROM format. This allows DVD discs to be used with computer operating systems that do not have a provision for UDF support.

In order to produce a UDF/ISO 9660-compliant bridge disc, your premastering software must support the format (see "DVD Premastering Software" on page 177). During the premastering step, the software builds an 8.3-compatible filename for every file on the volume.

The primary use for this format is in burning DVD content onto a CD-R disc for viewing on a broader range of systems, including those that do not support the UDF format. You can also master the content onto a Windows or Macintosh hard drive for playback.

Section II:
Disc-Based Architectures

CHAPTER 8

DVD Video

This chapter provides information that will help you to understand the challenges, choose your tools, and then create and distribute discs that conform to the DVD Video specification.

Part A: Background

Introduction

While DVD has been adopted at a faster rate than any other consumer format in history, with some 28 million units shipped worldwide in 2001, the one remaining issue for complete adoption of the DVD Video format in place of VHS, Video CD, or CD-ROM is player penetration. VHS players and CD-ROM drives, for example, are nearly ubiquitous and therefore remain the target platforms of choice for distribution of titles that must reach the largest possible audience right out of the box. That is expected to change in the next few years, as DVD player and DVD-ROM drive penetration finally reaches critical mass.

DVD Video is much more than an advancement over formats such as Video CD and VHS. DVD Video represents a quantum leap in quality and functionality. DVD Video brings together the high standards of quality found in the broadcasting and cable industries with the advanced interactivity and functionality found on the World Wide Web or in multimedia industries.

Some Comparisons

To date, DVD Video's closest kin is the Video CD, a format which never found a big audience in the United States but which remains popular throughout much of the world. Table 8-1 provides a quick comparison of the two formats.

Table 8-1: Video CD Versus DVD Video

Specification	Video CD	DVD Video
Disc size	12 cm	12 cm
Track size	1.6 micron	0.74 micron
Capacity	650.4 MB	3.75 to 15.9 GB
Data rate	Max 1.1519291 kbps	Max 9.8 kbps
Video formats	Composite digital MPEG-1	Component digital MPEG-2
Playing time	74 minutes	2+ hours (MPEG-2) 8+ hours (MPEG-1)
Copy protection	None	Macrovision, CGMS-A

Table 8-1: Video CD Versus DVD Video (Continued)

Specification	Video CD	DVD Video
Audio formats	224 kbps MPEG-1 layer II (44.1 kHz) 16-bit 44.1 kHz LPCM	64 to 384 kbps MPEG-1 layer II 64 to 914 kbps MPEG-2 (48 kHz) 64 to 448 kbps Dolby Digital (48 kHz) 16/20/24-bit 48/96 kHz LPCM

DVD also shared some heritage with the CLV Laser disc and VHS cassette. Some additional comparisons of features and functionality are listed in Table 8-2.

Table 8-2: DVD Video, Video CD, CLV Laser Disc, and VHS

Specification	DVD Video	Video CD	CLV Laser Disc	VHS Tape
Capacity	2+ hours video; 1,000+ still frames plus 20+ hours of audio	74 minutes video; limited stills	1 hour video; limited stills, no audio	2+ hours video and/or stills
Image Quality	Component, broadcast-quality video	Composite video; approximately 50 percent of DVD Video resolution	Composite video; approximately 66 percent of DVD Video resolution	Composite video; approximately 50 percent of DVD Video resolution
Sound Quality	Up to 8 tracks; sample rate up to 96 kHz, 24 bit	2 stereo tracks; sample rate 44 kHz, 16 bit	2 stereo tracks; sample rate 44 kHz, 16 bit	2 stereo tracks
Conveniences	Small disc size; small player size; no switching of discs for feature-length content	Small disc size; small player size; must switch discs for feature-length content; no rewinding	Large disc size; large player size; must switch discs for feature-length content; no rewinding	Small tape size; small player size; no switching of tapes for feature-length content; must rewind

Table 8-2: DVD Video, Video CD, CLV Laser Disc, and VHS (Continued)

Specification	DVD Video	Video CD	CLV Laser Disc	VHS Tape
Features and Functionality	Multiple languages; up to 32 subtitles; camera angles; menus; copy protection; regional codes; seamless branching; interactivity; Web links; instant rewind	Single language; 1 subtitle added to video; menus; interactivity; Web links; instant rewind	Single language; 1 subtitle added to video; instant rewind	Single language; 1 subtitle added to video; copy protection

DVD Video Development Timeline

Table 8-3 provides a brief overview of the evolution of the DVD Video specification.

Table 8-3: DVD Video Development Timeline

Date	Event
1993	Ten years after the compact disc was first introduced, prototypes of blue lasers with four times the storage capacity of the CD are first demonstrated.
1994	Seven international entertainment and content providers call for a single worldwide standard for digital video on optical media. The companies form the Digital Video Disc Advisory Group consisting of Columbia Pictures (now Sony); Disney; MCA/Universal (Matsushita); MGA/UA; Paramount; Viacom; and Warner Bros. (Time Warner).
Dec. 16, 1994	Sony and Philips and 14 supporting companies announce the single-sided, 3.7-billion-byte multimedia CD (MMCD).
Jan. 24, 1995	SD Alliance (Hitachi, Matsushita, Panasonic), Mitsubishi, Victor (JVC), Pioneer, Thomson (RCA/GE), Toshiba (partner of Time Warner), plus 10 supporting companies announce the superdensity double-sided 5-billion-byte SD-DVD standard.
Jan. 26, 1995	Sony calls Ministry of International Trade and Industry to arbitrate unification of the two into a third standard.
Feb. 23, 1995	Sony announces a two-layer, single-sided design with 7.4 billion bytes.
Apr. 1995	Five computer companies (Apple, Compaq, HP, IBM, Microsoft) form technical working group urging a compromise.

Table 8-3: DVD Video Development Timeline

Date	Event
Aug. 14, 1995	Computer industry group (with Fujitsu and Sun added) recommends adoption of the universal disc format (UDF) developed by the Optical Storage Technology Association (OSTA).
Aug. 1995	At the Berlin IFA show, the two rival camps announce that they will compromise and come up with one standard.
Aug. 24, 1995	Negotiations begin.
Sept. 15, 1995	SD Alliance announces willingness to switch to Philips/Sony method of bit storage.
Sept. 25, 1995	OSTA announces UDF file system interchange standard, a big improvement over ISO 9660.
Oct. 19, 1995	Interactive Multimedia Association (IMA) and Laser Disc Association (LDA) hold joint conference to determine requirements for "innovative video programming" capabilities of DVD.
Dec. 12, 1995	Final DVD-ROM format and video standards are announced; new alliance form DVD Consortium consisting of Philips, Sony, seven companies from the SD Alliance, and Time Warner.
1996 through 1997	Copy protection schemes are hammered out.
1997	First consumer DVD Video products enter the market.

DVD Video Specifications

As of April 14, 2000, the DVD Format/Logo Licensing Corporation (DVD FLLC, www.dvdfllc.co.jp) assumed all responsibilities for licensing the various DVD formats and logos. The official specification for DVD is documented in a series of five books covering read-only discs; recordable discs; rewritable discs; rerecordable discs; and DVD-RAM, DVD-RW, and DVD-R for general discs. Beginning November 11, 2001, a new DVD Multi license became available for development of DVD Multi drives that can handle all of the formats mentioned.

The DVD-ROM, DVD Video, and DVD Audio specifications fall under the Read-Only Disc book.

- For more information about the DVD-ROM spec, see Chapter 7.

- For more information about the DVD Audio spec, see Chapter 9.

As of June 2001, the DVD Video spec Version 1.1 includes:

- Reference information — Jacket Picture Format, version 1.0

- Reference information — IEC958 to convey non-PCM encoded audio bit streams, version 1.0

For more complete book information and instructions on how to order a DVD book specification, visit www.dvdfllc.co.jp.

About DVD Video and Audio Streams

DVD Video is based on a subset of the MPEG-2 Main Profile at Main Level. Constant bit rates (CBRs) and variable bit rates (VBRs) are both supported. DVD adds additional restrictions to the full MPEG-2 standard, with one video stream at a time, video data rates up to 9.8 Mbps, and a specific series of supported resolutions:

- MPEG-2 resolutions
  NTSC 720x480, 704x480, 352/480 (525/60)
  PAL 720x576, 704x576, 352x576 (625/50)

- MPEG-1 resolutions
  352x240 (525/60)
  352x288 (625/50)

DVD audio streams are based on three industry standards: MPEG-2, linear PCM (LPCM, similar to industry-standard audio tracks on a CD), and Dolby Digital. Discs containing NTSC video are required to include at least one audio track in Dolby Digital or PCM format. After that, any combination of formats is allowed.

Your encoding or authoring software and hardware might have additional requirements or limitations. Consult your documentation.

Part B: Tools

Introduction

This section describes development tools for authoring DVD Video discs. This section is divided into three parts covering entry-level tools, mid-range tools, and high-end tools. Defining such categories is a risky business; one developer's mid-range tool might be considered high-end to another. At the same time, pricing and feature sets are always in flux. In defining these categories, we've tried to follow as closely as possible a set of marketing categories into which the tool vendors seem to be targeting their products. These can be described as follows:

- **Entry-level:** Most DVD authoring tool vendors provide low-cost tools (from free bundled software up to about $4,000 USD software and hardware systems) that can author only a subset of features available in the DVD Video spec.

- **Mid-range:** The next step up for most DVD authoring tool vendors is mid-range professional tools, in many cases combining both software and hardware (from about $5,000 up to about $10,000) that allow you to include most or all of the features in the DVD Video spec while differing from the high-end tools primarily on issues of speed and/or quality.

- **High-end:** The high-end covers more costly professional tools ($10,000 to $100,000) that make no compromises in terms of speed, quality, or functionality.

This section does not specifically list MPEG encoding tools, except as they are included in a specific authoring system. For more information on MPEG as well as a complete list of stand-alone MPEG encoding tools, see Chapter 15.

Entry-Level Tools

Table 8-4 provides a summary and comparison of entry-level tools used in developing DVD Video discs.

Table 8-4: Entry-Level DVD Tools — Feature Comparisons

	Spruce Up	Apple iDVD	Daikin ReelDVD	Sonic DVDit!
Platform	Windows 98, NT4, 2000, ME	Macintosh, OS X.1 or greater	Windows 98, NT4, 2000, ME	Windows 98, NT4, 2000, ME
Configuration	Software	Software; ships with G4, iBook	Software; frequently bundled	Software; frequently bundled
Video I/O	System-dependent	FireWire	System-dependent	System-dependent

Table 8-4: Entry-Level DVD Tools — Feature Comparisons (Continued)

	Spruce Up	Apple iDVD	Daikin ReelDVD	Sonic DVDit!
DVD recording device	System-dependent	Apple SuperDrive	System-dependent	System-dependent
Premastering			DVD-R, DLT, disc image	DVD-R, DLT, disc image
Machine control	System-dependent	FireWire	System-dependent	System-dependent
Image file import		PICT, Photoshop	BMP, JPEG, MPEG Still (MPI), PICT, TIFF or YUV	Photoshop
Preview	Software simulation	Software simulation	Software simulation	Software simulation
MPEG encoding	MPEG-2, CBR, software	MPEG-2, CBR, software	MPEG-2, CBR, software	MPEG-2, CBR, software
Video import	AVI	QuickTime	AVI	AVI, QuickTime
Audio encoding	PCM (no AC3)	PCM (no AC3)	PCM, MPEG (no AC3)	PCM (no AC3)
Audio import			AC-3, MPEG, WAV, AIFF, 96KHz, 16- or 24-bit PCM	AC-3, WAV, MPEG
Muxing/ compiling	Built-in software	Built-in software	Built-in software	Built-in software
DVD Video streams	1	1	1	1
DVD Audio streams	1	1	1	3
DVD subtitle streams	0	0	0	3
DVD languages	1	1	1	3
DVD still menus	Yes	Yes	Yes	Yes

Table 8-4: Entry-Level DVD Tools — Feature Comparisons (Continued)

	Spruce Up	Apple iDVD	Daikin ReelDVD	Sonic DVDit!
Menus	Yes	Yes	Yes	Yes
Slideshows	Yes	Yes	Yes	Not supported
Camera angles	Not supported	Not supported	Not supported	Not supported
Scene/ chapter/stop definition	Yes	Yes	Yes	Yes
Widescreen	16:9	16:9	16:9	16:9
Dual-layer discs	Not supported	Not supported	Not supported	Not supported
WebDVD features	Not supported	Not supported	Not supported	Not supported
Region coding	Not supported	Not supported	Not supported	Not supported
Parental management	Not supported	Not supported	Not supported	Not supported
Copy protection	Not supported	Not supported	Not supported	Not supported
More info	www.spruce-tech .com	www.apple.com	www.dvd.ace-daikin.com.sg	www.sonic.com

Mid-Range Tools

Table 8-5 provides a summary and comparison of mid-range tools used in developing DVD Video discs.

Table 8-5: Mid-Range DVD Tools — Feature Comparisons

Product Detail	Spruce DVD Conductor	Apple DVD Studio Pro	Daikin	Sonic DVD Creator; DVD Fusion	Pinnacle DVD2000/ Impression
Platform	Windows NT	Macintosh OS 9.1	Windows 98, NT4, 2000, ME	Windows 98, NT4, 2000, ME	Windows 98, NT4, 2000

Table 8-5: Mid-Range DVD Tools — Feature Comparisons (Continued)

Product Detail	Spruce DVD Conductor	Apple DVD Studio Pro	Daikin	Sonic DVD Creator; DVD Fusion	Pinnacle DVD2000/ Impression
Configuration	Turnkey system	Software; requires dual-processor G4	Turnkey system	Turnkey system	Turnkey system
Video I/O	Serial digital NTSC/PAL; component analog; composite analog; S-video	FireWire	Serial digital NTSC/PAL; component analog (option); composite analog (option); S-video (option)	Serial digital NTSC/PAL; component analog (option); composite analog (option); S-video (option)	FireWire; component analog; composite analog; S-video
Video formats	NTSC, PAL, SECAM	NTSC, PAL	NTSC, PAL	NTSC, PAL, SECAM	NTSC, PAL
DVD recording device	Supports most DVD-R, DVD-RAM, DLT	Supports Apple Super-Drive and most DVD-R, DVD-RAM, DLT	Supports most DVD-R, DVD-RAM, DLT	Supports most DVD-R, DVD-RAM, DLT	Supports most DVD-R, DVD-RAM, DLT
Premastering	DVD-R, DVD-RAM, DLT, disc image	DVD-R, DVD-RAM, DLT, disc image	DVD-R, DVD-RAM, DLT, disc image	DVD-R, DVD-RAM, DLT, disc image	DVD-R, DVD-RAM, DLT, disc image
Machine control	RS-422	FireWire	RS-422	RS-422	RS-422
Image file import	Photoshop	Photoshop	BMP, JPEG, MPEG Still (MPI), PICT, TIFF or YUV	Photoshop	Photoshop
Preview	Hardware	Real-time software	Hardware	Hardware	Hardware
MPEG encoding	Hardware MPEG-1 and 2, VBR	Software MPEG-1 and 2, VBR	Hardware MPEG-1 and 2, VBR	Hardware MPEG-1 and 2, VBR	Hardware MPEG-2, MPEG-1, CBR

Table 8-5: Mid-Range DVD Tools — Feature Comparisons (Continued)

Product Detail	Spruce DVD Conductor	Apple DVD Studio Pro	Daikin	Sonic DVD Creator; DVD Fusion	Pinnacle DVD2000/ Impression
Video import	AVI, MPEG	QuickTime, MPEG	AVI, MPEG	AVI, Quick-Time, MPEG	AVI, MPEG
Audio encoding	PCM, MPEG, AC3	PCM, MPEG, AC3	PCM, MPEG, AC3	PCM, MPEG, AC3	PCM, MPEG, AC3
Audio import		PCM, MPEG, AC-3, Quick-Time, AIFF, WAV, SDII	PCM, MPEG, AC-3, WAV, AIFF	PCM, MPEG, AC-3, WAV	
Muxing/ compiling	Built-in hard-ware	Built-in soft-ware	Built-in hard-ware	Built-in hard-ware	Built-in hard-ware
DVD feature support	Full support for spec	Full support for spec	Full support for spec	Full support for spec	Full support for spec
Web features	SpruceLink (Windows only)	Not provided	DVD@ccess links (cross-platform)	eDVD (Windows-only)	Not provided
More info	www.spruce-tech.com	www.apple.com	www.dvd.ace-daikin.co.sg	www.sonic.com	www.pinnacle-sys.com

High-End Tools

Table 8-6 provides a summary and comparison of high-end tools used in developing DVD Video discs.

Table 8-6: High-End DVD Tools — Feature Comparisons

Product Features	Spruce DVDMaestro DVDPerformer	Panasonic LQ-VD2000S	Daikin	Sonic Scenarist
Platform	Windows NT	Windows NT	Windows 98, NT4, 2000, ME	Windows 98, NT4, 2000, ME
Configuration	Turnkey system	Turnkey system	Turnkey system	Turnkey system

Table 8-6: High-End DVD Tools — Feature Comparisons (Continued)

Product Features	Spruce DVDMaestro DVDPerformer	Panasonic LQ-VD2000S	Daikin	Sonic Scenarist
Video I/O	Serial digital NTSC/PAL; component analog (option); composite analog (option); S-video (option)	Serial digital NTSC/PAL; component analog (option); composite analog (option); S-video (option)	Serial digital NTSC/PAL; component analog (option); composite analog (option); S-video (option)	Serial digital NTSC/PAL; component analog (option); composite analog (option); S-video (option)
DVD recording device	Supports most DVD-R, DVD-RAM, DLT	Supports most DVD-R, DVD-RAM, DLT	Supports most DVD-R, DVD-RAM, DLT	Supports most DVD-R, DVD-RAM, DLT
Premastering	DVD-R, DVD-RAM, DLT, disc image	DVD-R, DVD-RAM, DLT, disc image	DVD-R, DVD-RAM, DLT, disc image	DVD-R, DVD-RAM, DLT, disc image
Machine control	RS-422	RS-422	RS-422	RS-422
Image file import	Photoshop	Photoshop	BMP, JPEG, MPEG Still (MPI), PICT, TIFF or YUV	Photoshop
Preview	Hardware	Real-time software	Hardware	Hardware
MPEG encoding	Hardware MPEG-1 and 2, VBR	Hardware MPEG-1 and 2, VBR	Hardware MPEG-1 and 2, VBR	Hardware MPEG-1 and 2, VBR
Video import	AVI, MPEG	AVI, MPEG	AVI, MPEG	AVI, MPEG
Audio encoding	PCM, MPEG, AC3	PCM, MPEG, AC3	PCM, MPEG, AC3	PCM, MPEG, AC3
Audio import		PCM, MPEG, AC-3, QuickTime, AIFF, WAV, SDII	PCM, MPEG, AC-3, WAV, AIFF	PCM, MPEG, AC-3, WAV
Muxing/ compiling	Built-in hardware	Built-in hardware	Built-in hardware	Built-in hardware
DVD feature support	Full support for spec	Full support for spec	Full support for spec	Full support for spec

Table 8-6: High-End DVD Tools — Feature Comparisons (Continued)

Product Features	Spruce DVDMaestro DVDPerformer	Panasonic LQ-VD2000S	Daikin	Sonic Scenarist
More info	www.spruce-tech.com	www.panasonic.com/PBDS/sub-cat/Products/mnu_dvd_authoring.html	www.dvd.ace-daikin.com.sg	www.sonic.com

Part C: Methods

Choosing Your Development Architectures

This section outlines a number of factors that affect your choice of tools and technologies.

Target Audience

Early in the investment stage, determine who the main target is for your DVD production efforts. There are a number of major audience categories for your titles:

- Consumer (personal video or photo archives such as family albums, video transfers, weddings, and so forth): Entry-level tools might be enough to produce this type of content, depending on how sophisticated you get with it. Before making the investment, look closely at any limitations in the packages listed in Table 8-4.

- Education (such as documentary or titles or language training): For simple educational titles, the entry-level tools listed in Table 8-4 might be enough. However, if you intend to evolve toward longer, more sophisticated titles that include branching navigational logic, testing and assessments, or Web links, for example, you should consider investing in mid-range tools. If your content is documentary programming, you should consider investing in mid-range or even high-end tools, at least for the encoding of source material, particularly if the footage was captured on film. Predictably, most of the low-end encoders produce average-quality video, and some do not include inverse telecine and other film-oriented encoding enhancements.

- Corporate (such as e-learning titles, hardware or software installations, new product introductions, and so forth): For corporate titles, the mid-range tools listed in Table 8-5 would make appropriate investments. Corporate titles can cover a wide range in terms of quality and sophistication. Since the video content rarely originates on film, mid-range tools for transcoding from DV source material or encoding of broadcast quality will do. As with educational titles, the one area where your budget might grow is in the authoring of interactivity. In applications such as corporate training, branching Boolean paths through content — sometimes with testing or other forms of assessment and feedback — are par for the course and will require some advanced scripting capabilities in your authoring tools as well as matching skills among developers. Web link technology is also a common element in corporate training titles.

- Entertainment (everything from movies to children's programs): If your goal is to serve a national clientele in DVD production of entertainment titles, you probably should plan on sparing no expense and acquire top-of-the-line systems that produce the most pristine results. Your budget and plans for sophisticated interactive programming can be smaller, as most entertainment titles use only the basics of DVD interactivity (menus, simple branching, and so forth), while the emphasis is on high-quality video content.

Windows or Mac

Aside from personal preference, there are some specific technical considerations when choosing platform-oriented tools. For example, most of the high-end DVD authoring systems at the moment exist on Windows only. That might change in the aftermath of Apple Computer's purchase of Spruce Technologies. It is possible that high-end Spruce products might migrate in some form onto the Macintosh OS X platform. For the time being, Apple's mid-range DVD Studio Pro product produces highly professional results for most personal, corporate, or educational media purposes, if you are more comfortable working on the Mac. For entry-level, you can more easily choose your platform based on personal preference.

Migration Paths

The availability of migration paths within product lines also affects your choice of tools:

- If your goal is to begin with an entry-level tool and eventually migrate to a mid-range tool set, then you have several excellent choices including Apple Computer tools on the Macintosh (iDVD to DVD Studio Pro) and Pinnacle turnkey systems such as DVD2000, as well as numerous flavors of Windows-based software from Sonic or Spruce Technologies.

- If your goal is to migrate over time to higher-end professional tools as your business grows, then you might want to begin with a Windows system from Sonic, Spruce Technologies, or Daikin.

DVD Production Workflow

This section describes the steps involved in authoring a DVD Video disc, with some tips along the way.

Step 1: Preproduction and Information Design

Some developers skip this step, which quite often turns out to be a big mistake. It is highly recommended that you plot out your project before you commit a single dollar or minute to the production effort. This is especially important when working with digital interactive media, which requires the precise interaction of many components in order to be successful. Include the following:

- **Create a map of the contents:** One place to start is to map out the contents of your disc. Some people create schematic drawings to illustrate the navigational structure. When you finally author the disc, this structure is often mirrored in one or more views available in authoring applications such as DVD Studio Pro. By mapping it out in advance, you can avoid situations in which an element is missing.

- **Design the structure of information:** Information design involves the process of carefully laying out the flow and hierarchy of information and interaction, always keeping the user's point of view in mind. Good information architecture, informed by usability studies and testing, can make the difference between a successful user experience and a frustrating one.

- **Involve a design director:** For a small shop, this might involve the developer merely switching hats, but in any case it's a good idea to work out design details as much as possible in advance, not only to improve the visual quality of the final product but also to discover details that will help you avoid shutting down production in the middle of a project in order to redesign elements that don't fit the technical or content requirements of the title.

Step 2: Preparing Source Materials

This step involves shooting and editing the video elements, designing and formatting image files, and recording and editing additional audio content.

Tips for preparing source video for encoding to MPEG-2 are the same as those you apply to streaming video formats, as described in Chapter 2.

Step 3: Organizing the Project

Your DVD title might involve hundreds of image, video, and audio files; therefore, good organization is a must to avoid confusion and errors. Prior to authoring your title, you might want to work out a folder structure, filenaming scheme, and system configuration that will simplify the process:

- **Folder structure:** You can devise a folder structure that matches the workflow of your authoring software. For example, if your software allows the import of entire folders into an asset database, you can group your assets in single-step procedures when importing them into the authoring environment, provided you have already placed your source files into appropriate folders.

- **Filenaming scheme:** You can use a filenaming scheme that allows you to view your source files in the order in which they will appear in the title, for example, by naming and numbering them alphanumerically (segment01.mpv, segment 01.pcm, segment01_menu.psd, and so forth). This will make it easier to find files and also to build your title quickly in a drag-and-drop environment.

- **System configuration:** In terms of system configuration, consider optimizing your setup for the encoding process. The proper setup depends on whether you will encode in software or in real time using hardware encoding. In all cases, if you can offload the encoding to another workstation, this will help you avoid tying up the authoring workstation at inconvenient times. If you must encode and author on the same workstation (for example, if your authoring system involves encoding and multiplexing of source video only at the end of the authoring process, or if you simply don't have a second system to use for encoding), try to leave the encoding and multiplexing stage for the end of the day in order to let the process run overnight. If you are encoding in software (no real-time MPEG encoding hardware), you can speed the encoding process by setting up your system so that the source and output content reside on separate drives. If you have two drives, place your source assets on the same drive that contains the authoring software (usually the boot drive), and target the second drive for the encoded output. If you have three drives, place your source assets, output content, and authoring software each on its own drive.

Here are a couple of additional tips for optimizing your encoding environment:

- Use the fastest computer available for software encoding. Encoding is CPU-intensive, but not memory-intensive. The more processing power your system has, the faster your clips will encode.

- Devote the system to the encoding task. Because encoding is CPU-intensive, the less activity that takes place on that system during encoding, the faster it will encode. Close all other applications, and turn off file sharing and networking during the encoding process.

Step 4 (Optional): Encoding in Advance

There are a number of circumstances in which you might want to encode in advance, rather than encode and multiplex at the end of the authoring process; these situations usually apply when you are using mid-range authoring tools:

- You have the opportunity to set up a dedicated encoding workstation.

- You have a hardware encoding device that is not integrated with the authoring environment. In general, hardware encoding is faster than software and so might provide a time-savings advantage.

- Your authoring software does not include encoding software, or you need to encode at a higher quality than your authoring software provides.

Here are additional tips for encoding:

- At lower data rates or with lower-quality encoders, minimize the use of shots that include lots of motion, zooms, and pans, and use variable bit-rate (VBR) encoding whenever possible.

- Consider editing out all detailed wide shots, and use VBR encoding.

- In sequences of diversely lit scenes, consider applying color correction to lessen the sudden shifts of light and color.

- Simplify the audio. If you want to dedicate more bandwidth to the video, consider encoding with stereo or mono audio, rather than AC-3, for example.

- Maintain relatively steady data rates among clips to avoid any playback issues with seamless branching of content.

Step 5: Authoring

Once all the source assets are prepared and organized, you can begin authoring. The details of this phase depend entirely on the features and capabilities of your authoring software (see Part B: Tools). One word of advice: If you can afford an authoring system that includes real-time previewing of your work in progress, this will save you a tremendous amount of time and money during this phase. A system that requires multiplexing (or worse, burning) of titles in order to test the accuracy of your authoring will also severely test your patience.

Step 6: Testing (Doing Quality Assurance)

Throughout the authoring process, the three fundamental rules of all digital media development apply equally to DVD production: Test, test, and test again. For the poorly tested title, ugly errors of programming or technology have a funny way of leaping out the minute you play that first copy you just received back from the duplication house.

Step 7: Recording and Mastering

You can undertake the process of recording or mastering your DVD title in a number of ways, depending on your application or system configuration:

- In-house recording and mastering: If you own a DVD-R burner, you can prepare your own discs for distribution in small quantities. Note that there are two primary media types for DVD-R recording: general-purpose, and authoring. There are also two sizes: 3.75 GB (authoring media only) and 4.7 GB (general-purpose and authoring). In a nutshell, authoring media came first to market, with general-purpose media arriving with the 2.0 DVD-R specification. Authoring media 3.75 discs play on the widest range of existing DVD players, while DVD general-purpose media has a longer list of incompatible DVD players. Some DVD burner models (such as the older Pioneer DVR-S201) burn only authoring media, while some newer, and generally less-expensive models will only burn general-purpose media discs. Check carefully before buying a burner, depending on your needs. See "Note on DVD Media Types and Replication Requirements" on page 205 for more information on the differences between the two media types.

- Copying to DVD-R for delivery to a replication facility: Many replication houses now accept DVD-R authoring media for duplication. Some will accept general-purpose media. See "Note on DVD Media Types and Replication Requirements" on page 205 for more information on the differences between the two media types.

- Copying to DLT: Digital Linear Tape (DLT) was the first widely accepted format for delivering a DVD title for creation of a glass master and duplication, and it includes all the information necessary for creating a glass master. If you have a DLT drive, you can use it to deliver your title to virtually any replication facility.

- Copying to a hard drive: You can also simply multiplex your title straight to an external hard drive, either for delivering to a replication house or for hooking up to a kiosk system or anywhere you want to present your one-off content.

- Copying to DVD-RAM or DVD-RW for testing or delivery of limited copies: Most replication houses will not accept these formats for copying and creating a glass master. Check with the facility.

Note on DVD Media Types and Replication Requirements

The differences between general-purpose media and authoring media have to do with the presence of additional information on authoring discs that gets used by replication houses. Authoring media has an available track for cut master format (CMF) encoding, whereas the general-purpose media does not. CMF encoding is necessary for a replication plant to make a glass master disc for pressing DVD disc replications.

Without the CMF track on a DVD-R disc, you must record your disc image onto a DLT to send to a replication plant. Recording CMF onto a DVD-R authoring disc might not become common in the future, because the demand for authoring drives at their price range is shrinking. In addition, more and more replication plants are now accepting general-purpose media and inserting the CMF encoding on the fly when reading the disc image onto a glass master disc.

Neither the authoring nor general-purpose drive will record CSS copy-protected disc images; however, you must send a DLT tape if you put your own CSS encryption into a disc image file. But you may arrange for the replication plant to insert a CSS key, thus enabling you to send either type of DVD-R media for replication with CSS protection. Check with your replication plant for details.

Guerrilla Authoring: Creating DVDs on a shoestring

Independent filmmakers have a long history of employing guerrilla tactics to get things done. Recent examples include the use of low-cost DV Video tools for production, and the World Wide Web for distribution. These new digital tools are truly revolutionizing — or should I say democratizing — the film industry. One of the biggest frustrations with Web distribution, however, is the poor quality of video in low-bandwidth situations. While we wait for broadband to arrive everywhere, filmmakers should not overlook existing forms of broadband delivery that are now well within the reach of the budget-conscious: CD-ROM, Video CD, and DVD.

DVD is no longer just an option for the big Hollywood studios. With the simple collection of guerrilla tactics and low-cost tools outlined in this section, you can now author, master, and package your own DVD Video discs to rival the slick titles available at your local Blockbuster.

The Matrix

What *is* the matrix, you ask? No, it's not a parallel universe of virtual studio execs conspiring to control the minds of MPEG encoding specialists (you can rent the movie or visit the Website for more information on *that* Matrix). We're talking about the matrix of interrelated tools and materials that you need to create a low-cost DVD title. These basic elements are shown in Figure 8-1.

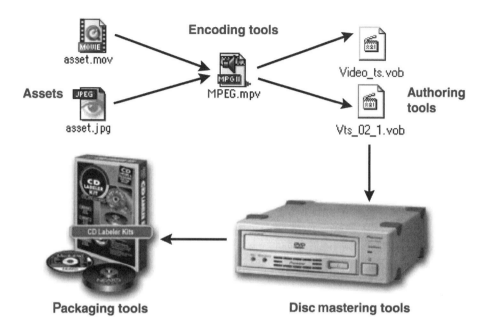

Figure 8-1 Low-Cost Production Matrix

With the right approach, you can assemble this simple production matrix in your basement studio and start creating your own discs for as little as $100 to $500.

If you would like to burn your own DVD discs, you'll have to spend an additional $300 to $3,000 or so for a DVD burner. For one-offs or small numbers of copies, you can find blank DVD-R media for under $8 apiece. If your goal is widespread DVD distribution (thousands of copies), you might want to make friends with someone at a DVD service bureau who can give you a break on duplication fees.

This process assumes that you already have finished film or video assets ready to author into a low-cost title using the kinds of tools and techniques described below. Here's how it works.

Free Assets

Start out by collecting free visual elements and assets — such as textures and clip art — that you can use for backgrounds, in the creation of buttons, and so forth. If you need additional visuals for supporting materials on the disc, such as historical or background information, collect these as well. These assets can come from any number of sources:

- **Scour your software discs:** Check all of your existing software discs for useful tutorial media or sample media.

- **Scan your own photos:** If you own a scanner, pull out that old photo album and take another look — you'll be surprised by what you might find. Or, use your still camera to capture your own cameos, textures, and patterns from the world around you.

- **Make your own textures:** If you own a scanner, there are amazing things you can do to capture striking patterns, designs, and textures. You can drop any towel, drapery, shirt, or brick (well, don't drop the brick) right onto the scanner and capture it. I once read about someone who placed sand right on top of the scanner and ran his fingers through it to create unusual shapes.

- **Look for deals:** Some software, hardware, or subscription purchases offer free CDs containing royalty-free images as incentives. Keep your eyes open.

- **Bother the government:** Most people don't realize that various U.S. government organizations such as the National Parks Service, the Library of Congress, and NASA collect visual resources that are available to us taxpayers royalty-free. Aside from basic duplication and shipping fees, footage or images from these sources are often free of charge.

- **Steal from yourself:** See if there are any materials you can reuse from your prior work. Same thing goes for future projects: If you hear a sound or see a visual during a production that you think might be useful somewhere down the road, export it or copy it off somewhere and save it for future use.

To prepare your visual assets prior to authoring, you don't necessarily have to spring for a full version of Photoshop. Check your computer for bundled applications that might allow you a basic level of image manipulation, such as the Paint application included with Windows, or a lite version of Photoshop or Adobe PhotoDeluxe that gets bundled with many scanners or nonlinear editing systems. If you can't find anything adequate on your desktop, search the Web for free or low-cost paint tools. You can easily find something useful in the sub-$100 range.

Cheap Encoding Solutions

Video encoding solutions have come down in price significantly in recent years, and for the shoestring production the least expensive solutions are the software encoders. Hardware encoding systems allow you to encode in real time in most cases but cost considerably more.

The good news is that software encoding does not necessarily mean lower quality of the encoded video. In some cases, in fact, software encoding can yield higher-quality results, particularly if the software employs a two-pass method in which the video is analyzed in the first pass and then encoded with greater precision on the second pass. The price you do pay for this kind of software encoding, however, is in time spent: software encoding can take 20 times real time or longer to encode a clip of video.

Some examples of MPEG encoding software in the under-$500 category include:

- MegaPEG from Digigami Inc. (MPEG-1 and MPEG-2), which can be purchased stand-alone or as a plug-in for Adobe Premiere.

- The LSX-MPEG family of encoding products (MPEG-1 and 2) from Ligos Corporation which can be purchased stand-alone or as a plug-in for other products such as Adobe Premiere or Discreet Cleaner.

- MPEG power professional products (MPEG-1 only for under $500) from Heuris.

- Media Cleaner EZ (video suitable for CD-ROM production) from Discreet for around $100. For around $500, the full-featured Cleaner 5 also includes MPEG encoding.

These encoding solutions also come bundled with various other products.

Lite DVD Authoring Tools

Once you've encoded your video and assembled enough visuals to build basic menus and informational screens, the next step is to author them into a form that you can burn onto a disc for playback in a CD-ROM player, DVD-ROM player, or DVD Video player.

When it comes to DVD Video — the kind you rent from a video store — the rules for authoring are relatively straightforward. You need to create a file and folder structure that strictly complies with the DVD Video specification from the DVD Forum (see "DVD Video Specifications" on page 189).

There are basically two ways you can achieve this. First, you can create DVD Video-compliant clips directly from your encoding software and then undertake raw coding of the file and folder structure on your computer drive. This route is the cheapest, of course, because it requires no additional software, but it is also error-prone and requires in-depth study of the DVD specification. In other words, it is not recommended.

Second, several very affordable and effective solutions are now available, thankfully, that allow you to author a DVD Video-compliant structure in a WYSIWYG authoring environment, such as Apple iDVD, Spruce Up, or DVDit! from Sonic (see "Entry-Level Tools" on page 192).

As you might suspect, for under $1,000 these applications do not include all the advanced capabilities of full-featured DVD authoring tools such as Minerva Impression or DVD Maestro from Spruce Technologies. But they do allow you to produce professional-quality DVDs with enough functionality for some situations. For example, even though you cannot create multiple video tracks, you can create multiple menus with chapter points in the video for easy navigation to various clips. And although you don't have advanced control over multiple languages, you can always build language paths into the menus or create a two-sided disc to handle at least two languages.

These applications solve a number of other challenges for you in filling in the "matrix" of tools. For example, DVDit also includes packages of "theme" art for creating backgrounds, buttons, and other assets. In addition, most of these applications provide their own transcoders for turning Quick-Time and AVI files into DVD Video-compliant MPEG streams.

Burners on the Cheap

For mastering and burning DVD Video titles, the simple solution is to get a burner. Most burners come with their own mastering software for completing the task.

In 2001 Pioneer introduced its second-generation DVD burner in the $1,000 range, which you can find for below $800 on the street. For the price, you buy a wonderful opportunity to burn DVD titles that play in nearly all current DVD players, just like the titles that come off the shelf at the local video store. Be aware of the issues of the various DVD-R formats, however, depending on your application, as described in "Note on DVD Media Types and Replication Requirements" on page 205. Some of these burners do not support all DVD-R formats.

If the price is too steep for your budget, you might be able to find a friend or someone in the production community in your area who has one of these burners and is willing to prepare a disc or two for a discount, in the spirit of your guerrilla effort!

To package your disc, inexpensive ink-jet printers are widely available now from manufacturers such as Epson or Hewlett-Packard. These printers allow you to produce high-resolution color output. Many of them come with bundled software for creating labels and other types of output. You can wrestle with your own templates for creating disc labels and jewel case inserts, or you can purchase premade templates such as the NEATO series of media labeling products from NEATO, LLC (www.neato.com).

Section II:
Disc-Based Architectures

CHAPTER 9

DVD Audio

This chapter provides information that will help you to understand the challenges, choose your tools, and then create discs that conform to the DVD Audio specification.

Part A: Background

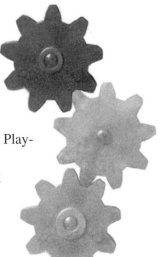

Introduction

Ever since DVD Video arrived on the scene to compete with VHS and Video CD players everywhere, music professionals have pondered the format's relationship to the compact disc. After several years of raging debate in music industry trades, among industry professionals, and within the DVD Forum working groups, the DVD Audio specification finally arrived in 2001. The music industry can be glad that so much time was spent perfecting the specification: even while a certain degree of compromise was necessary to satisfy all points of view in the debate, the DVD Audio spec overcomes most of the weaknesses of the CD while incorporating many excellent new features.

What Is DVD Audio?

In order to provide the music industry with a flexible, open, and highly compatible format, the developers of the DVD Audio specification (primarily the DVD Forum) included many of the same capabilities as DVD Video. In the early stages of adoption of DVD Audio, this has been a source of confusion. In a nutshell, although DVD Audio is a very close cousin of DVD Video, when played in a DVD Audio player, DVD Audio discs provide a handful of special features geared toward the music industry, such as super-high-fidelity audio and music album-oriented interactive capabilities. These features are described in greater detail in the following sections.

The DVD Audio Difference: Meridian Lossless Packing (MLP)

The key difference in DVD Audio is a special form of lossless compression applied to audio tracks called meridian lossless packing (MLP). The difference between MLP and lossy compressions used in MPEG formats, for instance, is that MLP does not discard any audio information. All of the audio content is completely and accurately reconstructed from an MLP file, achieving the ultimate in fidelity. Utilizing MLP lossless compression, a DVD Audio disc can deliver a single channel up to 192 kHz or up to six channels of perfectly reconstructed 96-kHz, 24-bit surround sound. DVD Audio also allows a higher data rate for audio tracks: 9.6 Mbps versus the 6.144 Mbps limit in DVD Video. DVD Audio also supports PCM audio, as well as Dolby Digital AC-3 and MPEG audio in the video portion.

The DVD Audio Difference: Longer Playing Time

Using the full 6-channel, 96-kHz, 24-bit surround sound, a single-sided DVD Audio disc has roughly the same playing time (79 minutes) as a conventional CD (74 minutes), albeit with much better fidelity. However, a two-sided DVD Audio disc or one that scales back from the maximum fidelity — using just two or even three channels, for example, or slightly lower sampling frequency — can contain much more content than a CD. This is especially helpful in avoiding multiple-disc titles for historical compilations, classical performances, or live event recordings, for example.

The DVD Audio Difference: Special Interactive Features

Perhaps the greatest difference between DVD Audio and a conventional CD is the addition of interactive visual content. Hooked up to a television, a DVD Audio player can offer most of the same features as a DVD Video disc, including stills, menus, video, and so forth. In fact, a DVD Audio disc can contain a Video_TS folder with content authored specifically for DVD Video. So why not just produce the content for DVD Video and avoid bringing a second family of players into the mix?

In fact, there are some useful features regarding interactivity and visual content in DVD Audio that are geared specifically toward the music industry. In addition, these features are not available for playback in DVD Video players (although they will work in a new generation of universal players; for more information on compatibility issues, see "CD, DVD Audio, and DVD Video Compatibility Chart" on page 218). The restrictions that apply to DVD Video-like features are necessary in order to avoid exceeding bandwidth limitations when using interactive features during playback of super high-fidelity audio. Special DVD Audio features include the following:

- **Still images:** Like DVD Video, DVD Audio discs can include still images that display during audio playback. But unlike DVD Video, the DVD Audio spec uses its own implementation (known as audio still video sequences or ASVs), which allows the images to be either presented as a slideshow with a continuous music track or provided as a gallery collection that the user can browse while the audio track continues to play. There are limitations on the number of still images you can use in the DVD Audio specification. Subpictures allow still images to be used as menus or for the display of lyrics.

- **Text:** DVD Audio allows for text elements that can be used for the contents, artists' names, Internet URLs, lyrics, etc.

- **Video:** Video clips follow the DVD Video specification but certain functions are limited or not supported (such as multiangle or seamless branching). The audio part of the video may be presented without the video.

- **Menus and navigation:** These also include some restrictions on the DVD Video specification.

- **Playlist:** A complete listing of all song titles is available on the disc.

- **Lyrics and linked lyrics:** This allows for the words for each song to be viewed on a continuous basis. Made popular by karaoke, linked lyrics highlight each word of a song as it is played.

- **Music markers:** These allow the user to jump to a specific point in a song.

- **Discography:** This provides a listing of other albums available by the artist(s) and can include cover art, song listings and clips of music.

CD Versus DVD Audio

A quick comparison of the technical specifications shows a vast improvement with DVD Audio over CD, as shown in Table 9-1.

Table 9-1: CD Versus DVD Audio

Specification	CD	DVD Audio
Disc size	12 cm	12 cm
Track size	1.6 microns	0.74 micron
Capacity	650.4 MB	3.75 to 15.9 GB
Data rate	Max 1.1519291 kbps	Max 9.8 kbps
Playing time	74 minutes	2+ hours (MLP) 8+ hours (PCM)
Audio formats	LPCM	LPCM MLP In DVD Video portion: MPEG-1 layer II MPEG-2 Dolby Digital AC-3
Sampling frequency	44.1 kHz	44.1, 48, 88.2, 96, 174, or 192 kHz
Bit rate	16 bit	16, 20, or 24 bit
Channels	1 channel (mono)" 2 channel (stereo)	1 channel (mono) 2 channel (stereo) multichannel (up to 6 channels)
Copy protection	None	Macrovision, CGMS-A

Flavors of DVD Audio

There are three basic types of DVD Audio discs:

- **DVD Audio (no video):** Like a conventional CD, these audio discs can play through the speaker system without any accompanying visuals. Unlike with CD players, however, you can hook up a television to a universal DVD player to view added visual features such as optional text, menus, and still pictures (but no video).

- **DVD Audio with video content:** A DVD Audio disc can include video and still comply with the DVD audio spec for playback on all DVD Audio players. Only the audio portion plays on an audio-only player (low-cost portable players or automobile systems, for example). The video portion of the disc, however, must be built from a subset of the DVD Video specification that allows for higher-bandwidth audio. For example, the video does not include seamless branching or multiangle viewing. This type of disc will play on a newer generation of universal DVD players, and the DVD Video portion (without the audio portion) can also play in a standard DVD Video player.

- **DVD Video:** This is a plain old DVD Video disc with the same characteristics as a Hollywood movie, but crafted to suit the purposes of an audio or music title. We include it here as a type of DVD Audio disc, however, because a number of music industry publishers sometimes forgo the greater audio fidelity and added album features of the DVD Audio spec in order to ensure backward-compatible playback capabilities in DVD Video players.

Perhaps the best way to consider the differences is through the actual file structure of the different disc types. There are two top-level folders involved in the construction of DVD Video and DVD Audio discs. DVD Video content resides in a folder named Video_TS. The majority of DVD Audio content resides in a folder named Audio_TS. When a DVD Audio disc also includes video, the DVD Audio specification allows for the presence of both folders side-by-side on the disc. Keep in mind, however, that the DVD Audio specification places some restrictions on the Video_TS contents for strict compliance with DVD Audio players.

CD, DVD Audio, and DVD Video Compatibility Chart

Table 9-2 provides a quick view of playback compatibility among the different types of audio and video discs.

Table 9-2: Playback Compatibilities: CD, DVD Audio, DVD Video

Device	CD	DVD Audio	DVD Audio with Menus, Stills	DVD Audio with Video	DVD Video
CD player	X				
DVD Audio-only player	X	X			
DVD Audio player	X	X	X	X (audio portion only)	
DVD Universal player	X	X	X	X	X
DVD Video player	X			X (video portion only)	X
Older DVD-ROM drives	X			X (video portion only)	X
New DVD-ROM drives	X	X	X	X	X

DVD Audio Speaker Systems

DVD Audio discs will work with most existing speaker systems. In order to experience a disc that includes high-fidelity multichannel audio, however, you will need a surround-sound system using high-quality amplifiers and speakers. The same surround-sound system used for DVD Video discs can be used for DVD Audio.

DVD Audio Specifications

As of April 14, 2000, the DVD Format/Logo Licensing Corporation (DVD FLLC, www.dvdfllc.co.jp) assumed all responsibilities for licensing the various DVD formats and logos. The official specification for DVD is documented in a series of five books covering read-only discs; recordable discs;

rewritable discs; rerecordable discs; and DVD-RAM, DVD-RW and DVD-R for general-purpose discs. Beginning November 11, 2001, a new DVD Multi license bacame available for development of DVD Multi drives that can handle all of the formats mentioned.

The DVD-ROM, DVD Video, and DVD Audio specifications fall under the read-only disc book.

- For more information about the DVD Video spec, see Chapter 8.

- For more information about the DVD-ROM spec, see Chapter 7.

As of June 2001, the DVD Audio spec Version 1.2 includes:

- Reference information — Packed PCM:MLP

- Reference information Version 1.0

For more complete book information and instructions on how to order a DVD book specification, visit www.dvdfllc.co.jp.

Part B: Tools

Introduction

DVD Audio (DVD-A) is a recently announced specification, and therefore only a handful of DVD-A tools are available on the market. Of course you can always hand-code to the DVD Audio specification. Here's a rundown of the WYSIWYG tools and technologies currently available for the creation of DVD Audio discs.

MLP Encoding Tools

While some high-end digital audio workstations and authoring systems allow you to encode MLP audio for use on DVD Audio discs, the following is a stand-alone encoder that you might use when encoding audio files and then coding the remainder of the disc separately.

Meridian MLP Encoder

Go to www.meridian-audio.com

Quick Review

This encoder can create content 100 percent compliant with the DVD Audio specification and can also be used for applications such as archiving. MLP provides a simple WYSIWYG approach to encoding, allowing you to organize, downmix, check, and decode MLP streams in a drag-and-drop interface.

MLP Encoder combines up to six channels (including mixed-rate and scalable content). Sample rates are between 44.1kHz and 192kHz with word sizes up to 24 bit. Each encoder is individually serial numbered and provides full content tracking through the use of MLP's metadata capacity.

It runs under Windows 95, 98, NT 4, or 2000.

DVD Audio Authoring Tools

SADiE DVD-A Direct

Go to www.sadie.com

Quick Review

DVD-A Direct is an accessory for SADiE's digital audio workstation solutions that provides a complete Windows-based authoring system for DVD Audio. DVD-A Direct adds optional MLP encoding while providing tools for the whole DVD-A production process, from editing and mixing in 5.1 surround to authoring the disc to DVD-R or DLT tape.

DVD-A Direct allows you to automatically create on-screen menus and provides a drag-and-drop interface for ordering of tracks on the disc to create an album playlist. Still-picture displays for each track are available with picture transition tools, and most popular graphic file formats are supported. The system is NTSC- and PAL-compatible with support for both 4:3 and 16:9 aspect ratio formats. All functions are accessible from menus, toolbars, or context-sensitive mouse clicks.

The program supports all audio formats in the DVD-A specification to create fully compliant DVD-A reference discs, which may be played directly on most DVD-A players for instant quality-control checking. DVD-A Direct also supports a range of DVD-R recorder operations including Record (test or write), Copy Disc, Verify, Create, and Write Image, Read Image.

DVD-A Direct Audio features the following:

- Support of all audio formats in the DVD-A specification:
  16-, 20-, or 24-bit WAV or AIFF
  44.1, 48, 88.2, 96, 176.4, or 192 kHz
  Meridian Lossless Packing (MLP)

- Individual mono WAV or AIFF files may be allocated to L, C, R, LFE, Ls and Rs

- Downmix parameters for playback of surround tracks in stereo

- Automatic creation of menu displays from album, group, and track information

- Create fully compliant DVD-A discs which may be played directly on most DVD-A players for instant quality-control checks

- Up to 9 groups of 99 tracks each

- Auto-play option for players without video output

- Master to DLT tape for replication

- 4.7 GB capacity

- MLP encoding from AIFF or WAV files (optional)

SonicStudio HD

Go to www.sadie.com

Quick Review

SonicStudio HD is a widely used system for advanced audio editing and disc premastering, with support for CD, DVD Audio, audio for DVD Video, and EMD mastering.

SonicStudio HD supports multichannel sampling rates up to 192 kHz and surround-sound mixing for preparation of DVD Audio tracks. You can include up to six channels of 24-bit, 96-kHz audio or four channels of 24-bit, 192-kHz input and output. SonicStudio HD includes integrated surround mixing, segment-based HDSP processing of EQ and gain, and high-quality HD multichannel sample-rate conversion.

SonicStudio HD supports both DVD Audio and audio for DVD Video publishing with Sonic's advanced DVD Audio authoring technology.

Sonic's NoNoise audio processing incorporates an all-48-bit data path used throughout the system, which preserves the original signal from initial recording to final output.

Part C: Methods

Managing Player Compatibility Issues

In most cases, the extent of interactivity that a record producer will add to a disc is directly proportional to the production budget. For the moment, DVD-A tools and technologies are fairly expensive and complex; therefore, early DVD Audio titles have tended to be fairly simple. As DVD-A tools and technologies become more efficient and user-friendly, expect to see an increase in rich and creative explorations of the medium.

As we move further down the path of interactivity, our explorations of the full range of DVD Audio features require careful consideration of the issues regarding player compatibility. As mentioned in "Flavors of DVD Audio" on page 217, there are three basic types of DVD Audio discs that you can author, each with different playback requirements. These differences affect your choice of development tools and techniques as well as the kind of audience you can reach with the title.

In choosing your target players, you must consider compatibility in all directions: forward compatibility (how the disc should work with upcoming technologies or new systems that will be more widespread in the future); backward compatibility (how the disc will play on legacy DVD systems); and lateral compatibility (how the disc will work on a variety of current players).

There is a "path of least resistance," where the distribution of certain players remains relatively widespread throughout the cycle, ensuring a broad audience as you gradually migrate toward more full-featured implementations of the DVD Audio specification.

Here's a summary of options, from the most universal to the least, for producing a disc at present:

- **Compact Disc:** Even while it lacks modern features, the standard compact disc will obviously reach the widest audience possible, although DVD Audio disc players will begin to replace CD players in cars and homes. The Enhanced CD format allows for rich, visual interactive content when played in a CD-ROM drive. However, this ill-fated format has suffered in the marketplace from a player identity crisis by forcing users to move the disc back and forth between the stereo system in the living room and the computer in the home office.

- **DVD Video:** Many early DVD Audio titles are simply conventional DVD Video titles designed to showcase music content. This allows record companies to reach the rapidly growing number of homes with DVD Video players. This helps with backward compatibility. Such titles will continue to play in DVD Video and DVD universal players in the future as well; however, these discs will not play in the DVD Audio-only players that will begin to appear in cars and boom boxes, for example. In other words, this format is best targeted toward the home theater system and therefore lacks portability. When designing such a disc, keep in mind that the user should be able to turn the television off and still enjoy the audio.

*   **DVD Audio with video:** In time this will be the most universal format; at present, the DVD Audio portion will only play in the small number of DVD Audio players that exist on the market. If the DVD Audio and DVD Video portions have the exact same content, this is not so important, aside from the lack of the super-high-fidelity audio playback in DVD Video players. If you want to cover all bases for the present and future, then this is the format to use, although it requires more production work to create the hybrid content.

*   **DVD Audio-only:** This format is best targeted at the music enthusiast. Few DVD Audio players have been sold to date. Within the next few years this audience will certainly grow, allowing you to reach a fairly refined niche market of listeners who demand the extremely high quality of uncompressed MLP audio, without much concern for visual or interactive features.

*   **DVD Audio with menus, stills, text, and lyrics:** This format will also suffer from a small distribution of players for the next couple of years, while the added interactive and visual features will only appear on an even fewer number of universal players with television attached or players that have built-in displays for showing menus, lyrics, or stills.

DVD Audio Production Workflow

The requirements of DVD Audio add some new twists to the common workflow for preparing DVD discs. Here's a summary of the steps.

Step 1: Preparing the Content

As with DVD, you must prepare all assets before authoring the disc. This involves editing and mixing the sound, as well as designing, producing, and gathering together all the visual elements.

Step 2: Downmixing Multichannel Audio

Downmixing in this case involves mapping the multiple channels in a DVD title to just two stereo channels in order to accommodate those players or systems that do not have multichannel surround-sound capabilities. This operation is only necessary when you wish to include more than two channels on the disc and is usually performed in a digital audio workstation with DVD Audio-specific authoring capabilities or in the MLP encoding software. This will be a new step for many in the industry because the CD involves only two channels (stereo) whereas DVD Audio allows up to six.

Step 3: Encoding MLP Audio Tracks

While it isn't mandatory for a DVD Audio title, MLP audio is one of the key reasons for making use of the DVD Audio format. MLP encoding is also a requirement in cases where the maximum DVD Audio bit rate would be exceeded (9.6 Mbps). It is likely that the most widely adopted multichannel digital audio configuration for DVD Audio will be six channels (5.1 channels) at 24 bit and 96 kHz.

Step 4: Testing the Audio

In conventional DVD authoring, this test is often conducted at the end of the authoring phase. This additional testing step (checking the audio mix, fidelity, and so forth prior to authoring) is due to the importance of the audio on a DVD Audio disc, as well as the unique challenges of MLP audio encoding and multichannel mixing and downmixing. The best way to test is to burn a DVD-R one-off disc and check on a true surround system. Computer-based testing is bound to suffer from lack of true representation of DVD Audio. Computer sound cards often do not exceed 48 kHz audio and usually lack multichannel surround-sound capabilities.

Step 5: Authoring

Unfortunately, just as DVD Video authoring tools have become robust and affordable, DVD Audio now requires its own set of tools. Well-developed DVD Video authoring tools do not yet work for DVD Audio, although support will likely be added to most tools in the near future. For now, the authoring phase might require both DVD Audio tools and DVD Video tools if you intend to create a hybrid disc.

You can simplify the hybrid authoring process by managing files carefully, with matching filenames and so forth, and by maintaining identical workflow for each format.

Step 6: Encrypting

This is also a new step for developers who are accustomed to authoring CDs, which include no copy protection. The DVD Audio specification includes provision for both the CSS approach used for DVD Video, and an encryption system called CPPM. This step can also be completed at the replication facility.

Step 7: Testing

Additional testing should be conducted after the authoring is complete.

Step 8: Mastering

After the title is thoroughly tested and verified, DVD Audio developers can create a DVD-R or DLT.

Section III: Distribution Architectures

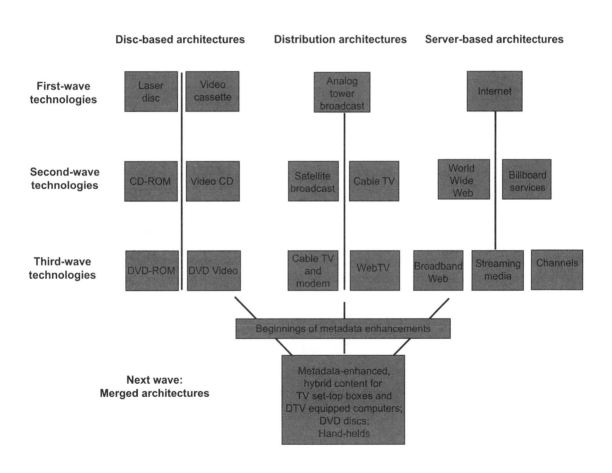

Disc-based architectures | Distribution architectures | Server-based architectures

First-wave technologies
- Laser disc
- Video cassette
- Analog tower broadcast
- Internet

Second-wave technologies
- CD-ROM
- Video CD
- Satellite broadcast
- Cable TV
- World Wide Web
- Billboard services

Third-wave technologies
- DVD-ROM
- DVD Video
- Cable TV and modem
- WebTV
- Broadband Web
- Streaming media
- Channels

Beginnings of metadata enhancements

Next wave: Merged architectures

Metadata-enhanced, hybrid content for TV set-top boxes and DTV equipped computers; DVD discs; Hand-helds

Section III:
Distribution Architectures

CHAPTER 10

Introduction

This section takes a look at distribution architectures for content. These architectures are more likely to be found in large-scale operations. However, the rapidly decreasing cost of both storage and bandwidth means that in the near future smaller operations will have an opportunity to install server-based systems that connect to broadband networks.

Chapters 10 to 13 serve as a reference and road map for individuals and organizations making the leap to larger digital systems that manage everything from single systems to entire workflows and organizations.

A Shifting Landscape

So far our focus has been largely on the technical ins and outs of digital media creation. However, all aspects of the media industry, including creation, management, and distribution, are undergoing change due to digital technology. These shifts are happening because the industry's entire management and distribution systems have been built around tape and film, along with analog broadcast and viewing equipment. Take, for example, the following advertisement, which recently appeared in a major broadcast trade magazine:

Broadcast Engineer

Will maintain and repair analog, digital, video and audio systems; including routers, switchers, automation systems, VTR's, cameras, and related broadcast technology. Must have ability and desire to develop skills in UNIX, Windows NT, and networking systems.

For those of you working in the media industry, this type of advertisement personally symbolizes the digital transition. Your clients and employers, the enterprises involved in broadcast, corporate, and entertainment media, are now expecting you to understand the old analog ways and also be willing to take center stage to develop new processes and methods of work based primarily on digital technologies.

Figure 10-1 gives an overview of the complexity of an integrated architecture that is designed to support:

- Creation of universal masters

- Integrated metadata created from automatic and human processes

- Connected rights management for security, transactions and ownership compensation

- Private and secure network to facilitate content creation using global talent

- Content distributed to the viewer on a built-to-order basis

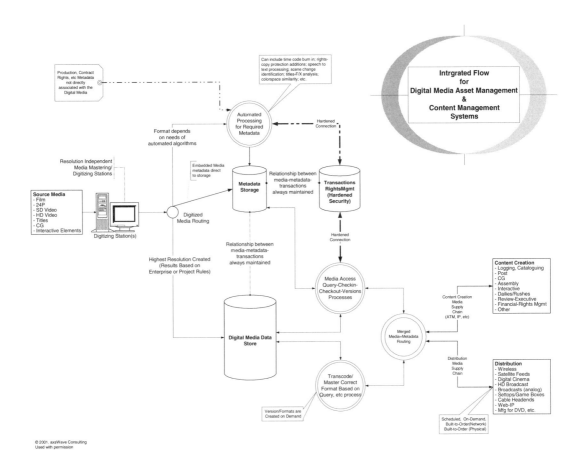

The following labels appear within the figure:

Production, Contract Rights, etc Metadata not directly associated with the Digital Media

Can include time code burn in; rights-copy protection additions; speech to text processing; scene change identification; titles-F/X analysis; colorspace similarity; etc.

Intrgrated Flow for Digital Media Asset Management & Content Management Systems

Automated Processing for Required Metadata

Format depends on needs of automated algorithms

Hardened Connection

Resolution Independent Media Mastering/ Digitizing Stations

Embedded Media metadata direct to storage

Metadata Storage

Relationship between media-metadata-transactions always maintained

Transactions RightsMgmt (Hardened Security)

Source Media
- Film
- 24P
- SD Video
- HD Video
- Titles
- CG
- Interactive Elements

Digitizing Station(s)

Digitized Media Routing

Highest Resolution Created (Results Based on Enterprise or Project Rules)

Relationship between media-metadata-transactions always maintained

Hardened Connection

Media Access Query-Checkin-Checkout-Versions Processes

Content Creation
- Logging, Cataloguing
- Post
- CG
- Assembly
- Interactive
- Dailies/Rushes
- Review-Executive
- Financial-Rights Mgmt
- Other

Content Creation Media Supply Chain (ATM, IP, etc)

Digital Media Data Store

Merged Media+Metadata Routing

Distribution Media Supply Chain

Transcode/ Master Correct Format Based on Query, etc process

Distribution
- Wireless
- Satellite Feeds
- Digital Cinema
- HD Broadcast
- Broadcasts (analog)
- Settops/Game Boxes
- Cable Headends
- Web-IP
- Mfg for DVD, etc.

Version/Formats are Created on Demand

Scheduled, On-Demand, Built-to-Order(Network) Built-to-Order (Physical)

© 2001. axsWave Consulting
Used with permission

Figure 10-1 Integrated Digital Media Flow Architecture

The Challenge

The complexity of integrated architectures is often very costly, requiring the resources of a large enterprise, and these systems are available to individuals and smaller operations only through service providers. Also, these systems often require significant organizational and process change. Every organization has processes that are the patterns of interaction — creation, communication, and decision making that have evolved in the enterprise or the industry. However, when seemingly efficient processes in the analog world are applied using digital media tools such as digital asset management, they are likely to prove slow and inefficient. For example, an archival process using analog tapes could become a liability when digital asset management is installed within the enterprise. Changing processes is often difficult because effective and established processes are not supposed to change, as process improvisation would introduce inefficiency. Consequently process change usually requires a series of controlled procedures managed separately from the process itself. Cross-organizational process changes are even more difficult, requiring upper management buy-in.

So why do it? Why are so many people and organizations fighting sometimes monumental battles to rebuild an entire infrastructure and industry? Quite simply, the business case for the industry changed when digital tools and networks began to be adopted. For those in the traditional media, cable, and broadcast industries, the business case for change began with a clear competitive assessment — what is likely to happen to you and/or your business in terms of customer growth, cost structure, new revenue streams, and your survival, if you stand still?

Think about it. In a very short time span, you saw digital nonlinear editors (NLE) become the standard; compositing, graphics, and F/X become a bigger part of the budget; digital cameras, native digital formats, LANs, WANs, the Internet, the Web, DSL, ISDN, digital satellite, and telco-backed digital networks all either come on line or be proposed. All of a sudden, when those of you in the traditional media and entertainment industries modeled your future scenarios, you saw potential customer losses and declining revenues due to technology and price competition. That's when the case for digital became compelling enough, through operating efficiency, new revenue streams, and scalability—and downright fear.

The "Holy Grail" is an integrated end-to-end digital system for creation and multiformat distribution. Whether you work on your own or are part of an enterprise, you must be concerned with enhancing your skill base in digital technologies in order to realize this goal and to compete in an increasingly competitive market.

The Media Industry in Transition

Accelerated changes and intense competition require the content industry to anticipate and drive change rather than merely adapt to it after someone else has shaped it. Following the introduction of the first digital NLEs, there was a period when adapting and combining strategies for a mixed digital/analog environment worked well. However, these times are disappearing, and when economic uncertainty exists, individuals and enterprises are better off with shaping-the-market strategies. The pace of change is too fast for developing successful adapting-to-the-market strategies. For example, in the distribution part of digital media, Qualcomm took the lead in its industry because it decided to drive and shape change by developing the code division multiple access (CDMA) wireless communications standard that is widely used in wireless networks in the U.S. and other countries. Back in the early 1990s, the founders and first employees of Avid Technology made the same decision when they decided to pursue NLEs.

With each new innovation, firms gained new possibilities for adding value to content. In a fully digital workflow, every step in the process has the potential to add value to a piece of content and increase profitability for the firms involved, as shown in Figure 10-2.

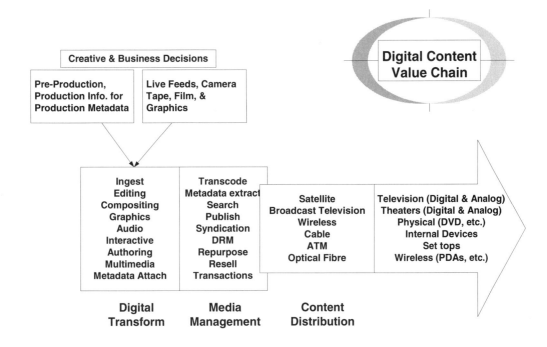

Figure 10-2 Digital Content Value Chain
Source: ©2001 axsWave Consulting. Used with permission.

What Will Drive the Leaders of the Digital Media Industry?

One of the major questions in our industry is whether the large integrated media corporations that are beginning to form will change their genetic code and evolve into creatures with rapid adaptability, or is that something that only smaller entrepreneurial organizations will be able to do? The classical wisdom says that only smaller entrepreneurial firms can spearhead new transitions. However, large companies such as Apple, Avid, and Thomson Multimedia have been untiring innovators, and many entrepreneurial ventures flamed out at the end of the 1990s. There are a number of forces driving the digital transition that make the answers to this question difficult. In this chapter and the three that follow, we will take a look at some of the major issues you and your enterprise (large or small) are likely to face as we move forward toward an all-digital media industry.

Six Forces Driving the Transition

Six forces, accelerated by digital media and network technology are driving the increase in competition:

1. Supplier power

*   Content owners are the suppliers of note in the digital media chain, and they are restructuring their vision to focus on their content as proprietary assets with a variety of uses. This new vision forces them to try and control all the different aspects of content creation, management, and distribution. This has been a longtime dream of content owners, ever since the big studio, publishing, and theater corporations of the early 1900s were dissolved. Digital media technologies support this vision.

*   Content creators, who by and large work for content owners, are reassessing their contributions and roles as the owners move to digital technology to manage the workflow distribution and archives. While creativity is still a premium, the reality is that you must now also demonstrate your ability to integrate with the content owner's digital systems.

*   Equipment and software vendors who sell to content creators are benefiting from digital technology in the sense that their costs for components are dropping and customers are looking to refit their facilities. However, the rapid pace of change and relentless competition put them in the precarious position of having to spend more on R&D while getting less for each product. The larger vendors, with diverse lines, are likely to look to mega-media corporation to standardize on their systems to buy breathing space.

2. People

*   Implementing digital solutions often is seen as a way to reduce costs, particularly people costs. In reality, you may have cut some part of your budget, but another part will have grown because you need in-house IT support.

*   Much of the media industry is dominated by various unions whose members are among the most creative and knowledgeable, whether directing a movie or fixing a broadcast switch. While these unions are often seen as an obstacle, in reality many are working very hard to train

members on the latest technologies, keenly aware of competition in Canada, Singapore, and elsewhere.

- The tool vendors are now working to hasten adoption by offering guild-approved training and certification. One of the major examples of this is Apple's new Final Cut Pro–based film editing classes authorized by the Motion Picture Editors Guild and offered in Los Angeles. Microsoft, Cisco, and many of the other large infrastructure providers also have expanded their certification offerings to address the needs of digital media creators and broadcasters.

3. Buyer power

- Resellers, packagers, syndicators, broadcasters, and other distributors are all in the process of reassessing both their roles in a restructured media business, and the ways they are going to continue to make money.

- Advertisers pay the bills for most of the media, and they are beginning to demand digital brand management, lower costs, and more effective metrics to track their expenditures and ROI.

- The mega-media firms can, again, begin to think about controlling it all. The Disney Channel is not advertiser-supported; the only advertiser there is Disney. It can call the shots for all its suppliers, whether it's a production company or a tool vendor, and Disney's efforts to standardize its digital workflow means it has the power to dictate everything from scripts to ingest stations to output systems and the standards they follow.

4. Technology — replacement, refinement, and open standards

- The government mandate to move to high-definition is driving broadcasters to reequip their physical plants to allow for this workflow.

- Analog equipment and parts are getting harder to find but are still the top choice for some individuals and enterprises. Vendors' attempts to refine how analog investments, past and future, integrate with digital technology are driving new thinking and new products.

- The first couple of generations of digital technology (primarily nonlinear editors used in postproduction) are getting long in the tooth, and every part of the industry, from television to film to physical (DVD, etc.) to interactive, is beginning to assess tools and potential migration strategies to new technologies.

- The assessment is happening at a time when there are large numbers of competitors in all areas of the business. Most of the prestige brands in content creation and broadcasting equipment have begun to lower prices and move to open standards such as MPEG..

5. New players

- Barriers to entry that once seemed insurmountable — huge facilities and plants, three major networks with no other option, and so forth — are now falling rapidly.

- The content-creation and broadcasting tools, vendors' cheap digital equipment, high-powered processors, and new software development methods are allowing new companies to ship competitive products at lower price points.

6. Industry rivalry

- Channels for distribution are proliferating, particularly as communities begin to allow multiple cable systems to enter a region, and an all-optical network combined with a new generation of laser satellites puts broadband in most businesses and a majority of affluent homes.

- Distributors will find it difficult to differentiate their services. They all will have digital pictures, good quality sound, pay-per-view, telephony, some level of interactive capabilities, Internet access, and easy-to-understand bills. *The key differentiator for these distributors will be content.* This is a dramatic difference! Distributors have been able to hold content owners hostage by making them pay for carriage on their systems or for their movies to be on the rental shelves. Distribution is on its way to becoming a commodity, and the distributors will now have to fight for content.

- New mega-media firms own most of the creation/distribution chain, and the access to quality content is going to be more competitive as content owners also become content providers. For example, AOL/Time Warner owns a very large content library and is in the process of buying a number of cable networks. The decision on how to allow proprietary content out of its network will be something it considers in terms of its overall position in the industry.

- Across the board, the tool vendors are faced with former partners turning into intense rivals as the content and broadcast industry shapes up to be a major driver of new technologies and market advantage.

The Killer App

Integration Efficiencies

While not as sexy as many parts of the media business, integration and successful deployment of digital technology will define the successful players in the next decade. Content that is compelling will always sell, but with a vast number of content choices, media firms will find it imperative to build end-to-end efficiencies where a firm owns all portions of the content, distribution, and any repurposing. The destruction of the great movie palaces in the 1950s and 1960s was symbolic of the growing dominance of television and the ending of end-to-end monopoly powers for many studios (see Figure 10-3). Now as end-to-end consolidation begins to reemerge, we are seeing attempts to rebuild these palaces in each individual viewer's home via the next generation of game boxes and home theater equipment.

Figure 10-3 End of the San Francisco Fox Theatre in 1963

Like the great movie palaces, digital media was all about a better experience, but the pattern of competing with more compelling and targeted programming quickly emerged. For example, Disney buys ads on the top broadcast and cable trade press Websites for its new cartoon channel rather than spend its entire promotional budget on consumer advertisement. These consumer ads, appearing on an industry-oriented site, act as a clear reminder to the cable systems (MSOs) that viewers are willing to buy digital satellite dishes to get certain channels to satisfy their children if the MSO fails to carry Disney's latest offering.

Finally, no other move could be more telling regarding the importance of content over hot technology than installing Richard Parsons as CEO of AOL/Time Warner at the end of 2001. Parsons came from Time Warner — the content side of the business. When AOL bought Time Warner, the industry pundits hailed it as a way to put more content on AOL and for the AOL management team to show old media how new media is done. Instead, we see management moving to the content side and the Internet playing a role as just another distribution channel for Time Warner's content library. Where the expertise of AOL is coming into play is providing an integrated approach to digital publishing and advertisement via the Web to promote properties across all distribution methods. This integration led to such newsworthy events as Harry Potter Day on CNN when hundreds of CNN reporters were reporting live from movie theater parking lots on opening day. While we can argue about the level of newsworthiness of the opening, it meant that *Harry Potter* was able to dominate a major cable system in a way no other film opening that week was. The movie opened as a blockbuster, and CNN updated its demographic by offering content that appealed to younger viewers. Central to supporting this effort was a marketing team working with the production team to capture, digitize, catalog, and archive (for quick retrieval) a large amount of on-set footage that could be repurposed for promotional material via all venues.

Digital Distribution Architectures: Both the Reigning Fad and Our Ultimate Future

Proprietary and closed analog systems are on their way out — the basic fact is that the long-term and large-scale growth of content creation, management, and distribution is in a digital and collaborative network that supports the creative process and streamlines numerous functions that have became inefficient during the days of analog architectures.

Benefits of Digital Media
• **Faster time to market**
• **Process times reduced via faster fixes and communication**
• **Fewer support personnel**
• **Lower facility costs and maintenance**
• **Long-term use of archived assets**
• **Direct contact between content owners and distributors and/or media consumers**

The Evolution to Digital

An Evolution of the Enterprise

One of the dilemmas you face as you move into digital creation, distribution, and archiving is that the processes you have established over the past fifty or more years aren't amenable to the digital generation. Although companies such as Avid, Discreet, Media 100 and Apple began the nonlinear editing revolution in the 1990s, the digital dominance in editing is by no means complete throughout the industry; even enterprises engaged in nonlinear editing still indicate that 30 percent of their networking is done via sneaker-net.

Eventually every organization in the media and content industries, and in the infrastructure industries that support them, will have to transition to digital — they will have no choice. There may be a few very-high-end boutiques that support analog media, but it will not be the standard, nor will it be where most of the money is made. For those of you involved in the change, it will require more than just using hard drives and networks instead of tapes and envelopes; it will require a new set of workflows and skills.

Virtual Organizations in the Digital Media Transition

Interacting with a variety of separate individuals and enterprises is an area where content creation has an advantage over other parts of the media industry. A large quantity of past and present content creation is accomplished within a virtual organization (VOrg). You can think of VOrg as a collection of individuals and enterprises coming together to complete a specific piece of content. They all perform different, sometimes extremely different, tasks, and their only common interest is the completion of the content.

The content-creation industry has a highly developed infrastructure to support this kind of organization, and professionals in the content industry know how to work this way. Various individuals' and organizations' success in this VOrg depend entirely on how well they can interact with one another and cope with the rapid changes of the creative process. Unlike assets such as bandwidth, which are easy to make into commodities, this method of working is very difficult to duplicate, because the work style goes to the very core of an individual's or organization's values and processes. This will ensure that the content-creation side of the industry becomes dominant, as other aspects of the industry (distribution, archiving, and so forth) become easier and less costly.

New Digital Media Supply Chains: Routes to Build-to-Order Content

A media supply chain (MSC) is a network of facilities focused on media creation, management and distribution. Content flows from the initial creators, on to the next tier of suppliers to be transformed into semifinished media products, then to the final assembly of completed media, on to the resellers or packagers, and then out the cable systems, satellite systems, and broadcasters for eventual end-user viewing/interaction. The goal is to develop systems that allow viewers to assemble build-to-order content (see Figure 10-4). In order for this to happen, content creation, management, and distribution must become completely digital and tightly integrated.

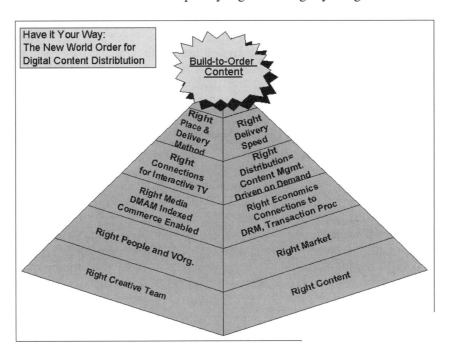

Figure 10-4   Build-to-Order Content
Source: ©2001 Janette Bradley and axsWave Consulting. Used with permission. Reproduction prohibited without consent.

Conclusion

The media, entertainment, set-top, gaming, and broadcast industries are at the very beginning of the various adoption curves for integrated digital solutions; because of that, the MSCs that they have all depended on for the past few decades are in flux.

Digital media asset management (DMAM) and content management (CM) are fundamental technologies changing the business, and as their use grows, our industry is beginning to think in terms of a type of digital value chain—a digital media supply chain (DMSC).

The change is happening because digital networks, digital media and sophisticated metadata architectures enable the *disaggregation* of older proprietary processes and a *reaggregation* of specialists into a more modern and flexible workflow, with greater efficiencies and potential to develop secondary income streams via new distribution outlets such as the enhanced-content DVDs, video on demand, or the Web.

A great example of the sources for new revenue that content owners are now using is the enhanced-content DVD, where content that would have ended up on the cutting-room floor is used for outtakes or reexpressed into a director's cut. The key to enabling this product to be done quickly and cheaply is embedding or including text information that describes the director's thought process, and often the editor's as well, in creating the content. The first level of customer, a distributor for a chain of movie theaters, may not see the need for a version that includes this information, and until recently they have been the primary outlet for this type of content. However, for the owners of the content, the editor's and director's thoughts might be very valuable in producing a DVD that they can sell directly, thus bypassing the distributors and keeping more of the revenue.

One of the mega-media corporations such as AOL/Time Warner could also make the decision to make the director and editor information and interviews available only to their cable subscribers or to the people who purchase a DVD directly from them. Strategies such as these allow these corporations to offer their content via other distribution channels but clearly differentiate that content by adding value when the content is distributed via their proprietary networks.

However, owning content is not the only way to succeed. Recently, we're seeing that innovative media enterprises, such as NeTune Communications (www.netune.com), are deciding that their real competitive advantage is their ability to quickly assemble creative and business knowledge and then apply it to managing a series of media and film projects — sometimes with specialists that are also competitors — to deliver new products and services to content creators. These enterprises have a deep interest in workflow technologies and standards to automate the rules for connecting and sequencing activities for a variety of media projects. In fact, workflow technologies are essential in building interenterprise value chains. NeTune's strong workflow technologies allowed it to support a globally diverse team of media specialists, all of whom were working primarily with digital media and networks, in order to get *Harry Potter* out in time.

In the short run, the ability to deliver build-to-order digital content will become a key differentiator for the companies involved in creation, management, and distribution. In the long run, it will be accepted that everyone can offer it, and the race will start again for the next generation of successful DMSC links.

The rest of the chapters in this section are designed to give you an overview of the challenges covered in the change from point products to integrated workflow as well as provide foundational material for those of you involved in making decisions about large-scale digital architectures.

Digital Media Technology Implementation Criteria

• Is the solution mature, or does it solve only part of my problem?

• Does it make my life easier?

• Does it cut out any steps in the process?

• Can I squeeze in more work?

• Can I reduce costs?

• Is it simple enough for me to use without much training, or does it add so much benefit that training is worthwhile?

• How protected is the digital material on the system?

• How reliable is the digital solution compared to my current solution?

• Will it help my creative team be more productive?

Additional Resources

Links to these resources, and more, can be found on the Developer's Digital Media Reference Website: www.dmmalchemy.com/digitalmediaguide.

Change Management in the Enterprise

- *The Death of "e" and the Birth of the Real New Economy: Business Models, Technologies and Strategies for the 21st Century* by Peter Fingar, Ronald Aronica, Bryan Maizlish

- *Digital Dimensioning: Finding the ebusiness in Your Business* by Samuel C. Certo, Matthew W. Certo

- *Evolve! Succeeding in the Digital Culture of Tomorrow* by R. M. Kanter

Workflow Modeling

- *Workflow Management Systems for Process Organisations* by Thomas Schael, Thomas Schal, Thomas W. Schaller

- *Workflow Modeling: Tools for Process Improvement and Application Development* by Alec Sharp, Patrick McDermott

Impacts in the Media Industry

- *Convergence in Broadcast and Communications Media: The Fundamentals of Audio, Video, Data Processing and Communications Technologies* by John Watkinson

- *Electronic Media Management* by Peter K. Pringle, Michael F. Starr, William E. McCavitt

Technical Libraries

- cyberlibrary.cpuniverse.com
  Contract Professional Universe CyberLibrary
  (Artificial Intelligence, Computing System Hardware, Consumer Electronics, Diagnostic and Test Hardware, Hardware, Information Security, Operating Systems, Information Technology Systems, Security Software, Information Technology Management, Software, Information Technology Workforce, Software Development, Internet, Storage Hardware, Network Management, Web Application Development)

- edtn.bitpipe.com
  EDTN e-Library
  (Communications, Computers and Peripherals, Consumer, Design,

Embedded Systems, Passives, Power Sources, Semiconductor: Discretes, Semiconductor: Integrated Circuits, Test and Measurement)

- techlibrary.commweb.com
  CommWeb Tech Library
  Timely and technical information on hot telecom and convergence issues such as VoIP, CRM, and the Voice Web (Call Center, Networking, Telecommunications, Voice/Data Convergence, Wireless)

- techlibrary.wallstreetandtech.com
  Wall Street & Technology Tech Library
  (Computer Hardware, Electronic Commerce, Enterprise Computing, IT Management, Market Research, Networking, Software Development, Telecommunications)

- whitepaperlibrary.m-commerceworld.com
  Internet World White Paper Library
  (eBusiness, ISP, Streaming Media Services, m-Commerce)

- whitepapers.interop.com
  N+I Whitepapers
  (Hardware, Network Management, Network/Systems, Software, Network Protocols, Wireless Systems)

- www.bbwlibrary.com
  Broadband Week Technical Library
  (3G Wireless Networks, Application Service Providers (ASPs), ATM, Bridges, Broadband Satellite Systems, Broadband Telecom Services, Broadband Video Services, Broadband Wireless Networks, Cable, Cable Modems, Communications Hardware, Data Networking Hardware, DSL, Frame Relay, Integrated Circuits, Internet Telephony, ISDN, ISPs, LAN Hardware, LAN Switches, Laws, Mobile Computing Systems, Network Management, Network Protocols, Network Security, Operations/Business Operations, Optical Storage, Quality of Service (QOS), Routers, Satellite Systems, Security, Standards, Testing, Video Conferencing Hardware, Virtual Private Networks, Voice Networking Hardware, Voice Over IP, Wireless Communication Hardware, Wireless Communications Systems, Wireless Internet, Wireless LAN)

Articles of Interest

- www.lbagroup.com/associates/lbatn106.htm
  "Technical Note 106: Wireless Cable: A Competing Technology"

- www.insight-corp.com/satellite.html
  "Satellite Communications for the Next Century: Global Markets for GMPCS, LEOs, MEOs, and GEOs 1999-2004"

Section III:
Distribution Architectures

CHAPTER 11

Metadata for Digital Media Distribution

We are on the verge of a metadata revolution. Get your data models clean and prepare for an interesting ride.
Tim Berners-Lee, 1999

It's Sunday night, and you're searching for something better than "Touched by an Angel" on the tube. Where do you turn? "Metadata Today"? Actually Metadata Today is available everywhere — only they call it "TV Guide." The TV Guide franchise was built on a few articles and a lot of metadata about who, what, where, and when. Metadata is derivative data, or to be recursive, data about data. The use of metadata throughout the media production process is a tremendously powerful and complex tool. Avid built a company by allowing editors to edit metadata (the digital media that was derived from the tape). The Avid editing process produced an edit decision list (EDL), yet another piece of metadata, which could then be used to complete the actual manipulation of the physical media.

Metadata is the fulcrum that turns a good idea — digital media asset management — into a competitive advantage. It is the glue that holds your digital management systems and processes — even the entire media supply chain — together. Get it right: opportunities. Get it wrong: investments as dormant monoliths realizing a fraction of their true value.

This chapter explains metadata in more detail and how to apply it in both your organization and your immediate supply chain.

Part A: Background

Introduction

Metadata is a very old concept. They even offer Ph.D.s that focus solely on metadata architectures; most of the people trained in this way come out of library science schools. However, the advent of widespread digital resources, databases, and data warehouses has led to a recognition of the importance of metadata in every curriculum that deals with data processing in some way. Visit your public library, and the lobby is filled with metadata in the form of millions of index cards summarizing books (and other media), when they were written, by whom, and where to find them in the library. Your driver's license and passport serve as metadata, credentials that summarize you in text and pictures (a thumbnail no less!) and help the police find your driving record after you run a red light. Movie listings are metadata.

What's common among all these examples? A small amount of data (metadata) summarizes a large amount of associated data and helps you quickly zoom in on the summarized data. If you get the metadata wrong, it will be much harder to find what you are looking for.

It's no accident that this is the first subject we're covering in detail for this section. Metadata must be the root of all planning in developing an end-to-end digital media creation and distribution system. Information provided to you by suppliers (for example, a media catalog) is in the form of metadata, and your clients will likely drive their processes off your metadata or enhancements to your vendors' metadata. Your automated workflow processes will operate on metadata, and so will your production crew as they shoot a TV sitcom episode.

The Digital Media Life Cycle

To understand why metadata is so important in digital media, take a look at the digital media life cycle in Figure 11-1.

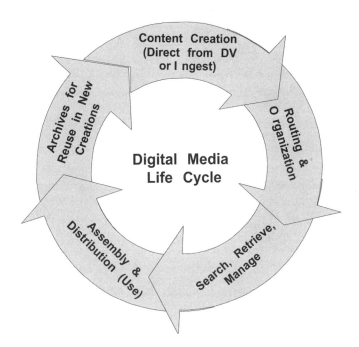

Figure 11-1 Digital Media Life Cycle

At each stage in the media life cycle, metadata is being modified and enhanced. Even in purging, it is not uncommon for the metadata to remain and grow over time, describing data that once was, for historical purposes. Yes, metadata can often be *more* important than the data it describes!

Take a simple television commercial created in a digital format. Clips become rough cuts, become final, become media library. The metadata surrounding a clip, such as the talent represented in that clip, is carried to each new stage in the life cycle. More importantly, whether that talent winds up in the final edit can drive talent payments for years (or decades) to come. Theoretically, a completely integrated system could calculate talent payments, based on an edit, in real time. Four frames cut could mean a savings of thousands of dollars in the long run. This is the true power of digital media systems, but it is tapped only when the metadata supports the process (and likewise, when the process supports the metadata).

Role of Metadata in Digital Media Supply Chains

Metadata lubricates a supply chain. That is to say, supply chains run on data, and when that data is properly managed metadata, and not the actual content itself, the chain operates much more rapidly. Conversely, incorrect or missing metadata can lead to supply-chain bottlenecks or complete disruption. If a cable movie channel orders Christmas Classics from the Disney library and Miramax's *Apocalypse Now* is delivered by mistake because of a metadata error (Miramax is a Disney unit), the results could be anywhere from annoying to embarrassing to very costly.

Clients base their buying decisions on the vendor's metadata. Vendors base their investments on the client's metadata. This is in essence the supply chain in action.

Metadata also serves other purposes:

- **Security:** Metadata provides a content sample without exposing the content itself.

- **Privacy:** Metadata summarizes aggregate usage metrics without exposing private consumer data.

- **Efficiency:** The 80/20 rule: 80 percent of the value is contained in 20 percent of the data (or less!). There's no need to transmit terabytes when kilobytes will do.

Using Metadata to Manage Digital Content Distribution

This year's Issue essays highlight a phenomenon that affects everyone with any role in moving intellectual property from creator to consumer. Focusing on two aspects of the sea change in the industry formerly known as the book business, they are designed to underline its imperatives. *Content Delivery*, by Jim Milliot of *Publishers Weekly*, is an essay that examines how members of the industry are using the Internet, and the value of the digitalization of information. Publishers, wholesalers, and others are now involved with producing content that is delivered to customers in a variety of formats through an ever-growing number of distribution channels.

"Contract Consequences," by Jonathan Kirsch, Kirsch and Mitchell, is an essay that examines changes in the industry and the need for publishers to address traditional contracts. The introduction of new technologies, including print-on-demand and e-books, poses new challenges for publishers who need to anticipate the rights required to compete effectively in the future. Publishers in the ever changing high-velocity world of multimedia publishing need visionary thinking to meet the challenges of providing content to customers in a variety of formats.

When metadata serves as a catalog of published content, it can drive an e-commerce business model. A simple model combines generic e-commerce with a filtered DMAM-based library to provide ad hoc content to local TV and cable channels. A more complex model allows syndicated shows to be auctioned in each local television market. These relationships are handled principally through direct sales and business development activities on a human level, and this is not likely to be deemphasized any time soon. However, when your sales force can tap into a rich, accurate metadata catalog, the returns per account representative can be far greater.

There are other ways metadata can help as well. For example, when programming is preempted unexpectedly, programming schedules have to be reset. Metadata can help to drive a programming scheduler that ensures that all subscribers are receiving correct and consistent content for air. Taking care of the exceptions automatically is an important workflow concept. Any time a workflow is effectively automated, the results are streamlined operations, cost savings, and acceleration of development and delivery.

Content distribution depends on digital rights management (DRM), which is also defined by metadata. Digital workflows will increasingly require that metadata be automatically added to protect the various rights holders. A more complete discussion of DRM is in Chapter 13.

Database Systems for Metadata Repositories

Truly managing large-scale metadata repositories requires sophisticated database tools. If you are going to be engaged in putting together a large media database, you will have to understand some of the key aspects of databases that manage metadata.

All database systems have their own proprietary way of creating, structuring, and storing data. Most of these systems also have their own proprietary database language for creating queries to access the data. However, most modern database products, such as IBM DB2, Informix, Microsoft SQL Server, Oracle, and Sybase, understand a standard query language called Structured Query Language (SQL). Despite the illusion that this is a standard, every database has its own idiosyncrasies that make application development on each platform unique. Programmers usually use SQL within the context of an application programming interface (API). These are the most common:

- ODBC, OLE-DB, and most recently ADO.NET for Windows programmers

- JDBC for Java programmers

Generally, unless you are writing a full-blown application or integration tool, you aren't going to be using these APIs. If you do, you'll have complete control over the database, or at least as much control as your database administrator will allow.

If your metadata is managed in an SQL database, you can get a pretty good picture of how it's configured for a given product by applying modeling tools to create an entity relationship diagram (ERD) of your database and therefore your metadata. Sometimes you may find relationships that you had not originally envisioned, and in some cases, find mistakes or mismappings of metadata.

More sophisticated modeling technologies can also be applied to SQL databases, but their main function will be to help with data mining and database optimization, not in structuring an enterprise metadata schema, principally because metadata is an abstract structure that often must be interpreted when applied in a relational database.

The general consensus is that various forms of extensible markup language (XML) will play a significant role in most of the new generations of databases. Just as with the case of SQL, however, even though it is considered an open standard, there are numerous flavors of XML and not all vendors support all features. Vendors also interpret the standards in different ways in order to optimize a solution.

It is a good idea to look at what other companies in the media and broadcast industries have selected as their database standards for metadata repositories. We have extremely unique challenges due to the temporal nature of media and the low latency requirements for real-time media access.

Role of XML in Metadata

XML is a standard for representing data between interoperable computer systems. It is not meant to be human-readable, although compared to binary formats, it is imminently decipherable by the average person. Practically all interoperation standards are being designed to use XML or are being adapted to XML. The advantages of XML include its extensibility, meaning its ability to easily add data points not originally designed into the original specification, and its ability to be easily read by a computer program. Microsoft, Sun, and a long list of computer software heavyweights as well as the W3C have embraced XML and are building XML-related programming tools.

Many of the standards reviewed in this chapter are XML-based. As an application user, XML is a technical detail that won't really affect your organization. However, as you plan for scalability, organizational growth, and technology advancement, the use of XML-based standards will ease integration woes between new and legacy systems.

XML is particularly applicable to metadata for several reasons:

- Metadata is often — but not always — represented as text. XML is fundamentally a text-based protocol, although it can represent binary data in certain circumstances (thumbnails, for example).

- Metadata is relational. XML is a fundamentally hierarchical data format, which gives it some relational capabilities. Other formats, such as comma-delimited formats, do not lend themselves as well to relational data.

- Metadata is dynamic. Not every object requires every attribute in the metadata schema. XML is well designed for dynamic schemas;

comma-delimited and binary formats can often suffer in efficiency under these circumstances.

There are some costs to using XML, primarily in the overhead of representing the attributes for each data point, but in metadata-based applications, this is generally not a major liability.

On the other hand, beware of programmers and vendors who seem overly enamored with XML and who use it everywhere, both in their marketing and in their implementation. Although XML is generally a good format for the representation of metadata, buy a product because it meets your requirements, not because it uses a specific technology.

Part B: Tools

Tools for working with metadata are often difficult to use. However, there is no getting around their use in digital media. The people who will be the most comfortable with metadata, the tools, and all the difficulties will likely be editors who have struggled with complex metadata since the first nonlinear editor (NLE) was introduced, the Web and print layout authors who have cried nightly over making the metadata work, and the librarians/archivists who are the original metadata toolmakers.

Much of the work on automatic capture of metadata is still only available in tools from research institutions. In addition, tools that work with the developing standards for metadata for multimedia are also few and far between. Two of the major standards contenders are the Dublin Core and MPEG-7 standards. Dublin Core is better developed and deployed in the area of bibliographical metadata on Web resources. MPEG-7 has more detail on metadata for the contents of audio and video. Unfortunately, very few commercial products support the proposed multimedia metadata model standards — most of the products use their own metadata model. Some of the products do mention Dublin Core, but few of them support specific metadata for multimedia. MPEG-7 is being discussed, but as yet no commercial product uses it as its fundamental metadata format. The transportation models using XML and resource description framework (RDF) are rarely used by commercial products either. Most of the products just use a proprietary database product to store the assets and the related metadata information.

Standards and Organizations

A variety of metadata-related standards and products (see Table 11-1) are under development and deserve consideration in your planning or upgrade of a digital media system. Your metadata model may need to integrate with these standards even if you and your tools don't use the standard formats directly within your enterprise, particularly if your customers or distributors expect data to be provided in a related format or with a defined set of attributes.

Note that the standards listed here are constantly changing. In fact, there are several current efforts to look at the hundreds of different standards and rationalize them into a few sets that are general-purpose and that focus on basic common functionality. Then, each industry or subject area can add extensions to those common definitions, knowing that they can count on the always being part of any standard implementation. Whether these standards bodies succeed or not is probably not relevant for a long time to come. The various standards organizations are lagging far behind industry and research innovation. Consequently, tool sets for metadata creation, editing, and repurposing are likely to be a difficult patchwork of proprietary, standard, and open-source resources that morph with the market and the technology.

Table 11-1: Metadata Standards

Standard	Description	URL
TV Anytime	A set of standards represented by nearly 150 companies, TV Anytime defines methods of storing and accessing digital media on consumer devices. Metadata is a major function of the standard, defining key attributes, media relationship, and usage metrics. A common usage of TV Anytime would be in personal video recorders (PVRs, also known as DVRs).	xml.coverpages.org/ tvAnytime.html
XMLTV	A more grassroots standard, XMLTV is an XML-based standard and set of tools for searching and browsing XML-based television program listings. It is similar to TV Anytime, except that it is designed from a consumer's viewpoint rather than a vendor's.	xml.coverpages.org/ xmltv.html

Table 11-1: Metadata Standards (Continued)

Standard	Description	URL
Encoded Archival Description (EAD)	The U.S. Library of Congress and several research level institutions have been engaged in the collaborative work of the EAD initiative for several years to create archival finding aids. Archival finding aids are descriptive bibliography or metadata tools that take the form of inventories, registers, indexes, guides, and similar resources created by museums, libraries, repositories, and other kinds of archives.	xml.coverpages.org/ ead.html
Resource Description Framework (RDF)	RDF is an extension of XML, designed to be more metadata-friendly. RDF is related to very basic metadata concepts, with its most powerful feature being the ability to define vocabularies for exchange of metadata between different schemas.	www.xml.com/pub/a/98/06/ rdf.html
eXtensible Metadata Platform (XMP)	XMP is Adobe's corporate metadata standard that has been published as an open-source software development kit. Based on RDF (and in turn, XML), XMP also adheres to a number of other standards, particularly Dublin Core, as well as schemas for digital rights management, asset management, and more. XMP also defines packets—ways of packaging a large data stream.	www.adobe.com/products/ xmp/pdfs/XAPv8.pdf
XML-based digital rights management standards	A number of XML-based DRM standards are in development. Each has a different scope and philosophy. Standards underway include XrML, DPRL, ODRL, XMCL, XACML, MPEG Rights Expression Language, Open eBook Initiative, EBX, IDRM Working Group, PRISM, INDECS, and DOI. As you can see from this alphabet soup, DRM is a major area of interest because it is the key to profitability and a cornerstone of a metadata architecture for any technology innovator in the digital rights space.	xml.coverpages.org/ drm.html

Table 11-2: Metadata Organizations

Organization	Description	URL
Open Media Framework (OMF) and Advanced Authoring Format (AAF)	OMF and the follow-on standard AAF are multimedia file formats that enable content creators to easily exchange digital media and metadata across platforms and between systems and applications. Video, sound, and music editors can work simultaneously on the same content without actually transmitting edited versions of the content itself. OMF and AAF simplify project management, save time, and preserve valuable metadata that was often lost when transferring media between applications in the past.	www.aafassociation.org/
DIG35	The DIG35 Specification: Metadata for Digital Images is proposed by the 80-member Digital Imaging Group and defines XML-based specifications for metadata in the digital imaging market. Just as in DRM, digital imaging has certain application-specific requirements that cannot be addressed with more generalized XML-based standards such as RDF.	xml.coverpages.org/dig35.html
Moving Pictures Experts Group (MPEG) [ISO/IEC JTC1 SC29 WG11]	A working group of ISO/IEC is in charge of the development of standards for coded representation of digital audio and video. Established in 1988, the group has produced MPEG-1, the standard on which such products as Video CD and MP3 are based; MPEG-2, the standard on which such products as Digital Television set-top boxes and DVD are based; MPEG-4, the standard for multimedia for the fixed and mobile Web; and MPEG-7, the standard for description and search of audio and visual content. Work on the new standard MPEG-21 Multimedia Framework started in June 2000. So far a Technical Report has been produced, and the formal approval process has already begun for two more parts of the standard. Several Calls for Proposals have already been issued, and two working drafts are still in development.	mpeg.telecomitalialab.com/ www.mpeg.org (MPEG pointers and resources, reference site for MPEG) www.mpeg.org/MPEG/ starting-points.html (MPEG starting points and FAQs) www.faqs.org/faqs/ compression-faq/part2/ section-2.html (introduction to MPEG)

Table 11-2: Metadata Organizations (Continued)

Organization	Description	URL
World Wide Web Consortium (W3C)	The World Wide Web Consortium was created in October 1994 to lead the World Wide Web to its full potential by developing common protocols that promote its evolution and ensure its interoperability. W3C has more than 500 member organizations from around the world and has earned international recognition for its contributions to the growth of the Web. The W3C is responsible for the development of the eXtensible Markup Language (XML). XML is the universal format for structured documents and data on the Web.	www.w3.org/ www.w3.org/XML/
Dublin Core Metadata Initiative (DCMI)	The Dublin Core Metadata Initiative is an open forum engaged in the development of interoperable online metadata standards that support a broad range of purposes and business models. DCMI's activities include consensus-driven working groups, global workshops, conferences, standards liaison, and educational efforts to promote widespread acceptance of metadata standards and practices.	dublincore.org/
Synchronized Multimedia Integration Language (SMIL)	SMIL (pronounced "smile") enables simple authoring of interactive audiovisual presentations. SMIL is typically used for rich-media/multimedia presentations that integrate streaming audio and video with images, text, or any other media type. SMIL is an easy-to-learn HTML-like language, and many SMIL presentations are written using a simple text editor.	www.w3.org/AudioVideo/

Research Projects

There are many universities and institutions supporting research projects that are attempting to provide useful tools for the automatic extraction of metadata from audio and video. A sample of the research that is underway is listed in Table 11-3.

Table 11-3: Metadata Research Projects

Institution	Description	Product(s)	URL
Informedia Project	The Informedia Digital Video Library project is a research initiative at Carnegie-Mellon University funded by the NSF, DARPA, NASA, and others that studies how multimedia digital libraries can be established and used.	Informedia Digital Video Library project	www.informedia. cs.cmu.edu/
Informedia Project	The purpose of the Multilingual Informedia project was to develop automated systems and tools enabling multilingual and multimedia information capture, search, retrieval, summarization, and reuse. The system, built on the underlying Informedia Digital Video Library system concepts, technology, and infrastructure, is designed to access textual, audio (radio), and video (TV) information to index, categorize, retrieve, summarize, and analyze it in one or multiple languages.	Multilingual Informedia project	www.informedia. cs.cmu.edu/mli/
Informedia Project	The Informedia system provides *full-content* search and retrieval of current and past TV and radio news and documentary broadcasts. This prototype database allows for rapid retrieval of individual *video paragraphs* that satisfy an arbitrary spoken or typed subject area query based on the words in the sound track, closed captioning, or text overlaid on the screen. There is also a capability for matching of similar faces and images.	Informedia-II	www.informedia. cs.cmu.edu/dli2/

Table 11-3: Metadata Research Projects (Continued)

Institution	Description	Product(s)	URL
Informedia Project	The Video Analysis and Content Extraction (VACE) program provides automatic content detection and recognition technologies for two primary video data sources: video scenes (of various indoor and outdoor activities involving people, meetings, and vehicles) and TV news broadcasts.	Video Information Summarization and Demonstration Testbed	www.informedia. cs.cmu.edu/arda-vace/
Informedia Project	The CCRHE project develops algorithms and systems enabling people to query and communicate a synthesized record of human experiences derived from individual perspectives captured during selected personal and group activities. This project assumes that within 10 years technology will be capable of creating a continuously recorded, digital, high-fidelity record of a person's activities and observations in video form.	Capturing, Coordinating, and Remembering Human Experience	www.informe-dia.cs.cmu.edu/ccrhe/ index.html
University of Kentucky	MOODS is an object-oriented application development framework for identifying, managing, and storing the *embedded content* found in multimedia data. Embedded content refers to any information that is contained in the data but is not directly accessible (akin to data mining). With an image, for example, this would be the features that appear in the image.	Modeling Object Oriented Data Semantics	www.dcs.uky.edu/ moods/
Centre for Telematics and Information Technology (CTIT)	The DMW project works with content-based retrieval techniques in large multimedia databases. It is focused on two media dimensions, video and audio, the discovery of relationships among their syntactic entities, their embedding in a query language geared at dealing with semistructured sources, and the architecture to maintain a feature database for fast multimedia searches.	DMW	www.ctit.utwente.nl/ projects/telemat-ica-instituut/dmw.html

Table 11-3: Metadata Research Projects (Continued)

Institution	Description	Product(s)	URL
Centre for Telematics and Information Technology (CTIT)	DRUID aims at the development of tools for the indexing and retrieval of multimedia content. In terms of the objects to be made available for retrieval, the project will cover continuous objects containing text and/or speech elements (for example, video and audio fragments) as well as static objects, ranging from paper documents and textually annotated images to Web pages.	DRUID	www.ctit.utwente.nl/
Distributed Systems Technology Centre	This paper describes an application that enables the computer-assisted generation of Dublin Core-based metadata descriptions and online digital visual summaries for videos. The generated metadata descriptions can be saved as RDF or HTML or saved to a database. They can be used to enable metadata interchange, searching across the Internet, or dynamic generation of detailed visual summaries for video browsing.	Veggie	archive.dstc.edu.au/ RDU/staff/jane-hunter/ INFOG99/paper.html
The Resource Discovery Unit of the Distributed Systems Technology Centre	The aim of the Reggie Metadata Editor is to enable the easy creation of various forms of metadata with one flexible program. As it stands, the Reggie applet can create metadata using the HTML 3.2 standard, the HTML 4.0 standard, the RDF (resource description Framework) format, and the RDF abbreviated format. The Reggie Metadata Editor uses a schema file to read in the details of all the elements in a set, their characteristics and descriptions. To create metadata based on a different element set or different language, one has simply to create a new schema file.	Reggie	metadata.net/dstc/

Table 11-3: Metadata Research Projects (Continued)

Institution	Description	Product(s)	URL
The Distributed Systems Technology Centre (DSTC) and Joint Information Systems Committee (JISC) and National Science Foundation (NSF)	The Harmony Project is an international collaboration funded by DSTC, JISC, and NSF. Its goal is to investigate a number of the key issues in describing complex multimedia resources in digital libraries.	Harmony Project	metadata.net/harmony/
Advanced Research and Development Activity (ARDA)	The initial focus of the ARDA-sponsored VACE program is on automatic content detection and recognition technologies for two primary video data sources: video scenes (of various indoor and outdoor activities involving people, meetings, and vehicles) and TV news broadcasts. Over time, VACE technologies will provide (1) significant improvement in indexing and retrieval performance for video data; (2) autonomous video understanding; (3) ancillary improvement for still-image processing; (4) enabling technologies for video data mining, filtering, and selection; and (5) a drastic reduction in volume for video storage and forwarding mechanisms.	Video Analysis and Content Exploitation (VACE)	www.ic-arda.org/InfoExploit/vace/index.html

Automated Media Analysis, Metadata Creation, and Cataloguing

When most people think of metadata, the most common data types envisioned are text, numbers, dates, and the like. With digital media, however, many more dimensions must be considered. Media is text (e-books, closed-captioned text), but it's also sound, pictures, video, 3D elements, and much more. Creating metadata around these various elements of a media object is tricky and expensive, often requiring sophisticated hardware and software systems. Return-on-investment (ROI) considerations for such metadata should be carefully considered. This section lists some of the automated metadata extraction tools you may want to investigate. One note of caution: While these technologies are promising, they are not perfect, so don't assume that your results are complete or even relevant; you must be the ultimate judge of whether automated systems are doing the job.

Text Analysis

- **Closed captioning:** Many final-edit media streams come with closed captioning streams embedded. This is a cheap and extremely valuable bit of data that should be used in certain types of metadata search. Not only is the vocabulary of the closed captioning data a great source of keywords, but the text itself can provide Society of Motion Picture and Television Engineers (SMPTE) pointers back to the media itself.

- **Automated keyword generation:** Using lexical analysis tools (computational linguistics), relevant keywords can be culled from a text stream and placed in the metadata. Keyword generation is a notoriously difficult manual task, partially because workers tend to use synonyms in a single context and spelling errors are introduced as well. Using keyword-generation tools allows you to automate the standardization of keywords within and across projects.

- **Clustering tools:** Assuming a large volume of text-based data, clustering tools allow an extremely large media library to be automatically interrogated for major themes and subjects. For example, when searching for the term "Star Wars" in a news library, you might get two different hits: the movie and the U.S. strategic missile defense system. Clustering tools can automatically determine which of these news themes a given media asset might belong to (perhaps using the closed-captioning text as input) and then present a choice to the user after a search.

Speech Analysis

In certain applications, speech analysis may be a key feature. For example, producing an automatic transcript of a news feed for which you do not have the original text can be tremendously valuable. Tools that have been developed to recognize continuous real-time speech, as spoken into a microphone, are often repurposed to recognize speech from audio or video feeds.

Image Analysis

Image analysis tools are the least developed of the automated tools because they have the hardest task. The easiest (although still difficult) analysis to provide is where the tool identifies some physical property of the video such as color, texture, scene changes, or motion and change through the scene. Finding the relevant content within a video stream would normally mean manually fast-forwarding through hours of video. What if you could display every scene change in a one-hour video at the touch of a button? Find some-one's face in a video by supplying a picture of him or her? Find all shots that are similar in the same stream? Resynchronize audio and video where they were previously out of sync? These capabilities are available with the current generation of tools.

The least developed are the tools that try to provide some sort of context for the images within the video stream. For example, is that scene with blue the sky or blue water? Is that orange sunset romantic or threatening? This level of analysis tool is still a dream of research institutions and, at this point, is best handled through manual entry of metadata.

Each vendor provides slightly different capabilities at a wide variety of price points. While it might be tempting to purchase the top-of-the-line image analysis tools, make sure that your organization is purchasing the features that are absolutely mission-critical and that you have properly valued the cost of the system and the organizational process change, training, and employee retention issues. These types of technologies typically fall in price over time; if you can't afford it this year, maybe you can next year. Table 11-4 provides information on image analysis tools.

Table 11-4: Image Analysis Tools

Company	Description	Product(s)	URL
Virage	The Virage Video Application Platform includes a suite of software products critical to organizations that create, manage, and distribute digital media on an enterprise scale. To optimize the creation and delivery of media-rich applications, the Virage platform includes products that allow content owners to capture, index, and encode video and to manage, publish, and distribute video.	Virage SmartEncode product suite includes: ControlCenter, VideoLogger, Video Application Server	www.virage.com/

Table 11-4: Image Analysis Tools (Continued)

Company	Description	Product(s)	URL
Voquette	The Content Enhancement Engine enables the automatic cataloging and categorization of content. In addition, metadata is automatically created by means of a growing knowledge base that is unique to the enterprise and is updated and maintained by the system. A semantic query engine is layered on top of the Content Enhancement Engine, allowing for the quick retrieval of content.	Content Enhancement Engine	www.voquette.com/
WordWave	WordWave provides end-to-end Web content enablement solutions. Its software captures, encodes, indexes, manages, and distributes digital media, making it accessible to wider audiences. Multimedia becomes searchable using standard text search engines.	WordWave	www.wordwave.com/index.html
Convera	Screening Room is a comprehensive integrated solution for fast, easy, and intelligent analog and digital video asset capturing, analyzing, indexing, browsing, accessing, and retrieving. It provides content-based, scalable, high-performance retrieval for multiple types of video assets in real time.	Screening Room	www.convera.com/Products/products_sr.asp

Table 11-4: Image Analysis Tools (Continued)

Company	Description	Product(s)	URL
Autonomy	Autonomy's technology forms an understanding of the actual content of any type of information, text- or voice-based, unstructured or structured, regardless of where it is stored, the format it has been created with, or the applications associated with the data. The technology allows applications to communicate with each other without any manual effort involved in setting up complicated connectors or using metadata.	IDOL	www.autonomy.com/ autonomy_v3/Content/ IDOL/
eVision	eVe (eVision Visual engine) is an advanced visual search engine that includes analysis, storage, indexing, and search/retrieval of images and video. Unlike a classical keyword-based search, eVision software retrieves images by analyzing their perceptual content. Images do not need to be viewed, interpreted, or keyworded by humans.	eVe (eVision Visual engine)	www.evisionglobal. com/tech/index.html
MediaSite (purchased by Sonic Foundry)	Provides tools to create customized rich media indexes, annotate and describe rich media, and encode video to different formats. Used in conjunction with the Rich Media Publisher Suite, Modules offer advanced indexing capabilities, including fully automated indexing and posting to the Web, PowerPoint slide indexing, and creating a searchable transcript.	Rich Media Publisher Suite Rich Media Publisher Suite Modules	www.mediasite.com/ corporateweb/products/ index.html www.sonicfoundry.com/
IBM	IBM's ViaVoice provides continuous speech recognition products for the PC. IBM offers a complete suite of products for every level of user — from beginners to seasoned voice recognition power users.	ViaVoice	www-4.ibm.com/ software/speech/ desktop/w9.html

Table 11-4: Image Analysis Tools (Continued)

Company	Description	Product(s)	URL
ScanSoft	Dragon NaturallySpeaking speech recognition software is fast, accurate, easy to use, powerful, and customizable. it recognizes words at up to 160 words per minute for several different languages.	NaturallySpeaking	www.lhsl.com/ naturallyspeaking/
Dremedia	Dremedia's software recognizes all aspects of broadcast content, including video, audio, and text. Dremedia's core video analysis technology enables an image to be segmented into its component parts in order that they may be identified, understood, labeled, and indexed. Dremedia's audio analysis technology uses a wide range of recognition technologies — from keyword spotting to small and large vocabulary continuous speech recognition and information retrieval from spoken documents — to enable speech and audio processing such as speech recognition, speaker recognition, language recognition, and speech enhancement. Dremedia uses Autonomy's technology to automatically handle large amounts of structured and unstructured text.	Dremedia	www.dremedia.com/ technology/
Humming-bird, Ltd.	Genio Suite is a data exchange solution that enables enterprises to extract, transform, and load data from any data source to any target. It transforms, cleanses, enriches, and directs information across the entire spectrum of decision support systems and enterprise applications. Genio Suite is particularly well suited for populating enterprise data warehouses and datamarts.	Genio Suite	www.humming-bird.com/products/dirs/ genio/index.html

Table 11-4: Image Analysis Tools (Continued)

Company	Description	Product(s)	URL
Automatic Duck	OMF import solution for composition for both Avid and Final Cut Pro users. It has low-end DMAM features for those on a budget.	Automatic Series	www.automatic-duck.com/
Avid Technology, Inc.	DigiTranslator offers OMF Interchange from within the Pro Tools 5.1.3 software environment. Developed in collaboration with working postproduction audio engineers, DigiTranslator allows translation of clip-based volume data, a choice between rendered audio effects or untreated sources, and options for media copying and consolidation.	DigiTranslator	www.digidesign.com/ products/ prd_specs.cfm?product _id=1040

Manual Metadata Generation and Editing

Automated tools are always improving, but most media systems will require some level of manual entry to really make the system useful. Most DMAM systems will have a way to manually enter metadata into the system or edit automatically generated metadata. In addition, most systems will have a number of required metadata fields when a media object is added to the repository. However, the more metadata information and the more steps users have to endure while getting media into a system, the less likely it will be that the metadata will be consistent and therefore useful. Requiring users to pick metadata from lists in required fields can be a big help, but users still improperly code attributes. Whenever possible, take the time to develop an approved set of metadata tags that users choose from a pull-down or checklist. If a metadata repository is a requirement for your organization, you can also restrict whether or not a project can be listed as completed without certain metadata being attached.

There are also tools available that are specifically designed to aid in the manual creation of metadata (see Table 11-5). Part of the mechanism by which many of them work creates a controlled vocabulary that is decided on either for the entire organization or for a particular project. For each project, a standard naming convention is used for each attribute of the media that is being tagged. Larger projects will often require both a controlled vocabulary and a "metadata crosswalk," or thesaurus. What the crosswalks and thesauri do is provide links from one type of metadata or term to another. This allows users to enter "fuzzy" queries that retrieve relevant results. The ability to easily add crosswalks and/or thesauri through open standards or readily available APIs should be a key factor in determining authoring, editing, management, and distribution software. The inclusion of this aspect in the digital products you choose will help you ensure that your systems will scale and adapt as the demands of the markets change. It is also a key selling point to content owners that your authoring systems will work with their metadata systems.

Table 11-5: Manual Metadata Creation Tools

Company	Description	Product(s)	URL
SoftQuad	XMetaL is an XML editor that can be quickly and cost-effectively customized to allow everyone in your organization to create and work with XML content. XMetaL simplifies the creation of reusable business content, making it possible for businesses to rapidly streamline the process of distributing information to the Web, print, and other media.	XMetaL	www.softquad.com/ top_frame.sq?page=products/xmetal/ content_xmetal.html
Hiawatha Island Software Company (HiSoftware)	TagGen Office is a sophisticated meta-tag generator. A tabbed dialog box steps you through creating keyword and description meta tags, customizing Web page meta tags (such as refresh, classification, copyright, robot handling, and so on), validating tags, establishing Microsoft Office compliance, and updating your files. TagGen works in single- and batch-file modes and also lets you build custom collections of meta tags, customize the rule base used to analyze tags, check the spelling of your tags, and use a thesaurus for developing more tags. TagGen supports the 15 essential Dublin Core elements.	TagGen Professional	www.hisoftware.com/ products.htm

Table 11-5: Manual Metadata Creation Tools (Continued)

Company	Description	Product(s)	URL
MKDoc Ltd.	MKDoc is a Website content management system that has been designed to make the creation of usable, accessible, semantically rich, and valid Websites as easy as possible. MKDoc provides different ways for the public to interact with and navigate between documents, including a site map, search facility, printer versions of pages, and Dublin Core RDF metadata for documents.	MKDoc	mkdoc.com/

Multimedia Search and Retrieval

The problem of searching multimedia data has received considerable attention in the last few years. Basic search engines will search for textual metadata associated with media. More advanced query systems typically take an image or a sketch as input, compute some visual features from it (for example, color histograms, texture, shape features), and search one or more indexes to return images with similar features. Alternatively, the user can specify values for these features and appropriate weights reflecting their relative importance. These systems are a big improvement over the method of manually annotating images and doing a text search to find relevant ones.

Multimedia search is a much harder problem than text or audio searching, so systems are both more expensive and less accurate. More recent systems focus on studying other types of features, such as wavelets, or localizing the features to subimage regions. By segmenting the images into their regions or objects and comparing images at the object level, such systems get closer to the mental model of the user of how image similarity is established. These systems should also be able to exploit not only visual feature similarity but also the relationships among the image objects, such as their spatial arrangements, for example.

The generation systems would compute the relevant constraints among the objects transparently to the user; therefore, the user had little control over the types of relationships used. Newer systems (see Table 11-6) give the user full control to specify arbitrary interobject constraints.

Table 11-6: Multimedia Search and Retrieval Tools

Company	Description	Product(s)	URL
dtSearch Corp.	dtSearch has more than two dozen text search options. It displays retrieved PDF and HTML files with highlighted hits, embedded links and images, and multiple hit and file navigation options. dtSearch converts other files — XML, word processor, database, spreadsheet, email, ZIP, Unicode, etc. — to HTML for browser display with highlighted hits and multiple navigation options.	dtSearch	www.dtsearch.com/index.html
LexiQuest	LexiQuest lets you access, manage, and retrieve textual information the way you speak by using advanced natural language technology. Not a search engine, LexiQuest's linguistic software solutions enhance your Internet, intranet, and extranet capabilities. You can rapidly identify, catalog, and retrieve unstructured textual information, regardless of where it resides.	LexiQuest Mine LexiQuest Categorize LexiQuest Guide LexiQuest Respond	www.lexiquest.com/index.html
Inktomi Corporation	Inktomi Enterprise Search is a comprehensive information retrieval platform that delivers access to information across an enterprise, regardless of location, language, or file format.	Enterprise Search	www.inktomi.com/products/search/enterprise.html
Convera	RetrievalWare enables users to index and search a wide range of distributed information resources, including text files, HTML, documents, relational database tables, more than 200 proprietary document formats (such as word processors and publishing systems), and groupware repositories. Advanced search capabilities include concept and keyword searching, pattern searching, and query-by-example.	RetrievalWare	www.convera.com/Products/products_rw.asp

Table 11-6: Multimedia Search and Retrieval Tools (Continued)

Company	Description	Product(s)	URL
doclinx	FT/XML Enterprise Search provides high-performance Enterprise Full-Text and XML Knowledge Retrieval Software. FT/XML Enterprise Search is designed for large-scale knowledge mining applications where handling terabytes of data with high performance and secure document retrieval are key requirements. FT/XML stores security information on a per-document basis, enabling secure knowledge retrieval applications.	FT/XML Enterprise	www.doclinx.com/ products/ftxml.html
Fast-Talk	Fast-Talk Communications has created audio searching technology that enables extremely accurate high-speed searching of audio and video content — without using speech-to-text conversion. Based on identifying phonemes, the smallest units of speech, Fast-Talk audio searching technology can identify and retrieve any word, proper name, or phrase, regardless of speaker or spelling, with up to 99 percent accuracy.	Phonetic Preprocessing Engine Phonetic Search Engine	www.fast-talk.com/ products.html
NextPage, Inc.	The Folio platform lets you search and navigate gigabytes of data, categorize disparate content, and gain secure access to information, regardless of where it resides — all from your Web browser. You share content across connected servers with partners, suppliers, customers, and employees to form an e-business content network.	Folio Views Folio Builder Folio Publisher Folio Integrator	www.nextpage.com/ section.asp?f= toc&section= Products&path= Products/additional%20products/ folio

Part C: Methods

Metadata Model

Modeling metadata in media is uniquely challenging. We want our metadata to do everything from assisting with the billing of a commercial spot that has a lifetime of a few seconds up to fully indexing a feature film and all the outtakes, each with a potential lifetime of years, if not decades.

If there's any hope of utilizing metadata across your entire supply chain, or even to automate processes within the organization, you're going to need a common data model. What does this mean?

- **Agreement on attributes:** The attributes of all systems must be aligned in data type, size, and meaning.

- **Agreement on data values:** The data values must mean the same thing in each system.

- **Agreement on business rules:** The meaning of status fields and routing information must be the same in each system, and the processing logic must be the same as well.

- **Agreement on interchange formats:** You will always need to exchange information with other divisions in your company or with other companies. The more agreement you have on common interchange formats, the easier the process will be.

To the extent that there is disagreement, transcoders are required for the metadata. When two systems come from the same vendor, this is usually handled internally or through professional services provided from the vendor. However, when a new infrastructure is put in place, significant effort must be applied to transcoding metadata between systems, even when you have put standards in place — standards have limits.

A good way to manage this is to design and manage a corporate metadata schema, usually using a DMAM system as a starting point. All information systems in the organization should then be adapted to this metadata model. While it may be difficult initially to conform to a common model, this effort will pay off in the long run.

Designing a common model is the domain of library science, not information technology. For a large and complex organization, handing this responsibility to the corporate records department is a smart move. Library scientists are trained in the design and production of indexes, catalogs, controlled vocabularies — all the standards necessary to accurately store and retrieve your valuable data.

Sometimes creating a common model can be extremely challenging, as different projects and organizational divisions have their own unique metadata needs. An editor repurposing content needs access to metadata that an interactive designer does not, and vice versa. When the differences in metadata become too great, this is often handled by completely segmenting systems. In some cases this is a reasonable choice. In less severe circumstances, a hierarchical metadata model can be created that defines a common corporate subset with organizational and project-specific extensions around the edges of the network. If a hierarchical metadata model is going to be required, then significant planning along with careful selection of customizable products is mandatory.

The metadata of a large organization can become so important that it becomes a corporate database and documentation of its own. Publishing and continuously updating the database will help to make it easier for individual projects and organizational divisions to build specialized services that integrate with the metadata. For example, if an organization wishes to build a custom search application to run on Palm handhelds, access to the metadata database not only would speed development but would help keep the application in sync with the rest of the organization, sometimes with no additional programming.

Metadata Analysis

When you are building your enterprise metadata schema — the über-schema — there are several design points to keep in mind:

- **Constituency:** Who is the customer for a given process, and how do they define effective results? Remember that your vendors can be considered customers of your digital media systems; giving them access to your content library will help them to offer products and services that are more aligned with your business, and giving them access to your production schedule may help them better plan their delivery schedules to you.

  There is a tendency to assume that systems are built to be used only by the worker bees in an enterprise. Treating your senior managers and executives as typical users not only puts a priority on the deployment task and budget, but it also helps to ferret out the desired metrics that define success within the whole system. For example, you may find that by including executive browsing in the system, production schedules should be measured not just in time but also in a balance between time and budget. Would doing so affect what metadata you were capturing? Absolutely!

- **Scope of the applications:** To get a good picture of the metadata you are going to need to capture today, you are going to need an understanding of the corporate systems that will be installed over the next 12 to 18 months. Even if the goals of the enterprise are unrealistic, having a vision and set of priorities will help you plan for the types of metadata that are needed to support an integrated system.

- **Scope of the enterprise:** Is your company planning any mergers or acquisitions, large or small? Will your infrastructure handle a rapid influx of new employees? Can your metadata cope with expansions into new media types or new business models? Are you limiting your metadata vision to that of the DMAM or DRM vendor?

- **Digital rights management:** Is your enterprise prepared to deal with the digital rights issues that will be required to support your media supply chain? Will you need to encrypt content? Watermark content? Who is the audience for your content, and what are the technologies that are appropriate and acceptable for them? What kind of metrics and personally identifiable information can you collect about your audience? What metrics will your distributor give back to you now or in the future?

- **Financial information:** Will your audience be paying you directly or through a distributor? What privacy concessions are you granting your audience? How will you secure credit card or bank information from outsiders and even your own employees? What kinds of payment options will you accept — credit cards, anonymous payments, third-party billers, micropayments? How are the payments related to the digital rights granted on the media? What media viewing or interaction options define the pricing structure of your content library?

Answering all these questions may be terrifically difficult at the beginning of a project because there is an urgency to get started on demonstrable deployment activities, yet that very deployment is dependent on the results of your analysis. Consider outsourcing for this type of requirements analysis. Many of your questions are shared by other enterprises in your market, and an experienced consultant knows the right questions to ask and the value of each answer from each constituency.

Metadata Extraction

One problem that has limited the reuse and repurposing of video and film material is the lack of effective video/film indexing methods (indices are either added manually or extracted automatically). The general reliance on just title and keyword information to identify material of interest means that valuable time is then wasted manually scanning the video to locate the most relevant portions. Your analysis with your organization or client will tell you:

- What pieces of data would they ideally like to capture?

- What is the minimum amount of data that is required to get the job done?

- How much time do people have available to spend on metadata extraction?

As discussed, there is a cost to metadata extraction. Balancing the three factors above, along with an evaluation of the capabilities of the authoring, analysis, storage, and query tools, will help you come to an optimum solution.

Be aware of valuable metadata stored on individual machines or local networks that are needed for special projects or media types. Many times integration of these systems into the general corporate-wide system is too expensive and only the end product can be profiled. This may create a risk, such as in the situation where manually profiled data might allow a rough cut to be marked as a final edit. Creating business rules that control how each user can apply metadata in these situations can help to prevent problems later.

Metadata Store

While DMAMs (discussed in Chapter 12) include both metadata and media storage, these cannot be seen as a monolithic system. Metadata is typically stored separately from the media itself. The analogy is not unlike a library where library cards are held in drawers and books are managed on shelves. Using either storage mechanism alone for both data types would be inefficient and costly.

Typically, metadata is stored in a relational database such as Oracle or Microsoft SQL Server. Media is typically managed by high-performance file systems that are tuned for the type of concurrent high-bandwidth retrieval tasks that are associated with media work. The metadata provides a pointer to the media as well as security credentials that are required to access the media. Metadata may also include ancillary information not stored in the relational tables, such as full-text indices of articles or separate thumbnails of the media, both of which may be stored separately on the hard drive.

Remember, the primary purpose of metadata is to serve as an index (a mechanism to speed queries whether they be automatic or user-initiated). Your metadata is not an archive but an active part of your entire digital media infrastructure. Speed of retrieval is paramount, and the metadata itself requires its own subindices to help it meet expectations. Often, the configuration suggested by a DMAM vendor may seem logical but may not hold up in practice once you've customized the metadata and integrated with third-party products. Keeping performance on par is a continual task, not only to optimize your queries but also to maintain the indices as their own entity. An index can become dirty or corrupt and affect performance or accuracy. It must be a crucial part of the job of the database administrator (DBA) to maintain these indices — even on a weekly or daily basis if necessary.

Because high-performance operating systems and storage systems are expensive and difficult to configure, it's generally not a good idea — nor is it necessary — to try to share storage and operating systems between the relational database and the media storage. Treat them as completely separate — let the metadata be the technical domain of a certified DBA. You may also find that you need a streaming media expert to focus on the performance of your storage systems as well as to help keep your media streaming services and related networking up and running — call this a digital media administrator (DMA).

Whatever the configuration, the key ingredients are performance and customizability. Some of you may be tempted to simplify the initial installation, but reconfiguring later can be much more costly than getting it right in the first place. The best way to avoid mistakes is to visit several existing customers who are happy with their installation and overall system value. Even if customers are currently happy, they'll no doubt have some horror stories that could help save you significant time and frustration.

Metadata isn't just title and owner information; it also includes licensing rights, security, and financial information. Most of these data types are highly sensitive and require special security. In some cases, these data types are so sensitive that they require their own physical storage. For example, in the case of credit card numbers, it is not uncommon to hire a third-party credit card processing company to maintain the data away from your own employees and with the service provider's specialized security mechanisms. These providers allow you to collect credit card revenue without ever touching the credit card number itself. Similarly, you may want to segment licensing rights and other security information in another database managed by a separate employee. It is often a good security measure to maintain interdependent but separate stores for security.

Creating Your Own Metadata Tools

If you have some programming or scripting expertise in-house, it is easy to create simple tools for the capture of metadata. For example, you could create a Web-based template (online fill-in forms) to collect metadata elements following a standard syntax such as the Dublin Core HTML. The metadata so collected would then be stored in a metadata repository. A simple repository can be created using XML files or a Microsoft Access database.

More complex systems can also be built around HTML forms. This is the approach taken by the Nordic Metadata Project. Briefly, the Nordic Metadata Project, which ran from 1996 to 1998, chose the Dublin Core element set as its metadata format, developed a template to collect and format metadata, and developed metadata harvesting and indexing applications, a Dublin Core-to-MARC converter, and a URN generator.

A simple example of an online form based on the Dublin Core set is shown in the following box.

Descriptive metadata for media resources

Describe your media using the form below.

If possible, please fill in as many fields as you can.

Note that it is possible to exceed the visible limitations of the input boxes.

TITLE of the resource to be described

| -- Select one from defined projects -- | ▼ |

Alternative title (Titles other than the main title)

| |

CREATOR (Name of the person or organization primarily responsible for creating the intellectual content)

| -- Select one from defined list -- | ▼ |

SUBJECT: Keywords (Select descriptive keywords)

-- Use project keywords --	▼
	▼
	▼

DESCRIPTION (Short description of the media)

| |

The Dublin Core metadata element set (dublincore.org/documents/1998/09/dces/) includes:

- Title
- Author or creator
- Subject and keywords

- Description
- Publisher
- Other contributor(s)
- Date
- Resource type
- Data format
- Resource identifier
- Source
- Language
- Relation
- Coverage
- Rights management

If you are building your own metadata repository, you should consider using this as a starting point before adding your own special metadata elements, as this will make interoperability with other metadata repositories much easier in the future.

Additional Resources

Digital Geospatial Metadata

- www.fgdc.gov/metadata/contstan.html
  Content Standard for Digital Geospatial Metadata (CSDGM)
- www.fgdc.gov/metadata/metadata.html
  FGDC Metadata
- www.fgdc.gov/clearinghouse/clearinghouse.html
  FGDC Geospatial Data Clearinghouse
- clearinghouse4.fgdc.gov/registry/clearinghouse_sites.html
  Websites Associated with FGDC Clearinghouse Participants
- www.fgdc.gov/standards/standards.html
  FGDC Standards
- gcmd.gsfc.nasa.gov/Aboutus/standards/
  Metadata Protocols and Standards
- gcmd.gsfc.nasa.gov/User/difguide/difman.html
  Directory Interchange Format (DIF) Writer's Guide

- www.lic.wisc.edu/metadata/metaprim.htm
  NSGIC Metadata Primer

National Information Standards Organization (NISO)

- www.niso.org/index.html
  NISO Home
- www.niso.org/standards/index.html
  NISO Standards Page
- ANSI/NISO Z39.2 – 1994 (R2001) Information Interchange Format (MARC)
- ANSI/NISO Z39.50 – 1995 Information Retrieval: Application Service Definition and Protocol Specification
- ANSI/NISO Z39.85 – 2001 Dublin Core Metadata Element Set
- www.niso.org/standards/std_info_retrieval.html
  NISO – Information Retrieval Documents
- www.niso.org/press/whitepapers/crsswalk.html
  Issues in Crosswalking Content Metadata Standards
- www.niso.org/standards/resources/Z39-85.pdf
  The Dublin Core Metadata Element Set
- www.niso.org/committees/committee_au.html
  Technical Metadata for Digital Still Images

Dublin Core

- dublincore.org
  Dublin Core Metadata Initiative (DCMI)
- dublincore.org/documents/
  Dublin Core Metadata Initiative (DCMI) Documents
- dublincore.org/resources/bibliography/
  Dublin Core Metadata Initiative (DCMI) Bibliography
- dublincore.org/resources/faq/
  Dublin Core Metadata Initiative (DCMI) Frequently Asked Questions (FAQs)
- dublincore.org/workshops/
  Dublin Core Metadata Initiative (DCMI) Workshops
- www.ukoln.ac.uk/metadata/dcdot/
  Dublin Core Metadata Editor

- www.lub.lu.se/cgi-bin/nmdc.pl
  Dublin Core Metadata Template

- archive.dstc.edu.au/RDU/staff/jane-hunter/ECDL2/final.html
  Application of Metadata Standards to Video Indexing

Data Documentation Initiative (DDI) (Social Science Metadata)

- www.icpsr.umich.edu/DDI/
  Data Document Initiative (DDI) Home

- www.nsd.uib.no/Cessda/
  Council of European Social Science Data Archives

IEEE Computer Metadata Conferences

- www.computer.org/conferences/meta96/meta_home.html
  Metadata '96 Proceedings

- computer.org/proceedings/meta97/
  Metadata '97 Proceedings

- computer.org/proceedings/meta/1999/
  Metadata '99 Proceedings

World Wide Web Consortium (W3C.Org)

- www.w3.org
  W3C Home

- www.w3.org/Metadata/
  Metadata at W3C

- www.w3.org/RDF/
  Resource Description Framework (RDF)
  (framework for describing and interchanging
  metadata for the Web)

Digital Libraries

- www.ifla.org/II/metadata.htm
  Digital Libraries Metadata Resources

- www.dli2.nsf.gov/
  Digital Libraries Initiative Phase 2

Library of Congress

- www.loc.gov/standards/metadata.html
  Introduction to Metadata Elements: Library of Congress

- www.loc.gov/standards/
  Standards (Library of Congress)

- memory.loc.gov/ammem/techdocs/libt1999/libt1999.html
  Online Access to Pictorial Images (Library of Congress)

Other Metadata Links

- www.cimi.org
  Consortium for the Computer Interchange of
  Museum Information (CIMI)

- www.ukoln.ac.uk/metadata/
  UKOLN (UK Office for Library and
  Information Networking) Metadata

- metadata.net/
  Metadata.Net Home (tools and resources — funded by Australian government)

- www.dstc.edu.au/RDU/
  DSTC Resource Discovery Unit Home

- www.lib.helsinki.fi/meta/
  Nordic Metadata Projects

- www.getty.edu/research/institute/standards/intrometadata/index.html
  Getty Institute — Introduction to Metadata

- www.pads.ahds.ac.uk/padsUserNeedsMetadataWorkshopsFilmBallantyne.html
  Moving Image Collections

- www.rlg.org/preserv/presmeta.html
  RLG Working Group on Preservation Issues of Metadata

- dis.lib.muohio.edu/documents/
  Miami University Digital Information Services
  Cluster Documents

Section III: Distribution Architectures

CHAPTER 12

Asset and Content Management Tools and Standards

This chapter provides information that will help you understand content and asset management tools and standards. Content and asset management are deeply related topics, but they serve two distinct purposes:

- Asset management: Digital media asset management (DMAM), as it is known in the digital media business, is a repository of metadata (see Chapter 11) and media assets, both digital and analog, along with capture, analysis, management, and archival tools. While the budget for DMAM is justified based on a transition to digital media, physical tape and document archives can play a critical role in the overall success of a DMAM implementation.

- Content management (CM): This widely used term generally refers to tools that can be used to dynamically assemble and distribute published digital content — often in real time. Content management always draws on some form of asset management during the assembly process: an internal repository or often a third-party DMAM system or document management product.

The rapidly decreasing cost of both storage and availability of the out-of-the-box content management and DMAM and CM systems will mean that in the coming few years these systems will be affordable for smaller operations. This chapter aims to help organizations better understand the complexities of implementation and maintenance of these systems and decide between an internal system and an application service provider as the most cost-effective route. One option that is not covered is that of not having a digital asset strategy; it is presumed that every organization in tomorrow's media supply chain will require various aspects of these technologies.

Part A: Background

Introduction

The media asset management task has been organized around the process of reorganizing small bits of film and sound shot out of sequence into a linear story line. This process is highly evolved and pervasive, allowing new teams to be assembled for each new project without hampering productivity. The relatively new world of digital capture, editing, storage, and delivery is offering new opportunities — and a wide variety of new problems. Now that everything is digital (or soon will be), the expectation is that the job of creating stories will be faster, cheaper, and better than in the past. Additional complexity is partially driven by the appetite of a younger, faster-paced audience that enjoys fast-cut sound bytes and video bytes interspersed with digital graphics and animation. On the other hand, allowing participants to create a cohesive product without sitting in the same editing room or giving you the opportunity to deliver instant content delivery has created new opportunities.

The benefits of a complete digital media chain are inescapable but require the deployment of new collaborative and management tools that are designed to automate the newfound complexity. In order to realize the true benefits of digital media, the old processes must be left behind for a new, yet undefined process. Creating great content, not change management, is the job of directors, editors, and Web producers. Fortunately, an entire technology industry has attacked this new complexity with two technologies covered in this chapter: digital media asset management and content management.

Asset Versus Content Management

When you first hear about asset and content management, they sound like they are same; after all, your assets are content. But the two technologies are trying to solve fundamentally different problems. DMAM solutions such as Documentum's Bulldog or IBM's Digital Library primarily focus on search, archive, and distribution. Content management vendors such as Vignette for Web content and Convera for multimedia address the problem of dynamically organizing the distribution of content. In the Web space, the problem is one of effectively delivering dynamic HTML or streaming media. Content management systems in the broadcast space manage the play-to-air process by taking digital video directly from editing systems or asset management systems and sending the digital video to air. Both technologies are important to help create an organized workflow and fluid collaboration of content, and they are essential to the success of digitally based media assets as a whole.

It is also important to note that it is often difficult to draw the technological line dividing DMAM and CM in an organization and that many vendors are offering integrated solutions. The key to understanding and success in implementation is to recognize that where the line is drawn is unique to your company, project, and/or need. The only real rule to follow is to modularize functionality as much as possible in order to give yourself the option of upgrading just one piece of your system as your needs change.

From Creation to Distribution

DMAM is an important part of the whole digital media supply chain, while CM is most critical at the end of the chain. In the creation of content, the dailies, rough cuts, and finals are captured by a DMAM repository and coded with appropriate metadata to assist in workflow, security, and distribution. Workflow and collaboration tools route the work product instantly to the desktops involved in content creation or reuse of that content. DMAMs also help with the distribution of content by providing a secure high-performance method of delivering the content to the final distribution point.

While a content management system provides many of the same workflow and collaboration tools found in a DMAM, its focus is squarely on the problem of packaging content for delivery to the consumer. Content can be text-based, embedded in HTML pages for Web delivery, or streamed out over broadcast networks. Where digital content management comes into its own is in its ability to compose dynamic and interactive content in real time, within the context of the consumer's worldview. For example, if a Website knows that a viewer is interested in skateboarding, the content manager can automatically deliver a skateboarding link or banner ad, even though the reader is currently viewing an article about water-skiing. A content management system can compose content for future publishing based on predefined rules or can use a set of loose guidelines to edit and publish content on demand. DMAM and content management intersect in that the content manager is concerned with the rules of publishing content stored and retrieved from a DMAM.

Content on Schedule

The deployment of DMAM and content management together can greatly speed the delivery of content to the viewer. A news editor who codes a clip as final in DMAM is instantaneously making that clip available to a content management system for publishing. Broadcast content management systems can then automatically insert the content into preplanned spaces in the news broadcast for play to air. A Web producer need only create pages that understand a general context; there is no need to explicitly insert the clip because the content manager can find and deliver it using metadata and rules set up in advance by the Web producer. This has a profound effect on schedules and, if set up correctly, greatly reduces the chance of error.

Content on Demand

Distributing content on demand is no easy task. For example, a standard server and file system can serve limited streaming video, but providing a large volume of streaming content from a typical Web server is a recipe for failure and viewer frustration. A CM system, backed up by a well-configured DMAM system, can make this task easier. A DMAM system can deliver precisely the correct format when given viewer specs, such as viewers' bandwidth and media format requirements. Media can be delivered either directly from a high-performance file system (specially designed for the DMAM) or from a content delivery network, such as Akamai, that puts the content delivery point closer to the viewer and therefore increases reliability and scalability of content delivery.

Build-to-Order Content

The major reason for deploying an expensive content management system, rather than a simpler Web server solution, is to provide build-to-order content. The concept of build-to-order is subtler than it probably sounds. Giving the viewers what they ask for is effective only to the degree that you've given them the choices they desire. For a complete Website, the number of choices can be in the thousands. On a small scale (say, for just one Web page), presenting dynamic content may be doable. However, what if you wanted your entire Website, or all of your streaming newscasts for that matter, to be dynamically generated? How much programming would that require? And how would you ever approach the problem of dynamically serving content via traditional broadcast methods? Capturing viewer preference into a DMAM system potentially allows you to automatically tailor content for each individual viewer.

Many so-called content management systems can present dynamic information driven from a database, business rules, and a DMAM. A much more powerful system will understand the *context* of the situation in which the content is being provided. For example, imagine a headline video newscast that is composed of stories built from a personal profile as well as keyword searches. If a user searches for "Mars lander" stories and then immediately views a general-purpose video newscast, you might want to feature the sci-tech story on Mars first. The next day, the same user may view sci-tech at the end of the newscast because he or she hasn't recently searched on a sci-tech story. With today's content management systems, such constructions are surprisingly simple, especially if they are married with a DMAM and a strong metadata model.

Lessons From Other Industries

The statement "Been there, done that" is definitely flip, but it is also often a clue that the person saying it is someone you should be talking to. In that spirit, let's briefly look at some other industries and operational areas that have been dealing with problems similar to our own for a while now: document/image management, workflow management, supply chain management, and customer relationship management.

- Document management: The goal of document management (a close sibling of DMAM) is to share critical corporate information assets by making them secure, accessible, retrievable, and interoperable. Documents must be shareable regardless of the authoring medium — paper or electronic.

- Storage management: Putting your documents, or your media for that matter, in a digital repository is a great idea until you start to run out of physical storage. Even in these times of cheap magnetic storage, there are processes that can reduce your overall storage costs within the IT system and provide a safe digital archival policy within your organization. Storage management is software and hardware systems working together to provide a balance between performance and storage costs.

- Records management: Records management is the application of library sciences to document management and storage management. Knowing what gets archived, why, when, where, and for how long — and even what gets purged — is a complex field that can require not only expert advice but sophisticated IT support. Records management is the traffic cop at the intersection of document management and storage management. Interestingly, many DMAM and CM concepts are forms of records management, but few seem to realize that they are practicing library science when they are using these systems.

  Records are arguably the most important assets of an organization. If managers managed assets as poorly as they manage records, they would soon be tossed out by angry stockholders and employees. For example, Enron (and Arthur Anderson) did not appear to have a well-researched and strictly implemented records management program. Comprehensive programs provide employees with specific instructions on the handling and retention of records. They provide for the systematic disposal of obsolete, outdated, and duplicate records as a normal business activity based on researched business and legal requirements. In addition, they have specific procedures that call for suspension of all document disposal or destruction when there may be legal or some other action. Too bad it takes an Enron to get the point across.

- Workflow management: Both rote and ad hoc processes these days are carried out online, whether it be through email, chat rooms, or a more structured system. Unfortunately, in most organizations, too many structured processes, including meetings and informal discussions, are managed through decidedly manual means. Workflow management is customized software that manages processes within an organization, providing faster cycle times and higher accountability than manual methods.

- Supply chain management: Supply chain management helps to transform customer demand into vendor action as rapidly as possible. For example, if you are making computers, an increase (or decrease) in sales could affect your orders of memory chips in real time. In fact, using complex mathematical formulas, you could predict your memory chip requirements for the next ninety days based on just one week's sales data, and adjust your ongoing orders by looking at each week's demand. In the media business, supply chain management might allow you to optimize production schedules automatically based on the supply of talent, crew, or equipment for given dates.

- Customer relationship management (CRM): CRM was a very hot area throughout the late 1990s, and while passé on Wall Street, the need for CRM will continue to be critical to customer-oriented businesses. CRM refers to software that can capture customer interaction–related information and help to manage the organization's employees and processes to fulfill customer requirements, measure success, and then adjust processes to improve overall customer satisfaction. CRM is most often associated with customer service call centers, but it also includes Web-based client review applications for media production.

Universal Requirements

When reviewing DMAM and CM vendors, you'll no doubt encounter aspects of the product categories previously discussed. Whatever system you look at, you will have to make a choice based on the following:

- Proprietary versus open technologies: While many customers are looking to maintain their future options through more open standards, vendors yearn to own the market with proprietary technologies. In most cases, you'll really want a bit of both. Truly innovative technologies are often proprietary. Where openness becomes critical is the need for interoperability, the need to integrate best-of-breed systems at the lowest possible cost. If your content manager pressures you to purchase their DMAM product because of lack of the ability to interoperate with competing products through prevailing industry standards, you may well want to reconsider the whole purchase decision.

- Scalability: Nearly all vendors in the DMAM and content management market tout their overall scalability. White papers, diagrams, PowerPoint slides, and a torrent of sales-speak will be thrown at you to convince you that the entirety of AOL/Time Warner could be run on just 50 percent of their power. Forget the sales pitch. Make the vendor prove it. Independent testing is a good start, but only customer references substantially larger than your planned installation will prove the point.

- Customization: Not only does your company run differently than your competitors, it may not even resemble today's company in 18 months. If the vendor's answer to customizability is $100,000 in professional services today, realize that you might be spending $250,000 in 18 months to deal with a merger or acquisition. The more that products have built-in customizability, the more that professional services and retrofitting costs are reduced.

Designing for Feedback

When creating your repository and your content management, design them such that you can collect metrics on the effectiveness of your new digitally driven processes. Content management should serve a more strategic purpose than throwing together a fast Website; it should actively solicit and collect data that either automatically adjusts the effectiveness of your message or allows your organization to fine-tune the content management and even the entire supply chain. Ultimately, if you can't measure how effective the delivery tools are in helping you accomplish your mission, you can't determine your return on investment from all these new tools.

Workflow and Rules

A primary function of DMAM and CM solutions is to either enable or in some cases provide workflow that automatically routes assets to the location where they are most needed in order to keep the process moving. Despite similar processes among media producers, the key to success for a workflow provider is flexibility. DMAM solutions often provide workflow as part of the solution, although sometimes only through an integrated product sold separately. Workflow can be a great help, but only when it is designed to fit or improve an existing process, is flexible enough to handle exceptions in tight situations, and can adapt to process change in the organization. These can be major hurdles for the pervasive deployment of workflow in the organization. While the benefits of DMAM aren't dependent on a fully developed workflow implementation in the organization, they aren't fully realized without workflow either.

Workflow is a specific problem within the larger question of business rules in your organization. The DMAM solution should model the rules of engagement for media in various stages of development. For example, you may not wish account managers to have access to dailies – an example of access control. Similarly, you may want to ensure that all final cuts are automatically converted to both RealVideo and QuickTime streaming formats in a variety of bit rates. While the complete implementation of these rules may depend on third-party or custom software, it is critical that the DMAM solution provide the flexibility to support these business rules and that the DMAM vendor provide the professional services support necessary to implement them.

There are some workflow standards, principally supported by the Workflow Management Coalition (www.wfmc.org), that spell out how a DMAM solution, content manager, and third-party workflow system might interoperate. The standards, while in development for many years, have not significantly eased the integration of tools from multiple vendors. When putting together a custom solution, it is critical to have the direct assistance of either the vendors themselves or the integrators who have a close relationship and long history with those vendors.

The Warehouse

The term "data warehousing" refers both to the storage of assets and to the controlled access to those assets. A DMAM warehouse consists of the following components:

- Operational storage: Data used for active processes, production, or frequently accessed data needs to be kept on high-performance operational storage. This is either a subset or a totally separate entity from the general media storage, depending on the application and the installation.

- Metadata storage: Most often, text-based metadata is managed in a database system such as Oracle or Microsoft SQL Server that provides reliability, scalability, and performance. Conceptually, metadata often exists in XML formats as well, but this is not considered so much a storage format as a communications protocol between repositories.

- Financial and rights storage: It may not be wise to maintain financial and rights-related information along with metadata storage. At a low level, security information is often managed by the operating system itself. At an application level, credit card numbers or public encryption keys might be managed in a secure and separate database or even by separate employees in extreme cases.

- Media storage: Because digital media is often huge (measured in gigabytes and terabytes), traditional operating systems and storage hardware are insufficient. Media storage therefore consists of software and components to provide reliable high-performance storage at the lowest possible cost per gigabyte. Costs can be difficult to determine because the vendors, such as EMC, that wrap their storage in high-performance fault-tolerant boxes charge a premium when compared to vendors who only measure cost by the gigabyte.

A competent DMAM vendor will provide very specific guidelines for hardware purchases as well as the professional services necessary to integrate the components into a working system. Some vendors will even provide the hardware itself for one-stop shopping. While it is tempting to treat DMAM as a black box, a word of caution is in order. The components may be as expensive to maintain as they are to purchase. Often, a highly developed maintenance staff is necessary. Individual vendors, such as storage hardware vendors, may not be available on two hours notice when your system is down during a tight deadline.

Once your enterprise switches to digital, reliable operation of your DMAM will become as important as the lights and caffeine. Cutting costs on components here will certainly ensure that the enterprise experiences extreme frustrations later. It is not uncommon for an installation to run hundreds of thousands of dollars in hardware, software, and services, and it is possible for a production facility to spend more than $1 million to get the implementation right. It is also common for the approved budget to be busted wide open halfway through the implementation. The lesson here is to make sure to have at least one experienced manager who has successfully deployed a similar implementation and can counsel on both costs and technology. While a nonlinear editing, system may seem complex, the variety of options offered by vendors involved in creating DMAM solutions is much larger, and that complexity leads to surprises in many cases.

Asset Management Requirements for Digital Media Content

When purchasing a DMAM system, there are certain basic functionality expectations you should have. It is critical that you not only determine that the vendor delivers the features you need, but that you understand the particulars of how those feature work and that the features important to you work as you expect. This will require checking with reference accounts and eventually testing an in-house pilot implementation.

High-Level Requirements

There are some basic attributes necessary for a successful DMAM implementation (Grimes article, DAM 101):

- Customizability: Given the complexity of the task, the lack of standard processes for handling digital media, and the rapidly changing technology environment, the ability to customize is critical to realizing a long-term gain out of your investment.

- Cross-referencing: Digital media exists in more than just one form. Even if the asset is not stored in the database, the DMAM system must be able to easily locate the relevant versions and renderings of a given media asset.

- Security: Because one of the principal benefits of a DMAM system is to build an extranet or even public Internet presence using the media assets, security capabilities are critical. Security should extend beyond the reach of the DMAM system and its access control to include digital rights management.

- Accessibility: There's no point in incurring the considerable expense of a DMAM infrastructure if access is limited. The DMAM system should provide strong PC and Macintosh support as well as Web and high-end workstation support. Furthermore, if the system does not integrate into relevant legacy applications, a software development kit must be available to allow integrators to build an acceptable interface.

Functional Requirements

The basic functional requirements for DMAM are as follows:

- Capture: A simplistic solution should allow simple import from the local file system into the repository and manual and automatic coding of metadata during the capture transaction. A more developed solution will provide for multiple methods of capture and batch transcoding from a production format to a distribution format.

- NLE integration: Many DMAM solutions integrate with specific NLE systems to provide import/export from within the NLE user interface. This is a tremendous benefit, as moving between an NLE and a Web-based interface can be crude and frustrating even though this is exactly what some DMAM vendors expect of the user.

- Searching and browsing: All DMAM systems allow you to perform simple searches on textual metadata. You should look carefully at the full-text and specific-attribute searches that are available to ensure they meet the needs of your business. For example, closed-caption text can be a powerful method for locating archival clips. More sophisticated searches even allow searching on a theme, finding related media even when a keyword cannot be expressly located. Any customized metadata attributes should be as searchable as the predefined system attributes. Browsing search results and even the entire repository by thumbnails should also be available; pictures and clips often provide the fastest method of identifying a precise asset.

- Hierarchical storage management: Storage for DMAM systems is expensive, especially when measured in terabytes. A hierarchical storage management feature ensures that performance is balanced with cost efficiently. Production media for current projects should be kept online on fast storage and be available as close to the client workstation as possible from a network bandwidth perspective. Archival media should be kept on reliable but cheaper storage that may be considered low-bandwidth on first retrieval, but becomes readily accessible for subsequent requests. In some cases, archival to digital tape or optical jukebox may be appropriate.

- Interoperability: Digital media is often transmitted in large quantities. Imagine the number of raw footage and audio assets necessary to edit just 10 minutes of a sci-fi thriller. Import and export of batches of content to third-party systems such as NLEs, content management systems, or programming platforms may be necessary. An appropriate solution will import and export both media and metadata using industry-standard formats, whether that is OMF, QuickTime, or XML.

- Content management integration: Truthfully, given today's convergence of vendors and solutions, if you are planning on publishing digital media from your DMAM, you should seek a DMAM solution that is fully integrated with a content management system and not assume interoperability between diverse pieces or have to depend on a software development kit. You can expect top-tier DMAM vendors to team with or be acquired by content management vendors. Examples include Documentum's acquisition of Bulldog and Artesia's partnership with Vignette.

- Annotation: A DMAM solution should provide adequate annotation capabilities for the types of media you will be managing. An image management system could use an off-the-shelf TIFF viewer with annotation features. Digital video annotation should allow keyframe commenting and sensible storage of that in metadata.

- Access control: Any DMAM system should have strong access control; more capable systems will have exclusionary security so that you can set up Chinese walls within your organization. Since various departments in your organization run their operations differently, investigate the customizability of the access control system. Sensitive data should be segmented onto private hardened storage and provide at least 128-bit encryption ciphers.

- Disconnected use/mobility: What facilities are in place for users, particularly reviewers, to view content offline? What kind of workflow processing is available offline?

- User interface (UI): Each department looks at its media differently. Some see projects where others see programming, and the various views can be orthogonal. Look at the UI from the perspective of every department and understand what kinds of customizations you'll have to make and what types of segmentation choices you'll have with the DMAM UI. Also look at the depth of the UI: Is the account manager's interface as complex as the editor's? Sure, the UI can handle video editing, but can it handle interactive videos with hot spots?

Miscellaneous Requirements

Other requirements you may want to consider:

- User-configurable light box layout (columns, rows, and thumbnail size)
- Real-time editing of metadata
- Batch offline editing of metadata
- Single file upload
- Batch file upload (probably handled as part of the vendor's conversion process)
- Multiple file download (useful in the editing process)
- Pass codes to invite customers or partners to a project
- Multiple user accounts per project
- Data mining and activity reports
- Search for images by color, shape, or texture

Content Management Requirements for Digital Media Content

When you've already selected a DMAM vendor and are looking at content management, you first have to decide what you are expecting out of content management. There are several classes of content management, which can be generalized as follows:

- Generalized publishing solutions: Vendors such as Vignette and Interwoven build content management solutions that help traditional media outlets and content aggregators build carrier-class Websites. An example is CNET, which helped develop the Vignette solution, and uses the StoryServer product to dynamically compose pages around its feature stories. CNET also produces video content for broadcast on cable and the Web, and its video clips are dynamically (by keyword matching) linked from related text-based stories. These pages are then syndicated to major Web portals such as Yahoo!

- Digital media content management: This is a relatively new area and there are many different perspectives, depending on the type of content and the media formats. For consumer applications such as online radio and newscasts, consider an application that can interrogate DMAM metadata and automatically construct a custom playlist on the fly. For e-learning, Webcasts, and other multimedia presentations, more complex or customized solutions may be required.

- E-commerce for media: Syndicators such as Sekani sell media content over the Web. The primary function of the company Website is to allow easy searching of stock footage that can be purchased on a royalty basis. The key here is that Sekani sells its content in a variety of analog and digital formats. Its e-commerce content management engine must link the purchase type to the desired format in the DMAM.

- Intranet/extranet solutions: Vendors such as Documentum primarily sell their content management solutions to big businesses such as pharmaceutical companies to manage the voluminous documentation associated with their products. Often, manufacturers need to publish product specifications, training, and marketing materials via the Web. Such a solution might allow a physician to view a marketing video regarding a new drug or an airline mechanic to see a training video on repairing a jet engine. While the problem is much the same as for the Web publishers, there are differences, and in many cases the content management component costs significantly less for this type of solution.

Within each of these categories, the requirements are as diverse as the customer base. The key requirement is that the content management vendor — through predefined integration points or professional services — provides consumers with just the digital media content they want.

Specific and in-depth requirements for content management for broadcast and cable, postproduction, and Web production is beyond the scope of this book. However, many of the vendors and resources listed in the next section provide extensive information, through both product literature and white papers, to get you started.

One piece of advice we can offer you is to understand that DMAM and CM implementations are people and organizational problems as well as technology problems. Those of us who have implemented a number of content management systems have learned that all implementations have three challenges in common:

1. Infrastructure problems (or the "Do you really *need* to handle 500 million Web page views a month?" types of questions)

2. Processes, or the complete lack thereof

3. People, who are often very territorial (as in "There is *no way* that I am going to make my project accessible to *anyone* I don't approve of until it expresses my true vision. And, on top of that, there is no way that I will allow anyone to modify my content either," followed by "*Particularly if they aren't part of my union*")

Part B: Tools

Digital Asset Management Vendors

The vendors represented here have solutions that range from as low as $25,000 to as high as $5 million. The solutions have been divided into three categories, depending on your budget and needs.

Building-Block Solutions

The tools described in Table 12-1 are designed to provide you with a core set of functionality that you can customize for your needs. Expect to hire programmers to develop solutions based on these tools.

Table 12-1: Building-Block Solutions

Company	Description	Product(s)	URL
Agari MediaWare	Agari MediaWare is a software company that has developed a middleware platform for the integration of rich media digital content applications. Product emphasis is on the development of Java 2 Enterprise Edition components that can be used to create custom digital management solutions.	Media Star Suite	www.agarimediaware.com/products/product.html
Chuckwalla	Chuckwalla produces a file management system component that supports rich media.	FileSmart	www.chuckwalla.com/products.html
Extensis	Extensis is widely known for its productivity software for graphic and media professionals. Extensis products are low-cost and do a lot to help with mixed-media environments where graphics are integral to the customer.	Extensis Portfolio 5	www.extensis.com/portfolio/

Table 12-1: Building-Block Solutions (Continued)

Company	Description	Product(s)	URL
SGI	SGI's entry into digital media asset management is the StudioCentral product. This product is fairly lightweight with only a basic feature set. For advanced users, SGI's integration of its Origin servers with Ascential's Media360 product suite is the preferred route (see Ascential in Table 12-3).	SGI StudioCentral Library	www.sgi.com/solutions/broadband/dam.html www.sgi.com/software/ascential.html

Middleware Solutions

The tools described in Table 12-2 are designed to provide a layer between a storage subsystem and a third-party database system. Depending on the underlying database, the tools can be very powerful.

Table 12-2: Middleware Solutions

Company	Description	Product(s)	URL
Artesia	Artesia provides a digital asset management middleware system based on an Oracle database. Designed to be easily integrated with third-party software packages that provide storage and distribution through the support of a number of standards, it provides a searching/metadata infrastructure within a nice user interface.	TEAMS	www.artesia.com/teams_overview.html
Documentum (BullDog)	BullDog has developed an integration layer between a number of third-party products such as Virage's VideoLogger, Convera's RetrievalWare, and Sony's NewsBase and PetaServe products, which in combination form a digital media asset management system.	Documentum 4i eBusiness Platform	www.bulldog.com/ www.documentum.com/

Table 12-2: Middleware Solutions (Continued)

Company	Description	Product(s)	URL
EMC	EMC is primarily a manufacturer of large-scale storage systems such as Optical Jukeboxes, RAID arrays, and CD/DVD systems. EMC has in recent years developed applications to leverage its storage sales by addressing various industry applications such as digital asset management, though this is not its core business.	Cellara Media Server Symmetrix	www.emc.com/ horizontal/ rich_content_products _mams.jsp
Enscaler, Inc.	Enscaler provides middleware to allow for the integration of digital media assets in applications. The middleware is organized into functional suites.	MediaScaler	www.enscaler.com/ solutions/ mediascaler.htm
Kasenna	Kasenna's rich-media platform is marketed under the product brand name MediaBase. Currently, two products are available: MediaBase Enterprise Edition powers centralized deployments where a single scalable server provides on-demand and live video delivery services on LAN and private networks. MediaBase Network Edition enables distributed deployments (origin-server/edge-server or NOC/head-end) where a group of coordinated servers provides services to a large geographically dispersed user community. The MediaBase products use either an Informix or Oracle database as their base on top of which the MediaBase middleware is added.	Kasenna MediaBase	www.kasenna.com/ products/

Complete Solutions

The tools described in Table 12-3 are designed to provide you with a suite of applications, tied to an underlying database system, that will give you all the functionality you require. Because these are complete tool sets, they are often very expensive.

Table 12-3: Complete Solutions

Company	Description	Product(s)	URL
Ascential	A very flexible DMAM system, Kasenna (see Middleware Solutions) partners with Ascential when the needs of the client exceeds Kasenna's MediaBase capabilities. SGI also partners with Ascential to provide the SGI DMAM solution using a combination of SGI Origin servers and Media 360.	Media 360	www.media360.com/ products/media360/ m360_core.html
Autodesk (Discreet)	A set of enabling technologies supports Discreet's Start-to-Finish Production Environment. These infrastructure technologies enable you to power up your workstations, better manage your workflow, and boost your facility's all-around productivity.	jobnet (designed to work with Discreet's product line and storage)	www.discreet.com/ products/infrastr/
Avid	A powerful browser-based media asset management application that allows easy facility-wide and remote searching, sorting, management, and retrieval of media.	Avid Unity Media Manager (designed to work with Avid's product line and storage)	www.avid.com/products/ unity_mediasvc/index.html
Broadcast Electronics	Broadcast Electronics, specifically the AudioVault division, specializes in audio digital asset management. Broadcast Electronics has been in business since 1959 when it developed tools for AM/FM radio broadcasting. The AudioVault division is BE's foray into the digital media space.	SonixStream WebVault VaultExpress AudioPoint	www.audiovault.com/

Table 12-3: Complete Solutions (Continued)

Company	Description	Product(s)	URL
Broadvision	Broadvision is a provider of a suite of integrated content management applications best known for managing complex enterprise Web systems. If you are involved in a deployment where you will be publishing significant amounts of mixed content to the Web, this is probably one to look at. It partners with most of the large vendors and top integrators, also offering support for other distribution venues including wireless. It provides sophisticated e-commerce and billing solutions.	BroadVision Content Management Solutions	www.broadvision.com
Convera	Convera products let users capture video; browse visual summaries; catalog content using metadata, annotations, closed-caption text, and voice sound tracks; search for precise video clips using text and image clues; create rough cuts and EDLs for further production; and publish those video assets to the Web for streaming. In addition to the Screening Room DMAM, Convera also develops content management software known as RetrievalWare and RetrievalWare WebExpress.	Screening Room	www.convera.com/ Products/index.asp
CYCLOP Intl.	CYCLOP produces six different variants of its digital media asset management system to satisfy the entertainment, museum, still image (photographic), tourism/ film, Internet, and library markets.	CYCLOPe CYCLOPm CYCLOPsi CYCLOPl CYCLOPl CYCLOPli	www.cyclop.ca/

Table 12-3: Complete Solutions (Continued)

Company	Description	Product(s)	URL
e-Motion	e-Motion provides a collaborative environment for storing and searching for digital assets in a project-based environment. e-Motion uses third-party storage options such as Oracle 8i, Avid Unity, and VERITAS.	MediaPartner Global Brand Manager	www.emotion.com/products/index.html
IBM	IBM has some of the most advanced management systems incorporating supercomputer technology built around the DB2 database engine. However, it is also building low-end systems for small and medium-size broadcasters and rich-media publishers. It also offers a strong consulting group to help with the installation.	Content Manager V7.1 VideoCharger V7.1 WebSphere	www.ibm.com/software/data/cm/cmgr/
IKnowledge	The ActiveContent Suite consists of 10 modules that support the entire application management process from content management and content aggregation to complete application archiving and application management. The modules are accessible via a customizable workflow engine that enables businesses to define their own workflow process and assign permissions to users to access the suite and participate in the process from any browser-based PC or MAC.	ActiveContent Suite	www.iknowledge.com/solutions/activecontentsuite.htm
Interwoven, Inc.	Interwoven has been building a portfolio of companies and products and is putting together solutions addressing content aggregation, content collaboration, content management, content intelligence, and content distribution. It aims at enterprise and brand management companies.	Interwoven TeamSite 5.5	www.interwoven.com/products/teamsite/

Table 12-3: Complete Solutions (Continued)

Company	Description	Product(s)	URL
Liberate Technologies	Liberate Technologies is the leading provider of interactive TV content production and management systems. Most major cable and satellite television operators, telecommunications companies, and Internet service providers use the Liberate software for their interactive services. These interactive digital services include enhanced TV broadcasts, electronic program guides, video-on-demand, personalized content (including local news, weather, and other information), TV chat, instant messaging, digital video recording, and more.	Liberate TV Producer Liberate TV Producer Compact Liberate VOD Gateway	solutions.liberate.com/products/tv_producer.html solutions.liberate.com/products/vod_gateway.html
Lysis	Lysis has been providing digital asset management solutions since 1993 specifically in the broadcast and interactive TV environment. Lysis is a direct competitor to Liberate.	Lysis On Demand Lysis Broadcast Lysis Smart Content	www.lysis.com/html/h_solutions/products.html
North Plains Systems	North Plains Systems is a provider of fully integrated and scalable digital asset management solutions. It is fairly new on the scene, but very savvy and working with some of the largest media holdings such as National Geographic.	Telescope Enterprise Telescope Workgroup	www.northplains.com/products/default.html
Sonic Foundry (MediaSite)	Sonic Foundry acquired Media-Site in mid-October 2001. The MediaSite product line consists of middleware layers that sit on top of a Web server to provide a basic DMAM system with emphasis on Web distribution.	Rich Media Application Server Suite	www.mediasite.com/corporateweb/products/application_server_suite.html

Table 12-3: Complete Solutions (Continued)

Company	Description	Product(s)	URL
thePlatform	thePlatform makes delivering media in the proven TV and radio playlist formats affordable. Features: Web-based playlist creation integrated with media management Dynamic real-time playlist creation Set-specific slots to be filled based on categories Creation of entire playlists in real time via the APIs Automatic synchronization of collateral media Automatic publishing (and updating) of all files in a playlist Automatic removal of unused content from delivery servers (to manage costs)	Digital media Web service	www.theplatform.com/digitalmediawebservice.asp.asp
Thomson Multimedia (purchased Grass Valley Group; expect integration of product lines)	The ContentShare platform presents an innovative approach to the complex problem of application integration and digital asset management. It establishes a common language that allows applications to request information and assets from each other without having to know how that information is stored. The ContentShare platform also decreases integration time and significantly reduces the costs associated with software development for integrated systems.	ContentShare	www.grassvalley-group.com/products/software/contentshare

Table 12-3: Complete Solutions (Continued)

Company	Description	Product(s)	URL
VideoSpheres	VideoSpheres VSP^{Plus} is an integrated digital media asset management, subscriber management, and workflow platform. The system is designed with built-in e-commerce features to enable telco-style billing and payments back to content providers. This product is designed to allow service providers to deploy rich-media asset services over broadband and wireless networks.	VideoSpheres VSP^{Plus}	www.videospheres.com/products.html
Vignette	Vignette is a provider of integrated content management applications best known for managing complex Websites. If you are involved in a deployment where you will be publishing significant amounts of mixed content to the Web, this is probably one to look at. It partners with most of the large vendors and top integrators and also offers support for other distribution venues including interactive TV and games. It has very rich personalization options and is very scalable.	Vignette Content Suite	www.vignette.com/
Virage	Virage provides organizations with advanced methods for automatically extracting metadata from content and for accessing media assets. Virage is a high-profile name in the image and video search area. It partners with a number of smaller companies and also makes its API available so it has a number of plug-ins to help customize its solutions.	Virage Video Application Server	www.virage.com/products/products-server.html

Content Management Vendors

The vendors represented here have solutions that range in price. These solutions have been divided into three categories, depending on your budget and needs.

Building-Block Solutions

The tools described in Table 12-4 are designed to provide you with a core set of functionality that you can customize for your needs. Expect to hire programmers to develop solutions based on these tools.

Table 12-4: Building-Block Solutions

Company	Description	Product(s)	URL
Chrystal Software	Chrystal Software provides XML content management software, and if you are in corporate media, might be one to look at.	Astoria	www.chrystal.com/
Lariat	Lariat has produced the StationManager product to allow content to be stored, arranged in playlists, and broadcast according to scheduling based on channels. Lariat has an electronic program guide (EPG) functionality that simulates television channel programming but for streaming media.	Lariat StationManager	www.lariat.com/ stationmgr/index.htm

Mid-Level Solutions

The tools described in Table 12-5 are designed to provide a layer between a storage subsystem and a third-party database system. Depending on the underlying database, the tools can be very powerful.

Table 12-5: Mid-Level Solutions

Company	Description	Product(s)	URL
Context Media	Context Media is a provider of syndication and licensing middleware to allow content providers to package their content and apply business rules to those packages to fulfill access and commercial requirements. Context Media also provides CDN support of Akamai through its EdgeShare product.	Interchange Platform Context Builder IBuilder EdgeShare	www.contextmedia.com/ products/index.html

Table 12-5: Mid-Level Solutions (Continued)

Company	Description	Product(s)	URL
Documen-tum (Bull-Dog)	BullDog was recently acquired by Documentum, Inc., as part of its enterprise content management (ECM) vision. Documentum plans to use the BullDog integration technology to provide brand new offerings within the Documentum ECM portfolio.	BullDog Two.Seven	www.bulldog.com/ www.documentum.com/
iVast	iVast is a vendor of delivery and content management systems for rich-media content using the MPEG-4 standard. The solution is designed to reach a wide range of end-user devices including PCs and consumer electronic devices such as cellular phones and set-top boxes.	iVast Server iVast System-ware iVast StudioTools	www.ivast.com/
Microsoft	Content Management Server 2001 empowers content providers to manage their own content, provides site users with a targeted and personalized experience tailored to their profiles and browsing devices, and enables IT departments to quickly deploy scalable dynamic sites.	Microsoft Content Management Server	www.microsoft.com/ cmserver/

Complete/High-End Solutions

The tools described in Table 12-6 are designed to provide you with a suite of applications, giving you a complete solution set. Because these are complete tool sets, they are often very expensive.

Table 12-6: Complete/High-End Solutions

Company	Description	Product(s)	URL
Avid	Avid AirSPACE video servers provide a high-quality, high-reliability ingest and play-to-air solution for broadcast news applications. Avid AirSPACE's flexibility allows it to be used in an Avid NewsCutter with Unity for News environment or as a stand-alone unit with traditional cuts-only editing equipment. It also can fulfill applications such as Spot and Program play to air, Feed Room Ingest, act as a key piece in asset storage and archival solutions, or as a high-quality multichannel media server.	Avid AirSPACE	www.avid.com/products/airspace/index.html
Broadcast Electronics	Broadcast Electronics, specifically the AudioVault division, specializes in audio digital asset management. Broadcast Electronics has been in business since 1959 when it developed tools for AM/FM radio broadcasting. The AudioVault division is BE's foray into the digital media space.	SonixStream WebVault VaultExpress AudioPoint	www.audiovault.com/
Convera	In addition to the Screening Room DMAM product, Convera also develops content management software.	Retrieval-Ware WebExpress	www.convera.com/Products/index.asp
Eprise (Divine)	Eprise has been recently acquired by Divine, Inc., as of December 5, 2001. Eprise provides content management solutions primarily for Web content. Divine has acquired Eprise to augment its other collaboration and e-commerce solutions. Divine is an enterprise system integrator.	Eprise Participant Server	www.eprise.com/ www.divine.com/

Table 12-6: Complete/High-End Solutions (Continued)

Company	Description	Product(s)	URL
IBM	IBM has some of the most advanced management systems incorporating supercomputer technology built around the DB2 database engine. However, it is also building low-end systems for small and medium-size broadcasters and rich-media publishers. It also offers a strong consulting group to help with the installation.	Content Manager V7.1 Video-Charger V7.1 WebSphere	www.ibm.com/software/data/cm/cmgr/
IKnowledge	The ActiveContent Suite consists of 10 modules that support the entire application management process from content management and content aggregation to complete application archiving and application management. The modules are accessible via a customizable workflow engine that enables businesses to define their own workflow process and assign permissions to users to access the suite and participate in the process from any browser-based personal computer.	ActiveContent Suite	www.iknowledge.com/solutions/activecontentsuite.htm
Interwoven, Inc.	Interwoven has been building a portfolio of companies and products and is putting together solutions addressing content aggregation, content collaboration, content management, content intelligence, and content distribution. It aims at enterprise and brand management companies.	Interwoven TeamSite 5.5	www.interwoven.com/products/teamsite/
Liberate Technologies	Liberate Technologies is the leading provider of interactive TV content production and management systems. Most major cable and satellite television operators, telecommunications companies, and Internet service providers use the Liberate software for their interactive services. These interactive digital services include enhanced TV broadcasts, electronic program guides, video-on-demand, personalized content (including local news, weather, and other information), TV chat, instant messaging, digital video recording, and more.	Liberate TV Producer Liberate TV Producer Compact Liberate VOD Gateway	solutions.liberate.com/products/tv_producer.html solutions.liberate.com/products/vod_gateway.html

Table 12-6: Complete/High-End Solutions (Continued)

Company	Description	Product(s)	URL
Odetics Broadcast	Odetics Broadcast, Inc., headquartered in Anaheim, CA, is a pioneer and leading supplier of enterprise content management and delivery solutions for the television, cable, and satellite industries. Odetics Broadcast provides sophisticated multichannel video management systems, including hierarchical asset management systems that couple the high-capacity archival advantages of tape libraries with the speed and immediacy of video servers.	AIRO Broadcast Automation System	www.odetics.com/ODETA/broadcast.html www.odeticsbroadcast.com
Sonic Foundry (MediaSite)	By using the Rich Media Publisher Suite product, digital assets can be combined in a manner not unlike Microsoft's Publisher product and then streamed from the MediaSite Application Server suite.	Rich Media Publisher Suite	www.mediasite.com/corporateweb/products/publisher.html
thePlatform	thePlatform makes delivering media in the proven TV and radio playlist formats affordable. Features: Web-based playlist creation integrated with media management Dynamic real-time playlist creation Set-specific slots to be filled based on categories Create entire playlists in real time via the APIs Automatic synchronization of collateral media Automatic publishing (and updating) of all files in a playlist Automatic removal of unused content from delivery servers (to manage costs)	Digital media Web service	www.theplatform.com/dynamicpresenta-tions.asp
Thomson Multimedia (purchased Grass Valley Group so expect integration of product lines)	NewsQ lets you enter a running order of stories and clips quickly, cue them, and trigger them for play to air. The WebAble tool suite offers a drag-and-drop method for creating streaming media from the content of a Profile XP Media Platform.	Grass Valley NewsQ Grass Valley WebAble	www.grassvalley-group.com/products

Standards Organizations

Three organizations are listed in Table 12-7. They are among the most widely known; however, there are hundreds of efforts going on across the globe having to do with content and asset management.

Table 12-7: Standards Organizations

Organization	Description	URL
Moving Pictures Experts Group (MPEG) (ISO/IEC JTC1 SC29 WG11)	A working group of ISO/IEC in charge of the development of standards for coded representation of digital audio and video established in 1988. The group has produced MPEG-1, the standard on which such technologies as Video CD and MP3 are based; MPEG-2, the standard on which such technologies as digital television set-top boxes and DVD are based; MPEG-4, the standard for multimedia for the fixed and mobile Web; and MPEG-7, the standard for the description and search of audio and visual content. Work on the new standard MPEG-21 Multimedia Framework started in June 2000. So far a Technical Report has been produced, and the formal approval process has already begun for two more parts of the standard. Several Calls for Proposals have already been issued, and two working drafts are being developed.	mpeg.telecomi-talialab.com/ www.mpeg.org MPEG Pointers and Resources (Reference site for MPEG) www.mpeg.org/MPEG/starting-points.html MPEG Starting Points and FAQs www.faqs.org/faqs/compression-faq/part2/section-2.html Introduction to MPEG
World Wide Web Consortium (W3C)	The World Wide Web Consortium was created in October 1994 to lead the World Wide Web to its full potential by developing common protocols that promote its evolution and ensure its interoperability. W3C has more than 500 member organizations from around the world and has earned international recognition for its contributions to the growth of the Web. The W3C is responsible for the development of the eXtensible Markup Language (XML). The eXtensible Markup Language (XML) is the universal format for structured documents and data on the Web.	www.w3.org/ www.w3.org/XML/
Workflow Management Coalition	It spells out how a DMAM, content manager, and third-party workflow system might interoperate.	www.wfmc.org

Part C: Methods

Implementation of DMAM and CM Systems

Server and Storage

The hardware requirements of DMAM/CM systems can be considerable. The most obvious expense is reliable storage, where a storage server, its specialized I/O equipment and software, can cost in the hundreds of thousands of dollars all by itself. The requirements for CPU and operating system, database servers, backups, Web server farms, and more can run the initial cost of the hardware alone above $1 million for a fully loaded solution. All of that equipment is often duplicated in other facilities backed by battery and fuel-driven power generation. It's not hard to see why smaller businesses must seriously consider outsourced solutions.

Small systems for simple Web content management and e-commerce can be much less, with no special requirements above and beyond a normal Web server. Couple this with inexpensive fault-tolerant storage and a small DMAM system and you could easily serve a few hundred visitors a day or a few Web-resolution video streams. Be aware, however, that as volume of data and simultaneous transactions increase, so does the complexity of the storage and server requirements.

At the very high end are vendors such as EMC and Hitachi that sell the Cadillacs of storage. Installation of these storage solutions is incredibly expensive, but the performance and capacity are unrivaled. Dell, IBM, and others are also competing in this market, with varying market share.

Databases

Most DMAM vendors support at least two database vendors for storing and searching on metadata and other relational database tasks, and many support other database vendors. Oracle is supported by practically every vendor as the industrial-strength solution, but a fully functioning Oracle installation is expensive to set up and maintain and should only be considered by sites with an extremely large transaction volume. Most vendors also support Microsoft SQL Server, which is a fine choice for the vast majority of installations, particularly for internal or extranet use and even for mid-tier Websites.

Access Tools

Editing tools to help control access are going to range from a stripped-down Final Cut Pro out in the field to a full-blown finishing station. In addition, any tool that adds metadata information about the media, such as logging tools for librarians or tools for financial modeling, will help the process of categorizing and cataloguing the media.

What is important to understand about any tool that adds metadata about the digital media you are working with is the ability of those tools and the metadata they generate to interoperate with all the other tools and metadata you use. Generating good metadata is critical, but just as critical is reading and using that metadata from within a variety of different tools.

Web browser–based user interfaces are the de facto standard with both DMAM and CM. This is a blessing and a liability. Browser technology benefits vendors because it can potentially provide a simple method of supporting a large number of client platforms with minimal testing. Multiplatform support is particularly important to DMAM vendors whose customers represent a large proportion of the Macintosh market.

The problem with browser technology is the rather difficult user interfaces presented to the end user. These interfaces — particularly the input of new media into a repository — are so troublesome to some users that they make infusion of the DMAM into existing processes painful and slow. Making sure that your end users are comfortable with the user interface, and that it does not slow down interactions with existing tools such as NLEs, is critical to a successful implementation.

Security

Security implementation is never straightforward. The most important thing to remember is that the security provided by the applications themselves is rarely as important as the security surrounding your network. If security is a critical factor to your implementation, make sure that you have IT security experts review your implementation plans and test each deployment to ensure that the latest security precautions are in place. If you are in a position where you could be sued by the people whose media you are working on, consider hiring an outside security audit firm to perform an in-depth analysis of your security and to show that you have engaged in the utmost due diligence to ensure your system is secure.

Media Archiving and Management

Understanding your management and organizational requirements first can save substantial money and time in the installation of DMAM and CM.

Digital media management is the discipline of determining the value of each asset to the organization, determining how they are filed, how long they must be retained, and when they must be purged. Another major issue is the archival format: In 50 years, how easy will it be to view a QuickTime 4 video clip? A combination of library sciences, general counsel, content producers, and other company directors and managers must agree on a basic digital media management framework and a change-management plan to deal with new media types and project types. For smaller organizations, these issues may be fairly simple to solve because there are a limited number of uses for the DMAM. But for larger organizations such as the growing number of mega-media giants, a team of digital media experts should be very much involved in the planning of the DMAM and CM installations.

One or Many Warehouses

How many repositories does an organization need? DMAM implementations are expensive, and the fewer the better, many would believe. It's also tempting to try to build an über-warehouse. Unfortunately, in a large organization, this is a recipe for disaster. The most obvious concern is access speed; the cost of providing high-bandwidth access to all users of a single DMAM repository may be more costly and unreliable than having multiple repository installations. Even in a single location, though, the differences in working styles and business rules between departments — and company politics — may dictate multiple installations, even when an enterprise DMAM license has been secured. This is because the customizations required for one department may conflict with the customizations for another.

To a certain extent, these decisions are driven by the limitations of the individual products. There is very little that customers can do about this other than continue to communicate with the vendors, letting them know where the opportunities for further flexibility in customization will help to simplify the enterprise implementations.

Network Choices for Creation and Management of Content

Internet

Smaller organizations can effectively rely on outsourcing for their DMAM and can use the Internet as their corporate WAN when security and network bandwidth aren't major issues. This covers a wide variety of businesses and is typical when there is only a handful of employees in each location. Just know that the bandwidth usage of even 10 users on a video library can consume all of your bandwidth at the worst possible time, such as during the last days of a project deadline.

Private Networks

Many DMAM hosting facilities operate their own private networks that provide high bandwidth. The issue here may be geography — not all private networks have the global reach that a business may require.

Extranets

Running an extranet, particularly to support the high-bandwidth requirements of digital media, means you're operating your own telecommunications department. This is sometimes necessary for mission-critical work or to reach geographic areas not handled by a private network.

Wireless

Support for wireless applications on cell phones and personal digital assistants (PDAs) — both for intranet workflow and consumer distribution—will require specialized networking equipment and management applications. Just because a content management vendor has a wireless strategy doesn't mean that it has the expertise to help you install a wireless infrastructure for your distribution channel.

Transaction and Commerce Planning

As you plan your DMAM and content management rollout, even as you construct a Request for Proposal (RFP) from vendors, understand that these systems aren't a Swiss Army knife. While vendors may recognize common ancillary requirements, and even acquire potentially best-of-breed vendors to meet those requirements, they may not meet *your* requirements. Here are some systems that you may want to consider from an alternate vendor:

- Digital rights management: See Chapter 13 for more information on this important topic.

- Clearinghouses: If you are involved in large transactions, you may want to consider some kind of escrow clearinghouse. The clearinghouse accepts the money for an item from the buyer, the seller is notified that the money is on deposit, and the seller then sends the item to the buyer. If the buyer finds the item acceptable, the escrow house releases the funds to the seller.

- E-commerce: Most Web-based content management vendors have a strong e-commerce connection, but if your primary reason for installing a content manager is e-commerce, you may want to consider an online catalog application that can interface to a strong DRM platform.

Legacy Concerns

DMAM and CM installations, if you haven't figured it out yet, take a lot of planning and can take a long time to implement. You *will* have to transition in new media with the old. Don't think you can abandon your analog gear; you're going to need most of that gear to continue your processes after the DMAM is in place, to maintain access to your analog library (which may be cataloged in the DMAM but probably won't be contained there), and to quickly respond to situations that weren't handled as part of your implementation planning.

If you already have a digital library and you are converting, you'll want to carefully understand what the batch conversion process will be, and what you'll lose in the process.

Outsourcing the Process

Part B of this chapter, detailing tools and implementation issues, should have thoroughly convinced you that DMAM and CM are difficult issues to tackle, even for experienced IT departments. A small networked installation will require a team composed of internal implementers and support staff from various vendors. A larger installation can easily involve 6 to 12 IT professionals for months. Ongoing maintenance will definitely require a network administrator and possibly a dedicated team.

For some facilities and integrated media organizations, the control and security provided by internal implementations make it well worth the trouble to keep implementation and maintenance in-house.

For smaller media producers, or organizations that are highly dispersed and whose business is based on relatively small projects — such as ad agencies — outsourcing may be the answer. Some of the factors to consider are the following:

*   Access speed: Hosted application service providers (ASPs) usually deliver their product via dedicated communications lines or virtual private networks (VPNs), although fully private network solutions are available. While these networks can provide adequate speed for streaming media and archival purposes, they do not necessarily scale to handle the most demanding applications. This is particularly true in media and broadcast production since most of these providers focus on the more traditional content and data processing applications. Many of the concepts, standards, and challenges necessary for managing media assets for production or broadcast are unknown to many ASPs. Latency, quality, and real-time response are some of the critical questions any service provider should be able to address. In many cases you will find that their expertise extends only to streaming media. Also realize that if critical media is hosted offsite and is only available via the network, then a failure point controlled by your service provider has been introduced.

*   Customizability: By their very nature, hosted applications have fewer customization choices. For straightforward applications, this may not matter, but picking a vendor and then requesting customization can be costly. However, having the service provider customize your systems for your workflow and media can be a cost-effective solution in the long run. The providers have access to network and programming talent that

may not readily be available, and many will also include support and upgrades as part of an overall package. Think of it as using an equipment rental house for your larger-scale networked applications and media management.

- Integration: Streamlining internal processes is one of the major benefits of digital media. Integration can become a challenge with hosting providers, particularly with workflow that changes with each project or media authoring applications that require a certain level of throughput. Where the challenges of integration with another organization become worthwhile is often in the areas of rights management and transaction management (discussed in Chapter 13). Another integration challenge that many facilities are facing now, or will be in the future, is that of complying with a large content owner's networked workflow. Many of the larger content owners and distributors are taking the first steps to define integrated workflows for their suppliers and partners in order to ensure an end-to-end digital media chain (see Chapter 14 for a more complete discussion).

- Cost: The major benefit of an ASP solution is the overall cost of implementation and maintenance. While the ASP fees may seem steep, when compared to an in-house implementation in a small to medium-size organization, they are often a great bargain.

- Speed of implementation: ASPs can often have an account set up in days or even hours, particularly if you are concentrating on streaming media and transaction processing. However, if the ASP is unfamiliar with media and broadcast requirements, the ASP may take longer than building your own solution.

When considering an ASP or even just an Internet provider, ask if it has a media and broadcast division. Many of the larger regional and global providers have set up specialized units for the media and entertainment industry. The local sales rep may not be able to answer your questions, but with a little digging you may get connected with a team that can satisfy you much better than going it alone.

Updating and Managing DMAM and Content Management Systems

Assuming that you've chosen to own your own systems, their complexity can require one or more full-time IT staff members for maintenance, and often a squad of consultants for updates and reconfigurations. Significant failures in DMAM or CM systems are nearly always a crisis, so you can imagine that updating software or supporting hardware, operating systems, and databases can result in critical downtime if there isn't adequate planning. You should also consider a solid network operations plan, particularly if you need a multisite installation; network operations can be as simple as pager alerts to the IT staff when a critical system goes down in any location or as complex as 24-hour in-person monitoring.

Number One Gotcha: Interoperability

In many cases, interoperability comes from hard work on the users' side as standards either don't exist or haven't matured. Here are a few tips for various media producers:

- If you are in Post, take a look at low-cost tools such as Automatic Duck (www.automaticduck.com/) to begin moving your work around without losing your metadata.

- If you have some programming expertise, consider "rolling your own" using scripting languages such as Python. Check out www.axs-wave.com/DMRG/tools for some examples.

- Apple is moving to reduce the interoperability challenges and expense of QuickTime with enhancements to Final Cut Pro.

- Avid, Discreet, and Thomson Multimedia have all launched work-group-oriented products for Post and Broadcast with a strong interoperability focus.

    See

    www.avid.com/products/unity_medianet/index.html

    www.discreet.com/products/infrastr/

    www.thomson-multimedia.com

- Thomson Multimedia has recently acquired companies such as Grass Valley Group (www.grassvalleygroup.com/) and formed a number of joint ventures with other key players such as Microsoft and DirecTV. Their moves and strategies indicate a strong awareness of the need to put together an integrated digital media chain.

It's important to remember that DMAM and CM are far more than the file and workflow management built into an editing or effects station, so look carefully at the claims for DMAM and CM functionality. What is needed to make true digital media supply chains function from end to end are solid partnerships and standards linking creation, DMAM, and CM systems as a cohesive system.

Metrics for Success

No organization is going to use exactly the same metrics to measure whether a DMAM and/or CM solution will be a success. There are some general measures that can be used, not only to determine how well the system works when it is implemented but also to create the requirements for a system that will match your needs:

- Collaboration systems beyond phone, fax, and email are critical in order to provide multidirectional digital workflows between organizations, and in the case of interactive TV, among viewers, distributors, and creators.

- Integration is a measure of how much of the company's methods, media, and information is shared across its sites, with its partners, and with other organizations. In the long-term, the digital workflow functionality and management of media assets must be integrated with the whole business in order for costs to go lower.

- How many people are contributing to the development and creation of new content and its distribution? This is where your money is made, and digital technologies should be used to focus your employees on these tasks.

- What is your cycle time for: Publishing content? For the high-end installations, this may need to measured in minutes, as opposed to hours or days.

- Reusing content? Do you have to send someone to the archive warehouse across the river, or do you have a streamlined process that, at the very least, allows you to use a keyword search to access browse-quality summaries of items in your archives?

- Are you, your people, and your systems able to respond faster to customers and market conditions than your competitors?

- Has the digital system you installed helped you to build a strong reputation and increase customer retention?

The items listed above are just a start. The range of digital systems and workflows needed to support the operations of a media enterprise will depend on where a particular institution sets the balance between point solutions and workflow support.

Additional Resources

Table 12-8 lists asset and content management resources.

Table 12-8: Asset and Content Management Resources

Title	Description	Author(s)	URL/ISBN/ Source
The Platform for Privacy Preferences 1.0 (P3P 1.0) Specification	The Platform for Privacy Preferences Project (P3P) enables Websites to express their privacy practices in a standard format that can be retrieved automatically and interpreted easily by user agents. P3P user agents will allow users to be informed of site practices (in both machine- and human-readable formats) and to automate decision making based on these practices when appropriate. Thus, users need not read the privacy policies at every site they visit.	Massimo Marchiori	www.w3.org/P3P/
SOAP Version 1.2 Part 0: Primer	SOAP Version 1.2 provides the definition of an XML document that can be used for exchanging structured and typed information between peers in a decentralized distributed environment. It is fundamentally a stateless one-way message exchange paradigm, but applications can create more complex interaction patterns (for example, request/response, request/multiple responses) by combining such one-way exchanges with features provided by an underlying transport protocol and/or application-specific information. SOAP is silent on the semantics of any application-specific data it conveys, as it is on issues such as the routing of SOAP messages, reliable data transfer, and firewall traversal. However, SOAP provides the framework by which application-specific information may be conveyed in an extensible manner. Also, SOAP provides a full description of the expected actions taken by a SOAP processor on receiving a SOAP message.	Nilo Mitra	www.w3.org/TR/ soap12-part0/

Section III: Distribution Architectures

CHAPTER 13

Digital Rights Management

In the 1980s, as distribution of content via digital technology began to proliferate, more and more attention started to be paid to methods to protect this content, or intellectual property (IP). This was particularly true for CD-ROMs with professional content. Slowly, an understanding started to develop that only in digital media does a content owner have the option of wide public distribution of content while simultaneously restricting access to the content and even determining access rights at the granular level (for example, you can only view the nude scenes if you have paid for the key to unlock them). The Web and e-commerce introduced a whole new level of concern over the protection of IP as ease of access, copying, and distribution of content and transaction information increased. Most industries have come to see digital rights management (DRM) solely as a method to control illegal distribution. However, in the professional content industry, DRM has an expanded definition, encompassing not only protection but the variety of rights associated with a production. This chapter examines some of the key issues, methods, and tools used to manage different aspects of DRM.

Part A: Background

Introduction

In networked digital environments, legal constraints and technological constraints may be interchangeable or even complementary in holding content proprietary. Content creators, who will be working on content that is perceived by the public to be valuable, can expect to be faced with increasingly difficult choices based on the degree of openness or constraint of the content, since with each additional constraint you place burdens on the consumer who may then choose to go somewhere else where things are simpler.

The important thing to remember, however, is that in professional digital content, the concept of DRM goes beyond just a secure transaction coupled with copy protection at the end of the digital media chain. Understanding authorship, ownership, and protected creative contributions is critical to understanding DRM issues in professional media. Within the professional content industry, entire enterprises are devoted to nothing but tracking who owns what part of the content and ensuring that they are correctly compensated and that written authorization is obtained. Without a clear owner, it is difficult to control the exchange of information. For our industry, authorship and ownership are not the stable one-dimensional concepts IT vendors and the popular press would have them be. Instead, they are complex, expensive, and fraught with tension and issues of security and risk management. In many cases, it is easier and cheaper to reshoot something than it is to track down all the clearances necessary to use a piece of content. Figure 13-1 gives an idea of the complexity of the problem and the various types of individuals and organizations that are now arguing a variety of issues in the courts, standards bodies, libraries, IT and engineering groups, and corporate boardrooms.

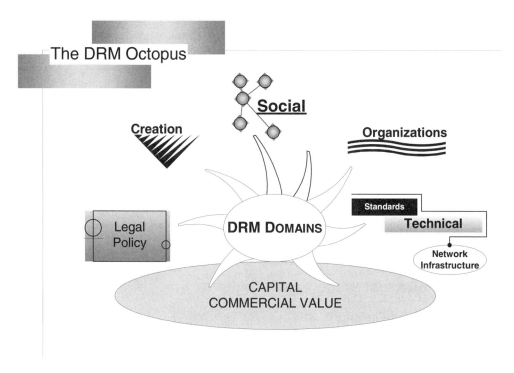

Figure 13-1 DRM Octopus (Bradley 2001)
©2001 axsWave Consulting. Used with Permission.

While DRM has been in development for more than 20 years — starting with software protected by hardware "dongles" — the overall technology has yet to prove itself. We hear regularly about methods of DRM being cracked and individuals with ownership rights being unable to collect revenues or track the different venues their content is being distributed on. Old-economy media such as music and video have frankly been under siege from illegitimate distribution. In response, the entertainment industry has rapidly made strange bedfellows with entrepreneurial mathematicians, various hackers, and hacker organizations. There is also a growing move to integrated document management systems that allow organizations such as Electronic Arts to manage their members' ownership rights.

Three Fundamental Principles of DRM

Vendors who promote their watermarking, encryption, biometric, and other technologies as answering the needs for DRM in professional content are missing the point. DRM is a multidimensional problem that cannot be solved by technology alone. There are a number of principles and techniques that must be examined by content owners before implementing a DRM strategy. The three most fundamental principles inherent in any definition/ implementation of DRM are: (1) protect the IP, not just the digitized media; (2) develop, protect, and automate a chain of trust that protects the media from start to finish; and (3) establish and track the identity of everyone who accesses the content.

Three Principles
The first fundamental principle on which to base your selection of a DRM strategy, tool set, and methodology is the principle of: *Protecting the individuals' or organizations' IP, not simply the digitized media.*
The second fundamental principle inherent in a DRM implementation is a defined and agreed-upon *chain of trust.*
The third fundamental principle inherent in a DRM implementation is a way to verify the identity of the content-creation professionals, content owners, rights holders, and those paying for the content.

Intellectual Property in a Digital World

The first fundamental principle on which to base DRM plans and methods is the principle of protecting the individuals' or organizations' IP, not simply the digitized media. The problems of distributing intellectual property are much the same for the digital and physical worlds, but the risk to digital assets is much greater. The obvious difference is that digital media can be rapidly duplicated and distributed around the world. Understandably, the ease of duplication and distribution is viewed by content owners as a potential Armageddon.

Supporting the prediction of Armageddon for media companies are the attitudes toward someone else's intellectual property prevalent in society. Whether it's using Napster for music or DueNow.com for a thesis, these casual attitudes are a key frustration to the owners of IP. Clearly, protecting digital assets is as much an issue of technology development as it is social education. The effectiveness of any DRM system is only as great as the owner's ability to detect unauthorized access, monitor use, and enforce her rights. This is partially accomplished through a variety of means:

- The content library must be protected by both traditional network security methods and cryptography.

- The distribution points, including distribution partners, aggregators, and finally the consumers, must be trusted and identified license owners, known to the content owner directly or indirectly.

- The technology, people, and organizations in both the creation and consumer distribution channels, including the content delivery network, must be protected and trusted.

- All participants in the digital media distribution supply chain must agree to the content owners' conditions within the law. For example, consumers must agree not to redistribute the content or create physical media copies such as CDs or tapes. Moreover, local and international statutes must protect owners' rights, and law enforcement must back up those statutes. Effective law enforcement is perhaps as much a barrier to profitability in digital media distribution as the technology issues.

DRM in the content marketplace is a very large topic. For the purposes of this chapter, we are going to discuss three fundamental principles at work in DRM. This does not mean that these three principles are the only ones, nor does it mean that they won't change as technology and social issues are resolved. However, this basic set of three principles — protection of IP, trust, and identity — will give any of you involved in DRM programs, planning, or implementation a good place to start.

Trust

The second fundamental principle that must be followed in order to increase the likelihood of legitimate distribution is to set up a chain of trust between all individuals involved in content creation, linked to the content owner's tracking of individuals' rights and residuals, and then finally to the ultimate consumers. Like the technology and strategies implementing methods for IP protection, a trust chain is an enabling principle. Its existence and implementation enable digital commerce via automated applications.

However, trust and trust chains are two of those necessary principles that are messy to define. One of the conceptual definitions that makes solid sense for our industry was developed by Kini and Choobineh (Kini and Choobineh 1998), who, drawing from the Webster's Dictionary definition, defined trust as having four aspects:

1. An assumed reliance on some person, thing, system, or technology by an individual or organization in the trust chain

2. A confident view of the character, ability, strength, and/or truth of someone's claims

3. A charge or duty imposed on an individual or organization either in confidence or as a condition of a relationship/transaction

4. Confidence in an entity to follow the conditions agreed upon in a timely and responsible manner

   Within a system, trust is "a belief that is influenced by the individual's opinion about certain critical system features."
   (Kini and Choobineh, 1998)

The above gives us a conceptual definition of trust and can be used to identify the key individuals and organizations you will link to your trust chain. but it needs to be expanded to support a business relationship. Figure 13-2 expands on the critical factors supporting a commercial trust chain in digital media. In this figure we see that trust is a vital component in every business transaction. We trust sellers to provide the services or goods they advertise in a timely and professional manner. For those selling services, there is a need to trust that the buyer can pay for the goods or services and is authorized to make the purchase and will deal with the seller concerning any problems in a fair and timely manner. The trust concept is at the foundation of all of our marketplaces, digital or not. Consequently, for digital content marketplaces to become major forces and not just add-ons to our "real" business, the issue of trust in an anonymous digital world must be resolved. Current solutions are prevalent in a variety of markets, with perhaps the most successful being PayPal, which processes millions of transactions per month for online auction sites.

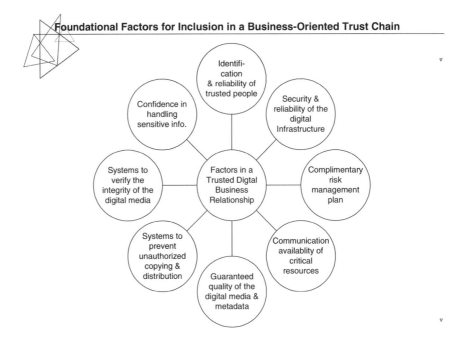

Figure 13-2 Foundational Factors

Identity

Identity is one of the key social issues facing all networked technologies today and is compounded by the steady growth away from centralized applications within the organizations' walls to applications that provide global and multiformat availability. A digital identity represents the key methodology for verifying an individual accessing content, a network, etc., but the nature of digital technology and networks means that both fraudulent identities and anonymity are not only possible but prevalent. At the foundation of all identity definitions are four concepts:

1. Something you know (password, user ID, etc.)

2. Something you are and are not likely to be able to change (biometric methods such as fingerprint locks)

3. Something you have (a smart card, keys, etc.)

4. Someone you know (physical recognition such as a guard not letting you pass without knowing you — obviously used only in highly secure environments; or using a trusted third party, such as PayPal, or a financial clearinghouse to verify your identity)

Gotcha: Even if you use all four methods, *you haven't protected anything* from an attack: Today's computers, using software readily available on the Internet, can run through every possible keyboard password in less than a day; biometric methods are only as good as the software code used to develop them; physical items can be stolen; and people and machines can be duped.

So how are you going to prove that the people accessing your digital media are the ones who have paid for that privilege? You aren't. The best you can hope to do is mix enough deterrents and identity technologies into your DRM methods to provide enough protection that your risks are minimized.

From a content owner's perspective, there are a vast number of identity classes that must be considered: creator, creative contributors, production teams, archivists, distributors, consumers, etc. For each, there are unique functional requirements for managing identity. Issues such as bulk licensing and auditing are important in distribution. Privacy and security balanced with convenience are the key issues for consumers. The end goal is the same — to ensure that content licenses are matched to specific instances of media in a verifiable and usable system that addresses the risks you are willing to take with your digital content.

DRM — A Strategic Program

Effective DRM requires comprehensive, well-designed, and reliable standards, plans, and methods within the organization. What that means is that DRM methods and strategies should *not* be considered primarily a technical function of the editor or the network/IT team, but an essential management function of the content owner and the organization as a whole.

The various dimensions involved in DRM make the problem one of the most difficult to solve as you move to digital media. In the end, though, there really is no other alternative. DRM has to exist in some form for digital media distribution and consumption to be ubiquitous. Otherwise, the market will never develop because the economics will not support it.

DRM Gotchas

GOTCHA: No one can define intellectual property...

"No one can define intellectual property in a way that is universally accepted. Inherent in the idea of intellectual property is the protection given by copyright laws, which vary from country to country and are still open to debate."

GOTCHA: It is impossible...

"It is impossible to design any DRM system without trust. Even the manufacturers of the hardware have to trust their chip suppliers and their cryptologists."

GOTCHA: You'll never prove it's them...

"You'll never prove it's them (your authorized users) logging on and accessing their files. The best you can hope for is to make it difficult for them to pretend to be someone else."

Part B: Tools

Standards for Digital Rights Management

Table 13-1 lists a number of emerging standards in various stages of market development designed to address the issues surrounding DRM.

Table 13-1: DRM Standards

Organization	Description	URL
Digital Orbit Identifier (DOI) Foundation	The purpose of the DOI Foundation is to support the needs of the intellectual property community in the digital environment by establishing and governing the DOI system, setting policies for the system, choosing service providers for the system, and overseeing the successful operation of the system. These systems acts like a registry of DOIs so that content can be registered to a specific provider.	http://www.doi.org/
Digital Transmission Content Protection (DTCP)	DTCP defines a cryptographic protocol for safeguarding audio/video entertainment content against illegal copying, intercepting, and tampering as it traverses high-performance digital networks. Use of this technology requires a license with the Digital Transmission Licensing Administrator (DTLA). With DTCP, the studios are able to protect prerecorded media, pay-per-view, and video-on-demand transmissions against unauthorized copying. In addition, DTCP purportedly does not allow unauthorized Internet retransmission of video.	http://www.dtcp.com/
DVD Copy Control Association (DVD CCA)	The DVD CCA is a not-for-profit corporation with responsibility for licensing CSS (Content Scramble System) to manufacturers of DVD hardware, discs, and related products. Licensees include the owners and manufacturers of the content of DVD discs; creators of encryption engines and hardware and software decrypters; and manufacturers of DVD players and DVD-ROM drives.	http://www.dvdcca.org/
eXtensible Media Commerce Language (XMCL)	An initiative led by RealNetworks, XMCL is an open XML-based language designed to establish industry-wide standards for Internet media commerce and interoperability of digital rights management commerce communications over the Internet.	http://www.xmcl.org/
High-Bandwidth Digital Content Protection System (HDCP)	HDCP is a specification developed by Intel Corporation to protect the video transmission between a digital visual interface (DVI) video transmitter and a DVI video receiver. HDCP is a specification that encrypts each pixel as it moves from the PC or set-top box to digital displays.	http://www.digital-cp.com/

Table 13-1: DRM Standards (Continued)

Organization	Description	URL
Moving Pictures Experts Group (MPEG) (ISO/ IEC JTC1 SC29 WG11)	A working group of ISO/IEC in charge of the development of standards for coded representation of digital audio and video established in 1988. The group has produced MPEG-1, the standard on which such products as Video CD and MP3 are based; MPEG-2, the standard on which such products as digital television set-top boxes and DVD are based; MPEG-4, the standard for multimedia for the fixed and mobile Web; and MPEG-7, the standard for description and search of audio and visual content. Work on the new standard MPEG-21, Multimedia Framework, started in June 2000. So far a Technical Report has been produced, and the formal approval process has already begun for two more parts of the standard. Several Calls for Proposals have already been issued, and two working drafts are being developed.	http://mpeg.telecomi-talialab.com/ http://www.mpeg.org MPEG Pointers and Resources (Reference site for MPEG) http://www.mpeg.org/ MPEG/start-ing-points.html MPEG Starting Points and FAQs http://www.faqs.org/faqs/ compression-faq/part2/ section-2.html Introduction to MPEG
Open eBook Forum (OEBF)	OEBF is an association of publishers and software and hardware vendors collaborating to establish standards for ebooks, including DRM requirements that will promote safe commerce of ebooks.	http://www.openebook. org/index.htm
Secure Digital Music	The Secure Digital Music Initiative is a working group comprised of more than 160 businesses and organizations that are working to develop a specification for the secure distribution of digital music. The impetus for the group's mission is the exponential explosion in the popularity of the MP3 compression format, widely used to facilitate the transfer of both legal and illegal digital music files online.	http://www.sdmi.org/
Trusted Computing Platform Alliance (TCPA).	A collaboration of Compaq, HP, IBM, Intel, and Microsoft, the TCPA specification aims to marry a set of hardware features with operating system services that will provide the low-level basis of DRM.	http://www.trustedpc.org/ home/home.htm

Managed Assets Collections

Table 13-2 provides information on managed assets collections.

Table 13-2: Managed Asset Collections

Company	Description	Product(s)	URL
Corbis	The Corbis Collection is the most definitive collection of news, editorial, sports, contemporary, historical, celebrity, and fine art imagery. The images come from the finest professional photographers, museums, cultural institutions, and public and private collections in the world. This collection may be accessed via the Web using an e-commerce-enabled platform. Some of the Corbis sources include Ansel Adams, Yann Arthus-Bertrand, Douglas Kirkland, Robert Holmes, Galen Rowell, David and Peter Turnley, Michael Yamashita, Mark Seliger, Michael O'Neill, the National Gallery-London, the Philadelphia Museum of Art, the State Hermitage Museum, Christies' and the Bettmann, Hulton-Deutsch, and Brett Weston Collections.	Corbis Corbis Stock Market	http://www.corbis.com/ http://www.corbis-stockmarket.com/
gettyimages	gettyimages is a service provider of stock digital material. It provides its material over the Web via an e-commerce-enabled platform where you may browse for photographs via a searchable interface and download the asset — your account is charged and appropriate rights are paid to the content provider.	gettyimages Creative	http://creative.gettyimages.com/source/home/home.asp
Sekani	Sekani is a comprehensive source for moving imagery and research rights and clearance services worldwide. In February 2000, Sekani was founded by bringing together Second Line Search, a respected source for research, rights, and clearances, and the well-respected group of stock footage companies Action Sports Adventure, Film Bank, and Hot Shots. Sekani is also partnered with Corbis to provide access to the Corbis highly recognized library of assets.	Sekani Network	http://www.sekani.com/

Encryption Technologies

Table 13-3 provides information on encryption technologies.

Table 13-3: Encryption Technologies

Company	Description	Product(s)	URL
Appligent, Inc.	Appligent's SecurSign is a server-based, command-line-driven application that applies standard Acrobat security features to large volumes of PDF documents automatically with encryption based on the RSA BSAFE cryptographics.	SecurSign	http://www.appligent.com/new-pages/secursign.html
FileOpen Systems	FileOpen Systems is a provider of stand-alone encryption products, which allow publishers to control distribution of their documents and retain 100 percent of their revenues. FileOpen products have made digital rights management a reality for publishers around the world since 1997.		http://www.fileopen.com/
Liquid Audio	Liquid Audio's Secure Portable Player Platform (SP3) provides consumer electronics companies, chip-set manufacturers, and embedded operating systems developers with a digital music DRM solution. SP3 is compliant with Secure Digital Music Initiative (SDMI) and uses standard, trusted security algorithms. With dynamic codec support, the firmware decoder software can be delivered securely with the music file providing a mechanism for supporting additional codecs without a firmware update. The infrastructure for secure firmware update and secure key management allows the device to be serviceable in the field, reducing customer support costs.	Liquid SP3	http://www.liquidaudio.com/products/sp3/
LockStream	LockStream's digital rights management (DRM) solutions enable the secure distribution, promotion, and sale of digital media content. The minimal client-side requirements enable LockStream to support virtually any type of device that is capable of playing digital media. LockStream is backed by such industry leaders as AOL/Time Warner, Artisan Entertainment, Audax Group, Encore Venture Partners, and ING.	VideoLock Secure Package Reader Secure Package Creator	http://www.lockstream.com/products.html

Table 13-3: Encryption Technologies (Continued)

Company	Description	Product(s)	URL
Permio	e-Border secures Internet-based (UDP) streaming media (real-time data feeds), video/audioconferencing, telephony, and multimedia. Firewalls cannot efficiently secure and manage UDP streaming, so the e-Border Server is a scalable access control gateway that supports thousands of simultaneous connections for any application through the e-Border Driver or applications with built-in SOCKS support. e-Border serves as a proxy, an application routing gateway, and complements all major firewalls.	e-Border	http://www.eborder.nec.com/products/products.htm
RSA Security	RSA Security Inc. is a trusted name in e-security, helping organizations build secure, trusted foundations for e-business through its authorization, encryption, and public key management systems.	RSA ClearTrust RSA BSAFE RSA Keon	http://www.rsasecurity.com/products/
SecureMedia	SecureMedia is a provider of secure digital media distribution solutions that enable protection of streamed and downloaded media, from source to point of rendering. Built on its patented high-speed, low-overhead, and embeddable encryption technology, SecureMedia's solutions are optimized for digital media distribution, where speed, scalability, consumer friendliness, and integration with multiple hardware platforms, DRM systems, and e-commerce applications are required.	SecureMedia for the Real-System G2 platform SecureMedia Software Toolkit Encryptonite Engine	http://www.rpkusa.com/product_server.php
ZipLabs Pte Ltd.	ZipLabs' SecureMP3 is a digital rights management (DRM) software solution developed to offer a universal DRM solution that enables secure copyrighted music protection, MP3 music distribution, track usage, and purchase of digital music via the Internet.	SecureMP3	http://www.zappee.com/secure.htm

Authentication

Table 13-4 provides information on authentication technologies.

Table 13-4: Authentication/PKI/Digital Signatures

Company	Description	Product(s)	URL
Baltimore Technologies	Baltimore Technologies develops and markets security products and services to enable companies to develop secure systems for e-business, the Internet, and mobile commerce. Baltimore is a provider of public key infrastructure (PKI) software including Baltimore's PKI technology for Microsoft Windows 2000.	SolutionsPlus for Windows 2000 UniCERT	http://www.balti-more.com/products/index.html
Certicom	Certicom was the original designer of the secure socket layer (SSL) encryption standard, which is now ubiquitous on the Internet. Certicom has now turned its attention to encryption and authentication of content in the mobile wireless and personal digital assistant (PDA) space.	movianCrypt MobileTrust SecurityBuilder	http://www.certi-com.com/products/index.html
Communication Intelligence Corporation (CIC)	CIC's Sign-it products represent a biometric authentication solution based on a client-server model. This technology ensures virtually tamper-proof security for electronically signing and securely transferring of PDF and Word documents.	Sign-it for Adobe Acrobat Sign-it for Microsoft Word	http://www.cic.com/products/signit/
Cyber-SIGN Inc.	Cyber-SIGN is a biometric authentication system that increases data security and enables trusted document authorization. Cyber-SIGN authenticates a person, not a machine or software key. Cyber-SIGN analyzes the shape, speed, stroke order, off-tablet motion, pen pressure, and timing information captured during the act of signing.	Cyber-SIGN	http://www.cybersign.com/product_app.htm#capture

Table 13-4: Authentication/PKI/Digital Signatures (Continued)

Company	Description	Product(s)	URL
DMDsecure	DMDfusion is a Java-based digital rights management (DRM) application that incorporates the technologies of Microsoft Corporation and Adobe Systems. The business logic of DMDfusion is based on the idea of separating content and licenses. Content is protected (or locked) using a key. Licenses contain the key to unlock content and the accompanying usage rights. Licenses are distributed separately from the content.	DMDfusion	http://www.dmdsecure.com/products/overview.html
Entrust Technologies Inc.	Entrust develops Internet security services that provide identification, entitlements, verification, privacy, and security management capabilities. Entrust has won numerous awards for its PKI software products including *Network Magazine*'s 2001 Product of the Year award in the Authentication and Access Control category.	Entrust Authority Entrust GetAccess Entrust TruePass	http://www.entrust.com/products
Lexign	Lexign ProSigner allows any computer-based document to be digitally signed from the desktop. Lexign ProSigner is integrated within MS Word, MS Excel, and Adobe PDF applications, providing software-based signing. Lexign ProSigner is also PKI-independent, so it can be easily deployed with any PKI infrastructure or with PIN password.	Lexign ProSigner	http://www.lexign.com/products/lexign_prosigner.htm

Table 13-4: Authentication/PKI/Digital Signatures (Continued)

Company	Description	Product(s)	URL
Microsoft	In addition to public key infrastructure (PKI) support in its Windows ME/2000/XP operating systems, Microsoft has developed its own DRM system including accessible APIs for developers. Microsoft Windows Media Rights Manager is an end-to-end DRM system that offers content providers and retailers a flexible platform for the secure distribution of digital media files. Windows Media Rights Manager Version 1 was first released in August 1999. The second-generation technology, Windows Media Rights Manager Version 7, includes both server and client software development kits (SDKs) that enable applications to protect and play back digital media files.	Microsoft Windows Media Rights Manager	http://www.microsoft.com/windows/windows-media/drm.asp
NTRU	NTRU develops public key cryptosystems (PKIs) that are not based on factorization or discrete logarithm problems. The computations performed in the execution of the NTRU algorithms involve simpler processes that can be performed very quickly, even on inexpensive 8-bit processors, at security levels comparable to or exceeding other public key cryptosystems.	NTRU Mobile Security for the TI OMAP Platform jNERI NERI	http://www.ntru.com/technology/tech.product.htm
Silanis Technology Inc.	Silanis Technology Inc. is a provider of electronic signature software. Silanis supports PKI technology from VeriSign, Entrust, and RSA, as well as any X.509 standard certificates.The ApproveIt technology is being used by a number of large customers including the U.S. Joint Chiefs of Staff.	ApproveIt	http://www.silanis.com/products/

Table 13-4: Authentication/PKI/Digital Signatures (Continued)

Company	Description	Product(s)	URL
VeriSign, Inc.	VeriSign has a number of security offerings including PKI, Website, and software signing certificates. It also has a digital asset monitoring service that scans the Web looking for infractions of copy-protected materials.	VeriSign Authentic Document IDs Digital Brand Management Services	http://www.verisign.com/products/index.html

Access Control

Table 13-5 provides information on managed assets collections.

Table 13-5: Access Control/Routing/Tracking

Company	Description	Product(s)	URL
Adobe Systems, Inc.	Adobe has developed the Content Server product with built-in digital rights management, which is supported by the e-Book format.	Adobe Content Server 2	http://www.adobe.com/products/contentserver/main.html
Alchemedia Technologies, Inc.	Alchemedia Mirage product line uses its patented SecureDisplay technology to control and audit the flow of information within an enterprise setting, much like the solution set from Authentica (see below).	Mirage Enterprise 3.0	http://alchemedia.com/
Authentica, Inc.	Authentica's product suite is designed for use within an enterprise to control and audit the flow of information around the enterprise. It limits access/manipulation rights with its Active Rights Management system that can be controlled within an enterprise setting from the centralized policy server.	MailRecall PageRecall NetRecall	http://www.authentica.com/products/default.asp
Digital Envoy	Digital Envoy provides geo-intelligent solutions and RealPath intelligent routing for the Internet. Digital Envoy's technology allows e-commerce, streaming media, online advertising, information sites, and others to customize, restrict, and target content based on the geo-location of an individual user.	NetAcuity	http://www.digitalenvoy.com/products/netacuity.shtml

Table 13-5: Access Control/Routing/Tracking (Continued)

Company	Description	Product(s)	URL
Entriq	Entriq Inc. provides content owners with information and solutions to protect Internet media rights and enable revenue using its Digital Rights Networks (DRNs) and Entriq Service Points (ESPs). Entriq Inc. is owned by the international subscriber platforms and software solutions group MIH Limited (NASDAQ & AEX: MIHL), which spans more than 50 countries delivering business services and entertainment to millions of viewers via TV or the Internet.	Digital Rights Network	http://www.entriq.com/
Intertrust Technologies	Intertrust has developed a general-purpose DRM platform, Rights/System, to serve as a foundation for providers of digital information, technology, and commerce services to participate in a global system for e-commerce. Intertrust also has developed integrated circuit (IC) technology for consumer devices.	Rights System	http://www.intertrust.com/main/products/index.html
Irdeto Access	Irdeto Access offers a conditional access content protection solution for the secure delivery of IP/Internet content over broadband networks. CypherCast secures multicast data that travels over open broadband networks including cable, satellite, telco, and terrestrial broadcast. CypherCast technology allows content to travel around the globe securely and efficiently without loss of quality. Deployed worldwide, CypherCast is used in applications such as virtual private multicast networks, distance learning, corporate training, and secure delivery of sensitive financial information.	Irdeto CypherCast Irdeto M-Crypt for Narrowcasting Irdeto M-Crypt for Broadcasting	http://www.irdetoaccess.com/

Table 13-5: Access Control/Routing/Tracking (Continued)

Company	Description	Product(s)	URL
Perimele	Perimele is a provider of end-to-end solutions for corporate content and digital information sales. Perimele's **rights**technologies solutions allow businesses to protect and manage their digital assets, track distribution, and prevent unauthorized access, copying, and piracy of their products or proprietary information.	**rights-**technologies Protector Series	http://www. perimele.com/content/ largebusinessprod- ucts.htm
RealNetworks	The RealSystem Media Commerce Suite provides secure media packaging, license generation, and content delivery to RealPlayer and RealOne players across all major platforms. Built on RealSystem iQ, it extends the RealSystem and RealPlayer open architecture to accommodate the incorporation of a wide range of rights management systems. It integrates into all types of existing infrastructures and back-end systems, and it supports a broad set of business models including purchase, rental, video-on-demand, and subscription services.	RealSystem Media Com- merce Suite	http://www. realnetworks.com/ products/commerce/ index.html

Other DRM Technologies

Table 13-6 provides information on managed assets collections.

Table 13-6: Other DRM Technologies

Company	Description	Product(s)	URL
Content- Guard	ContentGuard, Inc. is driving the stan- dards for interoperability in digital rights management for digital content and Web services. The company's digital rights language, XrML (eXtensible rights Markup Language), and its broad foun- dation patent portfolio were originally developed at the Xerox Palo Alto Research Center.	XrML 2.0	http://www.content- guard.com/xrml.asp

Table 13-6: Other DRM Technologies (Continued)

Company	Description	Product(s)	URL
Corporation for National Research Initiatives (CNRI)	CNRI undertakes, fosters, and promotes research in the public interest. The Handle System is a comprehensive free Java software system for assigning, managing, and resolving persistent identifiers, known as handles, for digital objects and other resources on the Internet. Handles can be used as uniform resource names (URNs). The Handle System includes an open set of protocols, a namespace, and an implementation of the protocols. The protocols enable a distributed computer system to store handles of digital resources and resolve those handles into the information necessary to locate and access the resources. This associated information can be changed as needed to reflect the current state of the identified resource without changing the handle, thus allowing the name of the item to persist over changes of location and other state information.	Handle System	http://www.handle.net/introduction.html
Digimarc Corporation	Digimarc develops digital watermarking technologies for use in identifying and securing content including movies, photographic or artistic images, and valuable documents such as financial instruments, passports, and event tickets. The technology used by Digimarc for audio and video watermarking was co-developed with Macrovision and Philips.	Digimarc Image-Bridge Philips Water-Cast	http://www.digimarc.com/imaging/default.asp http://www.digimarc.com/imaging/avideocap01.htm
eLiberation	eLiberation is an Internet software company that has developed comprehensive relational microtransaction management systems. Focusing on the entertainment industry, eLiberation has developed a system integrating digital rights management, rich information, and financial transaction technology.	Event Frame FTM	http://www.eliberation.com/aboutus/products-andservices/default.asp

Part C: Methods

DRM in the Content-Creation (Repurposing) Process

Content owners wishing to syndicate digital media have a dilemma in that DRM is characterized by vendors with proprietary solutions. Aggregators are often powerful enough to prescribe DRM solutions to the content owners, and yet most content owners are neither inclined nor equipped to deploy multiple DRM systems, nor is there an interoperability standard in place that would facilitate centralized control for the owner. This puts the aggregators in control, and it means that sales data may only be selectively available to those who need it the most, the content producers. Imagine a small book publisher trying to manage and measure sales of its content from several different online book retailers. How can you gauge your editorial success if you have limited access to trial use or viewing information?

Interoperability will be a significant challenge for DRM vendors, and there are many competing market forces that will shape the way industry standards develop. Content owners looking at DRM systems should discuss with their vendors how they will handle issues of management across a heterogeneous marketplace. There is no single right answer, but there is one requirement: DRM vendors must remain flexible and open to interoperating with competitive systems in the interest of commerce.

DRM in Digital Media Distribution

In addition to the control and interoperability issues paramount to content owners, distributors must also deal with a myriad of other issues:

- Full-featured e-commerce interfaces to meter the consumption of content

- Security of content storage as well as offline security to protect intellectual property rights

- Tracking, verifying, and accounting for all individual ownership rights in the content

- Balancing content owners' or owners' rights with ease of use and consumption (see the DRM Gotchas box)

- Geographic restrictions — determining the consumer's location and determining the rights that can be granted (for example, use of certain encryption technologies are restricted by the U.S. government)

- Identity of the consumer and assurance that each media use is restricted to the licensee (for example, tying a digital music file to a given portable music player)

Vendors such as IBM and Intertrust are providing fully developed solutions for managing distribution rights. For distributors of one or two media types to a limited audience, this is a manageable implementation. However, for handling worldwide distribution of a large number of media types to a consumer-oriented audience, the complexity of integrated implementations will make DRM an extremely difficult proposition. In such large installations, it may be easier to provide multiple DRM installations or even multiple vendor solutions in order to meet the varying needs of different media types, content creators, distribution channels, or consumer groups.

Built-in DRM

Built-in tools within DVD-ROM production packages (see Chapter 7) will help you take raw content and burn it onto a DVD-ROM master in its encrypted format. Another example includes the open DRM framework found in RealNetworks' Media Commerce Suite. However, using DRM systems that come bundled with content production, CM, and digital media asset management (DMAM) tools is convenient but has risks. These built-in tools or plug-ins can save you significant money because custom stand-alone systems are often very expensive and take much longer to implement. The issue with using these tools is that they are readily available to hackers interested in breaking the systems. Custom solutions that deal with security issues, metadata, embedded media encryption, and other issues may stand up longer than the widely distributed systems.

Handling of Content with Different Rights Systems

You may be compelled to use multiple DRM systems throughout the entire process of production, management, and distribution due to the mix of available equipment, lack of global standards, and varying laws for content protection. An example we may all have to face is the need to develop content for different set-top boxes, operating systems, or wireless devices, each using a proprietary DRM product or partner. The only hope is that the standards bodies can come together with a small set of standard solutions that the major vendors can agree on. Otherwise, this vision outlined in Microsoft's 2001 Letter to Shareholders will become a content creation nightmare.

> *Yet even greater technological advances are just ahead. XML Web Services will open up new possibilities in e-commerce, business planning, and customer service. Document and workflow management will become simpler and more comprehensive. Technologies such as the advanced speech and handwriting-recognition capabilities of the next-generation Tablet*

PC will transform the workplace for knowledge workers. Inexpensive high-capacity disk drives, powerful audio and video capabilities, and easy-to-use digital cameras will make the PC an entertainment and information hub for the home.

More than 500 million PCs are already in use around the world, and another 130 million or more were purchased in calendar 2001 — more than the number of TVs that will likely be purchased this year. Increasingly, the PC is moving to the center of an ever-expanding network of smart connected devices — from mobile phones to televisions and handheld devices, even household appliances. There has never been a more exciting time in the history of our industry.

The coming digital decade will be a time of enormous opportunity: for consumers, for the technology industry, and for Microsoft as we realize the vision of empowering people through great software — any time, any place, and on any device.

Limelight Demands: Digital Rights Metadata for All Authors and Creative Contributions

One of the most important sets of metadata for creative content involves authorship and creative rights, including complex relationships between big-name talent contracts, the film credits, and distribution. Questions you need to ask when implementing a comprehensive DRM strategy go beyond technology and encompass issues such as: How will you handle residual talent payments? deferred payments? What if those contracts and relationships change (and they will) over time? How will you manage those changes? What happens if you distribute the content digitally and it is hacked? How are you going to address the legitmate concerns of the authors?

The metadata systems required to track authorship and ownership rights are also complex and are currently handled by people, paper, and occaisionally custom IT solutions. Companies such as Getty Images and Corbis are creating their own tracking systems for royalties on vast libraries of still images. CNN is involved with IBM and Sony in a project to encode, archive, and make available for sale its vast media store. For them, key issues around areas such as talent releases, time of ownership of purchased video, and permissible distribution venues are going to be just as important as developing solutions to prevent digital theft and alteration. If your content library is fairly small, you may not need a complex system. A number of application service providers are promising to handle moderate royalty complexities on a contract basis, much the same way talent payments have been serviced in the past. No matter what route you decide to take, make sure that your IT people, system integrators, and vendors spend significant time with your legal and rights acquisition teams.

Protection Methods for Distribution

The more people gain access to unmetered and unprotected content, the more likely it is to be pirated. However, protection of content too early in the supply chain may make it difficult for partners to distribute content using their own DRM model. Here is a list of methods and where in the process you might consider implementation:

- **Metadata encoding:** While metadata doesn't protect against piracy, it's still a necessary step to further stake your claim on intellectual property. Whenever possible, use all available metadata capabilities of the digital format to provide copyright information for all the content sources. Use of metadata early in the process will increase chances that the media will be treated correctly further down the supply chain, especially when the media is handled with automated procedures. Refer to Chapter 11 for more on metadata tools and methods.

- **Watermarking:** Watermarking technology is far from perfect. It is also true that watermarking video is a complex and difficult problem. While it provides a way for you to mark your content before distribution to anyone, be aware that many watermarking technologies have been broken already, and some affect the quality of the video and audio. Early watermarking techniques aimed at identifying MP3 copies of music CDs have resulted in embarrassing recalls for the record labels that have used them.

- **Encryption:** Depending on your encryption technology and the context of your distribution, encryption will normally be applied at the point of distribution to the consumer. The reason for this is that the strongest encryption processes require different keys for each user, high levels of processing power, and often complex processes if applied in the middle of the content-creation process. When applied at the point of distribution to the consumer, it can be coupled with specialized consumer hardware to mitigate the effect on the consumer. Such individualized encryption isn't always used (see DVDs, for example), but you should consider it when protecting access to content that is of utmost importance. When content security is a priority, apply encryption as early in the workflow as possible, but realize there are costs.

Workflow Issues

When building data-driven workflow processes, the organization must make several decisions in regards to DRM. Should internal postproduction content be protected with DRM? In most cases, the answer to this is no. In certain secure installations (military intelligence, law enforcement, big-budget feature films, for example), you may want to protect content at every stage of the process, and simple access control isn't enough to protect the content at the storage level. If you decide to protect at this level, realize that the point of setting up an automated workflow and DMAM system is to allow controlled access to content. If your DRM system obstructs the automated flow of information through the organization, you may want to rethink your reasons for using DRM at this stage in the process.

What is workflow's role in DRM? If it is your intent to set up a fully managed content production workflow system, you may want to add DRM-related steps to the workflow. You may be able to automate some of these processes completely. For example, a workflow could automatically spawn an encryption process upon being marked final by the director and producer.

Increasingly, workflows move outside the corporate firewall to extranets and even the public Internet. In these instances, how far can you trust your vendors and distributors with the content prior to publication? Building DRM into the workflow process as it leaves the firewall may be necessary; however, it may be expensive to manage this process if your DRM vendor hasn't built this into the original DRM system. The parties outside the firewall will likely require some form of client software that must be licensed from the DRM vendor and that must be managed by your IT team. Even if you require such processes of your employees, getting people outside your organization to use the same processes may be difficult. Making the process convenient is essential to ensuring its use outside the organization.

Complexities of Media Assembly

Ask questions about how your media is composed. How deep do you need to track information? As an editor, do you care about archiving fonts used in graphics (and if so, in what format)? What about special transitions, perhaps the edit decision list (EDL)? As a music producer, are you going to archive outtakes and between-takes, and what are the rights on those media as opposed to the published media?

The deeper you go, the more expensive the digital rights problem becomes. There is a point of diminishing economic return in any system. However, if you at least don't capture the data now, you won't have substantial opportunities later when less expensive off-the-shelf software becomes available that can handle the job profitably.

Using Risk Management and Insurance

No DRM strategy or technology, no matter how well it's thoughtout, is perfect. In reality, the saying, "Your DRM and network security system are only worth as much as the network administrator's stock options," is probably more true than most of us want to admit.

So, the need to develop a risk management plan is essential. Watchers need to watch watchers, and outside watchers need to be employed. Remember that DRM methods are preventive measures — deterrents — but you have to plan for the deterrent to fail. The planning for failure is where risk management needs to be used. Some algorithm needs to be developed that balances how much is spent on DRM methods against the risks and costs of those methods' failure.

Businesses do this all the time, and they work with insurance companies to come up with a balanced plan of protection. However, we are in uncharted territory. No one really knows what it would mean in terms of lost revenues or damage if someone downloaded the latest blockbuster and sent it out two weeks before release. Luckily, the insurance industry usually can put a price on anything, and as we move ahead in digital content, insurance companies are likely to be regular visitors to production houses.

Global Issues

No discussion of DRM would be complete without including the additional nightmare of global copyright and security laws. Because copyright and other intellectual property laws and enforcement levels are different for each country, in many cases DRM systems will have to manage the access, management, and consumption rights differently. For example, a distributor may have rights to distribute one publisher's content worldwide but be prohibited from distributing other content to Asia, Africa, or other regions where piracy is prevalent. The DRM is responsible not only for verifying the location of the consumer through account and payment details but also for ensuring that the actual delivery destination matches the consumer's stated location. Levels of deterrents are also subject to change, with different countries allowed access to different levels of encryption. In addition, integrated media companies will have to think about balancing the kind of punishment doled out in various countries for violations with profits and public image. China has already put to death one hacker; a global enterprise might consider the damages from that kind of publicity more damaging than the loss of content.

DRM — Not a Complete Solution for Content Protection

Think about home security systems — they are never sold with a guarantee that they will *prevent* all break-ins. Instead, they function as both a deterrent and a detection system. DRM, from encryption to authorship metadata, has to be looked at in the same way. The problem content creators, owners, and distributors face is that detection in a global network is a lot of work. For example, tracking down everyone who ever used Napster to obtain a song they didn't pay for would not only be impossible, but it would likely result in a PR nightmare.

So any DRM vendors who come to you and say their technology can't be defeated, escort them to the door. There is no perfect solution, period — all it takes is one small, insignificant vulnerability and your DRM solutions will be compromised. Therefore, your only true protection is to plan for failure, institute good detection procedures, and have a back-up plan. Don't be in the situation content distributors are in with DVD encryption. The breaking of the code means that they have to either recall every DVD and DVD player sold or live with the problem. So the central goal is managing your risk, and the better you do that, the more profitable your move to digital media will be.

Additional Resources

http://www.cyberbee.com/copyrt.html
Adventures of CyberBee: Shockwave presentation on copyright and fair use issues. Authors: Virtual University Professional Development Partnership, Columbus Education Association, and Otterbein College

Section IV: Merged Architectures

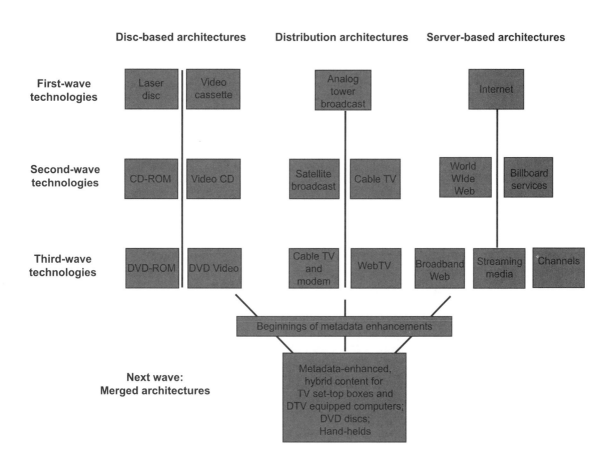

	Disc-based architectures	Distribution architectures	Server-based architectures
First-wave technologies	Laser disc / Video cassette	Analog tower broadcast	Internet
Second-wave technologies	CD-ROM / Video CD	Satellite broadcast / Cable TV	World Wide Web / Billboard services
Third-wave technologies	DVD-ROM / DVD Video	Cable TV and modem / WebTV	Broadband Web / Streaming media / Channels

Beginnings of metadata enhancements

Next wave: Merged architectures

Metadata-enhanced, hybrid content for TV set-top boxes and DTV equipped computers; DVD discs; Hand-helds

Section IV: Merged Architectures

CHAPTER 14

Introduction

Convergence or Divergence?

The theme of convergence that has suffered from overuse at the National Association of Broadcasters (NAB) convention and other industry events refers to the coming together of the television, film, and computer industries through shared digital technologies. The reality is that during the late 1990s digital technologies have, in fact, brought about the opposite effect in regard to distribution. A plethora of new formats and distribution mechanisms — from the World Wide Web to set-top boxes to wireless devices — threatened to overwhelm even the most well-equipped and well-staffed content development facilities. From the viewpoint of content creators at the end of the last decade, convergence more accurately referred to the coming together of creation tools on the desktop (such as the flatbed, effects workstation, tape bay, audio mix room, multimedia software, Website development tools, and so forth) while divergence more accurately described the new range of requirements for output.

Two Illustrations

The following two illustrations outline at a high level the evolution of creation paths, first toward divergent delivery formats and then toward merged architecture formats.

Figure 14-1 highlights the separate paths required to create the types of content that are common in the industry today. Until recently, production of various forms of media involved such distinct technologies and techniques that the translation of content required significant time and resources.

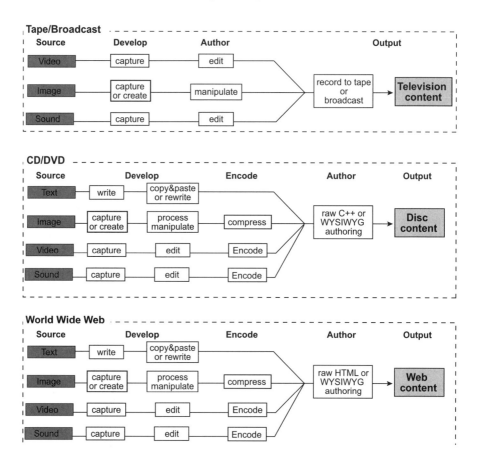

Figure 14-1 Traditional Development Paths: Divergent Creation, Divergent Output

The diversity of output requirements encouraged the evolution of development tools that brought video production, Website creation, and multimedia authoring together on the desktop (with the World Wide Web as a common focal point), with the ability to publish content across two or more formats in order to streamline the process. See Figure 14-2.

Step 1: Workstation Model
Convergent Creation, Divergent Output

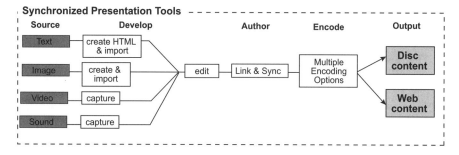

Step 2: Workgroup Model
Single-Source Creation & Storage, Divergent Output

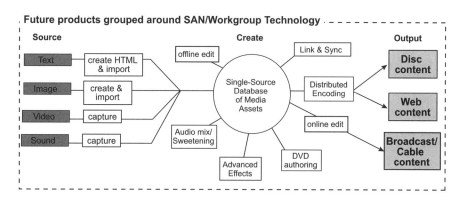

Figure 14-2 Create Once, Publish Everywhere (COPE) Paths

In the new millennium, true convergence at the distribution end is starting to take shape in the form of hybrid delivery mechanisms.

This section of the book describes the most prominent convergence points, such as interactive television (iTV) and hybrid DVDs. We conclude with a chapter on a new generation of Internet devices that includes everything from game consoles to set-top boxes to wireless devices. Interestingly, all of these convergent platforms rely heavily on Internet and World Wide Web technologies as their backbone. Thankfully, from the content development standpoint, even as delivery devices continue to multiply, the industry seems to be gradually settling on a mature set of standards and architectures.

Evolution of Cross-Media Content Creation

At the high end of production, interoperability between software applications handling video, audio, and effects has been a Holy Grail of content creators for some time. With the advent of hybrid formats and multiplication of Internet devices, there's also the new imperative to author content that can interop from one delivery mechanism to another, a process sometimes referred to as cross-media publishing.

The need for effective publishing across all barriers is giving rise to a new crop of tools to streamline the process. At all the big publishing industry gatherings such as the Seybold Conference held recently in Boston, the term cross-media publishing gets a lot of play in press and marketing materials surrounding the event. In some ways it is the print publishing/Web publishing industry answer to the convergence theme at NAB. The term cross-media publishing was originally coined to embody the efficient repurposing of content between print publications and the World Wide Web.

In the past, these two camps hailed from very different traditions. A Website that showed nothing but static pages naturally took its cues from the design concepts and principles of the print industry. In the traditions of motion media — from film to video — a different set of standards has prevailed for the most part, with font issues and color management lower down on the priority scale compared to manipulations of time, audio, or 3D capabilities, for example. During the late 1990s, motion-media professionals grappled with their own set of cross-media challenges, such as simultaneous broadcast and disc-based (CD and DVD) deployment of content.

Considering the growing viability of video, audio, and various forms of animation on the Web, we can now safely extend the cross-media imperative to include the NAB crowd as well. Broadcasters are starting to embrace the Web with genuine enthusiasm — not as a second-rate upstart but as a medium in its own right, with its own particular technical and aesthetic guidelines — while old-guard Web and multimedia developers are taking on the specific challenges of full-motion video and animation with gusto.

Convergence Tools

One easy solution right off the bat is to go with a suite of tools from a single vendor that has achieved some degree of compatibility between applications. Adobe and Macromedia are two leading examples of this. In the past few years these two powerhouses — along with just about every software vendor servicing the production community — have retooled their product lines to address the demands of the Web, and this has given rise to an interesting mix of cross-media capabilities. Table 14-1 presents a simple matrix that conveys the cross-media strengths of several leading vendors.

Table 14-1: Cross-Media Production Tools

Delivery format	Adobe Systems	Apple Computer	Avid Technology	Discreet	Macromedia	Media100	Microsoft	Pinnacle Systems
Print publishing	X						X	
Web authoring	X		X	X	X	X	X	
Web animation	X		X	X	X	X		
Film/TV animation	X	X	X	X		X		
CD-ROM authoring					X		X	X
Entry-level DVD authoring		X	X			X		X
Pro DVD authoring	X	X					X	X
Desktop video/audio	X	X	X	X	X	X	X	X
Pro video/audio	X	X	X			X		X
Web video/audio	X	X	X	X		X		X

Because these vendors have been building from their strengths, each one covers some areas of cross-media publishing, but no one vendor really has a total solution yet for moving between the big four delivery contexts: print, Web, video, and disc.

Adobe Systems (Print, Web, Video, Disc)

Adobe Systems seems to cover the broadest range, even if some of the tools are not the most popular. Now that Adobe has achieved a reasonable degree of compatibility and similarity between its old standards — Photoshop, Illustrator, Premiere, and Adobe After Effects — with late-comers Adobe GoLive, InDesign, and LiveMotion bolstering the Web end of things — it's a good starting point for any aspiring cross-media publisher. The biggest challenge for Adobe is to keep up with the competition while maintaining such a wide range of applications. Adobe GoLive, for example, competes hard with Macromedia Dreamweaver. The new LiveMotion makes an exciting entrance on the Web animation stage, while Flash continues to maintain a big lead. Adobe recently began a DVD authoring initiative but will once again have to compete with more established vendors for that market.

Apple Computer (Web, Video, Disc)

Apple has made use strides as a software provider for the production community with the increasingly sophisticated Final Cut Pro (now in its third generation) and elegant, user-friendly disc-authoring tools such as iDVD and DVD Studio Pro. Apple continues to push further toward the high end of production with improved color correction tools and integration of third-party tools for film editors as well as serial digital interface (SDI) and high definition (HD)-quality PCI cards and tools.

Avid Technology (Web, Video, Disc, iTV)

You might be surprised by a couple of the entries under the Avid heading in the above matrix. That's because Avid's Web strategy yielded some surprising results. Avid Xpress DV and the ePublisher suite cover some cross-media territory for which Avid is ideally suited: moving high-quality video from the desktop out to either the Web or onto disc (CD-ROM, DVD-ROM, and DVD Video). Avid Xpress DV takes the unmatched elegance of the Avid editing interface into the realm of DV authoring. Because of the affordable, lightweight, and no-hassle tools that have sprung up around this broadcast-quality format, DV has become the de facto standard for many cross-media publishing operations that involve video. Avid has attempted to give the DV author every possible option on output, including the ability to encode and author simple DVD Video titles using the bundled DVDit! software from Sonic Solutions, plus output to popular Web-streaming formats such as RealMedia G2, Microsoft Windows Media, and Quick-Time/Sorenson. Avid is working to develop iTV features within its industry-standard postproduction tools and is also working toward integration of DVD scripting technologies through its Advanced Authoring Format (AAF)-based meta data strategy.

Macromedia (Web, Disc, iTV)

Macromedia's strong emphasis on its Web strategy has taken it a long way since Director ruled the new media world for CD-ROM production. Flash continues to win converts (including arch-rival Adobe which supports Flash output in its LiveMotion application), and Dreamweaver consistently receives great reviews. If Macromedia had not sold its Final Cut video editing technology to Apple (the starting point for Apple's Final Cut Pro), it would cover an even more impressive swath of the above matrix. But Macromedia's careful focus on its strengths — multimedia authoring retooled for the Web — makes its suite of tools the best option if your cross-media publishing needs extend only between disc (CD-ROM and DVD-ROM) and Web-based delivery. The Dreamweaver exchange community also provides tools for interactive television authoring. We might see Macromedia grow more aggressively in the direction iTV should that medium begin to prosper.

Media 100 (Web, Video, Disc)

Avid's perennial competitor Media 100 offers the high-powered 844/X products as well as iFINISH for Windows and Media 100 i for Macintosh. iFinish and Media 100 i both interoperate with the Cleaner products, which Media 100 sold to Discreet in 2001. For Media 100 (and cross-media publishers who use their tools), this is a marriage made in heaven, though as the above matrix shows, you still need additional tools to fill in the disc-authoring piece of the puzzle. iFINISH allows you to perform every stage of the streaming media production workflow for Web delivery and also allows you to record broadcast-quality video to tape or for use in DVD authoring with third-party tools.

Pinnacle Systems Inc. (Web, Video, Disc)

Pinnacle made a strong entrance into the nonlinear editing arena last year with several new tools that were designed from the outset to solve some of the cross-media challenges of today's authors/editors. Pinnacle's strategy answers a basic question: If you had to choose one video compression scheme for cross-media deployment, what would it be? Pinnacle's answer is MPEG-2. Not a bad choice, when you consider that variations of MPEG are used for everything from DVDs to digital satellite broadcasts to digital television to Webcasting. What Pinnacle has done is solve the basic problem of MPEG-2 editing by employing a unique IBB encoding pattern that leaves the MPEG stream open to cuts. This form of encoding does require some additional reencoding, however, to make it compliant with the DVD Video spec, but it takes a fraction of the time with no loss of quality. Pinnacle has also found a way to author Windows-only CD-ROMs that use MPEG-2 without the need for additional plug-ins or installations on the user's system. Bundled with the full-featured DVD authoring tool Minerva Impression, these are formidable systems covering every output option, minus the ability to build Web pages.

Cross-Media Practices

While building up a collection of tools that best meets your cross-platform challenges, you can also develop standards and techniques for getting the job done more efficiently.

Everything's Relative

Those of us who started out with no computer background and a bunch of WYSIWYG tools learned a few good lessons from grappling with HTML in recent years. Two of the greatest benefits to cross-media publishers are the use of relative paths (versus absolute paths) and the building of uncompiled applications.

Relative paths (in HTML for example) tell the browser where to find source material for drawing the page relative to where the page itself lives on the server. An absolute path includes the full location including the name of the drive itself. Therefore, if the drive changes (when you move the top-level folder), the link is broken. Relative paths allow you to move the top-level folder to any location and maintain all internal links.

Hand-in-hand with relative paths is the fact that Websites are built as uncompiled applications, which means that all the elements of the Website remain in pieces. This can be a pain when trying to keep track of all the elements, of course, but it also means that you can revise and replace items in the source folders at any time, making sure to keep the same filenames, and the code calls them up automatically whenever the page is opened.

All Website development tools maintain this approach, and in fact many software vendors who once forced you to import elements into their applications now allow you to maintain source elements externally. Adobe has done a good job throughout its product line: Illustrator, InDesign, Premiere, and Adobe After Effects all keep track of source files, so you can make changes and your compositions are updated instantly. For example, if you are sharing a series of still images between a brochure (InDesign), a Website (GoLive), a video clip (Premiere), and an animation (After Effects), you can change a graphic once and replace it in all locations to update the image in all contexts.

Naming Schemes

To take this technique further, you can devise a naming scheme for your projects that allows you to replace source files from project to project (or between iterations of the same project) with completely different source material and instantly display a new design in the application.

One of the lessons we've learned in attempting this is that as much as we enjoy the ability to give meaningful labels to files using long filenames, the truth is that this gets in the way when you begin to swap out files in a project. Consider giving meaningful names to your source material at the folder level, while keeping your filenames generic.

Here's an example of a source folder for a recent project. In our naming scheme, the first number indicates the section of the presentation (section 01-, section 02-, etc.). The middle number indicates the scene (-01-, -02-, -03-, etc). The third character group indicates either a text element (-a, -b, -c, etc.) or a graphic element (-01, 02, 03, and so forth). With this naming scheme, all elements group together, making it easy to navigate when you view the folder by name. In addition, we can take the elements to different contexts or redesign them completely, and they will still show up appropriately in the various applications in which we use them.

Capture Size and Resolution

One basic problem with swapping outsource files is that when the size of the graphics changes, most applications don't automatically resize them. So you can end up with the task of readjusting each graphic for size within your Web pages or multimedia authoring tool. Automatic resizing would be a nice cross-media feature for vendors to add to development applications. One way to get around this, whenever possible, is to arrive at a standard size for as many elements in a piece as possible. Occasionally this might mean a little extra work in your paint or illustration tools (compositing foreground elements with a standard-size background, for example), but it will pay off when you start to change the source material from iteration to iteration, project to project, or delivery platform to delivery platform.

You should also choose your base resolution (the resolution in which you first capture and store the source) with an eye toward cross-media conversions. For example, if you know that you will be using images for both print and CD-ROM projects, scan or create the source artwork in high-resolution first (240 to 300 dpi minimum for most print applications). If you know that you will only use a set of graphics for Website work and in a video project, you can save drive space by capturing the source at screen resolution (72 or 96 dpi), 640 x 480 pixel dimensions or smaller. If you plan to produce iTV content that will also be available on the Web, make sure you conform to the design requirements of iTV first (see "Design Tips for Television Display" on page 431) then either provide an alternate page that includes additional elements for Web display or simply design the content to work adequately in both contexts. One popular solution among iTV developers is to create content in Flash, which displays well in either context and scales easily to any display size.

For video, capture the material at the highest resolution you can according to your cross-media requirements. For television and DVD Video situations, this is a given. If you know you will only use the material for CD-ROM and low-bandwidth Websites, you can get away with 320 x 240 dimensions. You never know when you might want to repurpose that video in a higher-bandwidth situation, so I still suggest at least 640 x 480. And maintain the video in a high-quality codec such as DV or MJPEG with as little transcoding as possible during its cross-media journeys. Reencode only at the last possible moment in each context.

Similarly, choose the file formats for your source images carefully so that they will go the furthest in the cross-media maze without the need for conversion. For example, a format such as JPEG is now supported by nearly every application out there, whereas your PNG files might hit a wall with some older applications. To accomplish conversions when they do become necessary, you should add to your cross-media arsenal as many automation tools as you can, with scripts in DeBabelizer, Actions in Photoshop, or scripting languages such as AppleScript.

Authoring Technology

Finally, your choice of basic technologies for authoring your projects can make a big difference in mastering cross-media situations. For greatest ease in cross-media translations, of course, the ideal situation is to author once and deploy in all contexts — another Holy Grail. This is all but impossible in most situations, but in one case, CD-ROM and Website deployments, you might just get away with it.

For example, we all know about Shockwave. Production companies often attempt to create Director titles that can also function reasonably in low-bandwidth situations so that they can deploy the material on the Web using the Shockwave plug-in.

If you deplore plug-ins, here's another radical idea: Go in the other direction. In other words, start authoring your titles with the Web browser as your target player, both on the Web and off CD-ROM. Considering the primacy of the Web and the presence of Web browsers on most desktops, this is probably the way to go and will probably become the trend of all future authoring methods and tools. And with technologies such as Flash and Dynamic HTML and new tools such as ePublisher, you can go a long way toward rivaling the effectiveness of titles authored using traditional tools such as Director.

The following chapters cover more specific tools and techniques for working with the various convergent media formats.

Section IV: Merged Architectures

CHAPTER 15

All About MPEG

This chapter provides information regarding MPEG technologies as well as available tools for encoding and working with various forms of MPEG, with a special focus on MPEG-4.

Part A: Background

Introduction

The founding of the Motion Pictures Experts Group (MPEG), established as an International Standards Organization (ISO) workgroup, dates back to the late 1980s. The workgroup's formal name is ISO/IEC JTC 1/SC 29/WG 11. MPEG standards produced by the group have created exciting new opportunities throughout the media production community. The impact of this working group reaches further than most of us realize. MPEG formats have been central to some of the most successful new digital media formats to arrive in the past decade, including multimedia CD-ROMs, Video CD, DVD, and various forms of digital television delivery including digital terrestrial, satellite, and wireless services.

As a multimedia video format, MPEG was overshadowed during the 1990s by the excitement over proprietary streaming video formats from Apple, Microsoft, and RealNetworks. There's a good chance that the MPEG workgroup will soon take center stage in this new arena as well, with the widespread adoption of the new MPEG-4 standard. According to an analysis report from Penton Media (www.penton.com) presented in November 2001, MPEG-4 is expected to become the streaming media standard within three years. Through surveys with member companies of the Internet Streaming Media Alliance (www.ISMA.org) and the MPEG-4 Industry Forum (www.M4IF.org), the report found that 65 percent of respondents expect MPEG-4 to become the standard for streaming media within three years and 93 percent expect it to become the standard for streaming media within five years. This accomplishment would restore MPEG standards to the core of nearly every digital delivery platform for video. For this reason, we've consolidated reference information on all MPEG formats here in the Merged Architectures section.

MPEG-4, in particular, could prove to be the cross-over format of choice for a whole variety of delivery mechanisms, from the World Wide Web to set-top boxes to wireless devices. MPEG-4, however, represents more than just digital video; the standard accommodates a wide range of current technology for animation and interactivity as well. For this reason, we give special treatment to this promising new format in this chapter.

Flavors of MPEG

Despite the fact that the numbering of MPEG specifications, either completed ones or works in progress, runs all the way up to MPEG-21, there are really only five. Table 15-1 provides a quick comparison.

Table 15-1: MPEG Specification — Quick Comparison

Specification	Description	Delivery Contexts	Special Features
MPEG-1	The first digital video and audio specification; also the source of the popular MP3 format for music and sound	Video CD, CD-ROM, Web	Allows VHS-quality video to fit on standard CD, with menu navigation
MPEG-2	Broadcast-quality digital video and audio that was meant to address HDTV and was eventually rolled into MPEG-2	DVD, television set-top boxes	Allows broadcast-quality video to fit on DVD disc; enabled digital terrestrial, cable, and satellite broadcasts
MPEG-4	Scalable, object-oriented, multi-track format accommodating video, audio, 2D animation, 3D animation, vector animation, synthetic voice, and more	Wireless devices, Web, possibly set-top boxes and DVD	Is meant to address needs of the streaming video arena while supporting a wide variety of media elements
MPEG-7	Builds rich metadata layers onto previous specifications	Archival facilities, video libraries and servers	Will provide a framework in which media objects can be identified, archived, searched, filtered, and reused
MPEG-21	Superset that accommodates former specifications and adds focus on deployment, pay-per-view, monetization, branding, and privacy	All former contexts	Will provide an all-encompassing environment for multimedia content development and deployment across platforms

MPEG-1

Go to http://mpeg.telecomitalialab.com/standards/mpeg-1/mpeg-1.htm

The MPEG-1 specification fulfilled the first mission of the MPEG workgroup: to enable the encoding of moving pictures and associated audio for digital storage media at up to about 1.5 Mbps. The reason for this particular target rate was the fact that it would allow distribution and playback of MPEG-1 content on the conventional compact disc (CD).

The standard consists of five parts, approved between November 1992 and 1994:

- Part 1 (Systems): Provides multiplexing and synchronization support to elementary audio and video streams

- Part 2 (Video): Provides efficient encoding of noninterlaced pictures with roughly VHS quality at 1.15 Mbps

- Part 3 (Audio): Provides encoding of stereo audio with transparency (subjective quality similar to the original stereo) at 384, 256, and 192 Kbps per Layer I, II, and III, respectively

- Part 4: (Conformance Testing): Provides methods and reference bitstreams that can be used to assess conformance of a bitstream or of a decoder, which was approved one year later

- Part 5: (Reference Software): Contains the C-code implementation of a systems multiplexer/demultiplexer and of encoders and decoders for audio and video

Both software and hardware players exist for MPEG-1. The video CD is a full application of MPEG-1, with more than 60 million hardware Video CD decoders sold worldwide, primarily outside of North America.

A more recent worldwide claim to fame is MPEG-1 Audio Layer III, also known as MP3. Many software packages now exist to rip a track from a CD audio and compress it in MP3.

MPEG-2

Go to http://mpeg.telecomitalialab.com/standards/mpeg-2/mpeg-2.htm

MPEG-2 was first discussed in July 1990, and was meant to address the need to provide digital encoding of broadcast-quality, component video. The 4:2:2 profile for video was approved in January 1996 and is an integral part of MPEG-2 video. The total specification was approved in parts between 1994 and 1996.

The first 5 parts of the specification cover areas similar to MPEG-1, while MPEG-2 adds additional parts for a total of 10parts:

- Part 1 (Systems): Transport Stream version of the Systems part provides support for efficient transmission over error-prone delivery systems, while the Program Stream version, similar to MPEG-1 Systems, is more useful for digital storage media.

- Part 2 (Video): It provides support for efficient coding of interlaced pictures at different spatial resolutions. These have been grouped in profiles to offer different functionalities, from simple VHS quality all the way to uncompressed 4:2:2 component video.

- Part 3 (Audio): MPEG-2 is backward-compatible with the MPEG-1 audio standard. Part 7 adds a multichannel extension for implementation of high-quality AC-3 audio surround sound.

- Part 4 (Conformance Testing): Like MPEG-1, it provides methods and reference bitstreams that can be used to assess conformance of a bitstream or of a decoder.

- Part 5 (Reference Software): Like MPEG-1, it contains the C-code implementation of a systems multiplexer/demultiplexer and of encoders and decoders for audio and video.

- Part 6 (Digital Storage Media Command and Control): DSM-CC provides protocols for session setup across different networks and for remote control of a server containing MPEG-2 content.

- Part 7 (Advanced Audio Coding): AAC provides a new multichannel audio coding that is not backward-compatible with MPEG-1 audio.

- Part 8 It was intended to support video coding when samples are represented with an accuracy of more than 8 bits, but its development was discontinued when the interest of the industry that had requested it did not materialize.

- Part 9 (Real-Time Interface): It provides a standard interface between an MPEG-2 transport stream and a decoder.

- Part 10 (DSM-CC Conformance Testing): It provides methods and reference bitstreams that can be used to assess conformance of a bitstream or of a decoder for DSM-CC.

Parts 1, 2, and 3 (this last one sometimes replaced with a proprietary solution) are used in some millions of digital television set-top boxes and DVDs. Some MPEG-2 encoders are very costly professional equipment, and some are very inexpensive PC boards that are sold with video editing software.

Several examples of DSM-CC are widely used in set-top boxes for satellite and cable. This part of the standard is also at the basis of provision of other set-top-box functionalities by other standards bodies and industry consortia. AAC has been adopted by Japan for a national digital television standard and by several manufacturers of secure digital music.

An important MPEG-2 amendment has been developed to support the carriage of MPEG-4 objects on MPEG-2 transport streams. This will enable rich multimedia applications in the television domain.

MPEG-4

Go to http://mpeg.telecomitalialab.com/standards/mpeg-4/mpeg-4.htm

The MPEG-4 standard, approved between 1998 and 2001, is based on Apple QuickTime and Virtual Reality Modeling Language (VRML). These technologies were chosen as the starting point because they met many of the goals of the new standard, specifically object-oriented, multitrack, multimedia capabilities. At the same time, MPEG-4 is also meant to surpass the broadcast-quality high-bitrate capabilities of MPEG-1 and MPEG-2.

Most importantly, MPEG-4 seeks to overcome the developer's current difficulties in dealing with a multitude of proprietary, incompatible formats and players by providing standardized ways to deliver interactive media across a number of high-profile applications such as Web streaming, wireless networking, and interactive television.

Work on the MPEG-4 standard Coding of Audiovisual Objects began in July 1993 in New York City and the first set of standards (so-called Version 1) was approved at the Atlantic City, NJ, meeting in October 1998. A major extension of the standard (so-called Version 2) was approved at the Maui, HI, meeting in December 1999.

Like all of the big three streaming media formats, MPEG-4 includes both a media spec and a server spec. The specification accommodates lossy environments, networks, and over-the-air broadcasts. Audio, video, and synthetic content such as animation, 3D elements, and synthetic speech are supported as well, making MPEG-4 the most wide ranging and most versatile MPEG standard to date. MPEG-4 can be used in many application areas, from Web browser delivery to interactive television to wireless devices, each with their own agendas and practices concerning the business models of how technology is actually deployed.

MPEG-4 shares many features with MPEG-1 and MPEG-2, although for low-bandwidth use, MPEG-4 provides better motion estimation and a deblocking filter. The standard supports interlaced content, with resolutions up to 4,096 x 4,096 and a data range from 5 kbps to 10 Mbps in version 1.

On the audio front, MPEG-4 provides new codecs for low-bitrate speech: Harmonic Vector eXcitation Encoding (HVXC) for the 2 kbps to 4 kbps range, and Code Excited Linear Predictive (CELP) for 4 kbps to 24 kbps. AAC (Advanced Audio Coding) from MPEG-2 and TwinVQ for general-purpose are also included.

MPEG-4 supports client-based and server-based interactions, with secure communications and pay-per-view through Intellectual Property Management and Protection (IPMP).

MPEG-4 also specifies a Java library for controlling content, called MPEG-J. With this library, a Java applet can be embedded in the MPEG stream, making it possible to include Java applets with the set-top box, for example.

On top of all that, MPEG-4 provides a wavelet-based still-image codec that is better than the perennial JPEG. MPEG-4 also includes a standardized file format based on VRML, called binary MPEG-4 format (BIFS). XMT is a textual format used in MPEG-4 that encompasses parts of other XML format such as SMIL and Web3D and that can be compiled to the binary MPEG-4 format.

Version 2 of the specification provides improved error correction and support for stereoscopic views, as well as codec enhancements (advanced coding efficiency), and additional profiles.

MPEG-4 and Rich-Media Capabilities

The rich-media capabilities of MPEG-4 truly set this standard apart from all others. From its VRML heritage, MPEG-4 handles media as objects. These object types can include audio, video, stills, text, synthetic speech, 3D models, textures, and more. MPEG-4 enables the coding of individual objects. This means that the video information need not be of rectangular shape as MPEG-1 and MPEG-2 video assume. In addition, the various types of media are mapped to objects in a scene. MPEG-4 includes an event model for triggering events or routing user actions to objects in a scene.

A media object in its coded form consists of descriptive elements that allow handling of the object in an audiovisual scene as well as of associated streaming data, if needed. It is important to note that in its coded form, each media object can be represented independent of its surroundings or background.

The coded representation of media objects is as efficient as possible while taking into account the desired functionalities. Examples of such functionalities are error robustness, easy extraction and editing of an object, or availability of objects in a scalable form. You can also group primitive media objects together. Primitive media objects correspond to leaves in the descriptive tree while compound media objects encompass entire subtrees. As an example, the visual object corresponding to a talking person and the corresponding voice are tied together to form a new compound media object containing both the aural and visual components of that talking person. Such grouping allows authors to construct complex scenes and enables consumers to manipulate meaningful sets of objects.

Media can include alpha channels. Vector-based elements, such as those used in Flash and scalable vector graphics (SVG), are also supported. In essence, MPEG-4 mixes the best of Shockwave, Flash, VRML, and video into single format, server, and player.

MPEG-4 Profiles

MPEG-4 players can support various subsets of the specification called profiles. Recent versions of the spec include a total of 19 visual, 8 audio, 4 graphics, and 5 scene graph profiles. These subsets are intended to address the needs of specific market segments in order to avoid the cost of complexity of implementing unnecessary aspects of this far-reaching specification.

- The visual part of the standard provides profiles for the coding of synthetic, natural, and synthetic/natural hybrid visual content.

- The audio part of the standard provides profiles for coding of natural and synthetic speech for various data rates.

- Graphics profiles define which graphical and textual elements can be used in a scene. These profiles are defined in the Systems part of the standard.

- Scene graph profiles (or scene description profiles), defined in the Systems part of the standard, allow audiovisual scenes with audio-only, 2D, 3D, or mixed 2D/3D content.

- MPEG-J profiles address the Java support and include a personal profile (a lightweight package for personal devices) and main profile (all the MPEG-J APIs).

- The object descriptor profile defines levels for the object descriptor (OD), sync layer (SL), object content information (OCI), and intellectual property management and protection (IPMP) tools.

Visual Profiles

- Simple Visual Profile provides efficient error-resilient coding of rectangular video objects, suitable for applications on mobile networks.

- Simple Scalable Visual Profile adds support for coding of temporal and spatial scalable objects to the Simple Visual Profile, allowing for efficient scaling on the Internet, for example.

- Core Visual Profile adds support for coding of arbitrary-shaped and temporally scalable objects to the Simple Visual Profile. It is useful for achieving relatively simple interactivity, on the Internet, for example.

- Main Visual Profile adds support for coding of interlaced, semitransparent, and sprite objects to the Core Visual Profile. It is useful for interactive and entertainment-quality broadcast and DVD applications.

- N-Bit Visual Profile adds support for coding video objects having pixel depths ranging from 4 to 12 bits to the Core Visual Profile. It is suitable for use in surveillance applications.

Synthetic and Synthetic/Natural Hybrid Visual Content Profiles

- Simple Facial Animation Visual Profile provides a simple means to animate a face model, suitable for applications such as audiovideo presentation for the hearing-impaired.

- Scalable Texture Visual Profile provides spatial scalable coding of still-image (texture) objects useful for applications needing multiple scalability levels, such as mapping texture onto objects in games and high-resolution digital still cameras.

- Basic Animated 2D Texture Visual Profile provides spatial scalability, signal-to-noise (SNR) scalability, and mesh-based animation for still-image (textures) objects and also simple face object animation.

- Hybrid Visual Profile combines the ability to decode arbitrary-shaped and temporally scalable natural video objects (as in the Core Visual Profile) with the ability to decode several synthetic and hybrid objects, including simple face and animated still-image objects. It is suitable for various content-rich multimedia applications.

- Advanced Real-Time Simple (ARTS) Profile provides advanced error-resilient coding techniques of rectangular video objects using a back channel and improved temporal resolution stability with the low buffering delay. It is suitable for real-time coding applications such as the videophone, teleconferencing, and remote observation.

- Core Scalable Profile adds support for coding of temporal and spatial scalable, arbitrary-shaped objects to the Core Profile. The main functionality of this profile is object-based SNR and spatial/temporal scalability for regions or objects of interest. It is useful for applications such as the Internet, mobile, and broadcast.

- Advanced Coding Efficiency (ACE) Profile improves the coding efficiency for both rectangular and arbitrary-shaped objects. It is suitable for applications such as mobile broadcast reception, the acquisition of image sequences (camcorders), and other applications where high coding efficiency is requested and small footprint is not the prime concern.

- Advanced Scalable Texture Profile supports decoding of arbitrary-shaped texture and still images including scalable shape coding, wavelet tiling, and error resilience. It is useful for applications that require fast random access as well as multiple scalability levels and arbitrary-shaped coding of still objects. Examples are fast content-based still-image browsing on the Internet, multimedia-enabled PDAs, and Internet-ready high-resolution digital still cameras.

- Advanced Core Profile combines the ability to decode arbitrary-shaped video objects (as in the Core Visual Profile) with the ability to decode arbitrary-shaped scalable still-image objects (as in the Advanced Scalable Texture Profile). It is suitable for various content-rich multimedia applications such as interactive multimedia streaming over the Internet.

- Simple Face and Body Animation Profile is a superset of the Simple Face Animation Profile, adding — obviously — body animation.

- Advanced Simple Profile looks much like the other Simple Profiles in that it has only rectangular objects, but it has a few extra tools that make it more efficient: B-frames, one-quarter pel motion compensation, and global motion compensation.

- Fine Granular Scalability Profile allows many scalable layers — up to 8 — so that delivery quality can easily adapt to transmission and decoding circumstances. It can be used with Simple or Advanced Simple as a base layer.

- Simple Studio Profile is a profile with very high quality for usage in studio editing applications. It only has I frames, but it does support arbitrary shape and multiple alpha channels. Bit rates go up to almost 2 gigabits per second.

- Core Studio Profile adds P frames to Simple Studio, making it more efficient but also requiring more complex implementations.

Audio Profiles

- Speech Profile provides HVXC, which is a very-low bit-rate parametric speech coder, a CELP narrowband/wideband speech coder, and a text-to-speech interface.

- Synthesis Profile provides score-driven synthesis using SAOL and wave tables and a text-to-speech interface to generate sound and speech at very low bit rates.

- Scalable Profile, a superset of the Speech Profile, is suitable for scalable coding of speech and music for networks, such as Internet and narrow band audio digital broadcasting (NADIB). The bit rates range from 6 kbps to 24 kbps, with bandwidths between 3.5 and 9 kHz.

- Main Profile is a rich superset of all the other profiles containing tools for natural and synthetic audio.

- High-Quality Audio Profile contains the CELP speech coder and the low-complexity AAC coder, including long-term prediction. Scalable coding can be performed by the AAC scalable object type. Optionally, the new error-resilient (ER) bitstream syntax may be used.

- Low-Delay Audio Profile contains the HVXC and CELP speech coders (optionally using the ER bitstream syntax), the low-delay AAC coder, and the text-to-speech interface (TTSI).

- Natural Audio Profile contains all-natural audio coding tools available in MPEG-4, but not the synthetic ones.

- Mobile Audio Internetworking Profile contains the low-delay and scalable AAC object types including TwinVQ and BSAC. This profile is intended to extend communications applications using non-MPEG speech coding algorithms with high-quality audio coding capabilities.

Graphics Profiles

- Simple 2D Graphics Profile provides for only those graphics elements of the BIFS tool that are necessary to place one or more visual objects in a scene.

- Complete 2D Graphics Profile provides two-dimensional graphics functionalities and supports features such as arbitrary two-dimensional graphics and text, possibly in conjunction with visual objects.

- The Complete Graphics Profile provides advanced graphical elements such as elevation grids and extrusions and allows creation of content with sophisticated lighting. The Complete Graphics Profile enables applications such as complex virtual worlds that exhibit a high degree of realism.

- 3D Audio Graphics Profile sounds like a contradiction in terms, but it really isn't. This profile does not propose visual rendering, but graphics tools are provided to define the acoustical properties of the scene (geometry, acoustics absorption, diffusion, transparency of the material). This profile is used for applications that do environmental spatialization of audio signals.

Scene Graph Profiles

- Audio Scene Graph Profile provides for a set of BIFS scene graph elements for usage in audio-only applications. The Audio Scene Graph rofile supports applications such as broadcast radio.

- Simple 2D Scene Graph Profile provides for only those BIFS scene graph elements necessary to place one or more audiovisual objects in a scene. The Simple 2D Scene Graph Profile allows presentation of audiovisual content with potential update of the complete scene, but no interaction capabilities. The Simple 2D Scene Graph Profile supports applications such as broadcast television.

- Complete 2D Scene Graph Profile provides for all the 2D scene description elements of the BIFS tool. It supports features such as 2D transformations and alpha blending. The Complete 2D Scene Graph Profile enables 2D applications that require extensive and customized interactivity.

- Complete Scene Graph Profile provides the complete set of scene graph elements of the BIFS tool. The Complete Scene Graph Profile will enable applications such as dynamic virtual 3D world and games.

- 3D Audio Scene Graph Profile provides the tools for three-dimensional sound positioning in relation to either the acoustic parameters of the scene or its perceptual attributes. The user can interact with the scene by changing the position of the sound source, by changing the room effect, or by moving the listening point. This profile is intended for usage in audio-only applications.

MPEG-J Profiles

- Personal Profile addresses a range of constrained devices including mobile and portable devices. Examples of such devices are cell video phones, PDAs, and personal gaming devices. This profile includes the following packages of MPEG-J APIs:

  - Network

  - Scene

  - Resource

- Main Profile addresses a range of consumer devices including entertainment devices. Examples of such devices are set-top boxes, and computer-based multimedia systems. It is a superset of the Personal Profile. Apart from the packages in the Personal Profile, this profile includes the following packages of the MPEG-J APIs:

  - Decoder

  - Decoder functionality

  - Section filter and service information

- Object Descriptor Profile includes the following tools:

  - Object descriptor (OD) tool

  - Sync layer (SL) tool

- Object content information (OCI) tool

- Intellectual property management and protection (IPMP) tool

Currently, only one profile is defined that includes all these tools. The main reason for defining this profile is not subsetting the tools but rather defining levels for them. This applies especially to the sync layer tool, as MPEG-4 allows multiple time bases to exist. In the context of levels for this profile, restrictions can be defined (for example, to allow only a single time base).

MPEG-7

Go to http://mpeg.telecomitalialab.com/standards/mpeg-7/mpeg-7.htm

MPEG-7, formally named Multimedia Content Description Interface, is an audiovisual information representation that is intended to advance the meta-data needs and requirements for archiving MPEG content in useful ways. MPEG-7 allows the creation of descriptors and description schemes for the various types of MPEG media, with reference software information for developing a wide range of applications for archiving, finding, retrieving, accessing, filtering, and managing MPEG content.

Work on the MPEG-7 Multimedia Content Description Interface standard started in April 1997 and extends through 2002. The technical content of the standard is as follows:

- Systems provides the architectural framework of the standard, the carriage of MPEG-7 content, and the binarization of MPEG-7 content.

- Description Definition Language allows creation of descriptors and description schemes.

- Visual provides standard descriptors and description schemes that are purely visual.

- Audio provides standard descriptors and description schemes that are purely audio.

- Multimedia Description Schemes provides standard descriptors and description schemes that are neither visual nor audio.

- Reference software has the same normative value as the MPEG-4 reference software and may be used for products at the same conditions.

In addition to description of the content, MPEG-7 can also make available other types of information about the multimedia data:

- Form: An example of the form is the coding scheme used (for example, JPEG or MPEG-2) or the overall data size. This information helps in determining whether the material can be read by the user.

- Conditions for accessing the material: This includes links to a registry with intellectual property rights information and price.

- Classification: This includes parental rating and content classification into a number of predefined categories.

- Links to other relevant material: The information may help the user to speed up the search.

- The context: In the case of recorded nonfiction content, it is very important to know the occasion of the recording (for example, Olympic Games 1996, final of the men's 200-meter hurdles).

MPEG-7 data may be physically located with the associated AV material, either in the same data stream or on the same storage system, but the descriptions could also live somewhere else on public or private networks. When the content and its descriptions are not colocated, mechanisms that link AV material and their MPEG-7 descriptions are needed; these links will have to work in both directions.

The main elements of the MPEG-7 standard are:

- Descriptors (D), or representations of features, that define the syntax and the semantics of each feature representation

- Description schemes (DS) that specify the structure and semantics of the relationships between their components (these components may be both descriptors and description schemes)

- A description definition language (DDL) that allows the creation of new description schemes, and possibly descriptors, and that allows the extension and modification of existing description schemes

- System tools that support multiplexing of descriptions, synchronization of descriptions with content, transmission mechanisms, coded representations (both textual and binary formats) for efficient storage and transmission, management and protection of intellectual property in MPEG-7 descriptions, and so forth

MPEG-21

Go to http://mpeg.telecomitalialab.com/standards/mpeg-21/mpeg-21.htm

MPEG-21 is a very ambitious initiative that will attempt to address the big-picture requirements for having an open framework that standardizes all forms of multimedia content creation and delivery. MPEG-21 will describe a multimedia framework and set out a vision for the future of an environment where delivery and use of all content types by different categories of users in multiple application domains will be possible. The vision for MPEG-21 incorporates all previous standards into a multimedia framework to enable transparent and augmented use of multimedia resources across a wide range of networks and devices used by different communities.

Work on the MPEG-21 Multimedia Framework standard started in the summer of 2000. Currently a Technical Report, Vision, Technologies and Strategy, has been approved that lays down the concepts on which the actual technologies will be developed. The Technical Report was approved in July 2001.

There are two documents at the CD level (Digital Item Declaration and Intellectual Property Management and Protection) that correspond to parts 2 and 4 of MPEG-1. They were approved in May 2002. One document is at the WD level (Digital Item Identification and Description). Responses to the latest Call for Proposals on Rights Expression Language and Rights Data Dictionary were considered at the December 2001 meeting with the goal to develop two new parts of MPEG-21 (part 5 and 6). A Call for Proposals on Terminals and Networks was due to be published in early 2002.

The seven key elements defined in MPEG-21 are:

1. Digital Item Declaration (a uniform and flexible abstraction and interoperable schema for declaring digital items);

2. Digital Item Identification and Description (a framework for identification and description of any entity regardless of its nature, type, or granularity)

3. Content Handling and Usage (the interfaces and protocols that enable creation, manipulation, search, access, storage, delivery, use, and reuse of content across the content distribution and consumption value chain)

4. Intellectual Property Management and Protection (the means to enable content to be persistently and reliably managed and protected across a wide range of networks and devices)

5. Terminals and Networks (the ability to provide interoperable and transparent access to content across networks and terminals)

6. Content Representation (ways the media resources are represented)

7. Event Reporting (the metrics and interfaces that enable users to understand precisely the performance of all reportable events within the framework)

MPEG Timeline

Table 15-2 provides a brief overview of the evolution of MPEG specifications.

Table 15-2: MPEG Timeline

Date	Event
1988	Motion Pictures Experts Group (MPEG) established as an International Standards Organization (ISO) workgroup
1992	MPEG-1 standard parts 1, 2, and 3 released
1994	MPEG-2 standard released; MPEG-1 standard part 4 released
1998	MPEG-4 Version 1 ISO/IEC-14496
1999	MPEG-4 Version 2
2000 – 2002	MPEG-4, Versions 3, 4, 5
2001	MPEG-7 international standard
2002 – 2003	MPEG-21 standardization

MPEG Specifications and Resources

The main resources for information about ISO MPEG standards can be found at the following locations:

- MPEG-1: http://mpeg.telecomitalialab.com/standards/mpeg-1/mpeg-1.htm

- MPEG-2: http://mpeg.telecomitalialab.com/standards/mpeg-2/mpeg-2.htm

- MPEG-4: http://mpeg.telecomitalialab.com/standards/mpeg-4/mpeg-4.htm

- MPEG-7: http://mpeg.telecomitalialab.com/standards/mpeg-7/mpeg-7.htm

- MPEG-21: http://mpeg.telecomitalialab.com/standards/mpeg-21/mpeg-21.htm

Internet Engineering Task Force (IETF)

Go to www.ietf.org

For information about Internet architectures as they relate to MPEG standards, visit the IETF Website. IETF is a large, open, international community of network designers, operators, vendors, and researchers concerned with the evolution of the Internet architecture and the smooth operation of the Internet.

MPEG-4 Industry Forum (M4IF)

Go to www.m4if.org

The M4IF has been established as a not-for-profit organization external to MPEG with the goal of promoting the adoption of the standard and in particular creating the conditions for organizations dealing with patent licensing to be set up.

Internet Streaming Media Alliance, Inc. (ISMA)

Go to www.ism-alliance.org

The ISMA is a nonprofit corporation formed to provide a forum for the creation of specifications that define an interoperable implementation for streaming rich media (video, audio, and associated data) over Internet protocol (IP) networks. The ISMA provides a forum for the creation and sponsorship of market and user education programs to accelerate the demand for products based on these specifications.

The ISMA maintains relationships and liaison with educational institutions, government research institutes, other technology consortia, and other organizations that support and contribute to the development of relevant specifications and international standards. In developing the specifications, the ISMA utilizes relevant established standards that exist and proposes additions or refinements as needed to relevant standards body efforts that are still in development.

Part B: Tools

Software MPEG-1 and MPEG-2 Encoding Tools

Table 15-3 provides information on software tools and vendors. For information on DVD authoring tools, see Section II of this book.

Table 15-3: Software MPEG-1 and MPEG-2 Encoding Tools

Product/ Company	Applications	Platforms	Description	Plug-ins
Apollo Series, DV Studio Technologies LLC www.dv-studios. com	DVD	Windows	Apollo D2D that provides an MPEG-2 software-based transcoding from DV-based AVI files to MPEG-2. With your preferred Firewire (IEEE1394) card or video capture card, Apollo D2D will enable you to significantly lower the cost of MPEG-2 encoding/decoding while preserving the quality you require. CPU speeds of 1 GHz or greater provide near-real-time performance.	Plug-in available for Adobe Premiere
LSX-MPEG Products, Ligos Corporation www.ligos.com	Web, CD-ROM, VCD, DVD	Windows	High-quality MPEG encoding solutions with motion estimation algorithm that combines speed with the best possible compression and quality. Includes both MPEG-1 and MPEG-2, constant and variable bit rates.	Plug-in available for Adobe Premiere

Table 15-3: Software MPEG-1 and MPEG-2 Encoding Tools (Continued)

Product/ Company	Applications	Platforms	Description	Plug-ins
MPEG Power Professional Series, Heuris Logic Inc. www.heuris.com	Web, CD-ROM, VCD, DVD, broadcast	Macintosh and Windows	Software MPEG encoder for compressing and converting video, animation, sound, special effects, and graphics to MPEG streams. The series covers encoding of MPEG-1 and MPEG-2, all the way up to the generation of transport streams for broadcast and satellite links. MPEG Power Professional 2 has been optimized to make full use of the G4's Velocity Engine and the Intel PIII MMX/SSE instruction set. It takes full advantage of all the new advances in processor technology so you can get the most out of the latest in computer technology. It includes support for DVB applications.	Export Engine available for Final Cut Pro, Avid Cinema, Adobe After Effects, and any other product that supports the QuickTime plug-in architecture
PixelTools, PixelTools Corporation www.pixeltools. com	Web, CD-ROM, VCD, DVD, broadcast	Windows	Multipass high-quality variable bit-rate MPEG-1 and MPEG-2 software video encoders and DVD-specific software encoding products. It also provides software products for encoding with transport streams for terrestrial and satellite broadcast applications.	Plug-in available for Adobe Premiere
Vitec Multimedia www.vitecmm. com	Web, CD-ROM, VCD, DVD	Windows	MPEG Maker-2 Module that allows you to convert AVI-1 video files into MPEG-1 and MPEG-2. This software can be purchased as a MODULE or as part of DVD TOOLBOX.	

Hardware MPEG-1 and MPEG-2 Encoding Tools

Table 15-4 provides information on hardware tools and vendors. For information on DVD authoring tools, see Section II of this book.

Table 15-4: Hardware MPEG-1 and 2 Encoding Tools

Product/Company	Applications	Description
Apollo Expert Plus, DV Studio Technologies LLC www.dv-studios.com	Archiving	Real-time MPEG-2 encoding/decoding. Includes Apollo Expert authoring and premastering software. Accepts inputs from a broad range of formats.The system control screens are intuitive and easy to use. The special scene indexing function automatically creates thumbnail chapter points for navigating the DVD's content without operator involvement.
DCM (DVD Cut Machine) and MPEGProfiler, Vitec Multimedia www.vitecmm.com	Web, CD-ROM, DVD, VCD	Cost-effective real-time MPEG-1 and MPEG-2 encoder, with frame accurate MPEG Editor DVD video authoring software. Includes DVD TOOLBOX 2.0.
FutureTel NS line, FutureTel Inc. www.futuretel.com	Web, CD-ROM, DVD, VCD, broadcast	Network video engine or publishing encoder based on advanced video compression silicon from C-Cube Microsystems. Single PCI slot, MPEG-1 and MPEG-2 encoders. Multiple encoders per PC, 24-hours-a-day, 7-days-a-week performance.
MediaPress Pro, Media 100 www.media100.com	Web, CD-ROM, VCD, DVD	Mac-based hardware encoder that delivers professional real-time MPEG-1 and MPEG-2 files. Includes software for controlling the encoding/transcoding process. Built-in presets simplify the creation of MPEG streams for DVD authoring.
Optibase Inc. www.optibase.com	Web, CD-ROM, DVD, VCD, broadcast, interactive television	Broadband media gateways, MPEG-1 and MPEG-2 encoding platforms, and DVB-PCI interface platforms. Optibase offers a line of MPEG-1, MPEG-2, and Dolby Digital encoding/decoding boards and MPEG-2 DVB-to-IP interface boards as well as various streaming software packages that allow the deployment of streaming applications based on open-system platforms.

MPEG-4 Development Tools

Table 15-5 provides information on MPEG-4 development tools and vendors.

Table 15-5: MPEG-4 Development Tools

Vendor	Description
Amphion Semiconductor (www.amphion.com)	Provides high-performance solutions for interactive motion image applications. This highly integrated application-specific core is fully compliant with ISO 14496-2 Natural Video Simple Profile Level 1 through Level 3, with error resilience and image post-processing. The CS6750 decoder is ideal for wireless applications that demand reduced CPU loading, low power, and small area. It also provides advantages for high-end solutions such as video-conferencing and Internet video streaming.
Celvibe www.celvibe.com	Provides hardware solutions for wireless carriers to facilitate streaming of live and stored video over erroneous and high variable networks such as the cellular one. Main product, the Cel-Feed, is a platform that transcodes in real time from previous formats such as MPEG-1, MPEG-2, H.261, and H.263, to MPEG-4 (including MPEG-4 to MPEG-4). This feature allows streaming video over cellular networks.
Cute Systems www.cutesystems.com	Provides solutions for delivery of video to mobile devices over wireless networks. Patented technology can use existing 2G infrastructure (GSM, CDMA, and TDMA) and 2.5G (HSCSD and GPRS) networks for real-time rich-media capture. Can upgrade to accommodate 3G (UMTS, CDMA-2000) networks as well. MPEG-4-compliant solutions have both low complexity and flexibility to allow for real-time implementation in mobile (or fixed-access) devices with limited processing power and battery life.
DiamondBack Vision www.dbvision.net	Develops MPEG-4 video processing solutions for delivering higher-quality video over the Internet. ObjectVideo provides high-quality technical performance through a combination of computer vision and video compression technologies. Computer vision techniques allow for segmentation of distinct objects within a video frame, a feature that enables more efficient video compression.
Dicas www.dicas.de	Provides components and applications for MPEG-based video coding.

Table 15-5: MPEG-4 Development Tools (Continued)

Vendor	Description
DivXNetworks, Inc. www.divxnetworks.com	Enables the distribution of DVD-quality video over Internet protocol networks. The company created the world-class patent-pending DivX digital video compression technology based on the ISO MPEG-4 standard. The latest generation of DivX video compression technology, the DivX 4.02 codec, serves as the basis for the company's product line. DivXNetworks"flagship product, the DivX Open Video System, is a complete solution for the distribution of video-on-demand (VOD) over broadband IP networks.
EnQuad www.enquad.com	Develops proprietary software and hardware systems that enable high-quality, low-bandwidth video to be streamed over any network, including wireless handsets, PDAs, PCs, and set-top boxes. EnQuad has developed an algorithm implemented on a hardware platform to efficiently compress and deliver MPEG-4 compliant, Core Profile, live, full-screen, full-frame rate video at 30kbps.
Envivio www.envivio.com	Develops end-to-end MPEG-4 interactive broadcasting solutions utilizing MPEG-4's integrated streaming media elements: high-performance audio and video, two- and three-dimensional graphics and animation, and rich interactive user experience. Envivio offers application suites with authoring, server, client, and DRM capabilities.
E-Vue www.e-vue.com	Provides secure multimedia streaming solutions based on MPEG-4 ISO/IEC standard. Offers a suite of MPEG-4 compliant encoding and authoring tools, server technology, and players with integrated digital rights management (DRM) tools.
Face2Face www.f2f-inc.com	Provides 3D facila analysis solutions for TV/film, electronic gaming, eBusiness, and wireless devices. Motion-capture solution that allows you to create life-like characters with precise lip synchronization and facial motion.
Fraunhofer IIS www.iis.fhg.de	Research laboratory in the area of audio coding. Involved in international standardization of several audio compression algorithms, including MPEG Layer 3 (MP3) and MPEG-2/4 AAC. Provides MPEG-4 audio and video software for PCs and digital signal processors (DSPs).
GEO Interactive Media Group Ltd. www.emblaze.com	Provides streaming video solutions over wireless and IP networks. Patented Emblaze technology enables encoding and playback of live and on-demand video messages and content on any platform: PCs, PDAs, video cell phones, and TV. Offers a commercial end-to-end solution for streaming of video over wireless networks from today's 2G networks (GSM, CDMA, TDMA) to 2.5G and 3G wireless networks for ISPs, content providers, wireless carriers, and handset manufacturers.

Table 15-5: MPEG-4 Development Tools (Continued)

Vendor	Description
Improv Systems www.improvsys.com	Develops and licenses configurable platform solutions for communications system-on-chip integrated circuits. Rhapsody media processing solution is optimized for Internet appliances and 3G wireless devices. For companies building ICs for media-rich application environments, Rhapsody includes MPEG-4 encoding and decoding.
IndigoVision www.indigovision.com	MainStream product is a high-performance MPEG-4 codec designed for system-on-chip applications. It encodes and decodes video to the MPEG-4 standard Simple Profile and goes beyond Simple Profile to support SVHS- and DVD-quality applications. Highly scalable, enabling the same design to support applications ranging from low-power mobile phones to PDAs and hard-disk camcorders to digital TV set-tops.
iVast www.ivast.com	Developer of interactive media technologies based on MPEG-4. Enables content owners to deliver enhanced rich-media experiences to a wide range of end-user devices including PCs and set-top boxes. Provides server, architecture and infrastructure, and player technologies. Currently developing iVAST Studio SDK to allow authoring tool vendors to create new authoring applications for MPEG-4 content creation by integrating iVAST proprietary technologies such as media encoding, compression, and scene creation.
PacketVideo www.packetvideo.com	Develops wireless multimedia software and services for mobile applications. Enables wireless carriers to deliver a variety of content and rich-media applications, not just data, to mobile devices over any digital wireless network. Air-interface and operating system independent technology, enabling the transmission of multimedia from narrowband (14.4 kbps) wireless networks to wideband (2.5G and 3G) networks in the future.
Philips www.philips.com	Provides ISO-compliant MPEG-4 solutions in the wireless IP market as well as broadband platforms. WebCine products and the VeonStudio authoring environment enable content creation and server-based delivery and playback.
PsyTEL Research www.psytel-research.co.yu	Provides real-time MPEG-4 video and audio encoding solutions. Primary focus on audio coding research and development was extended to complete MPEG-4 multimedia solutions. Also available as source code, MPEG-4 implementation can be ported to wide range of DSP devices for integration into consumer multimedia products.

Table 15-5: MPEG-4 Development Tools (Continued)

Vendor	Description
Serome Technology www.seromemobile.com	Develops a full lineup of solutions for end-to-end multimedia services in wireless networks as well as the Internet, based on the open standards of international standardization bodies including MPEG, IETF, and 3GPP. Provides media encoders, streaming servers, and players to wireless carriers, content providers, device manufacturers, and chip makers.
Sigma Designs www.sigmadesigns.com	Provides solutions for high-quality decoding of MPEG-1, MPEG-2 and MPEG-4. Cost-effective solution for streaming video clients, advanced digital set-top boxes, and next-generation interactive DVD players.
SolidStreaming www.solidstreaming.com	Provides a plug-and-play solution for delivery of streaming video or audio to and from mobile devices operating on current 2G networks as well as on future 2.5G and 3G networks. Designed to help wireless carriers deliver content across wireless networks with data speeds as low as 9.6 kbps, MPEG-4 solutions include GUI-based MPEG-4 encoding tool, MPEG-4 VOD and real-time streaming server, and MPEG-4 players running in various devices.
Soundball www.soundball.com	Provides MPEG-4 structured audio software and hardware development.
UB Video www.ubvideo.com	Develops both proprietary and standards-complaint (for example, H.263, MPEG-4) video codecs and network transport solutions for multimedia communications. Software solutions for both desktop and embedded platforms designed to support the diverse requirements of video communication applications such as videoconferencing and video streaming.

Section IV: Merged Architectures

CHAPTER 16

Interactive Television

This chapter provides information that will help you to understand the challenges, choose your tools, and then create interactive television geared toward a variety of devices.

Part A: Background

Introduction

As the slow burn of high-definition television (HDTV) adoption leaves some wondering whether mass acceptance of the big boxes might fizzle altogether, a much smaller type of box might end up stealing the show to become television's first real entry into the new digital economy. We're speaking, of course, about a new generation of set-top boxes, DVD players, and even game consoles that are — or will be — wired for interactive television (iTV). Informed more by the evolution of the Internet than the grand vistas of wide-screen Panavision, iTV is marrying the Web directly to conventional television for millions of viewers. Some form of interactive television is expected to reach more than 29 million households in the United States by 2005.

What Is iTV?

In this case, we're not talking about the kinds of modem-based Web television content that viewers have been enjoying for the past few years. Microsoft's WebTV — with its proprietary set-top device that adapts Web content to the specific limitations of an interlaced television display while negotiating the switch between modem and TV transmissions — has been an early echo of things to come. True interactive television involves a much tighter integration of digital broadcast and interactive browser-based technology. The hope for both content creators and content providers is that iTV will become a new medium in its own right, creating new demand for content and the services that support it.

Because of the sprawling development of numerous enhancements to television in recent years, the term "interactive television," taken literally, can refer to anything from digital satellite broadcasting services to personal digital recording devices such as TiVo to Microsoft's WebTV. Many industry professionals have begun to group the various technologies into three categories:

1. Personal television: This term refers to TiVo and similar devices that allow viewers to program their viewing schedule with great flexibility, including automated scheduling and recording of programs of interest, as well as the ability to pause and rejoin shows in progress.

2. Internet on television: This term refers to early forms of WebTV and similar technologies that take the first step toward the convergence of television and the Internet, by allowing users to take email and Web-browsing capabilities out of the home office and into the TV room. While Internet interactivity occurs on the television set, there are no direct technological links between television programs in progress and the interactive content.

3. Interactive television: This term refers to new forms of Web television that provide direct links, usually delivered through the vertical blanking interval, from television programming to the interactive content. Through the use of overlays and other iTV technologies, the Internet content can be closely integrated with the television programming.

This chapter describes true interactive television, as defined in the last item.

Competing Systems

iTV is not new. Some 25 years ago when cable television first arrived, all kinds of efforts were under way to tap the interactive potential of the new 50-channel universe. All of those efforts failed, largely as a result of rampant competition and confusion among technologies and standards.

Then, about 10 years ago, it was the 500-channel universe, which ended with a few video-on-demand experiments in the mid-1990s. These experiments failed for similar reasons.

After many false starts, iTV seems to be having more luck this time around as a result of three factors:

1. The explosive growth of the World Wide Web, which has trained a generation in the use of interactive tools and techniques

2. Cheap, powerful computing technologies, which just keep getting smaller and more affordable

3. The intervention of serious, determined standards organizations, the first and foremost being Advanced Television Enhancement Forum (ATVEF, at www.atvef.com)

As a result of these factors, iTV is back in the running with a number of new systems gaining widespread deployment in 2001 in the United States. In Europe, interactive television services have been growing steadily since the late 1990s.

Globally, there are a number of major players involved in the development and deployment of iTV. They include:

- AOLTV (www.aoltv.com): AOLTV brings the huge AOL community into the TV room, while adding new forms of interactivity to the television experience. Existing AOL members can carry over their screen names, buddy list groups, e-mail boxes, and parental control settings. AOL is working with DirecTV, Hughes Network Systems, Philips Electronics, and Liberate Technologies to develop the AOLTV service.

- Gemstar-TV Guide International (www.gemstar.com): It is involved in interactive services and e-commerce on the company's proprietary interactive platforms, primarily in electronic program guides (EPGs) and now interactive program guides (IPGs) built around the TV Guide brand name.

- Liberate Technologies (www.liberate.com): The Liberate TV Platform provides a software platform for cable, satellite, and telecommunications companies to build interactive television systems. Liberate products include client and server software that delivers a range of enhanced content and services to digital set-top boxes of various types. Liberate has its own browser called the Liberate TV Navigator, which became certified as Java technology-compliant under the Java 2 platform Micro Edition (J2ME) in 2001. Liberate software is also used by AOL and AT&T, among many other clients, to develop their own custom solutions.

- Microsoft TV (www.microsoft.com/tv): A complete family of software products for the television industry that merges technologies from Microsoft's core operating system software and the WebTV platform into an entirely new system designed specifically for today's set-top boxes and other devices including digital video recorders, integrated TVs, and combination devices.

- OpenTV (www.opentv.com): One of the earliest players, OpenTV claims distribution to more than 50 digital network operators in more than 50 countries; provides end-to-end systems designed to work across any type of system architecture, from phone line to cable and from thin client to advanced set-top box. OpenTV also provides authoring tools for application building and acquired Spyglass in order to expand into Internet and wireless applications.

- PowerTV (www.powertv.com): Provides iTV software solutions for the cable industry consisting of the PowerTV Platform, which includes the most widely deployed operating system in the cable industry today and standards-based middleware components, as well as the various e-commerce-oriented applications and management systems.

- RespondTV (www.respondtv.com): Provides robust, scalable network infrastructure that is optimized for TV-based transactions; developed to work within all the major software platforms and environments, including AOLTV, Liberate, Microsoft TV, OpenTV, PowerTV, WebTV, and WorldGate.

- Wink (www.wink.com): One of the first active players in the interactive television industry, for several years Wink has provided services that allow viewers to interact with the television shows and advertisements. Wink also provides companies and ad agencies direct feedback and various promotional opportunities based on user response and market research.

- WorldGate (www.wgate.com): Provides the Worldgate iTV service platform for delivering iTV content through cable set-top boxes.

During 2001 AT&T announced that it is teaming up with Liberate Technologies to perform pilot testing of interactive television content. Liberate's iTV systems, supported by Microsoft rivals Oracle and Sun Microsystems, were also chosen as the foundation for AOLTV, representing America Online's (and presumably Time Warner's) entry into the field. Microsoft, in the meantime, struck an agreement with AT&T the previous year to provide its competing Microsoft TV technologies for as many as 10 million set-top boxes.

Specifications to the Rescue

Judging from the heated competition, you might fear that the current generation of iTV dreams will fail as before based on a confusion of standards. Also during this same period, however, three of the key industry leaders (Microsoft and its rivals Liberate Technologies and Sun Microsystems) — with coaxing from Cable Television Laboratories, Inc., and the OpenCable movement (www.opencable.com/), among others — have agreed to cooperate as authors of the OpenCable Application Platform (OCAP), or middleware software, specification to be used in iTV set-top boxes. The rate of industry-wide cooperation and interaction seems to be accelerating, and this market is due to reach critical mass over the next few years.

The ATVEF Specification

Microsoft, Wink, and Liberate are all developing their systems in accordance with the ATVEF specification. ATVEF provides a foundation or common set of capabilities that allows developers to author content only once and deliver that content to the maximum number of devices. The ATVEF Specification 1.1 states that the foundation for all ATVEF content is the following set of Web standards:

- HTML 4.0

- CSS Level 1

- ECMAScript and DOM 0 (JavaScript 1.1)

For more information on these commonly used Web standards, visit the World Wide Web Consortium at www.w3c.org.

In terms of integration with video broadcasts, ATVEF works on both analog and digital video systems as well as IP networks. While ATVEF can run on any video network, a complete specification requires a specific binding to each video network standard in order to ensure true interoperability. Section three of the specification includes two bindings: the reference binding to Internet protocol (IP) and an example National Television Standards Committee (NTSC) binding. The IP binding is the reference binding both because it provides a complete example of ATVEF protocols and because most networks support the IP protocol. The NTSC binding is included as an example of an ATVEF binding to a specific video standard. It is not the role of the ATVEF group to define bindings for all video standards. The various video standards bodies define the bindings for PAL, SECAM, and so forth.

What Does iTV Look Like?

When you buy or acquire a new set-top box from your cable company, what can you expect to come out of it? Interactive television services are designed to be as flexible and unobtrusive as possible. Therefore, when you first turn on the television, you probably won't see anything other than the usual programming. Don't be disappointed. The first sign of interactivity will probably appear as a small icon somewhere on the screen. Icons like this are often programmed to appear at specific places in the programming where interactivity is encouraged. The icon is telling you that you are a click away from entering this brave new interactive world. Developers also have the option of placing you right into the interactive environment without first displaying an icon.

What you actually see when you enter the interactive space is entirely up to the developers of the interactive content. There are a number of features that developers can implement, including two formats for combining the video with the interactive elements, along with numerous content options.

Two iTV Formats

According to the Advanced Television Forum (www.atvf.org), there are two basic formats for interactive television, as shown in Figure 16-1.

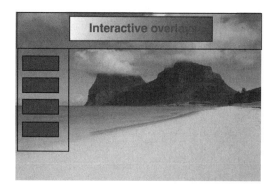

Figure 16-1 Two iTV Formats — Interactive Overlays and Reduced Picture

Using the remote, the user can choose to toggle between one of these interactive modes and normal full-screen television viewing. Once in interactive mode, the user can use hyperlinks to view additional content or depart from the television viewing altogether and spend some time viewing Web content full-screen.

The subtle differences in appearance are obvious, while under the hood the browser technology used to implement each format is entirely different. One format involves overlay of the interactive elements on top of the video stream using transparency. In this format, all elements are coded as a single HTML page that uses the DIV tag to achieve the layering. The reduced picture format involves resizing the television signal as an embedded object within a frameset (no use of transparency). Table 16-1 presents some of the pros and cons of each approach.

Table 16-1: iTV Interactive Overlays Versus Reduced Picture

	Pros	Cons
Interactive overlays	TV picture remains full-size, with no loss of detail. Integrates closely with conventional appearance of TV programming.	Enhancements might cover parts of the television picture. Viewers might experience screen refresh problems when content is updated. As new content gets loaded, the entire page reloads, which causes interruption of the picture.
Reduced picture	TV picture and enhancements are clearly separated on screen. TV image is not covered by enhancements. As with streaming video on the Web, you can swap out pages in a frameset by using additional links in the TV signal. When new content is loaded into a frame, the rest of the frameset, including the frame containing the embedded TV signal, does not get reloaded, and so there is no interruption of the picture.	Appearance is different from the normal viewing experience. TV signal is smaller on screen and might result in lost detail. Enhancements are not as closely integrated into the traditional look of television.

For more information on coding Web pages for each of these approaches, see Part C: Methods on page 429.

iTV Content Options

The actual content of the iTV elements that surround or overlay the video is left to the imagination of developers and producers. In this sense, iTV development is much like DVD Video development, with two exceptions:

1. The video is continuous, even during interaction with menus and other content. For this reason, it is recommended that iTV developers always emphasize the video programming by keeping it displayed within the interactive interface as much as possible.

2. With iTV, viewers are always linked to the Internet, allowing a broad range of interactive possibilities.

The perpetual Web connection makes iTV an attractive tool for enhanced advertisement, allowing click-through from television ads all the way to the final sale. This is likely to be the first killer app in iTV. However, networks such as PBS are also tapping the deep educational potential by providing immediate links from programming to related content, such as background information and research.

Developers have the option of bringing viewers gradually into the interactive content, by first displaying just a small information and control strip at the top or the side of the screen, for example. As the viewer explores further, the interactive content can take up more of the screen or even replace the video altogether until the user switches back to standard programming.

iTV Navigation

As with all forms of communications media, user-interaction with the content is shaped by the tools they are given. In the case of iTV, the primary tool is an advanced TV remote, rather like the remote used to control a standard DVD player. An iTV set-top box remote generally includes simple navigational buttons (up, down, left, right, select, and so forth) as well as the standard buttons for changing channels. In terms of content creation, developers should keep in mind the same set of rules as the one that applies to navigational elements in DVD titles: realizing that most viewers will be using arrow keys to make selections, keep the process simple by providing only a small number of selections at any one time, with large and easily identifiable buttons.

iTV Vocabulary

Though relatively new as a medium, iTV is already giving rise to a new vocabulary to describe elements of the interactive content. Here are a few terms to keep in mind:

- Constants: Refers to interactive prompts, icons, or informational elements that remain on screen throughout a program to remind viewers of the availability of program enhancements. Two examples of this would be a link that remains available throughout a program for getting more information on products or topics in the program, and a scrolling information area that provides timely news updates related to the subject of a documentary, with the option to follow a link for more information.

- Enhancements: Refers to interactive HTML or other Web-based elements that are added to the TV viewing experience.

- Links: This is the term commonly used to refer to URL links delivered through the vertical blanking interval (VBI) of the video signal.

- Synchronous elements: Refers to HTML or other Web-based elements that are synchronized to specific moments in the television programming. When the user is in interactive mode, these elements appear and change throughout the program to provide enhancements related to specific content. Synchronous elements can make programs compelling by providing new depths of information or resources for the user to explore at will. Examples can be anything from fully interactive pop-up videos in which the user can actually click on a pop-up for additional information, to news, documentary, or financial programs that provide continuously updated information and links based on specific topics.

- TV Object: Unlike DVD but more like streaming Web content, iTV provides the opportunity to embed the video signal within the interactive HTML content. The television signal becomes an object in the code, with special tags used to handle the video, as described in "Web-Side Authoring: Thinking Inside the Box" on page 430.

How Does It Work?

As you might guess from the participation of Microsoft and Sun, the new set-top boxes employ much of the same computer technologies used to power our Web surfing. The major difference is in accommodating the type of broadband video streams provided on cable systems and, in turn, encoding World Wide Web data and hyperlinking mechanisms directly into the video streams.

Figure 16-2 shows the basic layers of technology that allow set-top boxes to accomplish this feat.

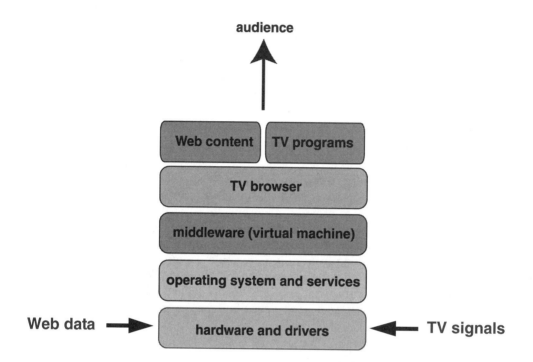

Figure 16-2 Home iTV Unit — Internal Workings

There are several important differences, however, between these new systems and what you experience on the computer. Going from the bottom of the illustration up, the hardware itself includes specific technologies for handling the new encoding schemes for interactive content, and there is also less built-in memory than you will find on the average personal computer. The iTV operating systems are also more lightweight than the operating systems on personal computers. The middleware, as mentioned previously, is being entirely rewritten by the industry leaders for this purpose. And finally, the browsers used in iTV, much like the WebTV browser, are specifically designed to handle the display differences between televisions and computer monitors.

Arriving at the top layer of content — where many developers hope to spend some time one day soon — the basic authoring technologies and techniques split into two sides of the coin: Web content and television content.

How Do iTV Links Work?

iTV links use the television signal's vertical blanking interval (VBI), or line 21, that is commonly used for closed captioning. The link messages are sent as text strings in the captioning service. Because there is only so much room in the VBI, the links must be carefully encoded. TV links might be slower and less responsive in programs that include a lot of closed captioning.

The interactive links in iTV require an Internet connection along with the cable, digital satellite, or broadcast reception of the television signal. The Internet connection can be established using a modem, but it can also be established with cable modem, DSL, or T-1 line. Because of the standard Internet connection, viewers can experience wait times during download, similar to the experience of surfing on a PC.

A second generation of iTV link technology is evolving along with digital television broadcasting. Fully digital iTV will forgo the analog VBI method and include more of the interactive data (perhaps some visual elements) within the digital signal, thereby overcoming wait times and other weaknesses of the public network.

Part B: Tools

iTV Authoring Tools

Authoring for iTV involves preparing the Web-based components (graphics overlays and other elements that appear on screen within the iTV browser) according to the production plans. The interactive content is triggered by links or events that are encoded into the television signal. Some of the products described in this section also encode the links. For more information on stand-alone encoding tools. see "VBI Video Encoding Software and Hardware" on page 424.

Avid Technology

Authoring platforms: Windows and Macintosh

Deployment platform: Microsoft TV

Go to www.avid.com

Avid Technology, Inc. delivers solutions for developing, producing, managing, and distributing media. Avid's products are used on a broad range of television and news shows, commercials, feature films, music and corporate productions.

   In 2002, Avid will began introducing meta-data-based iTV authoring features into its nonlinear editing products, such as Avid Symphony and Avid Media Composer. iTV authoring and tools for adding links are added right into the timeline display within the system for simple integrated authoring of links and previewing of iTV content throughout the editing process.

Chyron Lyric iTV

Authoring platforms: Windows 2000, Windows NT SP 4

Deployment platforms: Microsoft TV, AOLTV, Liberate TV, and more

Go to www.chyronitv.com

Lyric iTV was the Editor's Pick of Show at NAB 2001, and for good reason. Originally delivered as Chyron's broadcast graphics software solution, Lyric has been extended to encompass interactive television in Lyric iTV.

   Available for Windows 2000 and Windows NT, Lyric iTV allows producers and developers to maintain a consistent look and feel between television and iTV graphics. Lyric's flexibility is rooted in the Canvas, a 3D composition and animation space, allowing for the creation and import of 2D and 3D graphics. Elements can be assembled from basic components and combined into complex layouts, scripts, and templates.

Lyric also features full-page layout and extensive word processing capabilities. Template-oriented text fields allow attributes such as justification, shrink-to-fit, database links, and many more, including the assignment of iTV properties such as HREF, JavaScript, ActiveX, and Flash.

The Lyric Canvas is resolution independent and supports instant aspect-ratio scaling for NTSC, PAL, various HDTV, and custom scaling. In addition, Lyric supports a variety of iTV set-top-box resolutions including Microsoft TV, Liberate, AOLTV, and more.

Lyric includes the following iTV features:

- Quick definition of hot spots and images with such iTV attributes as HREF, DIV, JavaScript, ActiveX, and Flash.

- Automatic generation of the appropriate XML, HTML, and JavaScript pages that reference these objects.

- Rendering of graphics in JPG, GIF, or PNG (including alpha) and creation of HTML or XML pages referencing these images individually by position or as a single flattened graphic with overlaying hot spots. Generation of TV: objects, either as pulled-back video window or as full-screen video for graphic overlays.

- Optional playout capabilities, as a deployment platform. Via timeline control, you can create and deploy ATVEF links, packages and triggers for Transport A and Transport B and preview your links in an integrated Web browser window. You can also add triggers to Lyric's play list for playback as a sequenced rundown that can chase time code as well as loop for carousel applications.

Chyron CGInteractive

Authoring platforms: Windows 2000, Windows NT SP 4

Deployment platforms: Microsoft TV, AOLTV, Liberate TV, and more

Go to www.chyronitv.com

The CGInteractive package is an upgrade for Chyron iNFiNiT! or Duet character generator systems, allowing operators to create state-of-the-art synchronous iTV productions right from the control room, remote truck, studio, or edit suite. When the graphics are played back to air, the iTV insertion occurs automatically — no special operator training or workflow changes are required. CGInteractive easily integrates with existing production and master control switchers for complete iTV content synchronization.

CGInteractive allows iTV content to be automatically inserted into the television signal, linked to on-air graphics. CGInteractive works with virtually all interactive formats, including iTV-enabled set-top boxes and companion Websites, and supports a range of analog and digital broadcast, cable, and satellite transmission technologies.

The CGInteractive package includes the required additions to your iNFiNiT! or Duet family software, as well as Chyron's powerful iTV Gateway application, complete with switcher interface hardware.

Mixed Signals Technologies

Authoring platforms: Windows 2000, Windows NT SP 4

Deployment platforms: Microsoft TV, AOLTV, Liberate TV, and more

Go to www.mixedsignals.com

Mixed Signals Technologies produces a full range of iTV products, including authoring software, data encoding, as well as tools to aid in the broadcasting and monitoring of interactive programming.

In terms of authoring, Mixed Signals offers three products:

1. An entry-level encoder, the Insertalink iTV, inserts iTV links, captioning, and other VBI data.

2. The ITVinjector is a more advanced iTV data encoder. The versatile ITVinjector can encode the various formats of iTV links and triggers as well as all VBI services. The ITVinjector can also be remotely controlled by Mixed Signal's ITVauto automation server, for encoding of iTV data into pre-produced, real-time, or live video streams. Remote monitoring and control are accomplished through the ITVinjector's patent-pending API for IP network control.

3. The Interactive Producer Bundle is a combination of software and hardware tools that enables video, Internet, and multimedia producers to generate ATVEF-compliant broadcast-quality iTV content. It includes one Insertalink data encoding device and one TV Link Creator software license.

OpenTV Tools

Authoring platforms: Windows 2000, Windows NT SP 4

Deployment platform: OpenTV

Go to www.opentv.com

OpenTV's global iTV network reaches more than 50 million viewers in 50 countries. To meet the needs of this broad-based network, OpenTV provides its own development tools. These tools are available as stand-alone, or as part of a production suite:

• OpenTV Publisher: Combines the latest iTV technology with XML content and other standard Internet protocols. Publisher includes a server system with a merge engine for dynamic publishing, allowing developers to create interactive services that include real-time updating content.

• OpenAuthor: A visual authoring tool designed for content developers who want to create interactive television applications and who have little or no software programming experience. OpenAuthor features objects called Gadgets to define a scene, including its visual layout, timing, interactivity, and behind-the-scenes programming control. OpenAuthor provides content developers with the power to create media-rich, dynamic content without requiring knowledge of the specific capabilities of the audio, video, and graphics hardware that reside in digital set-top boxes.

• OpenTV Target Decoder: The OpenTV Target Decoder is a customized set-top box that developers can use to test interactive television content and services for OpenTV-enabled broadcast networks. OpenTV Target Decoder simulates a broadcast environment so that content developers can test the overall look and feel of their OpenTV applications directly on a television.

• OpenTV Player: OpenTV Player simplifies the process of viewing and testing interactive television applications by enabling a standard PC to send OpenTV applications in MPEG-2 format (using its parallel port) to the OpenTV Target Decoder set-top box. OpenTV Player eliminates the need for a licensed installation of the software development kit (OpenTV SDK) or OpenAuthor on a PC that is connected to a OpenTV Target Decoder. OpenTV Player is also capable of playing compressed MPEG-2 video and audio files on a OpenTV Target Decoder.

• OpenTV Frame: OpenTV Frame is an MPEG encoder that converts images of different formats, including JPEG and BMP, into professional-quality television-ready MPEG-1 or MPEG-2 pictures. Based on technology originally developed to create high-performance silicon chips, images created using OpenTV Frame take full advantage of the MPEG decoders that are at the heart of today's digital set-top boxes. OpenTV Frame enables developers to view a still picture before and after MPEG conversion. This allows for dynamic adjustment of contrast, brightness, and gamma correction. OpenTV Frame also accelerates the application development process with regard to variations of pixel width, bandwidth, and color display.

SpinTV

Authoring platforms: Windows 2000, Windows NT SP 4

Deployment platforms: Microsoft TV, AOLTV, Liberate TV, and more

Go to www.spin.tv

The SpinTV Studio Suite is expected to be released in 2002 as a full product line that enables customers to build iTV applications from beginning to end. SpinTV's first offering, available since 2001, is the SpinTV Studio Suite Kit, which is an extension for Macromedia Dreamweaver or UltraDev.

Available for use on Windows 98, Windows 2000, or Windows NT, the extension provides a rich tool set within Dreamweaver for building iTV browser layouts. Those who are familiar with Macromedia's authoring environments can hit the ground running rather than having to learn an entirely new tool set. The kit also includes tools for debugging iTV applications for use on set-top boxes that are currently deployed within the United States, based on ATVEF 1.1.

Features in Dreamweaver include the following:

- TV Embed Object
- Trigger Receiver Object
- Page Preload Object
- iTV Cache Object
- iTV Browser Sniffer (platform detection)
- TV Pilot Image
- TV Embed Object Translator
- TV Screen Sizes
- Automated TV Aspect Ratios
- Integrated iTV Platform References
- Middleware Content Guides
- Middleware Browser Code Error Reporting

VBI Video Encoding Software and Hardware

In regard to iTV, the VBI encoding software and hardware components allow developers to insert URL links into the VBI (line 21 in NTSC) of a television signal. Most VBI video encoders can also be used to insert closed captioning, and sometimes other forms of data. Authoring of the interactive content itself (URL content triggered by the encoded links) is covered in "iTV Authoring Tools" on page 420.

EEG Enterprises, Inc., iTV Xpress

Software only (requires additional hardware encoder)

Authoring platforms: Windows 98, 2000, Windows NT SP 4

Go to www.eegent.com

EEG offers a complete line of closed captioning, XDS (Vchip) and URL encoders, decoders, and software. The EEG iTV Xpress software package is a comprehensive suite for creating and encoding ATVEF Transport Type A broadcast data triggers on the VBI.

iTV Xpress consists of two applications, the Data Trigger Editor and the Encoder Controller. The two programs can reside on one PC or on separate machines linked through a network. The Data Trigger Editor allows the user to edit and save the URL data list. The Encoder Controller program provides the link between the URL Data list and the VBI data encoder. It also provides the interface to a timecode reader card. All current options for ATVEF Type A data transmission are supported.

iTV Xpress can operate in manual or automatic data insertion mode. In manual insertion mode, the triggers are manually sent to the encoder one at a time by clicking the Send Next URL button. Automatic mode can deliver URL data using a timecode input or a time offset from start. Timecode mode sends URLs to the encoder based on an input from a timecode reader. Offset mode uses an internal timer to trigger URL insertion based on the start time of the encode process. The mode of automatic delivery is set on a per-file basis. Both the start and end times, whether they are an offset or an absolute timecode, can be configured on a per-URL basis in the Data Trigger Editor program.

Leapfrog Productions CCaption

Software encoder (no hardware encoder required; integrates with NLEs)

Authoring platforms: Macintosh and Windows 98, 2000, Windows NT SP 4

Go to www.ccaption.com

CCaption from Leapfrog Productions enables a video non-linear editing system to directly create ATVEF Transport Type A Triggers without the need for a special hardware encoder. CCaption integrates with many popular NLE systems to allow editors and developers to add captioning and links within existing Avid-, Media 100-, or FireWire-capable computers. CCaption can also use the same captioning information to add text captions to QuickTime movies as well as RealText captions for RealVideo or generate a description file for adding captioning to a DVD using popular DVD authoring systems.

In addition to a range of closed-captioning features, CCaption features the following iTV support:

- Support for ATVEF Transport A Triggers

- Creation of URL, LID, Type, Name, Expires, Script, and View fields

- Arbitrary user data input

Microsoft ATVEF Player

Authoring platforms: Windows 98, 2000, Windows NT SP 4

Go to www.microsoft.com/tv

The ATVEF Player, available from Microsoft, is a simple stream player that can load an XML file formatted with link information for this purpose and insert it into line 21 of NTSC when connected to a Norpak TES 3 encoder. The encoded video content can be used on Microsoft TV services. Other types of networks will use different encoders and different stream players. The ATVEF Player is a free tool that provides you with a solution if you are using a Norpak TES3 encoder. You must join the Microsoft TV developer program to download the free software.

Norpak Corporation

Hardware encoding solutions

Authoring platforms: Windows 98, 2000, Windows NT SP 4

Go to www.norpak.ca

Norpak Corporation has a long history of delivering television data transmissions, going all the way back to the first teletext systems of the 1970s. The current generation of Norpak encoders is ATVEF-compliant and is used in all the major iTV initiatives including Gemstar, Liberate, Microsoft TV, RespondTV, WINK, and WorldGate. Norpak claims to have the only full family of data encoders supporting all the world's TV and data standards.

Encoders include the following:

- TES3: These are analog encoders that can be configured through software to support all data standards such as ATVEF A, ATVEF B, WINK, NABTS, WST, and Japanese. The encoders can insert into any of the world's 11 different TV systems including all variants of PAL, NTSC, and SECAM. The encoders are available with either RS232 serial or LAN interfaces, and a single encoder can simultaneously encode and insert up to 8 different data services of differing standards. Additional capabilities include bridging data services from one standard to another. Many first-generation software packages for iTV encoding — including Microsoft's ATVEF Player, for example — work with this encoder.

- TES5: This is a 270-Mbps serial digital family of encoders that provides the same SDI functionality as the TES3 family does for analog television. As with the TES3 family, these encoders can also simultaneously handle captioning, Vchip, XDS, TSID, and other data services.

- TES7: For working in HDSDI for high-definition television. These encoders follow the SMPTE334M standard for encoding and inserting data in the SMPTE292M 1.5 Gbs signal.

- TES8: MPEG-2 encoders that are based on Norpak's new MPEG Stream Controller PCI adapter designed to handle MPEG-2 transport streams. This adapter can perform the following functions: remultiplexing of MPEG transport stream, digital splicing, and data insertion. As a remultiplexer, it can receive a multiprogram transport stream (MPTS) at the input port, demultiplex it (to filter the selected programs), remultiplex the programs, and generate a new transport stream to be transmitted through the output port. Program streams received through the PCI interface can also be multiplexed into the transport stream on the output port. As a splicer, the adapter is capable of switching from one program stream to another one without generating video artifacts when the resulting transport stream is decoded. This is needed to support advertisement insertions into digital television broadcast feeds. As a data inserter, the adapter allows the insertion of data into a program stream to support services such as electronic program guides (EPGs) and interactive TV.

Norpak also offers iTV monitoring systems as well as a family of receivers and signal bridging solutions.

Part C: Methods

iTV Development Workflow

iTV adds new tasks to every stage of the traditional television production workflow, from initial concept to final broadcast. For scripted or preproduced shows (versus live programming), the additional steps are listed below:

- Preproduction phase

    - Concept: new iTV elements

    - Proposals: new iTV elements

    - Storyboards: new iTV elements; additional art direction

    - Schedule and budget: additional resources for iTV elements

- Production phase

    - iTV asset creation

    - Programming and HTML development

    - Testing

- Postproduction phase

    - Editing: adding encoding links during or after editing

    - Uploading HTML

    - Testing

Web-Side Authoring: Thinking Inside the Box

iTV is built on existing open standards, making it possible for developers to tap their knowledge of these common Web technologies:

- HTML
- XHTML
- XML
- HTTP
- UHTTP
- ECMA 262 (ECMAScript)
- JavaScript
- CSS
- DOM

• Macromedia Flash

There are two key components that make all the difference between your pages authored for iTV and those authored for the Internet: the television display and the television broadcast signal. The following two sections describe specific issues and tips for accommodating each in your development efforts.

Design Tips for Television Display

Even while iTV builds on existing standards for the Web elements, the display issues are entirely different. A television uses an interlaced display technology that is relatively low in resolution at 720 x 480 nonsquare pixels (the equivalent of 640 x 480 square pixels on a computer) versus a computer monitor, which uses progressive-scan technology that can go all the way up to 1,600 x 1,200 pixels and beyond. Add to this the fact that television sets generally crop about 10 percent of the image all the way around, and you end up with a display area of about 560 x 420 pixels.

Depending on your point of view, this can be a negative or a positive. On the negative side, you end up with much less screen real estate to work with. On the positive side, your display area is fixed, and, therefore, you can design specifically for one size without having to jump through hoops to accommodate various screen sizes and color-depth settings.

Speaking of color, there are a few limitations of color to contend with as well. Television uses a subtractive color technology (known commonly as YUV color space), while computer monitors use additive color technology (known as RGB). For developers, the primary difference is that some colors that are acceptable for the computer monitor do not display well on a television, usually by exceeding the maximum saturation levels of certain colors in the YUV color space.

These issues, along with tips for producing effective content for the television screen resolution, are covered in the following reminders:

• **Avoid small text and fine detail in graphics:** If you are coming from a television background, you are accustomed to the large, thick font styles used on the average character generator. Coming from a Web or CD-ROM development perspective, you must keep in mind that the interlaced television display tends to soften fine details, making it necessary to avoid line widths smaller than 2 pixels, for example, or text smaller than point size of 12. Also remember that users are not seated right in front of the television as they are with a computer monitor; instead, they might be up to 10 or even 20 feet away. A point size of 18 is considered ideal size for reading at various distances. Also, use sans serif fonts as often as possible.

• **Keep page titles short and descriptive:** Because of the lack of screen real estate and the need for large readable fonts, you will find it necessary to avoid long titles. It follows, then, that your titles need to say more with fewer words.

- **Write concise text:** Interactive developers working on iTV content must take a page from the experience of television CG operators. The video image is paramount; supporting text elements must be short and to the point.

- **Keep elements within the safe action, safe title areas for television:** The safe action area on a television screen, roughly 560 x 420, is the area in which you can be sure that the vast majority of televisions will not crop off the images or action of your scenes. The safe title area, roughly 526 x 388, is the recommended area in which you should place all text elements. This provides a safe margin for content, both to help appearance and to accommodate older televisions that might crop more than today's standard of 10 percent around the edges. Various iTV services provide their own specifications for designing to exact screen dimensions. For specific dimensions, consult with the services described in "iTV Authoring Tools" on page 420.

- **Avoid scrolling content:** Some interactive services do not support scrollable pages in TV mode. Any content that extends beyond the visible boundary of the television screen becomes inaccessible to viewers on those services. In addition, consider that some of your television viewers have never used a computer and therefore are not accustomed to the process of scrolling. To reach the largest possible audience with your content, consider designing in browsable page-by-page chunks of information, rather than in long topics that require scrolling.

- **Use safe colors:** The television YUV color space does not handle certain highly saturated colors as well as a computer monitor's RGB space. Bright red or bright white, for example, can bleed in a television image. In addition, the pure white and black levels used in television do not match these levels in RGB formats. Most up-to-date graphics design software, such as Adobe Photoshop, provides filters for designing safe color content for television. Consult the documentation that came with your software for more information. In addition, if you are developing hybrid content for delivery on both television and computer monitors, you should also observe the Web-safe guidelines that apply to all Web content. Web palettes are also included with most graphics design software.

- **Avoid complex tables or framesets:** Keep in mind that most iTV browsers are first- or second-generation browsers, and therefore suffer from some of the limitations we all experienced in the mid-1990s when it comes to the rendering of complex tables and framesets. Again, keep it simple.

- **Simplify forms:** Long, complex scrolling forms might fall outside the capabilities of some iTV browsers to deliver. Keep all forms simple. If your form requires many fields, plan a sequence of several pages for data entry.

- **Limit system memory requirements:** Television set-top boxes have less memory than the average computer. Avoid causing the iTV browser to download large files to memory, and also avoid complex games and other interactive devices that are memory-intensive.

- **Use supported code and file formats:** This goes without saying.

- **Test your pages:** Quality assurance with iTV content is, in some ways, even more important than it was during the fledgling days of the World Wide Web, to the extent that television viewers are not accustomed to experiencing bugs. Software issues in iTV are likely to cause viewer confusion and will likely generate many support phone calls. Things should just work, without a hitch. Most television programming executives will be even less pleased with kinks in the software. As with all interactive content development, test and test again, using all the various iTV services and browsers you can expect your audiences to be using.

The intention of the evolving iTV standards is to provide support for all existing World Wide Web technologies in the new iTV browsers, but only time will tell if the companies developing those browsers have the time and resources to carry that out. Microsoft TV is perhaps the most predictable, since it uses the Internet Explorer engine. Unfortunately, in the short term you will most likely end up with yet another subset of cross-platform features and a companion set of competing browsers to test your content in. As in the early days of the Web, the rule of thumb is to keep things simple.

Adding Real-Time Broadcasts to the Mix

According to the ATVEF specification 1.1, you can add a broadcast television channel to a Web page by specifying tv: as an attribute of the <OBJECT>, <IMG>, <BODY>, <FRAMESET>, <A>, <DIV>, or <TABLE> tag. It is that simple.

Although a variety of tags can be used, the most robust and most universal method for reaching all set-top boxes is the following syntax:

```
<OBJECT DATA="tv:" HEIGHT="x" WIDTH="x">
```

As mentioned in the Background section of this chapter, the ATVEF specification allows for two ways to display iTV enhancements (HTML or other Web-based elements) along with the television broadcast or cablecast signal: The interactive enhancements can overlay the video content at full size, or the video content can be reduced in size and embedded within the Web-based interface, much like a synchronized streaming presentation. The following sections describe codes and options for implementing each approach in your Web pages.

Implementing Interactive Overlays

The primary way to integrate the television signal with enhancements within iTV browsers is by using the tv: attribute. According to the ATVEF specification 1.1, tv: URL can be used anywhere that an image URL can be applied in HTML 4.0. For example:

* Both images and television signals can appear in-line within a page.

* Images and television signals can be pulled into frames within a frameset.

* Using the DIV tag, an image or TV object can be placed within a floating box.

* An image or television signal can be applied to the background property of the <BODY> tag (<BODY BACKGROUND="tv:">), and thus appear behind all content shown within the browser.

Some set-top boxes currently do not support use of the tv: attribute in the background property, so unless you know that your target audience uses the appropriate set-top boxes, you should use one of the first three implementations to reach the largest possible audience of set-top box owners.

The second option, using a frameset, will not work for interactive overlays. This is the preferred method of coding the reduced picture format for iTV. For more information, see "Implementing Reduced Picture Enhancements" on page 435.

The third option, the DIV tag, is the preferred method for coding interactive overlays. The code is simple:

```
<DIV
STYLE="position:absolute;top:0;left:0;z-index:-1">
<OBJECT DATA="tv:" HEIGHT="100%" WIDTH="100%"> </
OBJECT>
</DIV>
```

Pixels can be substituted for percentages of the height and width attributes, but percentages are recommended to ensure full-screen implementation of the video image.

Notice that the z-index attribute is set to –1. By first defining the z-index (layer number) of the television signal this way, you ensure that subsequent DIV items written in the code will appear on top of the television signal, since by default elements whose z-index values are not specified are implicitly assigned z-index values according to their source order in a document.

To code the first layer of enhancements, therefore, you would create another DIV object, which by default would have a z-index of zero, and place the elements within it. For example:

```
<DIV STYLE="position:absolute;top:240;left:0">
<IMG SRC="images/buttonrow.jpg" WIDTH="100%"
HEIGHT="180"
ALT="" BORDER="0">
</DIV>
```

Additional layers would be added with similar code.

For more information on use of the DIV tag, as well as CSS styles for positioning and z-indexing, visit www.w3c.org.

Implementing Reduced Picture Enhancements

The preferred method for coding the reduced picture format for iTV is to author a basic HTML frameset. Much like the pages used for some forms of synchronized presentation, the video runs in one frame while links in the video pull the HTML enhancements into surrounding frames, as shown in Figure 16-3.

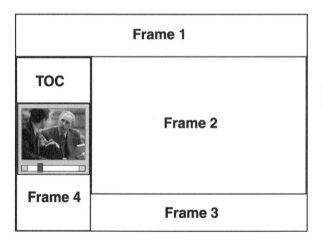

Frame 1: Header
Frame 2: Slides (static or dynamic)
Frame 3: Notes/text
Frame 4: Transcript
Video: Includes play controls
TOC: Table of Contents

Figure 16-3 iTV — Embedded Frameset

The HTML content used for Figure 16-3 consists of a simple frameset with three frames, with one or several additional HTML files that get pulled into each frame.

The TV frame contains the TV object:

```
<DIV STYLE="position:absolute;top:0;left:0">
<OBJECT

DATA="tv:" WIDTH="240" HEIGHT="180"
ALT="" BORDER="0">
</OBJECT>
</DIV>
```

When adding links to the television signal, as described in "How Do iTV Links Work?" on page 416, you can target the various frames for display of synchronized elements using the standard HTML target parameter in the encoded URL. However, avoid reloading the TV frame content as it will cause an interruption in the television signal. Also, remember that the HTML should be nonscrollable to reach all set-top boxes without cropping some of your content.

For more information on authoring of HTML framesets, as well as CSS styles for positioning and z-indexing, visit www.w3c.org.

Exiting Interactive Overlay or Reduced Picture Viewing

Whether you use overlays or embed your television signal in a frameset, you can allow users to jump out of these interactive modes and return to normal television viewing by providing a link with the tv: as the HREF of an anchor tag to return to full-screen TV. For example:

```
<A HREF="tv:">Return to Full Screen Viewing</A>
```

Using Style Sheets for Hybrid Content

For example, Microsoft provides this code sample for linking to alternate style sheets depending on whether the viewer is using WebTV or the Internet Explorer browser on a computer:

```
<!--links the cssTV.css stylesheet for WebTV-->
<LINK REL="stylesheet" TYPE="text/css"
HREF="cssTV.css">

<!--links the cssPC.css stylesheet for design-time
purposes-->
<SCRIPT type="text/JavaScript">
var bName = "navigator.appName"
if (bName = "Microsoft Internet Explorer")
```

```
{
document.write(<LINK REL='stylesheet' TYPE='text/
css' HREF='cssPC.css'>");
}
</script>
```

Adding Animation

The World Wide Web standards supported by the ATVEF specification allow you to add several types of animation. Here are the three primary types of animation you can use, with some notes on limitations:

1. Animated GIFs: These are fully supported for all set-top boxes that conform to the ATVEF standard and are the most reliable form of delivery.

2. Dynamic HTML: DHTML is included as part of the HTML 4.0 specification supported by ATVEF. However, you might experience a lot of variation in the way the various iTV browsers render DHTML; therefore, it is a good idea to keep dynamic HTML content simple and use it sparingly.

3. Macromedia Flash: Flash has a great following on the Web as a highly reliable, lightweight, and effective animation format. Flash is also considered by many to be an ideal format for interactive television, because it mirrors the rich graphical look of television, scales perfectly, produces crisp fonts at various sizes, downloads quickly, and displays consistently across all browsers that support the Flash player. However, the one issue with Flash in the early stages of iTV has to do with support for the player. Some set-top boxes do not support Flash at all, while others support the 2.0 player only, which means you must forgo the many improvements to Flash that have been incorporated into subsequent releases. When using Flash, again it's important to know which set-top boxes your audience will be using. If you must reach the largest possible audience, consider using animated GIFs instead.

Authoring on the Broadcast Side

Authoring on the broadcast side refers to the process of preparing and encoding the link information into the video that will be broadcast or cable-cast on the iTV system. Most of the industry leaders abide by the open standards developed by ATVEF for this purpose, providing various solutions for encoding URL links into television content. In some cases, encoding of this content might occur right at the distribution point: at the broadcasting facility. In that scenario, content developers will have to cooperate with the workflow of the broadcast institution to provide their Web content for inclusion in the video stream. Another scenario might involve products that allow you to perform the task directly within your NLE suite or on a separate workstation in your facility. The final output consists of a program recorded onto your tape that includes the links that will be delivered over line 21 of the VBI when broadcast.

For more information on specific encoding tools, see "VBI Video Encoding Software and Hardware" on page 424.

About iTV Links

Unlike Web browser URLs, iTV links have some limitations. Note that encoded TV links can be a maximum of 512 characters. Also iTV links do not take effect as quickly as computer-based links because the vertical blanking interval can transmit just 2 characters per frame and 30 frames per second. Therefore, if you had a link that was 60 characters long, it would take one second to download the link on a program with no closed captioning. Because TV links share line 21 of the vertical blanking interval with closed captioning, TV links will take even longer to download on heavily captioned programs. The bottom line is to allow for some delay when designing your program for interactivity. Table 16-2 lists information on iTV link attributes.

There are several types of links to plan for in your productions, with different behaviors depending on the actions taken by the viewer:

•   Presenting invitations: Any TV link that contains a Name attribute will present the viewer with the option to switch to interactive mode. Based on the type of service and set-top box, this option might be presented as an icon somewhere on the screen, or the viewer might be automatically switched to interactive mode. If the viewer is presented with an icon and chooses not to follow the link, subsequent TV links with the same URL attribute will be ignored and will not present the prompt again. If the viewer does follow the link, the set-top box will go about downloading and presenting the enhancements.

•   Understanding behavior of missed invitations: Some services provide viewers the ability to "go interactive" even if they didn't accept an earlier invitation. For Microsoft receivers, viewers can choose the Options button on their remote to go interactive for the current show.

•   Forcing multiple invitations: As mentioned in the last item, subsequent invitations with the same Name attribute are ignored if the viewer does not accept the first invitation. However, you force the system to prompt the viewer again as many times as you like by changing the Name attribute in the invitation.

•   Preparing links that do not present an invitation: If you do not want a TV link to act as an invitation, do not set the Name attribute.

- Understanding invitation behavior while viewing enhancements: If the viewer follows an invitation, subsequent TV links will be ignored unless they contain a matching URL attribute and a Script attribute. Therefore, if two interactive shows are being sent on the same broadcast and the viewer follows one invitation, other links will not present an invitation prompt.

- Changing channels while viewing enhancements: Depending on the service and set-top box, changing the channel might restore normal viewing mode, requiring the viewer to manually go back to interactive mode using the remote.

Table 16-2: iTV Link Attributes

Attribute	Description	Requirements
URL	Address of the interactive television content on the Web, located on a Web server. The domain portion of the URL attribute uniquely identifies a trigger.	Required attribute. The URL attribute must be listed first in a TV link. Most TV link generators, however, do this automatically.
NAME	Human-readable name that some iTV systems show to viewers in the invitation to go interactive.	Optional attribute. If this is not present, an invitation is not issued. Some receivers will not show more than 20 or 30 characters; the Name attribute can be abbreviated to n.
TVE	ATVEF content-level descriptor. Indicates the level of support a receiver should have to accept the TV link.	Required attribute. Example: [tve:1.0] [v:1]. In general, the content level should always be set to 1; setting the content level to 0 (zero) or w will cause some receivers to link to the Web (Web mode); Some receivers also support the View attribute name instead, along with a value of t for TV mode, but in general it should not be used.
SCRIPT	Allows ECMAScript (JavaScript) fragments to be delivered to a Web page specified by the URL attribute.	Optional attribute. A script is immediately executed once it is received. The Expires attribute helps determine whether a script is executed or not.

Table 16-2: iTV Link Attributes (Continued)

Attribute	Description	Requirements
EXPIRES	Specifies the last date the TV link is valid, after which the receiver should ignore it. This is an extremely useful attribute for limiting the life of the content. For example, if someone records your show onto a VHS tape, then plays it back months later, your TV links will not show up if you have set up the expires attribute to be one month after your air date.	Optional attribute. The format of the time conforms to International Standard ISO 8601 and is relative to Greenwich Mean Time (GMT). A valid compact format is yyyymmddThhmmss, where T separates the date from the time. The Expires attribute can be abbreviated to e.
CHECKSUM	A calculated field that verifies the accuracy of the string and detects data corruption. This field is usually automatically calculated for you after all of the desired trigger attributes have been created. Any changes in the TV link will require a new checksum value.	Required attribute. After calculating the checksum, do not change the case of any text, add or remove spaces, or format the string in any way; otherwise the checksum will fail, and the TV link will not work.

For more information on iTV links, see the Enhanced Content Specification at www.atvef.com.

Distribution, the Old-Fashioned Way

As far as distributing your iTV content goes, if you are used to Web development, don't expect that to resemble anything like your experience with developing for the Internet. Just another Web server, right? Think again. Most of the links to your Web content are embedded in the broadcast side of the equation, where your viewers will discover your brave new interactive content. Finding the opportunities to develop that broadcast content in the short term will require relationships with broadcasting and cablecasting producers and executives.

Section IV: Merged Architectures

CHAPTER 17

Hybrid DVDs

This chapter provides information that will help you to understand the challenges, choose your tools, and then create hybrid discs that work in a variety of players.

Part A: Background

Introduction

There are four basic areas of hybrid convergence that are possible on the DVD disc:

- DVD Video and DVD Audio: This form of DVD convergence involves integrating elements that play on a DVD Audio player only with elements that play on a DVD Video player only. Because this format is considered part of the DVD Audio specification, it is discussed in Chapter 9.

- DVD-ROM on a DVD Video Player: The format emphasizes DVD Video, with additional DVD-ROM elements thrown in for use on special playback units that support DVD-ROM. This is a futuristic format, requiring new set-top boxes or special PCs designed for the home theater environment that include both a DVD player and a PC desktop environment such as Microsoft Windows.

- DVD Video (or DVD Audio) on a PC: One of the first forms of DVD convergence, this involves integrating DVD-ROM and DVD Video (or DVD Audio) technologies. Elements of a DVD Video title, for example, might be combined with PC formats such as Macromedia Director titles or PowerPoint presentations. This category can also include DVD Video titles that simply add additional DVD-ROM files (Word documents, JPG images, and so forth) that can be opened on a PC. This format is covered in "DVD Video (or DVD Audio) on a PC" on page 447.

- WebDVD: Although this type of disc shares similar convergence technologies with the previous type of hybrid, we cover it as a special category that combines DVD Video elements into Web pages or DVD titles that include links for launching Web pages in a browser. Most WebDVD titles are designed for use on PCs, although a new generation of set-top boxes and DVD players promises to bring this form of convergence to the TV room. This format is covered in "WebDVD" on page 445.

There are also discs that mix and match several of these convergences, resulting in what have been called "tri-bryd" discs. For example, many new DVD Audio titles are designed for use in both DVD Video and DVD Audio players and also include WebDVD elements. Many DVD Video titles also include both WebDVD elements as well as various desktop files that can be accessed in a DVD-ROM drive.

There is one more hybrid format that involves placing DVD Video content onto a standard CD. Sometimes called cDVD, this kind of disc has the advantage of playing high-quality DVD Video and Audio on many CD-ROM drives for those audiences who do not have DVD-ROM drives. We don't discuss this format at length in this chapter for two reasons: First, the format is quickly becoming obsolete as the installed base of DVD-ROM drives approaches critical mass; secondly, it is an unreliable format, often requiring the installation of additional software or hardware to play DVD Video on CD-ROM systems that often are set up for DVD or that are not robust enough to handle the processing requirements.

WebDVD

While the DVD spec was under development in the early 1990s, the Internet explosion was a mere twinkle in the eye of Tim Berners-Lee. As a result, the 1.0 specification from the DVD consortium missed that boat entirely. A good number of DVD developers and technology companies have been striving ever since to provide DVD's missing link to the Web. This section describes the nature of these efforts, how they work, and how we can expect them to evolve in the years ahead.

Players and PCs

You might be wondering how the average DVD movie is going to make a Web connection from that new DVD player sitting in your home entertainment center. Unfortunately, it can't — at least until a new generation of Web-enabled DVD players finally takes hold in the market. The only place where the links on a Web-enabled DVD disc will function right now is in a personal computer equipped with a DVD-ROM drive.

That won't always be the case. While the remainder of this chapter covers technologies used primarily on corporate titles designed for the PC, there is still some hope for the home entertainment center. A new category of DVD player, known as iDVD, is under development through partnerships between companies such as Planet Web (www.planetweb.com) and various DVD chip and player manufacturers. These second-generation DVD players, combined with proprietary Web browsers such as the PlanetWeb Enhanced Content Viewer, allow you to play DVDs and follow links embedded in the DVD content to companion locations on the Web. For the first-time, consumers gain the advantages of DVD-ROM on family entertainment systems. The benefit of Web content is that it can be dynamic and changing, as opposed to the fixed content of the DVD disc. New versions of popular game consoles are also expected to provide similar features. These devices are expected to become widely available during 2002.

Hollywood is making more and more use of WebDVD technology, but where WebDVD really comes into its own is in the presentation of informational content for corporate or educational use. Those developers working on rich-media training and educational programming (ranging from travelogues to documentaries to corporate titles) seem to be breaking the most new ground with this category of hybrid disc, particularly in corporate communications where a captive audience is generally tied down to the PC.

Specs and Speculation

The biggest hurdle with WebDVD at the moment is the lack of a single specification. As a result, options for producing Web-enabled DVDs are splintered among several competing tools, each with different advantages depending on your target platform and audience.

A working group at the DVD association (www.DVDA.org) is trying to change that. Known as the Haiku Group, this collection of industry experts is developing an interactive DVD specification that they hope will be adopted in the next version of the industry-wide DVD standard. Until that day arrives, here are some technologies that deliver the first wave of WebDVD technology.

WebDVD Today

As you might expect, current WebDVD technologies allow you to develop a range of capabilities. In general, you can group them into three main categories:

- Simple Web links: Most DVD authoring systems provide tools that embed simple Web links into moments in the video or buttons on a menu that launch a browser and seek a location. Simple Web links within a DVD Video title are easy to implement and require less testing and support than other types of Web integration.

- Embedding in proprietary players: Several tools allow you to embed the DVD Video content inside a proprietary browser designed for simple DVD control and navigation combined with Web page content. The advantages include the fact that you can more tightly integrate the video with the Web content. For example, going beyond simple links to companion content, you can also go the other way with links and functions in the Web content that cause the DVD disc to display additional video tracks or menus that are hidden on the disc. The disadvantage is that you are forced to work with the player developed by the solution provider rather than working with more common and (in some cases) more robust browsers such as Microsoft Internet Explorer. Most Web video developers working with QuickTime, Windows Media, or Real are accustomed to complete control.

- Full-fledged browser integration: These tools allow you to integrate the DVD content into a standard browser such as Internet Explorer, along the lines of Web video formats such as QuickTime or Windows Media. One of the most attractive technologies for developing Web-enabled DVDs within Internet Explorer is Microsoft's MSWebDVD ActiveX control. The one drawback is that it is not cross-platform.

Specific tools are discussed in Part B: Tools.

DVD Video (or DVD Audio) on a PC

DVD Video and DVD-ROM hybrids, for use on PCs, can include a wide range of content and interactive features. Here are some examples:

- A DVD Video disc can include supplemental material in the form of Word, Excel, PDF, desktop video, or still-image formats that users can open from the disc in their DVD-ROM drive. Like a CD-ROM, this material can be in any format supported in the computer desktop environment.

- DVD Video can be incorporated directly into a PowerPoint presentation, using third-party tools.

- DVD Video content and MPEG-2 clips can be incorporated directly into a Macromedia Director title using a Director Xtra plug-in.

- Using C++ or other programming languages, developers can come up with their own custom solutions for integrating DVD Video into the PC environment.

Most WebDVD discs, discussed in the previous section, are fundamentally DVD Video and DVD-ROM hybrids. Specific tools and plug-ins are discussed in Part B: Tools.

The Secret Convergence Race

The question for the future is: After several years of competing with the World Wide Web for mindshare, will DVD finally live up to its full potential in a new generation of Web-enabled set-top boxes and game consoles? At the same time, there's another convergence race going on that is not so obvious. Even while DVD leans heavily toward the Web for new possibilities, the Web continues to strive toward broadband video capabilities that one day might just make the DVD obsolete. In addition, iTV seems to be taking off as a alternative, real-time convergence of broadcast-quality video with Web interactivity. So, while current WebDVD convergence technologies must point toward the disc to retrieve broadcast-quality video, it's not hard to imagine a day when all browsers will simply point to a location on the Web to receive the highest-quality video available — whether it's MPEG-2, MPEG-4, or some other video format altogether. At that point the integration will truly be complete. The question of whether Web and iTV standards and practices will eventually swallow the DVD spec altogether, or whether the DVD spec will successfully holds its own with new forms of Web functionality, is anyone's guess.

Part B: Tools

WebDVD Tools

For a general introduction to the various types of WebDVD tools, see "Web-DVD" on page 445.

General Comparisons

Table 17-1 provides a bird's-eye view of differences among the tools.

Table 17-1: General Comparisons of WebDVD Tools

Tool	Type	Development Platforms	Delivery Platforms	Compatible with WebDVD Players?
DVD@ccess (Apple Computer Inc.)	Simple Web links	Macintosh	Cross-platform	No
eDVD (Sonic Solutions, Inc.)	Embedded: Proprietary player	Windows and Macintosh	Windows only	Yes
InterActual Player 2.0 (InterActual Technologies, Inc.)	Embedded: Proprietary player	Windows and Macintosh	Windows only	Yes
MSWebDVD (Microsoft Corporation)	Embedded: ActiveX control integration	Windows	Windows only	No
OnStageDVD (Visible Light Holdings, Inc.)	Embedded: ActiveX control integration	Windows	Windows only	No

DVD@ccess (Apple Computer Inc.)

Go to www.apple.com/dvdstudiopro

Type: Simple Web links

Development platform: Macintosh

Playback platforms: Macintosh and Windows (requires a Web browser on each target system)

If you need to go cross-platform, Apple Computer's DVD authoring tool, DVDStudio Pro, includes a Web link technology called DVD@ccess, which allows you to create hot spots within a DVD title that link to URLs on both

Macintosh and Windows computers. You can embed URL links right into the DVD Video title to be triggered at chapter points, when various tracks play, or through menus. There is also no need for JavaScript or Visual Basic knowledge to author titles. However, there are no advanced scripting capabilities on the Macintosh for embedding and combining DVD content within a browser. If you need your Web links to work cross-platform (Macintosh and Windows), this is the way to go. If you seek more sophisticated Web integration, read about some of the Windows-only solutions in this section.

Apple Computer acquired Spruce Technologies in 2001. Spruce had its own WebDVD solution called SpruceLink, which in turn incorporated the InterActual Technologies solution described in "InterActual Technologies, Inc." on page 452. It will be interesting to see what Apple has in mind for integrating elements from Spruce into its DVD solutions. Don't be surprised to find more advanced capabilities in future upgrades of DVD Studio Pro.

eDVD (Sonic Solutions Inc.)

Go to www.sonic.com

Type: Integration with proprietary player

Development platforms: Windows (Macintosh with some Sonic Solutions authoring systems that include the eDVD option)

Playback platforms: Windows 95, 98, ME, NT, 2000 (requires Internet Explorer 4.02 SP2 or above); Web-enabled DVD players

Like DVD@ccess, Sonic's eDVD technology allows you to add URLs to your DVD titles. Through integration of InterActual Technologies Player 2.0, eDVD also provides an infrastructure for embedding and controlling DVD content within Web pages. For specific information about the capabilities of the InterActual solution, see "InterActual Technologies, Inc." on page 452.

The one advantage of eDVD over simply turning to the InterActual Technologies development resources is that you can do your Web integration authoring on the Macintosh platform, if that is your choice. To do so, you must own or purchase a Sonic DVD authoring solution for the Macintosh that supports the eDVD option. For more information, visit the Sonic Solutions Website (www.sonic.com).

InterActual Technologies, Inc.

Go to www.interactual.com

Type: Integration with proprietary player

Development platforms: Windows (Macintosh with some Sonic Solutions authoring systems that include the eDVD option)

Playback platforms: Windows 95, 98, ME, NT, 2000 (requires Internet Explorer 4.02 SP2 or above); Web-enabled DVD players

The most popular Windows playback solution for many years has been PCFriendly from InterActual Technologies. PCFriendly is basically a media player that can access DVD content from a DVD-ROM while allowing users to view assets on the disc, additional assets that can be copied over to their hard drives, or assets that are on the Web.

The latest version of the InterActual player, Player 2.0, provides many improvements over PCFriendly, including scalable window size, customizable skins, and a reduced footprint from approximately 40 MB (PCFriendly software) to about 6 MB (InterActual Player).

With Player 2.0, InterActual also introduces the Inventor Connection:, an online membership service that delivers essential programming information, support and training, and the latest InterActual software and tools including a Macromedia Dreamweaver plug-in, development and testing utilities, and new software and documentation shipped throughout the year. The one drawback for smaller production facilities is the cost: You must pay a licensing fee to distribute the player, and you must also pay a subscription fee to access some of the more advanced offerings of the Inventor Connection, including development support.

PCFriendly and InterActual Player do not provide their own software for DVD control capabilities, but instead they attack video playback challenges by linking users to the latest versions of the DVD playback software already on their systems. Each of the decoder manufacturers supported by InterActual allows the InterActual products to detect their DVD navigator software on the current system and launch it when the title is loaded. This also overcomes the fact that not all PCs have Microsoft's DirectShow installed, with its built-in DVD control features. In the meantime, PCFriendly supports a broad variety of proprietary DVD player software, and it also communicates with DirectShow.

InterActual is responsible for developing the closest thing to a standard at the moment — a set of JavaScript extensions to standard and embedded Web browsers called ITX. The ITX extensions, which have been adopted by various Hollywood studios and consumer electronics companies worldwide, define a standard language by which DVD players and browsers can communicate. ITX is also incorporated into many new Web-enabled DVD set-top boxes, which makes InterActual titles compatible with a new generation of DVD players as well as the vast majority of PCs (about 98 percent according to InterActual).

Popular authoring tools from Sonic Solutions (www.sonic.com) and Spruce Technologies (now owned by Apple Computer, www.apple.com) work with InterActual products to deliver integrated WebDVD solutions.

MSWebDVD and Windows Media Player (Microsoft Corporation)

For Windows Media Player information, go to msdn.microsoft.com/library/en-us/wmplay/mmp_sdk/ usingdvdwiththewindowsmediaplayercontrol.asp

For MSWebDVD information, go to msdn.microsoft.com

Type: Integration with Internet Explorer

Development platforms: Windows, or any Web page authoring or tool or text editor

Playback platforms: Windows (systems with DirectX 8 and Internet Explorer 5 or greater, and Windows Media Player 6.4 or greater)

Microsoft has been working hard to integrate DVD technology directly into the DirectShow capabilities of the Windows environment. A subset of the DirectX group of technologies that support the use of graphics and multimedia on the Microsoft Windows platform, Microsoft DirectShow is an architecture for streaming media. DirectShow provides for high-quality capture and playback of multimedia streams.

By intelligently integrating DVD supports right at the base level for multimedia functionality, Microsoft has made it possible to use a number of relatively simple schemes (including scripting for Internet Explorer, Windows Media Player, or programming with Visual Basic or Visual C++) to implement hybrid DVD solutions in a variety of ways on the Windows platform.

The one main drawback with MSWebDVD and the Windows Media Player implementation is that they are not cross-platform. ActiveX Controls and DirectShow are a Windows-only proposition, so if your audience must include Mac users, the Microsoft solutions are not for you. If you are developing for corporate communications or similar applications where you know the audience is using Windows PCs, this is a very effective option.

In addition, this technology will not work on a majority of first-generation Web-enabled set-top DVD players. In the future, however, it is quite likely that a new generation of devices — from Microsoft's Xbox game console to

Microsoft TV interactive television boxes — will fully support this form of DVD integration.

One of the most attractive technologies for developing Web-enabled DVDs is Microsoft's MSWebDVD ActiveX Control. First of all, it's free. It's included with DirectX Version 8. It's also available on many current installations of Windows 2000 and Windows XP.

The great thing about MSWebDVD is that it includes a plethora of scripting capabilities and follows all the scripting conventions common to other Microsoft applications. For example, if you are accustomed to scripting Web content that incorporates Windows Media, it's not a big leap to work with MSWebDVD to embed DVD Video directly into Web pages in Internet Explorer. You can mix your high-quality DVD content with Flash or Dynamic HTML elsewhere on the page to create an entire browser-based environment of your own making, or you can link to other locations on the Web. You can also create your own widgets within Web pages to control the DVD Video. For more information on scripting and building Web content with MSWebDVD, see "Working with MSWebDVD" on page 463.

Version 6.4 or greater of the Windows Media Player ActiveX control can also be used as a component in a Web page for playing DVD content. Through scripting, the Windows Media Player uses automation to expose the DVD Video-specific interfaces, methods, events, and properties of DirectShow application programming interface — although the MSWebDVD control is probably more robust and full-featured. For more information on integrating DVD into Web content using Windows Media Player, see "Working with Windows Media Player" on page 480.

OnStage DVD for ActiveX (Visible Light Holdings, Inc.)

Go to www.onstagedvd.com/products/activex/

Development platforms: Windows 95, 98, ME, 2000 (with any ActiveX-compatible authoring language)

Playback platforms: Windows 95, 98, ME, 2000 (with Internet Explorer, PowerPoint, or any Visual Basic or Visual C++ programmed application)

OnStage DVD for ActiveX has many of the same advantages as MSWebDVD and the Microsoft DirectShow environment because it can be used within any application or with any number of authoring languages that support communication with ActiveX controls. These include PowerPoint, HTML, Flash, Visual Basic, and C++.

OnStage DVD for ActiveX actually works with the same DirectShow technologies as MSWebDVD, but it provides developers with an easy-to-use interface for setting properties and functions and for controlling DVD content.

If you are familiar with ActiveX authoring in one of the supported programs or languages, then this product offers a good solution. One disadvantage is the price: Especially when compared with the free Microsoft solutions, the professional edition of this product seems expensive. Thankfully, a stripped-down version is also available at a more reasonable price. A second disadvantage is that these titles obviously will not work in DVD Video players. Basically, this solution is meant only for PC-based or kiosk delivery. One final issue to consider is that, like the Microsoft solutions, OnStage DVD for ActiveX might require some form of installation on the user's system — of the ActiveX control, Internet Explorer, and so forth. If you would like to deliver a title that also requires little or no installation, see "InterActual Technologies, Inc." on page 452.

DVD-ROM Hybrid Tools

Hybrid DVD Video/DVD-ROM applications are gaining importance as a way of combining the video and sound quality of DVD with the highly advanced authoring and programming that are possible on modern computers. All of the WebDVD tools described in the previous section can also be used for delivering basic DVD Video/DVD-ROM hybrid content through the browser. In other words, an Internet connection is not necessary for local files delivered through the browser. This section describes a few additional tools for delivering hybrid content in DVD-ROM drives.

OnStage DVD for Director and Authorware (Visible Light Holdings, Inc.)

Go to www.visiblelight.com/products/onstagedvd.com/odd4

Development platforms: Windows 95, 98, ME, 2000 (with Macromedia Director Version 7 or 8, Authorware Version 5)

Playback platforms: Windows 95, 98, ME, 2000

With a history of several years, OnStage DVD for Director and Authorware is a stable and robust Xtra that allows you to combine all the advanced authoring capabilities of Director or Authorware with DVD Video content. If you are accustomed to authoring with Macromedia tools, but have been craving top-notch video and audio, OnStage DVD provides a proven solution that adds a set of dialog boxes, Lingo functions, and properties to the familiar Director environment.

Aside from advanced authoring capabilities and the opportunity to continue working with familiar tools, the next biggest advantage of OnStage

DVD for Director is the fact that you can compile your application into an executable projector file that will launch straight off the disc with no installation required. For this reason alone, OnStage DVD for Director is worth considering over the various browser-based solutions that might, or might not, work straight off the disc.

Another good reason to use OnStage DVD, even for WebDVD implementations, is the fact that any Web links and content can be handled in any Web browser that the user has installed. As with any HTML content, developers still have to make sure the Web content appears and functions properly cross-browser, but because Director is able to spawn a Web page through use of Lingo, whatever browser the user has installed on their system will automatically open and display the content.

One disadvantage is the price: especially when compared with the free Microsoft solutions, the professional edition of this product seems expensive. But a stripped-down version is also available at a more reasonable cost. A second disadvantage is that these titles obviously will not work in DVD Video players. Basically, this solution is meant only for PC-based or kiosk delivery.

Obviously, OnStage DVD for Director provides all the flexibility of that venerable program. Display properties and complexity of your title are completely under the developer's control. At the same time the OnStage DVD API, in the more expensive professional edition, has more than 60 commands covering the full range of the DVD specification. You can even use a transparent Web connection (no browser) for advanced control and content updates over the Internet.

OnStage DVD for ActiveX (Visible Light Holdings, Inc.)

Go to www.onstagedvd.com/products/activex

Development platforms: Windows 95, 98, ME, 2000 (with any ActiveX-compatible authoring language)

Playback platforms: Windows 95, 98, ME, 2000 (with Internet Explorer, PowerPoint, or any Visual Basic or Visual C++ programmed application)

OnStage DVD for ActiveX offers many of the same DVD features in environments that support ActiveX Controls, including Internet Explorer, PowerPoint, Visual Basic, and Visual C++ programs. For more information, see "MSWebDVD and Windows Media Player (Microsoft Corporation)" on page 453.

Xtra DVD

Email: info@dvdbiz.co.jp

Development platforms: Windows 95, 98, NT (with Macromedia Director or Authorware)

Playback platforms: Windows 95, 98, ME, 2000, NT

Xtra for Macromedia Director Shockwave Studio Pro. Install this Xtra in Director and use DVD Video, including high-quality MPEG-2, within your projects. This is the first Xtra extension that enabled DVD Video playback in Director.

Active DVD (Zuma Digital Inc.)

Go to www.zumadigital.com

Development platforms: Windows 95, 98, NT (with PowerPoint)

Playback platforms: PowerPoint on Windows 95, 98, ME, 2000, NT

A software plug-in for Microsoft PowerPoint. It allows users to enhance their presentations with DVD material by playing a DVD title or parts of it from their PowerPoint presentation on a DVD-enabled PC. Active DVD can access and play back DVD content from a disc as well as the hard drive of the computer.

Part C: Methods

Choosing Your Hybrid DVD Technologies

As with all media technologies, your choices for development tools and delivery technologies are affected by both the purpose of your disc as well as the target audience. Various limitations of the technologies can narrow your choices quickly, like a funnel.

Do you need to reach the widest possible audience on all platforms?

The simplest approach is to build a DVD Video title and then supply some instructions and a series of companion files that users can open manually on DVD-ROM drives if they so choose. This approach can be developed with almost any of the tools listed in this chapter and will work on any computer with a DVD-ROM drive and DVD Video playback software. The DVD Video portion of this disc will also play on all set-top DVD players, although the ROM portion won't be available in a player unless you include an optional link in the title for launching additional companion WebDVD elements.

Do you need to create a WebDVD title that reaches users on both Macintosh and Windows computers?

In this case, you need to keep your design approach simple and your technologies open. For example, a simple DVD Video title with Web links authored in DVD Studio Pro can be used to launch companion Web pages on the ROM portion of the disc using any browser available on the target system. The DVD Video does not appear within the Web page in this scenario, but it plays in a separate window while the Web pages display or update. This kind of dual-display approach is not as effective from a usability standpoint, but it will get the job done cross-platform.

Do you need to reach the majority of Web-enabled players as well as DVD-ROM drives?

The best choice here is simply the InterActual Player 2.0 technology. InterActual Technologies boasts 98 percent compatibility on DVD-capable Windows computers and near-complete compatibility with up-and-coming Web-enabled DVD players. InterActual also has the closest thing to a WebDVD standard: the ITX group of browser extensions that helps ensure compatibility with most players going forward. The downside is that the interactive content does not work on the Macintosh. If you must also reach Mac users, you should plan on authoring accordingly, with button choices for linking to another set of Web elements that users can launch into a separate browser window in the Macintosh.

Does your audience fall primarily into the group of technologies developed by Microsoft?

Of course, this group of technologies includes a broad range of applications, from DVD-ROM content on the Windows desktop to PowerPoint to Internet Explorer to Microsoft TV (interactive television content) and, quite possibly, the Xbox game console (which includes a DVD player option that might be Web-enabled in the near future). The advantage here is that you have one development environment to work in, which helps to speed development and avoid compatibility problems across devices. The other advantage, of course, is that the development tools are very cheap or, in many cases, free.

WebDVD Workflow

The workflow for producing a WebDVD is similar to standard DVD production as described in Chapters 6 and 7, with the following additions:

- **Preproduction and information design:** It is especially important at this early stage to map out the structure of content as shared among the DVD Video elements and the HTML or other file formats. You also need to think about additional skills and resources required for the design and authoring of Web elements and how these affect the budget and scheduling.

- **Preparing source materials:** In addition to preparing the DVD Video elements, you must also prepare the HTML elements during this phase.

- **Organizing the project:** As you organize the project, you might want to begin structuring an additional folder for the HTML and other elements to reside on your DVD disc master next to the Video_TS folder containing the DVD Video elements. You also need to prepare for special testing needs of WebDVD, which might involve finding or setting up a set-top WebDVD player or one or more PCs with the appropriate configuration.

- **Authoring:** Obviously, the authoring stage involves the additional coding and authoring of the Web content.

- **Testing (quality assurance):** Quality assurance involves the additional testing of all Web links and Web content on the target platforms.

- **Recording and mastering:** Recording and mastering are similar to basic DVD; however, you must also include your additional Web elements on the disc outside of the Video_TS folder, as well as the appropriate installers if required. Some DVD authoring systems automatically place the necessary installers for using Web links into a folder on the disc when you run the build process.

WebDVD Authoring Tips

Here are a few tips for authoring of WebDVD titles:

- Consider installing your HTML content onto the local hard drive: Users might experience performance problems on some systems when DVD Video playback and Web interactivity are occurring at the same time. This happens because the DVD-ROM drive is attempting to stream the video data from one location on the disc while seeking the HTML or other data from another location on the disc. The best solution is to include an installer that places the HTML content, or any other files that the program will attempt to access locally, onto the playback system's hard drive. This way the DVD-ROM drive remains devoted to the task of delivering the DVD Video content.

- Use relative links for all local HTML files: If you will be including some of the HTML files along with the DVD disc, make sure to avoid absolute references to files; use relative referencing instead. This is a standard Web technique for referencing external files and links relative to the location of the current HTML file in the folder hierarchy. Consult your Web authoring HTML reference documentation for more information.

- Consider rerouting links to locations on the Web that might change: Since the content of your DVD disc is fixed once it is completed and Web locations sometimes change, you can overcome this hazard by having your links seek URLs on your company's Website, which then automatically relink to the appropriate Web address. This way, when you become aware of broken links or changed URLs, you can make the changes on your Website and keep the DVD links on the disc functional.

Working with Proprietary Tools

Proprietary WebDVD authoring tools and resources include programs such as InterActual Player 2.0 and the Inventor Connection from InterActual Technologies (see "InterActual Technologies, Inc." on page 452) or OnStage DVD from Visible Light Holdings, Inc. (see "OnStage DVD for ActiveX (Visible Light Holdings, Inc.)" on page 454). Consult the documentation and other resources provided by these manufacturers for specific information on authoring steps and techniques. In the case of InterActual Player 2.0, you must become a member of the Inventor Connection developer community (inventor.interactual.com) in order to download software and begin using the tools.

These tools save you time and money in the development phase but involve more up-front cost. On the Windows platform at least, if you have a mind for scripting languages and would like to save some money on development and delivery tools, you can develop your own custom WebDVD programs targeted to the Windows environment using techniques described in the following sections.

Working with MSWebDVD

MSWebDVD is an ActiveX control that interfaces with Microsoft Direct-Show, an architecture for streaming media on the Microsoft Windows plat-form. For some time now, DirectShow has included DVD control capabilities. DirectShow provides MSWebDVD, as well as the Windows Media Player, with access to the underlying stream control architecture for applications that require custom solutions. You can use MSWebDVD and DirectShow to create custom DVD players or complex WebDVD applica-tions that play directly in Internet Explorer. You can also leverage these capabilities in other programs that support ActiveX controls, such as Microsoft PowerPoint, as discussed in "Integrating DVD into PowerPoint" on page 488.

DirectShow is part of the group of DirectX technologies. DirectX Version 8 and greater include the MSWebDVD control by default, so many recent systems — including many Windows 2000 systems and all Windows XP systems — will not require installations, although you should plan to include an installer for those systems that do not include it. Also, DirectX 8.1 is not supported on Windows 95 or Windows NT. Remember that your target systems will require a DVD-ROM drive.

Working with MSWebDVD is much like working with the Windows Media Player in Internet Explorer. You follow a similar workflow of embed-ding the object into a Web page, adding buttons or other elements, and scripting the functionality that you wish to incorporate. As with the synchro-nized presentations discussed in Chapter 2, you can embed DVD Video within a frameset and use URL flips to synchronize the video to content in other frames.

The Microsoft developer network library (msdn.microsoft.com/library) provides a wealth of information and resources for developing with MSWebDVD, DirectShow, and Windows Media Player. The following top-ics provide a high-level run-through of the process. These procedures require some knowledge of HTML and JavaScript.

MSWebDVD Methods and Properties

Authoring with MSWebDVD involves a combination of HTML and JavaScript that closely resembles the type of code you might experience when working with the Windows Media Player within Web pages (with many additional elements specific to DVD, however). This section provides a reference resource for the specific JavaScript methods and properties sup-ported for the MSWebDVD object, as well as the events that various types of events (internal events or that you can respond to with code. These comprise the building blocks of your interactive DVD applications. The following tables provide a list of MSWebDVD methods and properties. Visit msdn.microsoft.com/library to view examples of each.

Table 17-2: MSWebDVD Methods and Properties: Playback

CanStep	Determines whether the MPEG-2 decoder on the local system can perform frame stepping.
Eject	Ejects or inserts a disc from or into the drive.
FramesPerSecond	Retrieves the video frame rate for the current DVD title.
Pause	Pauses playback at the current location.
Play	Plays the current DVD title.
PlayAtTime	Starts playback in the current title at the specified time.
PlayAtTimeInTitle	Starts playback at the specified time within the specified title.
PlayBackwards	Starts backward playback from the current location at the specified speed.
PlayChapter	Starts playback from the specified chapter in the current title.
PlayChapterInTitle	Plays the specified chapter in the specified title.
PlayChaptersAutoStop	Starts playback at the specified chapter in the specified title, for the number of chapters specified.
PlayForwards	Starts forward playback from the current location at the specified speed.
PlayNextChapter	Starts playback from the next chapter in the current title.
PlayPeriodInTitleAutoStop	Starts playback at the specified time in the specified title until the specified stop time.
PlayPrevChapter	Starts playback from the previous chapter in the current title.
PlayTitle	Starts playback at the beginning of the specified title.
ReplayChapter	Starts playback at the beginning of the current chapter.
Resume	Resumes playback after a menu has been displayed.
StillOff	Resumes playback, canceling still mode.
Step	Advances the DVD Video stream by the specified number of frames.
Stop	Stops playback.

Table 17-3: MSWebDVD Methods and Properties: Menus

ActivateAtPosition	Activates the menu button at the specified position.
ActivateButton	Activates the selected menu button.
ButtonsAvailable	Retrieves the total number of buttons on the current menu.
CurrentButton	Retrieves the number of the selected button.
DefaultMenuLanguage	Retrieves the default menu language from the disc.
GetButtonAtPosition	Retrieves the number of the button at the specified coordinates without selecting or activating it.
GetButtonRect	Retrieves the rectangle for the specified button, in window coordinates.
ReturnFromSubmenu	Returns display from a submenu to its parent menu, or to the current title if the menu is a top-level menu.
SelectAndActivateButton	Selects and activates the specified button.
SelectAtPosition	Selects the menu button at the specified position.
SelectLeftButton	Selects the left directional button from the displayed menu.
SelectLowerButton	Selects the lower directional button from the displayed menu.
SelectRightButton	Selects the right directional button from the displayed menu.
SelectUpperButton	Selects the upper directional button from the displayed menu.
ShowMenu	Displays the specified menu on the screen.

Table 17-4: MSWebDVD Methods and Properties: Audio Stream

AudioStreamsAvailable	Retrieves the number of audio streams available in the current title.
Balance	Sets or retrieves the speaker balance for the audio stream output.
CurrentAudioStream	Sets or retrieves the number of the enabled audio stream.
DefaultAudioLanguage	Retrieves the default audio language from the disc.
DefaultAudioLanguageExt	Retrieves the default audio language extension from the disc.
GetAudioLanguage	Retrieves a string indicating which language is available on the specified audio stream.

Table 17-4: MSWebDVD Methods and Properties: Audio Stream (Continued)

IsAudioStreamEnabled	Retrieves a value indicating whether the specified audio stream is enabled in the current title.
Mute	Turns the audio stream output on or off.
SelectDefaultAudio-Language	Sets the current default audio language in the DVD Navigator.
Volume	Sets or retrieves the audio volume level.

Table 17-5: MSWebDVD Methods and Properties: Subpicture Stream

CurrentSubpictureStream	Retrieves the selected subpicture stream.
DefaultSubpictureLanguage	Retrieves the default subpicture language from the disc.
DefaultSubpictureLanguageExt	Retrieves the default subpicture language extension from the disc.
GetSubpictureLanguage	Retrieves the language for the specified subpicture stream.
IsSubpictureStreamEnabled	Retrieves a value indicating whether the specified subpicture stream is enabled in the current title.
PreferredSubpictureStream	Sets or retrieves the user's preferred subpicture stream for the current viewing session.
SelectDefaultSubpictureLan-guage	Sets the current default subpicture language in the DVD Naviga-tor.
SubpictureOn	Sets or retrieves the current subpicture state (on or off).
SubpictureStreamsAvailable	Retrieves the number of subpicture streams available in the cur-rent title.

Table 17-6: MSWebDVD Methods and Properties: Video Rectangle

AspectRatio	Retrieves the aspect ratio of the current video stream as authored on the disc.
BackColor	Sets or retrieves the color of the bars that appear around the edges of the video rectangle when the aspect ratio of the native video is not the same as that of the object's display area.

Table 17-6: MSWebDVD Methods and Properties: Video Rectangle (Contin-

Capture	Captures a still image from the video frame when the MSWebDVD object is in windowless mode.
FullScreenMode	Sets or retrieves a value indicating whether the display is in full-screen mode.
GetClipVideoRect	Retrieves the clipping rectangle defined for the video display.
GetVideoSize	Retrieves the native video dimensions.
SetClipVideoRect	Sets the clipping rectangle occupied by the video display.
Zoom	Zooms the video display in or out, centered on a given set of screen coordinates.

Table 17-7: MSWebDVD Methods and Properties: Closed Captioning

CCActive	Sets or retrieves the current status of closed captioning.
ColorKey	Sets or retrieves the color key used in closed captioning.
CurrentCCService	Sets or retrieves the current closed-captioned service.

Table 17-8: MSWebDVD Methods and Properties: Angle Blocks

AnglesAvailable	Retrieves the number of angles available.
CurrentAngle	Sets or retrieves the current angle in an angle block.

Table 17-9: MSWebDVD Methods and Properties: Karaoke Audio

GetKaraokeChannelAssignment	Retrieves a value that indicates how the karaoke channels are assigned to the left and right speakers.
GetKaraokeChannelContent	Retrieves a value that indicates the type of content in the specified karaoke channel in the specified stream.
KaraokeAudioPresentationMode	Sets or retrieves the right-left speaker mix for the auxiliary karaoke channels.

Table 17-10: MSWebDVD Methods and Properties: Text Strings

GetDVDTextLanguageLCID	Retrieves the locale identifier (LCID) for the specified text string block.
GetDVDTextNumberOf-Languages	Retrieves the number of text languages available in the current DVD directory.
GetDVDTextNumberOfStrings	Retrieves the number of text strings available for the specified language.
GetDVDTextString	Retrieves the specified text string from the disc.
GetDVDTextStringType	Retrieves a value that indicates the type of information contained in the specified DVD text string.
GetLangFromLangID	Retrieves a human-readable string when given a primary language identifier (ID).

Table 17-11: MSWebDVD Methods and Properties: Parental Management

AcceptParentalLevelChange	Instructs the DVD Navigator to accept or reject the new temporary parental management level.
GetPlayerParentalCountry	Retrieves the current country/region as set in the DVD Navigator.
GetPlayerParentalLevel	Retrieves the parental management level set in the DVD Navigator.
GetTitleParentalLevels	Retrieves the parental management levels for the specified title.
NotifyParentalLevelChange	Enables or disables the event handling for temporary parental management level commands.
SelectParentalCountry	Sets the specified parental country/region for subsequent playback.
SelectParentalLevel	Sets the specified parental level for subsequent playback.

Table 17-12: MSWebDVD Methods and Properties: Disc Info

CurrentChapter	Retrieves the number of the chapter currently playing.
CurrentDiscSide	Retrieves the current side of the DVD.
CurrentDomain	Retrieves the DVD domain that the DVD Navigator is in.

Table 17-12: MSWebDVD Methods and Properties: Disc Info (Continued)

CurrentTime	Retrieves the current playback time.
CurrentTitle	Retrieves the number of the title currently playing.
CurrentVolume	Retrieves the volume number for the current root directory.
DVDDirectory	Retrieves or sets the root directory of the current DVD volume.
DVDTimeCode2bstr	Retrieves a string indicating the current time on the disc.
DVDUniqueID	Retrieves a system-generated number that uniquely identifies the current DVD.
GetNumberOfChapters	Retrieves the number of chapters in the specified title.
TitlesAvailable	Retrieves the number of titles available on the DVD.
TotalTitleTime	Retrieves the total playback time for the current title.
UOPValid	Retrieves a value that indicates whether the specified user operation is currently valid.
VolumesAvailable	Retrieves a value specifying the number of volumes in the disc set.

Table 17-13: MSWebDVD Methods and Properties: Object Initialization and Control

DisableAutoMouseProcess-ing	Enables or disables the object's mouse-processing functionality.
DVDAdm	Provides access to the MSDVDAdm object containing methods and properties for saving application and user information.
EnableResetOnStop	Sets or retrieves a value that determines how play will resume when the filter graph transitions out of a stopped state.
PlayState	Retrieves the current play state.
ReadyState	Retrieves the ReadyState of the MSWebDVD object.
RegionChange	Displays a system dialog box that enables the user to change the region associated with the DVD drive.
Render	Initializes the DVD filter graph.
WindowlessActivation	Initializes the MSWebDVD object at design time for either windowed or windowless mode.

Table 17-14: MSWebDVD Methods and Properties: Bookmarks

DeleteBookmark	Deletes the current bookmark.
RestoreBookmark	Moves the DVD Navigator to the point on the DVD as specified in the current bookmark, with all audio, video, and subpicture settings restored.
SaveBookmark	Saves the current disc position and state of the DVD Navigator to disc so that the user can return to the same place later.

Table 17-15: MSWebDVD Methods and Properties: Cursors and Tooltips

CursorType	Sets or retrieves the current cursor type.
GetDelayTime	Retrieves the delay time for the ToolTip associated with the MSWeb-DVD object.
SetDelayTime	Sets the delay time for the ToolTip associated with the MSWebDVD object.
ShowCursor	Makes the mouse pointer visible when the DVD Navigator is in full-screen mode.
ToolTip	Sets the text for the ToolTip that will appear when the mouse pointer is over the MSWebDVD Video rectangle.
ToolTipMaxWidth	Sets or retrieves the maximum width for the ToolTip associated with the MSWebDVD object.

Table 17-16: MSWebDVD Methods and Properties: GPRMs and SPRMs

GetGPRM	Retrieves the specified general parameter register.
GetSPRM	Retrieves the specified system parameter register.
SetGPRM	Sets the specified general parameter register to the specified value.

MSWebDVD Events

Events can occur on the user's system either internally (when the user clicks something or performs some other operation) or externally (when certain information is encountered on the DVD disc). You can then write code to respond to these events. There are three events that relate to operation of the DVD disc itself (not user operations). Visit msdn.microsoft.com/library to view examples of each of the following events:

- **DVDNotify** event notifies your application of many different types of DVD-related events, which are identified in the EventCode parameter.

- **ReadyStateChange** event notifies your application of changes in the MSWebDVD ReadyState property, which is a property common to all ActiveX controls.

- **UpdateOverlay** event is sent to applications only if they are hosting MSWebDVD in windowless mode. Applications need to respond to this event only if they are displaying floating buttons over the video rectangle in full-screen mode. Table 17-17 lists MSWebDVD events.

Table 17-17: MSWebDVD Events

Event	Description
ChangeCurrentAngle	Sent when the disc enables or disables changing the angle.
ChangeCurrentAudioStream	Sent when the disc enables or disables changing the audio stream.
ChangeCurrentSubpictureStream	Sent when the ChangeCurrentSubpictureStream command has been enabled or disabled.
DVDNotify	Notifies an application of many different DVD events and disc instructions.
PauseOn	Sent when the Pause command has been enabled or disabled.
PlayAtTime	Sent when the PlayAtTime command has been enabled or disabled.
PlayAtTimeInTitle	Sent when the PlayAtTimeInTitle command has been enabled or disabled.
PlayBackwards	Sent when the PlayBackwards command has been enabled or disabled.
PlayChapter	Sent when the PlayChapter command has been enabled or disabled.
PlayChapterInTitle	Sent when the PlayChapterInTitle command has been enabled or disabled.
PlayForwards	Sent when the PlayForwards command has been enabled or disabled.

Table 17-17: MSWebDVD Events (Continued)

Event	Description
PlayNextChapter	Sent when the PlayNextChapter command has been enabled or disabled.
PlayPrevChapter	Sent when the PlayPrevChapter command has been enabled or disabled.
PlayTitle	Sent when the ReturnFromSubmenu command has been enabled or disabled.
ReadyStateChange	Sent when the ReadyState property of the MSWebDVD control has changed.
ReplayChapter	Sent when the ReplayChapter command has been enabled or disabled.
Resume	Sent when the Resume command has been enabled or disabled.
ReturnFromSubmenu	Sent when the ReturnFromSubmenu command has been enabled or disabled.
SelectOrActivatButton	Sent when the disc enables or disables the selection or activation of menu buttons.
ShowMenu	Sent when the disc enables or disables the showing of a menu.
StillOff	Sent when the StillOff command has been enabled or disabled.
Stop	Sent when the Stop command has been enabled or disabled.
UpdateOverlay	Sent when the overlay surface has been moved or resized or its color key has changed.

Embedding the MSWebDVD Object

The methods, properties, and events of the MSWebDVD object enable an application both to control all aspects of DVD Video navigation and playback and to retrieve information from the disc. To access these capabilities, you must first embed the MSWebDVD object into a Web page. The process is much like embedding the Windows Media Player object into a page. Here is sample HTML code:

```
<OBJECT
CLASSID=clsid:38EE5CEE-4B62-11D3-854F-00A0C9C898E7
ID=DVD
STYLE="height:480px; width:640px">
<PARAM NAME="BackColor" VALUE="navy">
<PARAM NAME="EnableResetOnStop" VALUE="0">
<PARAM NAME="ColorKey" VALUE="1048592">
</OBJECT>
```

The EnableResetOnStop parameter determines how playback will resume after the program has been stopped. The ColorKey parameter relates to background color for captions.

Embedding a Custom DVD Controller

Unlike the Windows Media Player ActiveX control, MSWebDVD does not allow you to simply enable a controller to reveal buttons in the embedded object. You need to embed button images and include JavaScript to enable basic DVD controller functions.

Fortunately, MSWebDVD uses similar names and syntax as the Windows Media Player object for the various standard playback methods. Here are two examples:

```
<INPUT ID=button1 NAME="playButton" TYPE=button
VALUE="Play" onClick='Play();'>
<INPUT ID=button2 NAME="pauseButton" TYPE=button
VALUE="Pause" onClick='Pause();'>
```

As with all form-based buttons, you must also add the appropriate function after the body tag to execute the method, for example:

```
<SCRIPT LANGUAGE="JavaScript">
function Play(){
  DVD.Play();
}
```

```
function Pause(){
 DVD.Pause();
}
</SCRIPT>
```

Handling DVD Event Notifications

To capture the various DVD event notifications, enter the following HTML SCRIPT tag below the OBJECT tag for the MSWebDVD object. For a list of all event codes, see "MSWebDVD Events" on page 470.

```
<SCRIPT LANGUAGE="JScript"
FOR=DVD EVENT="DVDNotify(EventCode, Param1, Param2)">
ProcessDVDEvent(EventCode, Param1, Param2)
</SCRIPT>You must then define the event codes and the
ProcessDVDEvent function, as shown in the next code
example.
<SCRIPT LANGUAGE="JScript">
// DVD event codes are valued 257 through 283
var EC_DVDBASE = 256;
var EC_DVD_DOMAIN_CHANGE = (EC_DVDBASE + 1);
var EC_DVD_TITLE_CHANGE = (EC_DVDBASE + 2);
var EC_DVD_CHAPTER_START = (EC_DVDBASE + 3);
var EC_DVD_AUDIO_STREAM_CHANGE = (EC_DVDBASE + 4);
var EC_DVD_SUBPICTURE_STREAM_CHANGE = (EC_DVDBASE +
5);
var EC_DVD_ANGLE_CHANGE = (EC_DVDBASE + 6);
var EC_DVD_BUTTON_CHANGE = (EC_DVDBASE + 7);
var EC_DVD_VALID_UOPS_CHANGE = (EC_DVDBASE + 8);
var EC_DVD_STILL_ON = (EC_DVDBASE + 9);
var EC_DVD_STILL_OFF = (EC_DVDBASE + 10);
var EC_DVD_CURRENT_TIME = (EC_DVDBASE + 11); // not
used by MSWebDVD
```

```
var EC_DVD_ERROR = (EC_DVDBASE + 12);
var EC_DVD_WARNING = (EC_DVDBASE + 13);
var EC_DVD_CHAPTER_AUTOSTOP = (EC_DVDBASE + 14);
var EC_DVD_NO_FP_PGC = (EC_DVDBASE + 15);
var EC_DVD_PLAYBACK_RATE_CHANGE = (EC_DVDBASE + 16);
var EC_DVD_PARENTAL_LEVEL_CHANGE = (EC_DVDBASE + 17);
var EC_DVD_PLAYBACK_STOPPED = (EC_DVDBASE + 18);
var EC_DVD_ANGLES_AVAILABLE = (EC_DVDBASE + 19);
var EC_DVD_PLAYPERIOD_AUTOSTOP = (EC_DVDBASE + 20);
var EC_DVD_BUTTON_AUTO_ACTIVATED = (EC_DVDBASE + 21);
var EC_DVD_CMD_START = (EC_DVDBASE + 22);
// not used by MSWebDVD
var EC_DVD_CMD_END = (EC_DVDBASE + 23);
// not used by MSWebDVD
var EC_DVD_DISC_EJECTED = (EC_DVDBASE + 24);
var EC_DVD_DISC_INSERTED = (EC_DVDBASE + 25);
var EC_DVD_CURRENT_HMSF_TIME = (EC_DVDBASE + 26);
var EC_DVD_KARAOKE_MODE = (EC_DVDBASE + 27);


var nCurDomain;
var nCurParentalLevel;


function ProcessDVDEvent(EventCode, Param1, Param2)
{
 switch (EventCode)
 {
 case EC_DVD_DOMAIN_CHANGE:
  nCurDomain = Param1;
  // do something
  break;
 case EC_DVD_PARENTAL_LEVEL_CHANGE:
  nCurParentalLevel = Param1;
  // do something
```

```
    break;


// handle any other events you are interested in


default:
 break;
 }
 }
</SCRIPT>
```

Handling User Operations

The MSWebDVD object sends UOP event notifications to inform an application when a specific user operation (UOP) has been enabled or disabled by the disc. Each user operation has its own event, with a single Boolean parameter indicating whether that operation is now enabled or disabled.

For each event that you wish to handle, specify an event handler (you can call your handler method anything you like) as shown in the following example.

```
<SCRIPT LANGUAGE="JScript" FOR=DVD
EVENT="PlayForwards(bEnabled)">
 PlayForwardsEventHandler(bEnabled)
</SCRIPT>
```

Now define your handler method to respond appropriately to the event. Assume that the "button_Play" variable here is the id attribute of the "Play" button in your application.

```
function PlayForwardsEventHander(bEnabled)
{
 if(bEnabled == true)
 button_Play.disabled = false;
 else
 button_Play.disabled = true;
}
```

For a list of all event codes, see "MSWebDVD Events" on page 470.

Working with DVD Menus

MSWebDVD automatically handles menu commands when the user clicks DVD menu buttons with the mouse. You can override this default mouse behavior in order to script additional actions into a button click. This is one example of how DVD-ROM can provide richer content than standard DVD Video. For example, user clicks can be programmed to display additional HTML content to elsewhere in a frameset, along with causing the standard relocation to a track within the DVD content. To implement custom mouse handling, use the MSWebDVD menu-related methods such as SelectAndActivateButton, GetButtonAtPosition to determine scripted responses to user clicks.

MSWebDVD also offers a set of methods (for example, SelectUpperButton) that allows you to display an image map on your Web page representing a DVD remote control, with buttons that move the current menu selection up, down, right, and left, just as they do in a DVD player connected to a television. Unlike the standard DVD Video menus which appear within the DVD Video object area, these buttons can be placed anywhere within the browser interface.

Working with Multiple Streams and Other Features

In order to handle multiple titles, angles, audio and subpicture streams, or parental management levels (PMLs), you need to establish the proper numbering scheme and to script using the appropriate numbers. Table 17-18 shows the default numbering for these elements of DVD content. In order to allow for selection of items within the browser interface, you can use the numbers to enable the user to select the preferred item.

Table 17-18: MSWebDVD Numbering of Multiple Streams

DVD Feature	Maximum Allowed	Numbering
Angles	9	1 to 9
Audio streams	8	0 to 7
PMLs	8	1 to 8
Subpicture streams	32	0 to 31
Titles	Varies	1 to x

For an MSWebDVD application to be notified of PML markers on the disc, it must call NotifyParentalLevels(true). MSWebDVD will then inform your application when it encounters PML information on the disc. To enforce PMLs, your application must implement some form of password control logic that associates users with levels and respond to EC_DVD_PARENTAL_LEVEL_CHANGE events to allow or disallow access as appropriate.

Working with LCIDs

The locale identifer (LCID) is a 32-bit data type into which are packed several different values that help to identify a particular geographical region. One of these internal values is the primary language ID, which identifies the basic language of the region or locale, such as English, Spanish, or Russian.

MSWebDVD requires a complete valid LCID as an input parameter for two methods: SelectDefaultAudioLanguage and SelectDefaultSubpicture-Language. This can be any valid LCID recognized by Windows, and even some that are not recognized by Windows. (It is not necessary that the host system actually support the locale with fonts, keyboard mappings, and so on.) For more information, visit msdn.microsoft.com.

Synchronizing HTML Content with the Video

Much like a synchronized presentation using one of the standard streaming video formats (see Chapter 2), you can use DVD Video to drive display of synchronized HTML content within a frameset. In this case you script the interface to handle timecode events from the disc. In fact, you can use time-code events to drive any variety of scripted behaviors in your browser-based interface.

The following code snippet (provided by Microsoft at msdn.microsoft.com) shows one way to synchronize JScript function calls to timecode events:

```
//DVDTriggerPoints array holds frame count for each
trigger. Must be in ascending order.

//Use timecode2frames() to convert timecodes
(hh:mm:ss:ff) to total number of frames.


var DVDTriggerPoints = new Array(
  timecode2frames("01:15:24:00"),
  timecode2frames("01:23:02:00"));
```

```
//DVDTriggerProcs array holds functions to be called
at each trigger point defined in DVDTimePoints.
var DVDTriggerProcs = new Array(
 "showDogPic();",
 "showCatPic();");


//DVDTriggerIndex keeps track of current trigger (it
indexes DVDTriggerPoints and DVDTriggerProcs).
var DVDTriggerIndex = 0;


//Handle DVD Events
function ProcessDVDEvent(EventCode, Param1, Param2) {
 switch (EventCode) {
  case EC_DVD_CURRENT_HMSF_TIME:
   if(MSWebDVD.CurrentDomain == 4) { //Don't bother
checking unless disc is playing.
    if (DVDTriggerIndex < DVDTimePoints.length) { //
Are there trigger points left to check?
    currentDVDTime =
(MSWebDVD.DVDTimeCode2bstr(Param1));
     if (timecode2frames(currentDVDTime)>=
DVDTriggerPoints[DVDTimeIndex]) {
      // if trigger point has passed, execute the
associated function
      eval(DVDTriggerProcs[DVDTimeIndex++]);
     }
    }
   }
  break;

  // handle other events
 }
}
```

```
function timecode2frames(timeCode) {

  if (timeCode != "undefined") {
   return timeCode.substring(0,2)*108000
   + timeCode.substring(3,5)*1800
   + timeCode.substring(6,8)*30
   + timeCode.substring(9,11);
  } else {
   return 0;
  }
}
```

Saving and Restoring Bookmarks

Bookmarks are another feature that sets the DVD-ROM application apart from the basic DVD Video title. Unlike a DVD Video title, your DVD-ROM application can use the internal data structure that the MSWebDVD object uses to create a snapshot of the current user session, including information such as the present location on the disc, the parental level of the person who was viewing at the time, and the selected audio and subpicture streams, and so on, and restore these characteristics the next time the user returns to view the disc, after any length of time. The SaveBookmark and RestoreBookmark methods are used to achieve this.

Only one bookmark can be stored at a time. Calling SaveBookmark twice will cause the first bookmark to be overwritten. Bookmarks are specific to a computer. Running the same HTML page on a different computer and calling RestoreBookmark will restore the last-saved bookmark on that computer or will return an error if no bookmark was previously saved.

Working with Windows Media Player

The Windows Media Player control uses automation to expose the DVD Video specific interfaces, methods, events, and properties of the Microsoft DirectShow API. If you prefer working with the Windows Media Player object in Internet Explorer rather than learning the script information required to work with MSWebDVD, you can script DVD control with Windows Media Player (Version 6.4 or greater).

To use DVD playback with the Windows Media Player control, you need to have Microsoft Internet Explorer 5, the Microsoft Windows 98 OEM Service Release (OSR), or Microsoft Windows 2000 installed.

The Microsoft developer network library (msdn.microsoft.com/library) provides a wealth of information and resources for developing with MSWebDVD, DirectShow, and the Windows Media Player. The following sections provide a high-level run-through of the process. This process requires some knowledge of HTML and JavaScript.

Seeking in DVD with Windows Media Player

The Windows Media Player control enables you to seek at several different levels within DVD content. The DVD Video disc format includes special data for seeking and navigation.

DVD Video streams consist of .vob files and associated .ifo files that contain information for navigation and data searching, including random access, fast-forward and fast-reverse play, angle switching, and seamless branching. In the case of One_Sequential_PGC_Titles, a time map table enables time-based seeking. For titles not authored in One_Sequential_PGC format, such as those with branching or multiple ratings, time-based seeking is not supported.

In contrast, MPEG-2 files play from the beginning or require access points to be specified as byte offsets into the file to Group of Pictures (GOP) headers. You can access any GOP without prior authoring of entry points, as is required in the case of DVD Video chapters. Table 17-19 shows the Windows Media Player control DVD Video methods exposed for seeking at various levels.

Table 17-19: Windows Media Player Control — DVD Video Methods

Seeking Level	Control Data	IMediaPlayerDvd Methods
Title Seeks	Video Title Set (VTS), Title, Program Chain (PGC)	TitlePlay
Chapter Seeks	Chapter/Part of Title (PTT), Program (PG)	ChapterPlay (specifying title and chapter number), ChapterSearch (search for a chapter within the same title), PrevPGSearch, TopPGSearch, NextPGSearch
Time Seeks	Interleave Unit (ILVU), Video Object Unit (VOBU)	TimePlay (start playing specified title from specified time), TimeSearch (start playing from specified time within the same title)

Methods, Properties, and Events with Windows Media Player

Because Windows Media Player uses the DVD capabilities built into Direct-Show, the supported methods, properties, and events are the same as for the MSWebDVD ActiveX control. For a list of specific methods, properties, and events, see "MSWebDVD Methods and Properties" on page 463, or visit msdn.microsoft.com for more complete explanation and examples.

DVD-specific properties are called on the Windows Media Player control DVD property, which then resolves to a MediaPlayer object, as indicated in the following syntax:

```
MediaPlayer.DVD.AnglesAvailable
```

DVD-specific methods are called on the Windows Media Player control's DVD property, which then resolves to a MediaPlayer object, as indicated in the following syntax:

```
MediaPlayer.DVD.ChapterPlay( Title, Chapter )
```

For standard playback functionality (pause, play, and stop), DVD-specific methods have not been created. Use the following Windows Media Player control methods:

- Pause

- Play

- Stop

In most cases, the standard Windows Media Player control Pause, Play, and Stop methods function correctly. However, when toggling between Play and the DVD methods BackwardScan and ForwardScan, the methods will not interact. To correctly implement these methods in tandem, add a flag to track whether your application is scanning through the DVD when the Play method is called.

For example, the following code uses a flag called isScanning to determine whether the DVD is being scanned. If it is, ForwardScan is called with a parameter of 1 to reduce the scanning speed to standard playing speed; otherwise, the Play method is called.

```
Dim isScanning

isScanning = False

Sub cmdPlay_OnClick()
 If isScanning Then
  MediaPlayer1.DVD.ForwardScan(1)
 Else
  MediaPlayer1.Play()
 End If

 isScanning = False
End Sub
```

Call this when you want to fast-forward through the DVD:

```
Sub cmdFastForward_OnClick()
 isScanning = True
 MediaPlayer1.DVD.ForwardScan(5)
End Sub
```

Call this when you want to rewind through the DVD:

```
Sub cmdRewind_OnClick()
 isScanning = True
 MediaPlayer1.DVD.BackwardScan(5)
End Sub
```

Using the Stop method is not recommended because it discontinues DVD playback. To continue DVD playback, you must restart the video from the beginning by calling the Play method or refreshing the page. To avoid this, use the Pause method to stop the video and the Play method to resume the video.

Using the Windows Media Player Object to View DVD in a Web Page

The OBJECT tag is used to embed ActiveX objects, such as the Windows Media Player control, into an HTML page. You can also set the properties of a control in a Web page by adding PARAM tags between the OBJECT tags. The following code is an example of using the OBJECT tag to insert the Windows Media Player control:

```
<OBJECT
CLASSID="CLSID:22D6F312-B0F6-11D0-94AB-0080C74C7E95"
 WIDTH="652"
 HEIGHT="382" ID="MediaPlayer1">
<PARAM NAME="AutoStart" VALUE="0">
<PARAM NAME="Filename" VALUE="DVD:">
<PARAM NAME="ShowControls" VALUE="0">
</OBJECT>
```

The following OBJECT tag attributes are required:

* ID: Name used to reference this instance of the control.

* CLSID: Class Identifier (CLSID) of the Windows Media Player control. A CLSID is a component object model (COM) object identifier.

DVD playback is triggered by setting the FileName property to DVD:, which instructs the Windows Media Player control to search for the DVD drive on the local system. If the AutoStart property is set to true (or 1 rather than zero, the default value), the Windows Media Player control will then begin DVD playback; otherwise, an event must be associated with DVD playback, such as the selection of a button. Note that none of the DVD-specific properties can be set by using the PARAM tag.

A value of 1 by default enables a parameter, while 0 disables it; therefore, the Windows Media Player controller is hidden with the previous code. You can use the basic play, pause, stop, and seek controls of the Windows Media

Player, or in this case, you can hide the controller and embed your own custom control buttons, as follows:

```
<INPUT TYPE="BUTTON" STYLE="WIDTH:60" NAME="cmdPlay"
VALUE="Play">

<INPUT TYPE="BUTTON" STYLE="WIDTH:60" NAME="cmdPause"
VALUE="Pause">

<INPUT TYPE="BUTTON" STYLE="WIDTH:60" NAME="cmdStop"
VALUE="Stop">

<INPUT TYPE="BUTTON" STYLE="WIDTH:60"
NAME="cmdResume" VALUE="Resume">

<INPUT TYPE="BUTTON" STYLE="WIDTH:60"
NAME="cmdShowMenu" VALUE="Menu">

<INPUT TYPE="BUTTON" NAME="cmdPrevChapter"
VALUE="|<<">

<INPUT TYPE="BUTTON" NAME="cmdRewind" VALUE="<<">

<INPUT TYPE="BUTTON" NAME="cmdFastForward"
VALUE=">>">

<INPUT TYPE="BUTTON" NAME="cmdNextChapter"
VALUE=">>|">
```

The following code creates the button controls to handle the selection of menu items from the DVD menu screen:

```
<INPUT TYPE="BUTTON" STYLE="WIDTH:70"
NAME="cmdTopSelect" VALUE="Top">

<INPUT TYPE="BUTTON" STYLE="WIDTH:70"
NAME="cmdLeftSelect" VALUE="Left">

<INPUT TYPE="BUTTON" STYLE="WIDTH:70"
NAME="cmdRightSelect" VALUE="Right">

<INPUT TYPE="BUTTON" STYLE="WIDTH:70"
NAME="cmdBottomSelect" VALUE="Bottom">

<INPUT TYPE="BUTTON" STYLE="WIDTH:70"
NAME="cmdButtonActivate" VALUE="Select">
```

The following code demonstrates how each subroutine is attached to the OnClick event of a specific button that was previously defined. When an event is triggered by a button being clicked, the code makes a call (or series of calls) to the Windows Media Player control, specifying the action to be taken. Put the SCRIPT tag anywhere within the BODY of your HTML file and embed the comment-surrounded code within the opening and closing SCRIPT tags.

```
<SCRIPT LANGUAGE="VBScript">
<!--
Dim isScanning

isScanning = False

Sub cmdPlay_OnClick()
 If isScanning Then
  MediaPlayer1.DVD.ForwardScan(1)
 Else
  MediaPlayer1.Play()
 End If
isScanning = False
End Sub


 Sub cmdPause_OnClick()
 MediaPlayer1.Pause()
End Sub


Sub cmdStop_OnClick()
 MediaPlayer1.Stop()
End Sub


Sub cmdResume_OnClick()
 MediaPlayer1.DVD.ResumeFromMenu()
End Sub


Sub cmdShowMenu_OnClick()
 MediaPlayer1.DVD.MenuCall(3)
End Sub
```

```
Sub cmdPrevChapter_OnClick()
 MediaPlayer1.DVD.PrevPGSearch()
End Sub


Sub cmdNextChapter_OnClick()
 MediaPlayer1.DVD.NextPGSearch()
End Sub


Sub cmdFastForward_OnClick()
 isScanning = True
 MediaPlayer1.DVD.ForwardScan(5)
End Sub


Sub cmdRewind_OnClick()
 isScanning = True
 MediaPlayer1.DVD.BackwardScan(5)
End Sub


Sub cmdTopSelect_OnClick()
 MediaPlayer1.DVD.UpperButtonSelect()
End Sub


Sub cmdLeftSelect_OnClick()
 MediaPlayer1.DVD.LeftButtonSelect()
End Sub


Sub cmdRightSelect_OnClick()
 MediaPlayer1.DVD.RightButtonSelect()
End Sub


Sub cmdBottomSelect_OnClick()
 MediaPlayer1.DVD.LowerButtonSelect()
End Sub
```

```
Sub cmdButtonActivate_OnClick()
 Dim buttonNumber
 buttonNumber = MediaPlayer1.DVD.CurrentButton

MediaPlayer1.DVD.ButtonSelectAndActivate(buttonNumbe
r)
End Sub


//-->
</SCRIPT>
```

Integrating DVD into PowerPoint

You can use the MSWebDVD ActiveX control to add DVD Video playback and functionality to PowerPoint presentations. This has several advantages:

- You can repurpose existing DVD Video content within PowerPoint.
- You can use high-quality MPEG-2 video.
- You can use the familiar PowerPoint authoring environment to add complex functionality to a DVD Video title to create rich DVD-ROM applications.

To use the MSWebDVD object in a Microsoft PowerPoint presentation:

1. Open the View menu, point to Toolbars, and then click Control Toolbox palette.
2. Choose the Insert Object icon.
3. Insert the MSWebDVD control.
4. Drag to size.

Scripting must be done in Visual Basic Scripting Edition.

Preparing a DVD-ROM Master Disc

There are several details to consider that are specific to creating a hybrid DVD-ROM disc image or recording, as described in the following topics.

Create an Autorun File

An autorun.ini file should be included on the disc so that Windows will launch the specified executable rather than automatically launching the DVD player to handle the DVD Video content.

Create a text file with appropriate autorun information, and place it at the top level of your DVD-ROM structure. Here's an example:

```
[autorun]
open=DVDtitle.exe
icon=DVDtitle.exe
```

This will cause the system to first launch your title and bypass the automatic initialization of the DVD Video playback software.

If you are launching Web pages, you cannot launch an HTML page on its own using this method. Instead, you will need an executable that will then launch the Web page. A good example might be a Macromedia projector file, either a Flash projector or a Director projector, that will introduce the title and allow the user to launch the HTML content.

Use the Correct Recording Software

When creating the DVD-ROM disc image or writing to a DVD-R, DLT, or DVD-RAM disc, be sure to use image formatting software that properly recognizes the DVD Video zone and places it at the physical beginning of the disc (before any additional ROM content).

Using Optional Microsoft's DVD-ROM Boilerplate Video

Microsoft provides a DVD-ROM boilerplate video that developers can use on DVD-ROM titles that contain no DVD Video formatted data. A disc without a proper DVD Video zone may behave unpredictably when placed in a stand-alone DVD Video player, possibly ejecting the disc or locking up. This can be avoided by adding the DVD-ROM boilerplate video to the disc. When the disc is inserted into a DVD Video playe,r it will display a message informing the user that the disc is designed to work in a DVD-ROM.

The DVD-ROM boilerplate video files may be used on any DVD-ROM title in accordance with the Distribution Requirements of the SDK End-User License Agreement.

To acquire the boilerplate video, go to msdn.microsoft.com/downloads/default.asp.

APPENDIX

Additional Resources

Table A-1: Conferences

Organization/ Event(s)	Description	URL
National Association of Broadcasters (NAB)	The National Association of Broadcasters(NAB) is a full-service trade association that promotes and protects the interests of radio and television broadcasters in the United States and around the world. NAB is the broadcaster's voice before the US Congress, federal agencies, and the courts. It also serve a growing number of associate and international broadcaster members. The association's spring convention, known simply as NAB, and the annual NAB Radio Show are the finest broadcast-related expositions in the world and welcome thousands of visitors each year from the United States and abroad.	www.nab.org
National Cable and Tele-communications Association (NCTA) Conference	The National Cable and Telecommunications Association (NCTA), formerly the National Cable Television Association, is the principal trade association of the cable television industry in the United States. Founded in 1952, NCTA's primary mission is to provide its members with a strong national presence by providing a single voice on issues affecting the cable and tele-communications industry. NCTA hosts the industry's annual trade show, which typically features more than 300 exhibiting companies and attracts more than 30,000 attendees.	www.cable2002.com/

Table A-1: Conferences (Continued)

Organization/ Event(s)	Description	URL
Streaming Media East Streaming Media West Streaming Media Asia Streaming Media Europe Streaming Media Japan Streaming Media Berlin	Streaming Media, Inc., a subsidiary of Penton Media, Inc., is a diversified, international media company serving and educating the streaming media industry. Streaming Media organizes the Streaming Media conferences throughout the year that are the premier events for people in the convergence and streaming markets. This Website is an excellent online resource for news and information about the industry as well as the schedules for the upcoming Streaming Media Conferences.	www.streamingmedia.com

Table A-2: Standards Organizations

Organization	Description	URL
American National Standards Institute (ANSI)	American National Standards Institute (ANSI) is a private, non-profit organization (501(c)3) that administers and coordinates the U.S. voluntary standardization and conformity assessment system	www.ansi.org
Motion Pictures Experts Group (MPEG) [ISO/IEC JTC1 SC29 WG11]	Motion Pictures Experts Group (MPEG) is a working group of ISO/IEC in charge of the development of standards for coded representation of digital audio and video. Established in 1988, the group has produced MPEG-1, the standard on which such products as Video CD and MP3 are based; MPEG-2, the standard on which such products as Digital Television set top boxes and DVD are based; MPEG-4, the standard for multimedia for the fixed and mobile Web; and MPEG-7, the standard for description and search of audio and visual content. Work on the new standard MPEG-21 (Multimedia Framework) has started in June 2000. So far a Technical Report has been produced and the formal approval process has already begun for two more parts of the standard. Several Calls for Proposals have already been issued, and two working drafts are being developed.	mpeg.telecomitalialab.com www.mpeg.org MPEG Pointers and Resources (Reference site for MPEG) www.mpeg.org/MPEG/starting-points.html (MPEG Starting Points and FAQs) www.faqs.org/faqs/compression-faq/part2/section-2.html (Introduction to MPEG)

Table A-2: Standards Organizations (Continued)

Organization	Description	URL
National Committee for Information Technology Standards (NCITS)	The mission of the National Committee for Information Technology Standards (NCITS) is to produce market-driven voluntary consensus standards in the area of information technology. Some of its best-known activities are multimedia (MPEG/JPEG), intercommunication among computing devices and information systems (including the Information Infrastructure, SCSI-2 interfaces, geographic Information systems), storage media (hard drives, removable cartridges), database (including SQL3), security, and programming languages (such as C++).	www.ncits.org/index.html
National Information Standards Organization (NISO)	The National Information Standards Organization (NISO), a nonprofit association accredited by the American National Standards Institute (ANSI), identifies, develops, maintains, and publishes technical standards to manage information in our changing and ever-more digital environment. NISO standards apply both traditional and new technologies to the full range of information-related needs, including retrieval, repurposing, storage, metadata, and preservation.	www.niso.org/
Society of Motion Picture and Television Engineers (SMPTE)	The Society of Motion Picture and Television Engineers (SMPTE) is the leading technical society for the motion imaging industry. There are more than 10,000 SMPTE members spread throughout 85 countries. SMPTE was founded in 1916 to advance theory and development in the motion imaging field. Today, SMPTE publishes ANSI-approved standards, recommended practices, and engineering guidelines, along with the highly regarded SMPTE Journal and its peer-reviewed technical papers.	www.smpte.org/ mpeg.telecomitalialab.com/events/mpeg-21/Morgan/ppframe.htm

Table A-3: Professional Organizations

Organization/ Event(s)	Description	URL
EDItEUR	EDItEUR is the Pan-European Book Sector EDI Group, recognized by the Commission of the European Union and by the Western European EDIFACT Board, supported by the European Federations of Library, Booksellers, and Publishers Associations (EBLIDA, EBF, and FEP, respectively). EDItEUR's brief is to coordinate the development, promotion, and implementation of EDI in the books and serials sectors.	http://www. editeur.org http://www. eblida.org http:// www.ebf-eu.org http:// www.fep-fee.be
MPEG-4 Industry Forum	The MPEG-4 Industry Forum is forum for industry members with the direct responsibility to promote the use of and disseminate information on MPEG-4 outside of the MPEG organization. Information on MPEG-4 press releases, licensing terms, and industry adoption are available on this site.	www.m4if.org
National Association of Broadcasters (NAB)	The National Association of Broadcasters(NAB) is a full-service trade association that promotes and protects the interests of radio and television broadcasters in the United States and around the world. NAB is the broadcaster's voice before the US Congress, federal agencies, and the courts. It also serve a growing number of associate and international broadcaster members.	www.nab.org

Table A-3: Professional Organizations (Continued)

Organization/ Event(s)	Description	URL
National Cable and Telecommunications Association (NCTA) Conference	The National Cable and Telecommunications Association (NCTA), formerly the National Cable Television Association, is the principal trade association of the cable television industry in the United States. Founded in 1952, NCTA's primary mission is to provide its members with a strong national presence by providing a single voice on issues affecting the cable and telecommunications industry. NCTA represents cable operators serving more than 90 % of the nation's cable television households and more than 200 cable program networks, as well as equipment suppliers and providers of other services to the cable industry. In addition to offering traditional video services, NCTA's members also provide broadband services such as high-speed Internet access and telecommunications services such as local exchange telephone service to customers across the United States.	www.ncta.com
Pro-MPEG Forum	The Pro-MPEG Forum is an association of broadcasters and program makers, equipment manufacturers, and component suppliers with interests in realizing the full potential offered by MPEG-2 as an open international standard for compressed digital content. The Pro-MPEG Forum focuses on MPEG-2 equipment interoperability according to the implementation requirements of broadcasters and other end users. The Forum currently has over 130 members from all over the world.	www.pro-mpeg.org

Table A-3: Professional Organizations (Continued)

Organization/ Event(s)	Description	URL
XrML Forum	Based on years of research at Xerox Palo Alto Research Center (PARC), which invented the digital rights language concept, and backed by patented technology, XrML is currently governed by ContentGuard, Inc. XrML is the only rights language being used in commercially deployed solutions, including the DRM solutions from Microsoft. ContentGuard has confirmed its intent to transfer the governance responsibilities of XrML to an international standards organization. By allowing the development of XrML to be managed by an independent body, ContentGuard is seeking to open up XrML's future development to broad industry participation. ContentGuard also plans to propose XrML to any standards organization seeking a rights language and has recently submitted the specification to MPEG-21 and *TV-Anytime* for consideration.	http://www.xrml.org

Table A-3: Professional Organizations (Continued)

Organization/ Event(s)	Description	URL
XMCL Initiative	XMCL is a rights specification language, as defined by the Association of American Publishers. The purpose of XMCL is for interchange of business rules to be applied to media between business systems (e.g., Web storefronts, customer tracking and management) and trusted delivery and playback systems (for example, a DRM implementation that will enforce the rights described in the XMCL document). Through the use of XMCL, business systems are completely free of knowledge of specific trusted system implementations. This separation of the business systems and the trusted systems allows businesses to support one or more trusted systems and provides the option of changing trusted systems as conditions change without changes to the business systems.	http://www.xmcl.org
	XMCL describes the minimum self-complete set of business rules under which digital media is licensed for consumer use. These business rules support multiple business models including rental, subscription, ownership, and video-on-demand/pay-per-view. When a business system authorizes a customer transaction for digital media, it generates an XMCL document that is then acted upon and enforced by a specific trusted system. The generated XMCL document is submitted to the trusted system through the APIs of the system (for example, HTTP POST, RPC call, API call).	

Bibliography and List of Internet Sources

Chapter 1

www.ngi.gov

www.internet2.edu

www.ipv6.org

www.cdt.luth.se/I3

Chapter 2

Deutsche Media Metrix Report, BT Alex Brown Research, March 2000

www.w3c.org

RealNetworks

www.realnetworks.com

www.akamai.com

www.infolibria,com

www.activate.com

www.digitalisland.net

www.ibeam.com

www.cidera.com

Jupiter MediaMetrix, June 2001

www.microsoft.com/windows/windowsmedia

www.realnetworks.com/products

www.apple.com/quicktime/

www.adobe.com

www.avid.com

www.movieworks.com

www.media100.com

www.totallyhip.com

www.sorenson.com

www.macromedia.com

www.totallyhip.com

www.tribeworks.com

www.megaseg.com

www.commotionpro.com

www.discreet.com

Chapter 3

www.macromedia.com

Browser News, 2001

www.adobe.com

www.macromedia.com/exchange/dreamweaver/
Extensions for Dreamweaver

www.macromedia.com/support/dreamweaver/

www.actionxchange.com/

www.adobe.com/support/main.html

www.actionext.com/

www.goliveheaven.com/

www.adobe.com/svg/

www.w3c.org

- TextPad.com
- www.levien.com

Chapter 4

www.filemaker.com

www.microsoft.com

www.oracle.com

www.w3c.org

www.xml.com

www.xml.org

www.adobe.com

www.brainshark.com

www.centra.com

www.digitallava.com

www.outstart.com

www.placeware.com

www.tekadence.com

www.webex.com

Chapter 5

www.yahoo.com

www.eloquent.com

www.presenter.com

www.horizonlive.com

www.digitallava.com

www.adobe.com

www.avid.com

www.apple.com

www.macromedia.com

www.microsoft.com

www.microsoft.com/windows/ie/

www.w3.org/TR/2001/WD-XHTMLplusSMIL-20010807/

www.microsoft.com/windows/ie/

msdn.microsoft.com/library/en-us/dntime/html/htmltime.asp

www.realnetworks.com

www.smilmedia.com

www.fluition.com

www.wgbh.org

www.realnetworks.com/solutions/ecosystem/
realone.html

www.oratrix.com/GRiNS/SMIL-2.0/

www.microsoft.com/windows/ie/

www.w3.org/TR/2001/WD-XHTMLplusSMIL-20010807/

www.microsoft.com/windows/ie/

msdn.microsoft.com/library/en-us/dntime/html/htmltime.asp

www.apple.com/quicktime/authoring/qtsmil.html

www.realnetworks.com

www.helio.org

smil.nist.gov/player

www.salzburgresearch.at/suntrec/schmunzel

www.xsmiles.org

www.discreet.com/products/cinestream

www.avid.com/products/avidxpressdv/

www.microsoft.com/windows/windowsmedia/technologies.asp

www.oratrix.com

www.sonicfoundry.com

msdn.microsoft.com/library/default.asp?url=/nhp/
Default.asp?contentid=28000411

www.apple.com/quicktime/authoring/embed.html

www.apple.com/quicktime/authoring/qtsmil.html

www.apple.com/quicktime/products/tutorials/
preparingtostream.html

www.realnetworks.com/resources/media_creation.html

Chapter 6

www.instat.com

www.dvdfllc.co.jp/

www.dvdforum.org/tech-dvdbook.htm

www.mpeg.org/MPEG/DVD/)

www.news.philips.com/whatsup/19971204-00.html

www.dolby.com/dvd/sel-code.html

www.icdia.org/

www.opendvd.org

www.efd.lth.se/~e95jla/soundpic/dvd/Jeffletters.html

www.columbia.edu/cu/moment/040396/dvdside.html

DVD Demystified, by Jim Taylor. McGraw-Hill, 1998, 2000

Chapter 7

www.dvdfllc.co.jp.

www.pioneerusa.com

www.pioneerusa.com

www.toshiba.com

www.Toshiba.com

www.Toshiba.com

www.Panasonic.com

www.hival.com

www.hp.com

www.hitachi.com

www.hitachi.com

www.ymi.com

www.softarch.com

www.gearsoftware.com

www.vob.de/us/

www.prassi.com

www.roxio.com

DVD Demystified, by Jim Taylor. McGraw-Hill, 1998, 2000

Chapter 8

DVD Demystified, by Jim Taylor. McGraw-Hill, 1998, 2000

www.dvdfllc.co.jp

www.spruce-tech.com

www.apple.com

www.dvd.acedaikin.com

www.daikin.com

www.sonic.com

www.pinnaclesys.com/

www.neato.com

Chapter 9

www.dvdfllc.co.jp.

www.meridian-audio.com

www.sadie.com

Chapter 10

Kanter, R. M. (2001). Evolve! : Succeeding in the Digital Culture of Tomorrow

Digital Dimensioning: Finding the ebusiness in Your Business
by Samuel C. Certo, Matthew W. Certo

The Death of "e" and the Birth of the Real New Economy : Business Models, Technologies and Strategies for the 21st Century
by Peter Fingar, Ronald Aronica, Bryan Maizlish

Workflow Modeling: Tools for Process Improvement and Application Development
by Alec Sharp, Patrick McDermott

Workflow Management Systems for Process Organisations
by Thomas Schael, Thomas Schal, Thomas W. Schaller

Electronic Media Management
by Peter K. Pringle, Michael F. Starr, William E. McCavitt

Convergence in Broadcast and Communications Media : The Fundamentals of Audio, Video, Data Processing and Communications Technologies by John Watkinson

techlibrary.wallstreetandtech.com:
Wall Street & Technology Tech Library
(Computer Hardware, Electronic Commerce, Enterprise Computing, IT Management, Market Research, Networking, Software Development, Telecommunications)

edtn.bitpipe.com
EDTN e-Library
(Communications, Computers and Peripherals, Consumer, Design, Embedded Systems, Passives, Power Sources, Semiconductor: Discretes, Semiconductor: Integrated Circuits, Test and Measurement)

techlibrary.commweb.com
CommWeb Tech Library
Timely and technical information on hot telecom and convergence issues such as VoIP, CRM and the Voice Web. (Call Center, Networking, Telecommunications, Voice/Data Convergence, Wireless)

www.bbwlibrary.com
Broadband Week Technical Library
(3G Wireless Networks, Application Service Providers (ASP), ATM, Bridges, Broadband Satellite Systems, Broadband Telecom Services, Broadband Video Services, Broadband Wireless Networks, Cable, Cable Modems, Communications Hardware, Data Networking Hardware, DSL, Frame Relay, Integrated Circuits, Internet Telephony, ISDN, ISPs, LAN Hardware, LAN Switches, Laws, Mobile Computing Systems, Network Management, Network Protocols, Network Security, Operations/ Business Operations, Optical Storage, Quality of Service (QOS), Routers, Satellite Systems, Security, Standards, Testing, Video Conferencing Hardware, Virtual Private Networks, Voice Networking Hardware, Voice Over IP, Wireless Communication Hardware, Wireless Communications Systems, Wireless Internet, Wireless LAN)

whitepapers.interop.com
N+I Whitepapers
(Hardware, Network Management, Network/Systems, Software, Network Protocols, Wireless Systems)

cyberlibrary.cpuniverse.com
Contract Professional Universe CyberLibrary
(Artificial Intelligence,Computing System Hardware, Consumer Electronics, Diagnostic and Test Hardware, Hardware, Information Security, Operating Systems, Information Technology Systems, Security Software, Information Technology Management, Software, Information Technology Workforce, Software Development, Internet, Storage Hardware, Network Management, Web Application Development)

whitepaperlibrary.m-commerceworld.com
Internet World White Paper Library
(eBusiness, ISP, Streaming Media Services, m-Commerce)

www.lbagroup.com/associates/lbatn106.htm
Technical Note 106: Wireless Cable: A Competing Technology

www.insight-corp.com/satellite.html
Satellite Communications for the Next Century: Global Markets for GMPCS, LEOs, MEOs, and GEOs 1999-2004

Chapter 11

www.fgdc.gov/metadata/contstan.html
Content Standard for Digital Geospatial Metadata (CSDGM)

www.fgdc.gov/metadata/metadata.html
FGDC Metadata

www.fgdc.gov/clearinghouse/clearinghouse.html
FGDC Geospatial Data Clearinghouse

clearinghouse4.fgdc.gov/registry/clearinghouse_sites.html
Websites Associated with FGDC Clearinghouse Participants

www.fgdc.gov/standards/standards.html
FGDC Standards

gcmd.gsfc.nasa.gov/Aboutus/standards/
Metadata Protocols and Standards

gcmd.gsfc.nasa.gov/User/difguide/difman.html
Directory Interchange Format (DIF) Writer's Guide

www.lic.wisc.edu/metadata/metaprim.htm
NSGIC Metadata Primer

www.niso.org/index.html
NISO Home

www.niso.org/standards/index.html
NISO Standards page

ANSI/NISO Z39.2 - 1994 (R2001) Information Interchange Format
(MARC)

ANSI/NISO Z39.50 - 1995 Information Retrieval : Application Service Definition & Protocol Specification

ANSI/NISO Z39.85 - 2001 Dublin Core Metadata Element Set

www.niso.org/standards/std_info_retrieval.html
NISO – Information Retrieval documents

www.niso.org/press/whitepapers/crsswalk.html
Issues in Crosswalking Content Metadata Standards

www.niso.org/standards/resources/Z39-85.pdf
The Dublin Core Metadata Element Set

www.niso.org/committees/committee_au.html
Technical Metadata for Digital Still Images

dublincore.org
Dublin Core Metadata Initiative (DCMI)

dublincore.org/documents/
Dublin Core Metadata Initiative (DCMI) Documents

dublincore.org/resources/bibliography/
Dublin Core Metadata Initiative (DCMI) Bibliography

dublincore.org/resources/faq/
Dublin Core Metadata Initiative (DCMI) Frequently Asked Questions (FAQ)

dublincore.org/workshops/
Dublin Core Metadata Initiative Workshops

www.ukoln.ac.uk/metadata/dcdot/
Dublin Core Metadata Editor

www.lub.lu.se/cgi-bin/nmdc.pl
Dublin Core Metadata Template

archive.dstc.edu.au/RDU/staff/jane-hunter/ECDL2/final.html
Application of Metadata standards to Video Indexing

www.icpsr.umich.edu/DDI/
Data Document Initiative (DDI) Home

www.nsd.uib.no/Cessda/
Council of European social science data archives

www.computer.org/conferences/meta96/meta_home.html
Metadata'96 Proceedings

computer.org/proceedings/meta97/
Metadata'97 Proceedings

computer.org/proceedings/meta/1999/
Metadata'99 Proceedings

www.w3.org
W3C Home

www.w3.org/Metadata/
Metadata at W3C

www.w3.org/RDF/
Resource Description Framework (RDF) (a framework for describing and interchanging metadata for the Web)

www.ifla.org/II/metadata.htm
Digital Libraries: Metadata Resources

www.dli2.nsf.gov/
Digital Libraries Initiative Phase 2

www.loc.gov/standards/metadata.html
Introduction to Metadata Elements: Library of Congress

www.loc.gov/standards/
Standards (Library of Congress)

memory.loc.gov/ammem/techdocs/libt1999/libt1999.html
Providing Online Access to Pictorial Images

www.cimi.org
Consortium for the Computer Interchange of Museum Information (CIMI):

www.ukoln.ac.uk/metadata/
UKOLN (UK Office for Library and Information Networking) Metadata

metadata.net/
Metadata.Net Home (tools, resources – funded by Australian Gov't)

www.dstc.edu.au/RDU/
DSTC: Resource Discovery Unit Home

www.lib.helsinki.fi/meta/
The Nordic Metadata Projects

www.getty.edu/research/institute/standards/intrometadata/index.html
Getty Institute – Introduction to Metadata

www.pads.ahds.ac.uk/padsUserNeedsMetadataWorkshopsFilmBallantyne.html
Moving Image Collections

www.rlg.org/preserv/presmeta.html
RLG Working Group on Preservation Issues of Metadata

dis.lib.muohio.edu/documents/
Miami University Digital Information Services Cluster Documents

Chapter 12

www.agarimediaware.com/products/product.html

www.chuckwalla.com/products.html

www.extensis.com/portfolio/

www.sgi.com/solutions/broadband/dam.html

www.sgi.com/software/ascential.html

www.artesia.com/teams_overview.html

www.bulldog.com/

www.documentum.com/

www.emc.com/horizontal/rich_content_products_mams.jsp

www.enscaler.com/solutions/mediascaler.htm

www.kasenna.com/products/

www.media360.com/products/media360/m360_core.html

www.discreet.com/products/infrastr/

www.avid.com/products/unity_mediasvc/index.html

www.audiovault.com/

www.broadvision.com

www.convera.com/Products/index.asp

www.cyclop.ca/

www.emotion.com/products/index.html

www.ibm.com/software/data/cm/cmgr/

www.iknowledge.com/solutions/activecontentsuite.htm

www.interwoven.com/products/teamsite/

solutions.liberate.com/products/tv_producer.html

solutions.liberate.com/products/vod_gateway.html

www.lysis.com/html/h_solutions/products.html

www.northplains.com/products/default.html

www.mediasite.com/corporateweb/products/
application_server_suite.html

www.theplatform.com/digitalmediawebservice.asp.asp

www.grassvalleygroup.com/products/software/contentshare/

www.videospheres.com/products.html

www.vignette.com/

www.virage.com/products/products-server.html

www.chrystal.com/

www.lariat.com/stationmgr/index.htm

www.contextmedia.com/products/index.html

www.bulldog.com/

www.documentum.com/

www.ivast.com/

www.microsoft.com/cmserver/

www.avid.com/products/airspace/index.html

www.audiovault.com/

www.convera.com/Products/index.asp

www.eprise.com/

www.divine.com/

www.ibm.com/software/data/cm/cmgr/

www.iknowledge.com/solutions/activecontentsuite.htm

www.interwoven.com/products/teamsite/

solutions.liberate.com/products/tv_producer.htm

solutions.liberate.com/products/vod_gateway.html

www.odetics.com/ODETA/broadcast.html

www.odeticsbroadcast.com/

www.mediasite.com/corporateweb/products/publisher.html

www.theplatform.com/dynamicpresentations.asp

www.grassvalleygroup.com/products/

mpeg.telecomitalialab.com/

www.mpeg.org

www.mpeg.org/MPEG/starting-points.html

www.faqs.org/faqs/compression-faq/part2/section-2.html

www.w3.org/

www.w3.org/XML/

www.wfmc.org

www.w3.org/P3P/

www.w3.org/TR/soap12-part0/

Chapter 13

Bradley, J. B. (2001). Digital Media Trust Chains: Essential to the Market. Boston, axsWave Consulting.

Bradley, J. B. (2001). Digital Media: New Ideas for Efficient Asset Management. Lowell, MA, axsWave Consulting.

Kini, A. and J. Choobineh (1998). <u>Trust in Electronic Commerce: Definition and Theoretical Considerations</u>. 31st Annual Hawaii International Conference in System Sciences, Hawaii, IEEE.

Microsoft (2001). Microsoft 2001 Online Annual report. Redmond, Microsoft Corporation.

Chapter 14

www.adobe.com

www.avid.com

www.discreet.com

www.macromedia.com

www.media100.com

www.microsoft.com

www.pinnaclesys.com

Chapter 15

www.ISMA.org

www.M4IF.org

mpeg.telecomitalialab.com/standards

www.ietf.org

www.ism-alliance.org

www.amphion.com

www.enquad.com

www.envivio.com

www.e-vue.com

www.dicas.de

www.iis.fhg.de

www.emblaze.com

www.improvsys.com

www.indigovision.com

www.ivast.com

www.packetvideo.com

www.philips.com

www.seromemobile.com

www.solidstreaming.com

www.soundball.com

www.f2f-inc.com

www.psytel-research.co.yu

www.sigmadesigns.com

www.ubvideo.com

www.heuris.com

www.ligos.com

www.pixeltools.com

www.vitecmm.com

www.dv-studios.com

www.futuretel.com

www.optibase.com

www.vitecmm.com

www.media100.com

www.amphion.com

www.celvibe.com

www.cutesystems.com

www.dbvision.net

www.divxnetworks.com

Chapter 16

www.atvef.com

www.aoltv.com

www.liberate.com

www.microsoft.com/tv

www.wink.com

www.gemstar.com

www.respondtv.com

www.opentv.com

www.powertv.com

www.wgate.com

www.opencable.com

www.avid.com

www.chyronitv.com

www.mixedsignals.com

www.opentv.com

www.spin.tv

www.eegent.com

www.ccaption.com

www.microsoft.com/tv

www.norpak.ca

Chapter 17

www.DVDA.org

www.apple.com/dvdstudiopro/

www.sonic.com

www.interactual.com

msdn.microsoft.com/

www.onstagedvd.com/products/activex/

www.visiblelight.com/products/onstagedvd.com/odd4

www.zumadigital.com

Index